# SIX ELIZABETHAN PLAYS

## RIVERSIDE EDITIONS

RIVERSIDE  EDITIONS

*Under the General Editorship of*

*Gordon N. Ray*

# SIX ELIZABETHAN PLAYS

## (1585-1635)

EDITED BY

## R. C. BALD

*University of Chicago*

HOUGHTON MIFFLIN COMPANY · BOSTON
The Riverside Press Cambridge

# CONTENTS

# INTRODUCTION

## *by R. C. Bald*

EVEN IF Shakespeare had never lived, the last fifteen years of Queen Elizabeth's reign and the reign of King James I would still be the greatest period in the history of the English drama. The six plays in this volume were all written by contemporaries of Shakespeare, some for the same theatre and company for which his were written, others for rival theatres and companies. The earliest play, *Tamburlaine*, was written four or five years before Shakespeare is first heard of as a working dramatist in London; the latest, *The Broken Heart*, appeared on the boards sixteen or seventeen years after his death. Taken together, the six plays illustrate a number of important phases of the drama of the period, some already familiar from Shakespeare's plays, some scarcely touched by him; they also illustrate the growth and decay of the drama over the relatively short period of half a century.

The first part of *Tamburlaine* was Marlowe's first great success and heralded the coming of a new era to the popular theatre. As Tucker Brooke has pointed out, the play is designed for a simple platform stage; Marlowe had not yet learned to make full use of the resources of the Elizabethan theatre as he did in some of his later plays. The action is single, uncomplicated by any underplot; there are no subsidiary episodes, nor is there even any comic relief. The plot rises by a series of steps, and it is accompanied by a growing sense of tension, until the reconciliation is effected at the end. First the foolish Mycetes is overcome; from this victory Tamburlaine passes on to the defeat of Cosroe, whom he takes unawares. Then comes the real trial of strength against Bajazeth, in which he overthrows an empire. Finally, all the forces of Africa and the East are mobilized against him, but the cruel subjugation of Damascus establishes Tamburlaine's invincibility and forces the reconciliation, in which Zenocrate acts as mediator. Tamburlaine, in fact, passes from triumph to triumph in a crescendo of victory.

Though the play is simple, even rudimentary, in structure, it is remarkable for the sense of power that it conveys. Most of this is to be found in the character of Tamburlaine himself; the play is, of course, essentially a one-man play. It should be noted that even when Tamburlaine is not on the stage he still dominates the play; he is still its theme, and the scenes in which he is not present are none the less *about* him. Individual episodes are sensational (witness those involving the encaged Bajazeth), but the force of the language rises to an even higher pitch than the action. Nor is Marlowe's range a narrow one, spanning as it does bombastic bluster at one extreme and flights of superb poetry at the other.

Equally important is Marlowe's blank verse, a medium which he did more than any other writer to acclimatize on the popular stage. Before his time dramatic verse had usually been rhymed, but Marlowe's sense of style gave the new measure a strength and dignity previously lacking in dramatic verse. The prologue to the play is a manifesto:

> From jigging veins of rhyming mother wits,
> And such conceits as clownage keeps in pay,
> We'll lead you to the stately tent of war,
> Where you shall hear the Scythian Tamburlaine
> Threat'ning the world with high astounding terms.

The "high astounding terms" gave Marlowe's lines a power lacking in the jig-jog metres of the rhymers; and though his verses do not have the flexibility that dramatic blank verse was later to attain, he, more than any other man, brought about a reform which made Shakespeare's work possible.

*The Shoemakers' Holiday* was written at about the same time as Shakespeare's *Henry IV* plays, and *As You Like It,* and *Twelfth Night.* Dekker's play has something in common with the plays just named, though its comedy is closer to that of Falstaff and his crew than to that of the more romantic plays, for Dekker has chosen a wholly contemporary English setting, and the notion that he is dealing with the historical past is little more than a fiction. The success story of Simon Eyre, who makes a fortune by a lucky purchase and then advances through the various civic dignities until he achieves the highest office attainable by a Londoner, would be little enough in itself were it not for the vivid glimpses of the shoemaker's shop and the portrayal of the characters who live and work there.

In Eyre and his wife one perceives the emergence of a new

kind of comic characterization. Eyre is a "merry madcap" even
when Lord Mayor and in the presence of the King; his wife's
habitual sourness is mollified only by a certain smugness as she
rises in the world with her husband. One or two salient eccentricities are underlined by oft-repeated oddities of speech and by
the use of tags, such as "Prince am I none, yet am I princely born"
from Eyre, but "But let that pass" from Margery. The same kind
of mannerism can be observed in Shakespeare's treatment of Falstaff's followers — in the bombastic quotations of Pistol, in Nim's
"That's the humour of it," and in the eccentricities of Dr. Caius
and Sir Hugh Evans in *The Merry Wives of Windsor*. This type
of characterization is a simplification of that found in Ben Jonson's
comedy of humours, and reminds us that at this time his *Every
Man in his Humour* and *Every Man out of his Humour* were still
fresh in the memory of dramatists and playgoers alike.

The two subsidiary plots involving the wooing of Lacy (or
Hans) and the affairs of Jane and Rafe have a pleasant vein of
sentiment in them. They also emphasize the fact already apparent
in the story of Eyre's rise that the play was designed to attract a
narrower audience than Shakespeare's plays. In spite of the fact
that *The Shoemakers' Holiday* was performed before the Queen,
Dekker's primary appeal was to the London citizenry. Matches
between members of the aristocracy and rich merchants' daughters were often looked at askance not merely by the nobility but,
as in the play, by the merchant classes. Rafe, it should be noted,
is bidden to fight in the French wars not for St. George and England but for "the honour of the gentle craft, . . . the mad knaves
of Bedlam, Fleet Street, Tower Street and Whitechapel." The
patriotism is purely local, and of the same sort as that around
which G. K. Chesterton three hundred years later built his romance *The Napoleon of Notting Hill*. Lacy, who is apparently
heir to the Earl of Lincoln, is engaging only because he plays so
well the part of a Dutch shoemaker in order to win Rose; yet to
do this he leaves his post in the army and has to win the King's
pardon for his act of desertion. Such a plot, however much it
might appeal to citizen sentiment, can scarcely be said to mirror the
aristocratic ideal of honor, and is, in fact, the very antithesis of the
feeling expressed in Lovelace's lines:

> I could not love thee, dear, so much
> Loved I not honor more.

If *The Shoemakers' Holiday* is the best surviving example of the type of play specifically written to appeal to the London citizenry, *The Knight of the Burning Pestle* is to some extent a satire on this type. *The Knight of the Burning Pestle* was written for a boys' company and performed at one of the "private" theatres before a more select and fashionable audience than formed the majority of the audience at the Globe or Fortune. The play is also valuable for the glimpses it gives of a performance at a private theatre, with the gallants sitting on the stage and smoking their pipes, the frequent songs worked into the play, and the intervals between the acts, filled in with music or acrobatic dancing.

The Citizen and his wife are portrayed with insight and sympathy; almost all the rest is parody. The play to which the spectators are supposed to have come is *The London Merchant*, a piece professedly based on citizen life. At the opposite pole to this pseudo-realism is the action generated by the Citizen and his wife, consisting almost wholly of the adventures of Ralph. Simon Eyre had praised his man Rafe by declaring (p. 77) that

> Hector of Troy was an hackney to him, Hercules and Termagant scoundrels; Prince Arthur's Round Table — by the Lord of Ludgate — ne'er fed such a tall, such a dapper swordsman,

and in this speech he had shown how well acquainted he was with legends and tales of knight-errantry, which were evidently a favorite form of reading among simple folk. Certainly in Beaumont and Fletcher's play such tales have captured the imagination of the Grocer's household, so that it seems natural for Ralph to act out some of the stuff of which his dreams were made and go a-questing as the Knight of the Burning Pestle in a manner that strongly recalls some of the adventures of Don Quixote. Not only are there parallels with some of the episodes in Cervantes' work, but something of its tone has also been caught in the juxtaposition of the absurdities of knight-errantry with the realities of everyday life. For a time the adventures of the Knight of the Burning Pestle are combined with those of the Merrythoughts, but eventually he goes his own way to woo the King of Moldavia's daughter, play the part of a May-lord, review the trained bands, and finally to die — all for no other reason than to obey the whim of the Citizen's wife. This part of the play becomes completely formless, and deliberately so, for Beaumont and Fletcher well knew what they were satirizing. Yet, alongside this surrender to a kind of dream life, there is in the Citizen's wife, not surprisingly, a vein of everyday shrewdness and respect for the *mores* of her class, as when she expresses her prejudices and shows her disapproval of the young lovers who defy parental marriage arrangements. *The Knight of the Burning Pestle* is an astonishingly good-tempered protest by a pair of young intellectuals against the popular fare of the day with which they had to compete.

One's strongest impression after reading Jonson's *Epicoene* is of superb craftsmanship. In many ways Jonson was an isolated figure in the theatre of his time. Like Bernard Shaw three hundred years later, he challenged the preconceptions of his audiences, and preferred to risk failure and unpopularity rather than compromise his standards. He eventually established for himself a following, and towards the end of his life became the grand old man of English letters, but to the average theatre-goer of his time he must have appeared something of a highbrow. Whereas the ordinary man was satisfied to be entertained and cared little about dramatic theory, Jonson was a highly articulate critic who had strong views about the social function of comedy and adhered strictly to the rules formulated by the ancients. Moreover, he lost no opportunity of telling his audiences that whether they cared or not they *ought* to care about such things. Yet if Jonson seemed a highbrow in his concern for the craft of the playwright, he was far from being one in his choice of subjects and characters, in his astonishingly keen ear for the turns of popular speech, and in the robust vitality of his plays. Jonson's comedies are primarily comedies of contemporary London life. They have none of the idealized background and atmosphere of Shakespeare's comedies, and none of the sentiment with which Dekker and Heywood regarded bourgeois domesticity. Jonson is not a realist in the modern sense of the term; his insistence on the didactic purpose of comedy and his theory of character prevented him from achieving the realist's detachment; but he looked at the life of his age with very few illusions, and put down what he saw without any of the glamour in which nearly all his contemporaries clothed it.

Much has been written about Jonson's theory of humors, but the best account of them is probably that given long ago by Dryden:

> by humour [he wrote] is meant some extravagant habit, passion, or affection, particular (as I said before) to some one

person, by the oddness of which he is immediately distinguished from the rest of men.

It is a critical truism that Jonson's characters lack the depth and roundness of Shakespeare's, but it must be realized that, holding as he did that it was the function of comedy to display and correct anti-social eccentricities, Jonson was compelled to emphasize one, or at most two, aspects of a character; anything more would have been irrelevant to the purposes of the play. In *Epicoene* the whole plot revolves around Morose's eccentricity, but the humours of the others are clearly marked: the collegiate ladies, the Otters, and the fops Daw and La-Foole all have their obvious affectations. The exceptions are Dauphine and his two friends, all three lively young men about town, whose wit and high spirits add an air of gaiety not always present in Jonson's comedies.

The construction of the plot is deserving of careful study. No detail has been neglected. The action all takes place on a single day, and within a narrow area. With great skill Jonson suggests early in the play that some scheme is afoot, especially when Dauphine is on tenterhooks lest Truewit's indiscretion should have spoilt it all, but Truewit has only precipitated it, and the rapid development of the action makes us forget immediately about Dauphine's fears. Jonson's greatest skill is in the manipulation of a number of groups of characters, so that in his comedies there is always a greater variety of characters and of action than is to be found in the classical comedies he so much admired. The conclusion of the play, coming as it does when Morose's fate seems altogether hopeless, is a brilliant climax. The revelation of Epicoene's true sex not merely frees Morose from all his difficulties but reinstates Dauphine as his heir and shows up the pretences of Daw and La-Foole. The whole situation is a topsy-turvy reversal of the situation at the end of the romantic comedies of the period, where, as in more than one of Shakespeare's plays, the heroine casts off her boy's clothing to be united to the man she loves. But there is one important difference; Jonson has kept the disguise secret until the end. The surprise *dénouement* was especially popular about the time this play was written, but nowhere was it used with such startling effect as here. To quote Dryden again:

for the untying of it [the plot], 'tis so admirable that, when it is done, no one of the audience would think the poet could

have missed it; and yet it was concealed so much before the
last scene, that any other way would sooner have entered into
your thoughts.

The *Duchess of Malfi* provides an example of tragedy as it was
being written by a contemporary at the close of Shakespeare's
dramatic career. Yet Webster, for all his power, was a very uneven
writer. He wrote slowly, and he was referred to as "crabbed."
Careful scrutiny suggests that his plays were put together in a
piecemeal fashion, almost like a mosaic, and it has been shown
that he kept a commonplace book, into which he copied extracts
from his reading that he versified whenever he thought he could
use them. He is fond, too, of formal set pieces, such as character
sketches and fables, introduced into the dialogue of his plays. Yet
his character sketches often prove inconsistent with one another,
and with the characters themselves. Similarly his rhymed passages accord ill with the rhythm of his blank verse, and his moral
tags are out of place alongside the flashes of insight to which he
sometimes rises. His plot construction is also open to criticism.
He tends to concentrate on individual episodes rather than on the
narrative line of his plot. This tendency is even more pronounced
in his other great tragedy, *The White Devil*, but it can be seen
in *The Duchess of Malfi* too. The scene at Loretto (III.iv) exists
mainly for its spectacle, and the beautiful echo scene (V.iii),
which does not forward the plot in any way, is dramatically super-
fluous.

Webster's choice of an Italian setting for his tragedies was no
accident. His choice was not merely determined by the simple
romantic notion that stranger things can happen in a foreign land
than at home; for the Elizabethans, Italy had more special associa-
tions. It was the land of unnatural vices and subtle crimes; it was
the home of the Borgias and, above all, of Machiavelli, who in his
own century was regarded as the proponent of a nihilistic philosophy as sinister as that of a Hitler or Stalin, and whose first
name became a nickname for the devil himself. Webster was un-
doubtedly fascinated by stories of Italian crime, and his tragedies
express some of the revulsion felt in the more puritanically-
minded parts of Northern Europe against the corruption it saw in
contemporary Italian life.

Some of the combined attraction and revulsion that Webster

felt towards his subject matter is embodied in the character of Bosola. Insofar as he fills the role of a commentator he is a variant of what had become a familiar type of character on the stage of the period — the malcontent; but he is unusual in being much more than a satirical mouthpiece because of the share he takes in shaping the course of the action. The dualism in his character is emphasized from the outset; on the one hand he is analytical enough to perceive sharply and critically the corruption of the society to which he belongs; on the other hand, he tries to be utterly cynical about himself and, as the only means to self-advancement, allows himself to become an active tool of Ferdinand and the Cardinal. Under the extreme pressure of the suffering he has to inflict on the Duchess he revolts against his employers and turns against them, with the ironical result that his attempt at reparation is more disastrous than if he had merely remained passive.

There has been a good deal of discussion of Webster's use of horrors. Some critics have shuddered deliciously, but others, like William Archer and Bernard Shaw, have derided. Yet much of the debate misses the real point, that the tortures inflicted on the Duchess are to be regarded as the products of Ferdinand's diseased mind. Ferdinand is the central character of the play, as the actor list reveals when it informs us that this part was played by Richard Burbage, the leading actor of the company. Part of the reason for the persecution of the Duchess by her brothers is given as their arrogance and pride of birth; they wished, too, to control her duchy; but in the case of Ferdinand the motivation is complicated by other feelings. From the beginning there is something abnormal about him; his mind is hovering on the borders of sanity. As the play develops he becomes obsessed with what one can only call a combination of sadism and repressed incestuous passion. This is the diseased mind which inflicts its tortures on the Duchess. When she is dead Ferdinand's passion no longer has an object, and the remains of his sanity collapse.

The relations of the Duchess, Antonio, and Cariola are drawn with great truth of feeling and no little charm. They are honest and sincere with one another; the genuineness of their feelings is in vivid contrast to the treachery of the surrounding world, which overwhelms them. The world of the play, then, is a cruel and hard one; what stand out are the brief happiness of Antonio and the Duchess, and the courage with which she meets suffering and death. In her courage and resignation Webster reveals the triumph of the human spirit over adversity.

*The Knight of the Burning Pestle, Epicoene,* and *The Duchess of Malfi* were all written within three or four years of each other (1609–13); *The Broken Heart* is about twenty years later. Ford's play shows the influence of two very popular types of drama not otherwise represented in this collection: the tragedy of revenge and tragicomedy. The tragedy of revenge traces its descent from *The Spanish Tragedy* by Thomas Kyd, a play originally produced about the same time as *Tamburlaine;* it had a numerous progeny, of which *Hamlet* is the best known, and remained influential right up to the closing of the theatres in 1642. Tragicomedy was largely the creation of Beaumont and Fletcher; in this type of play, though there was a happy ending, the events were sensational, even melodramatic, and the sentiments expressed by the leading characters were lofty and ideal. Ford has combined elements of the two types of play, but in such a way as to suggest that the vigorous creative impulse of twenty and thirty and forty years previously is in a decline. It is as though all the possible situations have been used and re-used, and the dramatist's only hope is to play on the knowledge and expectations of the audience by taking familiar *clichés* of action and behavior, and trying to give them a sudden and unexpected twist. The same phenomenon can be observed in the detective thriller of our own day; the form is so worked out that little originality is possible any longer, and writers still using the form try desperately to find fresh variations of the old situations. Ford had real skill in finding such variations. There is no room to analyze Ford's technique in detail, but a couple of examples may be given. Orgilus in *The Broken Heart* is clearly the revenger; the spectator who had already seen a dozen or more revenge plays would at once sense something sinister in the promise he exacts from Euphranea that she will not marry without his consent, and would expect him to wreak some of his vengeance on Ithocles' friend Prophilus as well as on Ithocles himself; thus his ready consent to his sister's marriage comes as a shock. Again, Bassanes is at first held up as an almost wholly ridiculous figure; he is the foolishly jealous husband, no fit mate for Penthea, and deserving only to be cuckolded. But Penthea's rigid sense of honor preserves his good name; when she dies he is beside himself with grief and remorse, and becomes in the end a pathetic figure. In both these instances Ford has taken advantage of the expectations of his audience in order to surprise them.

Ford is not, however, without his virtues. One can feel that Bassanes, after all, may be truer to human nature than if he had been portrayed throughout merely as a jealous cuckold, and even if Calantha's assumed gaiety in the striking last scene is not true to human nature one could almost wish it were. It is impossible to achieve the effects Ford achieves without being a master of dramatic technique. His use of language, too, is more Shakespearian than that of any of his contemporaries; his poetry and rhetoric are not merely effective but often very moving. Nevertheless, the dominant tone in all his plays is that of the *fin de siècle*, the decline of the great age that will soon be coming to an end.

THE TEXT. Spelling and punctuation have, of course, been modernized, although in the title pages of the individual plays the actual spelling as well as the wording of the original editions has been reproduced. Each text has been checked either with the earliest edition or with a standard modern edition in old spelling. Editorial insertions (e.g., additional stage directions) have been kept to a minimum and, since the plays were originally written for performance on a stage without scenery, no attempt has been made to indicate the location of the scenes.

BOOKS. The two standard reference books for the period are E. K. Chambers, *The Elizabethan Stage*, 4 vols., 1923, and G. E. Bentley, *The Jacobean and Caroline Stage*, 5 vols. to date, 1941–. Besides giving full information about dramatists and their plays, these books also contain accounts of the theatres, acting companies, and individual actors. Brief histories of the drama are those by H. W. Wells, *Elizabethan and Jacobean Playwrights*, 1939, and T. M. Parrott and R. H. Ball, *A Short View of Elizabethan Drama*, 1943. Also of interest are two books by F. S. Boas, *An Introduction to Tudor Drama*, 1933, and *An Introduction to Stuart Drama*, 1946. Outstanding critical studies involving more than a single dramatist are: M. C. Bradbrook, *Themes and Conventions of Elizabethan Tragedy*, 1935, U. M. Ellis-Fermor, *The Jacobean Drama*, 1936, and R. Ornstein, *The Moral Vision of Jacobean Tragedy*, 1960. Studies of the individual authors of the plays included in this volume are listed at the end of the note preceding each play.

# TAMBURLAINE
## the Great.

*Who, from a Scythian Shephearde,*
by his rare and woonderfull Conquests,
became a most puissant and migh-
tye Monarque,

And (for his tyranny, and terrour in
Warre) was tearmed,
The Scourge of God.

*Deuided into two Tragicall Dis-*
courses, as they were sundrie times
shewed vpon Stages in the Citie
of London,

By the right honorable the Lord
Admyrall, his seruantes.

Now first, and newlie published.

LONDON.
Printed by Richard Ihones: at the signe
of the Rose and Crowne neere Hol-
borne Bridge. 1590.

# Tamburlaine the Great

 CHRISTOPHER MARLOWE
was born in 1564, the son of a shoemaker in Canterbury. He was
educated at the King's School attached to the Cathedral, and from
there went with a scholarship to Corpus Christi College, Cambridge. He took his B.A. in 1584 and his M.A. in 1587, and there
exists the record of a letter from the Privy Council commanding
the University not to withhold the higher degree for lack of sufficient residence, since Marlowe had been abroad on the Queen's
service. The nature of this service is not known. Later in the
same year (1587) Marlowe made his first appearance in London
as a dramatist, and the initial success of *Tamburlaine* was followed
by that of other plays equally successful: *Dr. Faustus*, *The Jew of
Malta*, and *Edward II*. Marlowe also became acquainted with
many of the chief literary figures of the age, including Sir Walter
Ralegh, and gained a reputation as a daring free-thinker. In 1593
an information was lain against him accusing him of atheism, but
before any proceedings were taken against him he was stabbed to
death in a tavern at Deptford by one Ingram Frezer in a dispute
over the reckoning.

In spite of the fact that *Tamburlaine* is universally attributed to
Marlowe, the contemporary evidence for his authorship is slight.
No author's name appeared on the title pages of any of the early
editions, but Robert Greene in his *Perimedes* couples "that athe-
ist Tamburlan" with "spirits as bred of Merlin's race." "Merlin"
and "Marlin" were alternative spellings of Marlowe's name, so the
punning reference points to him more clearly than might at first
appear. The allusion in *Perimedes* also gives a valuable clue to the
date of *Tamburlaine;* since *Perimedes* came out in 1588 and Marlowe had returned from abroad in 1587, the winter of 1587–88 is
usually regarded as the time of the play's first performance. It
must have been followed fairly soon by the second part, and both
parts were published together in 1590.

On 14 August 1590 "the twooe commical discourses of Tomber-
lin the Cithian Shepparde" were entered in the Stationers' Register, though when the book was published later in the year the
piece was said to be "Deuided into two Tragicall Discourses." The
title page of the quarto also states that the plays had been "sundrie

times shewed vpon Stages in the Citie of London, By the right honorable the Lord Admyrall his seruantes." The part of Tamburlaine was played by Edward Alleyn, the leading actor in the Admiral's company, and the dramatist Thomas Heywood subsequently stated that it was in this part that Alleyn first "wan the Attribute of peerelesse." The *Diary* of Alleyn's father-in-law, the theatrical manager and financier Philip Henslowe, records a series of performances of *Tamburlaine* in 1594.

Tamburlaine is better known to modern historians as the Mongolian conqueror Timur Khan, who in 1402 overthrew Bajazet, the head of the Turkish Empire, and himself died in 1405. Over forty books have been identified in which Marlowe could have read accounts of Tamburlaine, but the two he is most likely to have used are a compendium of history and geography by Pedro Mexia first published in Spanish in 1542 under the title *Silva de varia lection*, and a life of Tamburlaine in Latin by Petrus Perondinus entitled *Magni Tamerlanis Scythiarum Imperatoris Vita* and published at Florence in 1553. From these two books Marlowe could have learned all the available historical facts about Tamburlaine, though he altered and arranged them for the purposes of the play.

BOOKS. *The Works and Life of Christopher Marlowe*, London, v.d., under the general editorship of R. H. Case, contains a life by C. F. Tucker Brooke and an edition of both parts of *Tamburlaine* by U. M. Ellis-Fermor. The most elaborate study of Marlowe is to be found in J. E. Bakeless, *The Tragicall History of Christopher Marlowe*, 2 vols., Cambridge, Mass., 1942; books on certain specific aspects of Marlowe's life are Leslie Hotson, *The Death of Christopher Marlowe*, London, 1925, and Mark Eccles, *Christopher Marlowe in London*, Cambridge, Mass., 1934. More general studies are: F. S. Boas, *Christopher Marlowe, a biographical and critical study*, Oxford, 1940; U. M. Ellis-Fermor, *Christopher Marlowe*, London, 1927; P. H. Kocher, *Christopher Marlowe, a study of his thought, learning, and character*, Chapel Hill, N.C., 1946; Harry Levin, *The Overreacher, a study of Christopher Marlowe*, Cambridge, Mass., 1952; F. P. Wilson, *Marlowe and the Early Shakespeare*, Oxford, 1953.

[*Dramatis Personae*

MYCETES, King of Persia
COSROE, his Brother
ORTYGIUS,
CENEUS,
MEANDER,        } Persian Lords and Captains
MENAPHON,
THERIDAMAS,
TAMBURLAINE, a Scythian Shepherd
TECHELLES,      } his Followers
USUMCASANE,
BAJAZETH, Emperor of the Turks
KING OF ARABIA
KING OF FEZ
KING OF MOROCCO
KING OF ARGIER
SOLDAN OF EGYPT
GOVERNOR OF DAMASCUS
AGYDAS,         } Median Lords
MAGNETES,
CAPOLIN, an Egyptian Captain
PHILEMUS, a Messenger

ZENOCRATE, Daughter of the Soldan of Egypt
ANIPPE, her Maid
ZABINA, Wife of Bajazeth
EBEA, her Maid

Virgins of Damascus; Bassoes, Lords, Citizens, Moors, Soldiers, and Attendants]

## The Prologue

From jigging veins of rhyming mother wits,
And such conceits as clownage keeps in pay,
We'll lead you to the stately tent of war,
Where you shall hear the Scythian Tamburlaine
Threat'ning the world with high astounding terms,
And scourging kingdoms with his conquering sword.
View but his picture in this tragic glass,
And then applaud his fortunes as you please.

## Actus 1. Scæna 1.

*Mycetes, Cosroe, Meander, Theridamas,*
*Ortygius, Ceneus, [Menaphon,] with others*

*Myc.* Brother Cosroe, I find myself aggriev'd,
Yet insufficient to express the same,
For it requires a great and thund'ring speech.
Good brother, tell the cause unto my lords;
I know you have a better wit than I.

*Cos.* Unhappy Persia! — that in former age
Hast been the seat of mighty conquerors,
That, in their prowess and their policies,
Have triumph'd over Afric and the bounds
Of Europe, where the sun dares scarce appear
For freezing meteors and congealed cold, —
Now to be rul'd and governed by a man
At whose birthday Cynthia with Saturn[1] join'd,
And Jove, the Sun, and Mercury[2] denied
To shed their influence in his fickle brain!
Now Turks and Tartars shake their swords at thee,
Meaning to mangle all thy provinces.

*Myc.* Brother, I see your meaning well enough,
And through your planets I perceive you think
I am not wise enough to be a king;
But I refer me to my noblemen
That know my wit, and can be witnesses.
I might command you to be slain for this:
Meander, might I not?

*Meand.* Not for so small a fault, my sovereign lord.

*Myc.* I mean it not, but yet I know I might.
Yet live; yea, live, Mycetes wills it so.
Meander, thou, my faithful counsellor,
Declare the cause of my conceived grief,
Which is, God knows, about that Tamburlaine,
That, like a fox in midst of harvest time,
Doth prey upon my flocks of passengers;[3]
And, as I hear, doth mean to pull my plumes:
Therefore 't is good and meet for to be wise.

[1] Unfavorable planets. [2] Favorable planets.
[3] Caravans of traders and travelers.

7

*Meand.*   Oft have I heard your majesty complain
Of Tamburlaine, that sturdy Scythian thief,
That robs your merchants of Persepolis[4]
Treading by land unto the Western Isles,
And in your confines with his lawless train
Daily commits incivil outrages,
Hoping (misled by dreaming prophecies)
To reign in Asia, and with barbarous arms
To make himself the monarch of the East;
But ere he march in Asia, or display
His vagrant[5] ensign in the Persian fields,
Your grace hath taken order by Theridamas,
Charg'd with a thousand horse, to apprehend
And bring him captive to your highness' throne.

*Myc.*   Full true thou speak'st, and like thyself, my lord,
Whom I may term a Damon[6] for thy love:
Therefore 't is best, if so it like you all,
To send my thousand horse incontinent[7]
To apprehend that paltry Scythian.
How like you this, my honourable lords?
Is it not a kingly resolution?

*Cos.*   It cannot choose, because it comes from you.

*Myc.*   Then hear thy charge, valiant Theridamas,
The chiefest captain of Mycetes' host,
The hope of Persia, and the very legs
Whereon our state doth lean as on a staff,
That holds us up, and foils our neighbour foes.
Thou shalt be leader of this thousand horse,
Whose foaming gall with rage and high disdain
Have sworn the death of wicked Tamburlaine.
Go frowning forth; but come thou smiling home,
As did Sir Paris with the Grecian dame.[8]
Return with speed — time passeth swift away;
Our life is frail, and we may die to-day.

*Ther.*   Before the moon renew her borrow'd light,
Doubt not, my lord and gracious sovereign,
But Tamburlaine and that Tartarian rout
Shall either perish by our warlike hands,
Or plead for mercy at your highness' feet.

*Myc.*   Go, stout Theridamas! thy words are swords,
And with thy looks thou conquerest all thy foes.

[4] Capital of Persia in ancient times, though not in the Middle Ages.
[5] Wandering, moving.          [6] Type or model of friendship.
[7] Immediately.          [8] Helen.

I long to see thee back return from thence,
That I may view these milk-white steeds of mine
All loaden with the heads of killed men,
And from their knees even to their hoofs below
Besmear'd with blood, that makes a dainty show.

 *Ther.* Then now, my lord, I humbly take my leave.
 *Myc.* Theridamas, farewell! ten thousand times.

            *Exit [Theridamas].*

Ah, Menaphon, why stay'st thou thus behind,
When other men press forward for renown?
Go, Menaphon, go into Scythia;
And foot by foot follow Theridamas.

 *Cos.* Nay, pray you let him stay; a greater task
Fits Menaphon than warring with a thief.
Create him Prorex⁹ of all Africa,
That he may win the Babylonians' hearts
Which will revolt from Persian government,
Unless they have a wiser king than you.

 *Myc.* "Unless they have a wiser king than you!"
These are his words; Meander, set them down.

 *Cos.* And add this to them — that all Asia
Lament to see the folly of their king.

 *Myc.* Well, here I swear by this my royal seat, —
 *Cos.* You may do well to kiss it then.   *[Aside.]*
 *Myc.* Emboss'd with silk as best beseems my state,
To be reveng'd for these contemptuous words.
Oh, where is duty and allegiance now?
Fled to the Caspian or the Ocean main?
What shall I call thee? Brother? — No, a foe;
Monster of nature! Shame unto thy stock!
That dar'st presume thy sovereign for to mock!
Meander, come: I am abus'd, Meander.

   *Exit [with Meander, &c.]. Manent Cosroe and Menaphon.*

 *Men.* How now, my lord? What, mated¹ and amaz'd
To hear the king thus threaten like himself!

 *Cos.* Ah, Menaphon, I pass² not for his threats;
The plot is laid by Persian noblemen
And captains of the Median garrisons
To crown me Emperor of Asia.
But this it is that doth excruciate
The very substance of my vexed soul —
To see our neighbours, that were wont to quake

---

  ⁹ Viceroy.     ¹ Stupefied.    ² Care.

And tremble at the Persian monarch's name,
Now sits and laughs our regiment[3] to scorn;
And that which might resolve me into tears,
Men from the farthest equinoctial line
Have swarm'd in troops into the Eastern India,
Lading their ships with gold and precious stones,
And made their spoils from all our provinces.
 *Men.* This should entreat your highness to rejoice.
Since Fortune gives you opportunity
To gain the title of a conqueror
By curing of this maimed empery.
Afric and Europe bordering on your land,
And continent to your dominions,
How easily may you, with a mighty host,
Pass into Græcia, as did Cyrus[4] once,
And cause them to withdraw their forces home,
Lest you subdue the pride of Christendom.  [*Trumpet within.*]
 *Cos.* But, Menaphon, what means this trumpet's sound?
 *Men.* Behold, my lord! Ortygius and the rest,
Bringing the crown to make you Emperor.

*Enter Ortygius and Ceneus, bearing a crown, with others*

 *Orty.* Magnificent and mighty Prince Cosroe,
We, in the name of other Persian states
And commons of this mighty monarchy,
Present thee with th' imperial diadem.
 *Cen.* The warlike soldiers and the gentlemen,
That heretofore have fill'd Persepolis
With Afric captains taken in the field,
Whose ransom made them march in coats of gold,
With costly jewels hanging at their ears,
And shining stones upon their lofty crests,
Now living idle in the walled towns,
Wanting both pay and martial discipline,
Begin in troops to threaten civil war,
And openly exclaim against the king.
Therefore, to stay all sudden mutinies,
We will invest your highness Emperor,
Whereat the soldiers will conceive more joy
Than did the Macedonians at the spoil
Of great Darius[5] and his wealthy host.
 *Cos.* Well, since I see the state of Persia droop
And languish in my brother's government,

---

[3] Rule.    [4] Founder of the ancient Persian Empire.
[5] Defeated by Alexander the Great at Issus in 333 B.C.

I willingly receive th' imperial crown,
And vow to wear it for my country's good,
In spite of them shall malice my estate.

   *Orty.* And in assurance of desir'd success,
We here do crown thee monarch of the East,
Emperor of Asia and of Persia;
Great Lord of Media and Armenia;
Duke of Africa and Albania,
Mesopotamia and of Parthia,
East India and the late-discovered isles;
Chief Lord of all the wide, vast Euxine sea,[6]
And of the ever-raging Caspian lake.
Long live Cosroe, mighty Emperor!

   *Cos.* And Jove may never let me longer live
Than I may seek to gratify your love,
And cause the soldiers that thus honour me
To triumph over many provinces!
By whose desires and discipline in arms
I doubt not shortly but to reign sole king,
And with the army of Theridamas,
(Whither we presently will fly, my lords)
To rest secure against my brother's force.

   *Orty.* We knew, my lord, before we brought the crown,
Intending your investion[7] so near
The residence of your despised brother,
The lords would not be too exasperate
To injure or suppress your worthy title;
Or, if they would, there are in readiness
Ten thousand horse to carry you from hence,
In spite of all suspected enemies.

   *Cos.* I know it well, my lord, and thank you all.

   *Orty.* Sound up the trumpets, then. God save the King!
                  *[Trumpets sound.] Exeunt.*

## Actus 1. Scæna 2.

*Tamburlaine leading Zenocrate: Techelles, Usum-
casane, [Agydas, Magnetes and] other Lords, and
Soldiers, loaden with treasure*

   *Tamb.* Come, lady, let not this appal your thoughts;
The jewels and the treasure we have ta'en
Shall be reserv'd, and you in better state,

---

[6] The Black Sea.                  [7] Investiture.

Than if you were arriv'd in Syria,
Even in the circle of your father's arms,
The mighty Soldan[8] of Egyptia.

    *Zeno.*   Ah, shepherd! pity my distressed **plight,**
(If, as thou seemst, thou art so mean a man,)
And seek not to enrich thy followers
By lawless rapine from a silly maid,
Who travelling with these Median lords
To Memphis, from my uncle's country of **Media,**
Where all my youth I have been governed,
Have pass'd the army of the mighty Turk,
Bearing his privy signet and his hand
To safe conduct us thorough Africa.

    *Mag.*   And since we have arriv'd in Scythia,
Besides rich presents from the puissant Cham,[9]
We have his highness' letters to command
Aid and assistance, if we stand in need.

    *Tamb.*   But now you see these letters **and commands**
Are countermanded by a greater man;
And through my provinces you must expect
Letters of conduct from my mightiness,
If you intend to keep your treasure safe.
But, since I love to live at liberty,
As easily may you get the Soldan's crown
As any prizes out of my precinct;
For they are friends that help to wean my state
Till men and kingdoms help to strengthen it,
And must maintain my life exempt from servitude. —
But, tell me, madam, is your grace betroth'd?

    *Zeno.*   I am, my lord — for so you do import.

    *Tamb.*   I am a lord, for so my deeds shall **prove:**
And yet a shepherd by my parentage.
But, lady, this fair face and heavenly hue
Must grace his bed that conquers Asia,
And means to be a terror to the world,
Measuring the limits of his empery
By east and west, as Phœbus doth his course.
Lie here, ye weeds that I disdain to wear!
This complete armour and this curtle-axe[1]
Are adjuncts more beseeming Tamburlaine.
And, madam, whatsoever you esteem
Of this success and loss unvalued,

---

[8] Sultan.       [9] Emperor of the Tartars.       [1] Cutlass.

Both may invest you Empress of the East;
And these that seem but silly country swains
May have the leading of so great an host,
As with their weight shall make the mountains quake,
Even as when windy exhalations,[2]
Fighting for passage, tilt[3] within the earth.

*Tech.*   As princely lions, when they rouse themselves,
Stretching their paws, and threat'ning herds of beasts,
So in his armour looketh Tamburlaine.
Methinks I see kings kneeling at his feet,
And he with frowning brows and fiery looks,
Spurning their crowns from off their captive heads.

*Usum.*   And making thee and me, Techelles, kings,
That even to death will follow Tamburlaine.

*Tamb.*   Nobly resolv'd, sweet friends and followers!
These lords, perhaps, do scorn our estimates,
And think we prattle with distemper'd spirits;
But since they measure our deserts so mean, —
That in conceit[4] bear empires on our spears,
Affecting thoughts coequal with the clouds, —
They shall be kept our forced followers,
Till with their eyes they view us emperors.

*Zeno.*   The gods, defenders of the innocent,
Will never prosper your intended drifts,
That thus oppress poor friendless passengers.
Therefore at least admit us liberty,
Even as thou hop'st to be eternized
By living Asia's mighty Emperor.

*Agyd.*   I hope our lady's treasure and our own
May serve for ransom to our liberties.
Return our mules and empty camels back,
That we may travel into Syria,
Where her betrothed lord Alcidamus,
Expects th' arrival of her highness' person.

*Mag.*   And wheresoever we repose ourselves,
We will report but well of Tamburlaine.

*Tamb.*   Disdains Zenocrate to live with me?
Or you, my lords, to be my followers?
Think you I weigh this treasure more than you?
Not all the gold in India's wealthy arms
Shall buy the meanest soldier in my train.
Zenocrate, lovelier than the love of Jove,

---

[2] Blasts.            [3] Battle.            [4] Imagination.

Brighter than is the silver Rhodope,[5]
Fairer than whitest snow on Scythian hills, —
Thy person is more worth to Tamburlaine,
Than the possession of the Persian crown,
Which gracious stars have promis'd at my birth.
A hundreth Tartars shall attend on thee,
Mounted on steeds swifter than Pegasus;
Thy garments shall be made of Median silk,
Enchas'd with precious jewels of mine own,
More rich and valurous[6] than Zenocrate's.
With milk-white harts upon an ivory sled,
Thou shalt be drawn amidst the frozen pools,
And scale the icy mountains' lofty tops,
Which with thy beauty will be soon resolv'd.[7]
My martial prizes, with five hundred men
Won on the fifty-headed[8] Volga's waves,
Shall all we offer to Zenocrate, —
And then myself to fair Zenocrate.
    *Tech.*   What now! — in love?
    *Tamb.*   Techelles, women must be flattered:
But this is she with whom I am in love.

*Enter a Soldier*

    *Sold.*   News! news!
    *Tamb.*   How now, what's the matter?
    *Sold.*   A thousand Persian horsemen are at hand,
Sent from the king to overcome us all.
    *Tamb.*   How now, my lords of Egypt, and Zenocrate!
Now must your jewels be restor'd again,
And I that triumph'd so be overcome?
How say you, lordings, — is not this your hope?
    *Agyd.*   We hope yourself will willingly restore them.
    *Tamb.*   Such hope, such fortune, have the thousand horse.
Soft ye, my lords, and sweet Zenocrate!
You must be forced from me ere you go.
A thousand horsemen! — We five hundred foot! —
An odds too great for us to stand against.
But are they rich? And is their armour good?
    *Sold.*   Their plumed helms are wrought with beaten gold,
Their swords enamell'd, and about their necks

---

    [5] Mountain range in Thrace.
    [6] Costly, valuable.
    [7] Melted.
    [8] A reference to the delta of the Volga, not to its sources.

Hangs massy chains of gold, down to the waist,
In every part exceeding brave and rich.
   *Tamb.*    Then shall we fight courageously with them?
Or look you I should play the orator?
   *Tech.*    No; cowards and faint-hearted runaways
Look for orations when the foe is near.
Our swords shall play the orators for us.
   *Usum.*    Come! let us meet them at the mountain foot,
And with a sudden and an hot alarm,
Drive all their horses headlong down the hill.
   *Tech.*    Come, let us march!
   *Tamb.*    Stay, Techelles! ask a parley first.

*The Soldiers enter*

Open the mails,[9] yet guard the treasure sure;
Lay out our golden wedges to the view,
That their reflections may amaze the Persians;
And look we friendly on them when they come.
But if they offer word or violence,
We'll fight five hundred men-at-arms to one,
Before we part with our possession.
And 'gainst the general we will lift our swords,
And either lanch[1] his greedy thirsting throat,
Or take him prisoner, and his chain shall serve
For manacles, till he be ransom'd home.
   *Tech.*    I hear them come; shall we encounter them?
   *Tamb.*    Keep all your standings and not stir a foot,
Myself will bide the danger of the brunt.

*Enter Theridamas with others*

   *Ther.*    Where is this Scythian Tamburlaine?
   *Tamb.*    Whom seek'st thou, Persian? — I am **Tamburlaine.**
   *Ther.*    Tamburlaine! —
A Scythian shepherd so embellished
With nature's pride and richest furniture!
His looks do menace Heaven and dare the gods:
His fiery eyes are fix'd upon the earth,
As if he now devis'd some stratagem,
Or meant to pierce Avernus' darksome vaults
To pull the triple-headed dog[2] from hell.
   *Tamb.*    Noble and mild this Persian seems to be,
If outward habit judge the inward man.

---

[9] Trunks, bags.        [1] Cut.        [2] Cerberus.

*Tech.*  His deep affections make him passionate.
*Tamb.*  With what a majesty he rears his looks!
In thee, thou valiant man of Persia,
I see the folly of thy emperor.
Art thou but captain of a thousand horse,
That by charácters graven in thy brows,
And by thy martial face and stout aspect,
Deserv'st to have the leading of an host!
Forsake thy king, and do but join with me,
And we will triumph over all the world.
I hold the Fates bound fast in iron chains,
And with my hand turn Fortune's wheel about:
And sooner shall the sun fall from his sphere
Than Tamburlaine be slain or overcome.
Draw forth thy sword, thou mighty man-at-arms,
Intending but to raze[3] my charmed skin,
And Jove himself will stretch his hand from Heaven
To ward the blow and shield me safe from harm.
See how he rains down heaps of gold in showers,
As if he meant to give my soldiers pay!
And as a sure and grounded argument,
That I shall be the monarch of the East,
He sends this Soldan's daughter, rich and brave,
To be my Queen and portly[4] Emperess.[5]
If thou wilt stay with me, renowmed man,
And lead thy thousand horse with my conduct,[6]
Besides thy share of this Egyptian prize,
Those thousand horse shall sweat with martial spoil
Of conquer'd kingdoms and of cities sack'd.
Both we will walk upon the lofty clifts,[7]
And Christian merchants that with Russian stems[8]
Plough up huge furrows in the Caspian sea,
Shall vail[9] to us, as lords of all the lake.
Both we will reign as consuls of the earth,
And mighty kings shall be our senators.
Jove sometime masked in a shepherd's weed,
And by those steps that he hath scal'd the Heavens
May we become immortal like the gods.
Join with me now in this my mean estate,

---

[3] Graze, scratch.          [4] Stately.
[5] Marlowe's metre often demands the addition of a syllable in such words.
[6] Under my direction.          [7] Cliffs.
[8] Ships.          [9] Salute.

(I call it mean because, being yet obscure,
The nations far remov'd admire me not,)
And when my name and honour shall be spread
As far as Boreas[1] claps his brazen wings,
Or fair Boötes[2] sends his cheerful light,
Then shalt thou be competitor with me,
And sit with Tamburlaine in all his majesty.

*Ther.*   Not Hermes, prolocutor[3] to the gods,
Could use persuasions more pathetical.[4]

*Tamb.*   Nor are Apollo's oracles more true
Than thou shalt find my vaunts substantial.

*Tech.*   We are his friends, and if the Persian king
Should offer present dukedoms to our state,
We think it loss to make exchange for that
We are assur'd of by our friend's success.

*Usum.*   And kingdoms at the least we all expect,
Besides the honour in assured conquests,
Where kings shall crouch unto our conquering swords,
And hosts of soldiers stand amaz'd at us;
When with their fearful tongues they shall confess:
These are the men that all the world admires.

*Ther.*   What strong enchantments 'tice my yielding soul
As these resolved noble Scythians?
But shall I prove a traitor to my king?

*Tamb.*   No, but the trusty friend of Tamburlaine.

*Ther.*   Won with thy words, and conquer'd with thy looks,
I yield myself, my men, and horse to thee,
To be partaker of thy good or ill,
As long as life maintains Theridamas.

*Tamb.*   Theridamas, my friend, take here my hand,
Which is as much as if I swore by Heaven,
And call'd the gods to witness of my vow:
Thus shall my heart be still combin'd with thine
Until our bodies turn to elements,
And both our souls aspire celestial thrones.
Techelles and Casane, welcome him!

*Tech.*   Welcome, renowmed Persian, to us all!

*Usum.*   Long may Theridamas remain with us!

*Tamb.*   These are my friends, in whom I more rejoice
Than doth the King of Persia in his crown,
And by the love of Pylades and Orestes,
Whose statues we adore in Scythia,

---

[1] North wind.          [2] A northern constellation.
[3] Spokesman.          [4] Moving.

Thyself and them shall never part from me
Before I crown you kings in Asia.
Make much of them, gentle Theridamas,
And they will never leave thee till the death.
    *Ther.*   Nor thee nor them, thrice noble Tamburlaine,
Shall want my heart to be with gladness pierc'd
To do you honour and security.
    *Tamb.*   A thousand thanks, worthy Theridamas.
And now, fair madam, and my noble lords,
If you will willingly remain with me,
You shall have honours as your merits be;
Or else you shall be forc'd with slavery.
    *Agyd.*   We yield unto thee, happy Tamburlaine.
    *Tamb.*   For you then, madam, I am out of doubt.
    *Zeno.*   I must be pleas'd perforce. Wretched Zenocrate!

                                          *Exeunt.*


### *Actus 2.  Scæna 1.*

#### *Cosroe, Menaphon, Ortygius, Ceneus, with other Soldiers*

    *Cos.*   Thus far are we towards Theridamas,
And valiant Tamburlaine, the man of fame,
The man that in the forehead of his fortune
Bears figures of renown and miracle.
But tell me, that hast seen him, Menaphon,
What stature wields he, and what personage?
    *Men.*   Of stature tall, and straightly fashioned,
Like his desire, lift[5] upwards and divine;
So large of limbs, his joints so strongly knit,
Such breadth of shoulders as might mainly[6] bear
Old Atlas' burthen; 'twixt his manly pitch,[7]
A pearl, more worth than all the world, is plac'd,
Wherein by curious sovereignty of art
Are fix'd his piercing instruments of sight,
Whose fiery circles bear encompassed
A heaven of heavenly bodies in their spheres,
That guides his steps and actions to the throne,
Where honour sits invested royally:
Pale of complexion (wrought in him with passion)
Thirsting with sovereignty, with love of arms.

---

[5] Lifted.                [6] Strongly.                [7] Breadth of shoulder.

His lofty brows in folds do figure death,
And in their smoothness amity and life;
About them hangs a knot of amber hair,
Wrapped in curls, as fierce Achilles' was,
On which the breath of Heaven delights to play,
Making it dance with wanton majesty.
His arms and fingers, long, and sinewy,
Betokening valour and excess of strength —
In every part proportioned like the man
Should make the world subdu'd to Tamburlaine.

    *Cos.*    Well hast thou portray'd in thy terms of life
The face and personage of a wondrous man;
Nature doth strive with Fortune and his stars
To make him famous in accomplish'd worth;
And well his merits show him to be made
His fortune's master and the king of men,
That could persuade at such a sudden pinch,
With reasons of his valour and his life,
A thousand sworn and overmatching foes.
Then, when our powers in points of swords are join'd
And clos'd in compass of the killing bullet,
Though strait the passage and the port[8] be made
That leads to palace of my brother's life,
Proud is his fortune if we pierce it not.
And when the princely Persian diadem
Shall overweigh his weary witless head,
And fall like mellow'd fruit with shakes of death,
In fair Persia, noble Tamburlaine
Shall be my regent and remain as king.

    *Orty.*    In happy hour we have set the crown
Upon your kingly head, that seeks our honour
In joining with the man ordain'd by Heaven
To further every action to the best.

    *Cen.*    He that with shepherds and a little spoil
Durst, in disdain of wrong and tyranny,
Defend his freedom 'gainst a monarchy,
What will he do supported by a king,
Leading a troop of gentlemen and lords,
And stuff'd with treasure for his highest thoughts!

    *Cos.*    And such shall wait on worthy Tamburlaine.
Our army will be forty thousand strong,
When Tamburlaine and brave Theridamas
Have met us by the river Araris;

   [8] Gate.

And all conjoin'd to meet the witless king,
That now is marching near to Parthia,
And with unwilling soldiers faintly arm'd,
To seek revenge on me and Tamburlaine,
To whom, sweet Menaphon, direct me straight.
  *Men.*   I will, my lord.                                        *Exeunt.*


## *Actus 2.   Scæna 2.*
### *Mycetes, Meander, with other Lords and Soldiers*

  *Myc.*   Come, my Meander, let us to this gear.
I tell you true, my heart is swoln with wrath
On this same thievish villain, Tamburlaine,
And of that false Cosroe, my traitorous brother.
Would it not grieve a king to be so abus'd
And have a thousand horsemen ta'en away?
And, which is worst, to have his diadem
Sought for by such scald[9] knaves as love him not?
I think it would; well then, by Heavens I swear,
Aurora shall not peep out of her doors,
But I will have Cosroe by the head,
And kill proud Tamburlaine with point of sword.
Tell you the rest, Meander; I have said.
  *Meand.*   Then having past Armenian deserts now,
And pitch'd our tents under the Georgian hills,
Whose tops are cover'd with Tartarian thieves,
That lie in ambush, waiting for a prey,
What should we do but bid them battle straight,
And rid the world of those detested troops?
Lest, if we let them linger here awhile,
They gather strength by power of fresh supplies.
This country swarms with vile outrageous men
That live by rapine and by lawless spoil,
Fit soldiers for the wicked Tamburlaine;
And he that could with gifts and promises
Inveigle him that led a thousand horse,
And make him false his faith unto his king,
Will quickly win such as are like himself.
Therefore cheer up your minds; prepare to fight;
He that can take or slaughter Tamburlaine
Shall rule the province of Albania:
  [9] Scurvy.

Who brings that traitor's head, Theridamas,
Shall have a government in Media,
Beside the spoil of him and all his train:
But if Cosroe, (as our spials say,
And as we know) remains with Tamburlaine,
His highness' pleasure is that he should live,
And be reclaim'd with princely lenity.

[*Enter a Spy*]

*A Spy.* An hundred horsemen of my company,
Scouting abroad upon these champion[1] plains,
Have view'd the army of the Scythians,
Which make reports it far exceeds the king's.
*Meand.* Suppose they be in number infinite,
Yet being void of martial discipline
All running headlong after greedy spoils,
And more regarding gain than victory,
Like to the cruel brothers of the earth,
Sprung of the teeth of dragons venomous,[2]
Their careless swords shall lanch their fellows' throats,
And make us triumph in their overthrow.
*Myc.* Was there such brethren, sweet Meander, say,
That sprung of teeth of dragons venomous?
*Meand.* So poets say, my lord.
*Myc.* And 't is a pretty toy to be a poet.
Well, well, Meander, thou art deeply read,
And having thee, I have a jewel sure.
Go on, my lord, and give your charge, I say;
Thy wit will make us conquerors to-day.
*Meand.* Then, noble soldiers, to entrap these thieves,
That live confounded in disorder'd troops,
If wealth or riches may prevail with them,
We have our camels laden all with gold,
Which you that be but common soldiers
Shall fling in every corner of the field;
And while the base-born Tartars take it up,
You, fighting more for honour than for gold,
Shall massacre those greedy-minded slaves;
And when their scatter'd army is subdu'd,
And you march on their slaughter'd carcases,
Share equally the gold that bought their lives,

---

[1] Level.
[2] The armed warriors who sprang out of the earth from the dragon's teeth sown by Cadmus, and who proceeded to slay one another.

And live like gentlemen in Persia.
Strike up the drum and march courageously!
Fortune herself doth sit upon our crests.

    *Myc.*   He tells you true, my masters: so he does.
Drums, why sound ye not, when Meander speaks?

                         *Exeunt* [*drums sounding*].


### *Actus 2.   Scæna 3.*

*Cosroe, Tamburlaine, Theridamas, Techelles, Usumca-*
*sane, Ortygius, with others*

    *Cos.*   Now, worthy Tamburlaine, have I repos'd
In thy approved fortunes all my hope.
What think'st thou, man, shall come of our attempts?
For even as from assured oracle,
I take thy doom for satisfaction.

    *Tamb.*   And so mistake you not a whit, my lord;
For fates and oracles of Heaven have sworn
To royalize the deeds of Tamburlaine,
And make them blest that share in his attempts.
And doubt you not but, if you favour me,
And let my fortunes and my valour sway
To some direction in your martial deeds,
The world will strive with hosts of men-at-arms,
To swarm unto the ensign I support:
The host of Xerxes, which by fame is said
To drink the mighty Parthian Araris,[3]
Was but a handful to that we will have.
Our quivering lances, shaking in the air,
And bullets, like Jove's dreadful thunderbolts,
Enroll'd in flames and fiery smouldering mists,
Shall threat the gods more than Cyclopian wars:
And with our sun-bright armour as we march,
We'll chase the stars from Heaven and dim their eyes
That stand and muse at our admired arms.

    *Ther.*   You see, my lord, what working words he hath;
But when you see his actions top his speech,
Your speech will stay or so extol his worth
As I shall be commended and excus'd
For turning my poor charge to his direction.
And these his two renowmed friends, my lord,
Would make one thrust and strive to be retain'd

   [3] The Persian army under Xerxes was said to have been so **huge that**
it drank dry the river Araris, or Scamander.

In such a great degree of amity.

    *Tech.*   With duty and with amity we yield
Our utmost service to the fair Cosroe.

    *Cos.*   Which I esteem as portion of my crown.
Usumcasane and Techelles both,
When she[4] that rules in Rhamnus' golden gates,
And makes a passage for all prosperous arms,
Shall make me solely Emperor of Asia,
Then shall your meeds and valours be advanc'd
To rooms of honour and nobility.

    *Tamb.*   Then haste, Cosroe, to be king alone,
That I with these, my friends, and all my men
May triumph in our long-expected fate.
The king, your brother, is now hard at hand:
Meet with the fool, and rid your royal shoulders
Of such a burthen as outweighs the sands
And all the craggy rocks of Caspia.

*[Enter a Messenger]*

    *Mess.*   My lord, we have discover'd the enemy
Ready to charge you with a mighty army.

    *Cos.*   Come, Tamburlaine! now whet thy winged sword,
And lift thy lofty arm into the clouds,
That it may reach the King of Persia's crown,
And set it safe on my victorious head.

    *Tamb.*   See where it is, the keenest curtle-axe
That e'er made passage thorough Persian arms.
These are the wings shall make it fly as swift
As doth the lightning or the breath of Heaven,
And kill as sure as it swiftly flies.

    *Cos.*   Thy words assure me of kind success;
Go, valiant soldier, go before and charge
The fainting army of that foolish king.

    *Tamb.*   Usumcasane and Techelles, come!
We are enough to scare the enemy,
And more than needs to make an emperor.   *[Exeunt] to the battle,*

[Scene IV]

*and Mycetes comes out alone with his crown in his
hand, offering to hide it*

    *Myc.*   Accurs'd be he that first invented war!
They knew not, ah, they knew not, simple men,

    [4] The goddess Nemesis, who had a famous temple at Rhamnus.

How those were hit by pelting cannon shot
Stand staggering like a quivering aspen leaf,
Fearing the force of Boreas' boisterous blasts.
In what a lamentable case were I,
If Nature had not given me wisdom's lore!
For kings are clouts[5] that every man shoots at,
Our crown the pin[6] that thousands seek to cleave;
Therefore in policy I think it good
To hide it close; a goodly stratagem,
And far from any man that is a fool:
So shall not I be known; or if I be,
They cannot take away my crown from me.
Here will I hide it in this simple hole.

*Enter Tamburlaine*

*Tamb.*   What, fearful coward, straggling from the camp,
When kings themselves are present in the field?

*Myc.*   Thou liest.

*Tamb.*   Base villain! dar'st thou give the lie?

*Myc.*   Away; I am the king; go; touch me not.
Thou break'st the law of arms, unless thou kneel
And cry me "mercy, noble king."

*Tamb.*   Are you the witty King of Persia?

*Myc.*   Ay, marry am I; have you any suit to me?

*Tamb.*   I would entreat you to speak but three wise words.

*Myc.*   So I can when I see my time.

*Tamb.*   Is this your crown?

*Myc.*   Ay, didst thou ever see a fairer?

*Tamb.*   You will not sell it, will ye?

*Myc.*   Such another word and I will have thee executed. Come,
give it me!

*Tamb.*   No; I took it prisoner.

*Myc.*   You lie; I gave it you.

*Tamb.*   Then 't is mine.

*Myc.*   No; I mean I let you keep it.

*Tamb.*   Well; I mean you shall have it again.
Here; take it for a while: I lend it thee,
'Till I may see thee hemm'd with armed men;
Then shalt thou see me pull it from thy head.
Thou art no match for mighty Tamburlaine.                    [*Exit.*]

*Myc.*   O gods! Is this Tamburlaine the thief?
I marvel much he stole it not away.

*Sound trumpets to the battle, and he runs in.*

5 White centres of archery targets, bull's eyes.
6 Peg at very centre of target to hold it in place.

## [Scene V]

*Cosroe, Tamburlaine, Theridamas, Menaphon, Mean-*
*der, Ortygius, Techelles, Usumcasane, with others*

*Tamb.*    Hold thee, Cosroe! wear two imperial crowns.
Think thee invested now as royally,
Even by the mighty hand of Tamburlaine,
As if as many kings as could encompass thee,
With greatest pomp, had crown'd thee emperor.

    *Cos.*    So do I, thrice renowmed man-at-arms,
And none shall keep the crown but Tamburlaine.
Thee do I make my regent of Persia,
And general lieftenant of my armies.
Meander, you, that were our brother's guide,
And chiefest counsellor in all his acts,
Since he is yielded to the stroke of war,
On your submission we with thanks excuse,
And give you equal place in our affairs.

    *Meand.*    Most happy Emperor, in humblest terms,
I vow my service to your majesty,
With utmost virtue of my faith and duty.

    *Cos.*    Thanks, good Meander: then, Cosroe, reign,
And govern Persia in her former pomp!
Now send ambassage to thy neighbour kings,
And let them know the Persian king is chang'd,
From one that knew not what a king should do,
To one that can command what 'longs thereto.
And now we will to fair Persepolis,
With twenty thousand expert soldiers.
The lords and captains of my brother's camp
With little slaughter take Meander's course,
And gladly yield them to my gracious rule.
Ortygius and Menaphon, my trusty friends,
Now will I gratify your former good,
And grace your calling with a greater sway.

    *Orty.*    And as we ever aim'd at your behoof,[7]
And sought your state all honour it deserv'd,
So will we with our powers and our lives
Endeavour to preserve and prosper it.

    *Cos.*    I will not thank thee, sweet Ortygius;
Better replies shall prove my purposes.
And now, Lord Tamburlaine, my brother's camp
I leave to thee and to Theridamas,

   [7] Profit.

To follow me to fair Persepolis.
Then will we march to all those Indian mines
My witless brother to the Christians lost,
And ransom them with fame and usury.
And till thou overtake me, Tamburlaine,
(Staying to order all the scatter'd troops,)
Farewell, lord regent and his happy friends!
I long to sit upon my brother's throne.
   *Meand.*  Your majesty shall shortly have your wish,
And ride in triumph through Persepolis.
    *Exeunt.  Manent Tamb., Tech., Ther., Usum.*
    *Tamb.*  "And ride in triumph through Persepolis!"
Is it not brave to be a king, Techelles?
Usumcasane and Theridamas,
Is it not passing brave to be a king,
And ride in triumph through Persepolis?
   *Tech.*  O, my lord, 't is sweet and full of pomp.
   *Usum.*  To be a king is half to be a god.
   *Ther.*  A god is not so glorious as a king.
I think the pleasure they enjoy in Heaven,
Cannot compare with kingly joys in earth.
To wear a crown enchas'd with pearl and gold,
Whose virtues carry with it life and death;
To ask and have, command and be obeyed;
When looks breed love, with looks to gain the prize, —
Such power attractive shines in princes' eyes!
   *Tamb.*  Why say, Theridamas, wilt thou be a king?
   *Ther.*  Nay, though I praise it, I can live without it.
   *Tamb.*  What says my other friends?  Will you be kings?
   *Tech.*  Ay, if I could, with all my heart, my lord.
   *Tamb.*  Why, that's well said, Techelles; so would I,
And so would you, my masters, would you not?
   *Usum.*  What then, my lord?
   *Tamb.*  Why then, Casane, shall we wish for aught
The world affords in greatest novelty,
And rest attemptless, faint, and destitute?
Methinks we should not: I am strongly mov'd,
That if I should desire the Persian crown,
I could attain it with a wondrous ease.
And would not all our soldiers soon consent,
If we should aim at such a dignity?
   *Ther.*  I know they would with our persuasions.
   *Tamb.*  Why then, Theridamas, I'll first assay
To get the Persian kingdom to myself;

Then thou for Parthia; they for Scythia and Media.
And, if I prosper, all shall be as sure
As if the Turk, the Pope, Afric, and Greece,
Came creeping to us with their crowns apace.
  *Tech.*  Then shall we send to this triumphing king,
And bid him battle for his novel[8] crown?
   *Usum.*  Nay, quickly then, before his room be hot.
   *Tamb.*  'T will prove a pretty jest, in faith, my friends.
   *Ther.*  A jest to charge on twenty thousand men!
I judge the purchase more important far.
   *Tamb.*  Judge by thyself, Theridamas, not me;
For presently Techelles here shall haste
To bid him battle ere he pass too far,
And lose more labour than the gain will quite.[9]
Then shalt thou see the Scythian Tamburlaine
Make but a jest to win the Persian crown.
Techelles, take a thousand horse with thee,
And bid him turn him back to war with us,
That only made him king to make us sport.
We will not steal upon him cowardly,
But give him warning and more warriors.
Haste thee, Techelles; we will follow thee.    [*Exit Techelles.*]
What saith Theridamas?
   *Ther.*        Go on for me.            *Exeunt.*

### Actus 2.  Scæna 6.

*Cosroe, Meander, Ortygius, Menaphon, with other
Soldiers*

  *Cos.*  What means this devilish shepherd to aspire
With such a giantly presumption
To cast up hills against the face of Heaven,
And dare the force of angry Jupiter?[1]
But as he thrust them underneath the hills,
And press'd out fire from their burning jaws,
So will I send this monstrous slave to hell,
Where flames shall ever feed upon his soul.
  *Meand.*  Some powers divine, or else infernal, mix'd
Their angry seeds at his conception;
For he was never sprung of human race,

---

[8] Newly won.              [9] Repay.
[1] An allusion to the fabled wars between Jupiter and the Titans.

Since with the spirit of his fearful pride
He dares so doubtlessly resolve of rule,
And by profession be ambitious.

 *Orty.* What god, or fiend, or spirit of the earth,
Or monster turned to a manly shape,
Or of what mould or mettle he be made,
What star or state soever govern him,
Let us put on our meet encount'ring minds
And in detesting such a devilish thief,
In love of honour and defence of right,
Be arm'd against the hate of such a foe,
Whether from earth, or hell, or Heaven he grow.

 *Cos.* Nobly resolv'd, my good Ortygius;
And since we all have suck'd one wholesome air,
And with the same proportion of elements
Resolve,[2] I hope we are resembled,[3]
Vowing our loves to equal death and life.
Let's cheer our soldiers to encounter him,
That grievous image of ingratitude,
That fiery thirster after sovereignty,
And burn him in the fury of that flame,
That none can quench but blood and empery.
Resolve, my lords and loving soldiers, now
To save your king and country from decay.
Then strike up, drum; and all the stars that make
The loathsome circle of my dated life,
Direct my weapon to his barbarous heart,
That thus opposeth him against the gods,
And scorns the powers that govern Persia!  *[Exeunt.]*


### [SCENE VII]

*Enter to the battle, and after the battle enter Cosroe,
wounded, Theridamas, Tamburlaine, Techelles, Usumcasane, with others*

 *Cos.* Barbarous and bloody Tamburlaine,
Thus to deprive me of my crown and life!
Treacherous and false Theridamas,
Even at the morning of my happy state,
Scarce being seated in my royal throne,
To work my downfall and untimely end!

  [2] Dissolve.      [3] Alike.

An uncouth pain torments my grieved soul,
And death arrests the organ of my voice,
Who, ent'ring at the breach thy sword hath made,
Sacks every vein and artier[4] of my heart. —
Bloody and insatiate Tamburlaine!

    *Tamb.*   The thirst of reign and sweetness of a crown,
That caus'd the eldest son of heavenly Ops[5]
To thrust his doting father from his chair,
And place himself in the empyreal Heaven,
Mov'd me to manage arms against thy state.
What better precedent than mighty Jove?
Nature that fram'd us of four elements,
Warring within our breasts for regiment,[6]
Doth teach us all to have aspiring minds:
Our souls, whose faculties can comprehend
The wondrous architecture of the world,
And measure every wand'ring planet's course,
Still climbing after knowledge infinite,
And always moving as the restless spheres,
Wills us to wear ourselves, and never rest,
Until we reach the ripest fruit of all,
That perfect bliss and sole felicity,
The sweet fruition of an earthly crown.

    *Ther.*   And that made me to join with Tamburlaine:
For he is gross and like the massy earth,
That moves not upwards, nor by princely deeds
Doth mean to soar above the highest sort.

    *Tech.*   And that made us the friends of Tamburlaine,
To lift our swords against the Persian king.

    *Usum.*   For as, when Jove did thrust old Saturn down,
Neptune and Dis gain'd each of them a crown,
So do we hope to reign in Asia,
If Tamburlaine be plac'd in Persia.

    *Cos.*   The strangest men that ever nature made!
I know not how to take their tyrannies.
My bloodless body waxeth chill and cold,
And with my blood my life slides through my wound;
My soul begins to take her flight to hell,
And summons all my senses to depart. —
The heat and moisture, which did feed each other,
For want of nourishment to feed them both,
Is dry and cold; and now doth ghastly death,

---

[4] Artery.
[6] Rule.
        [5] Wife of Saturn and mother of Jupiter.

With greedy talons gripe my bleeding heart,
And like a harpy tires on my life.
Theridamas and Tamburlaine, I die:
And fearful vengeance light upon you both!
  [*Cosroe dies.   Tamburlaine*] *takes the crown and puts it on.*
 *Tamb.*   Not all the curses which the Furies breathe
Shall make me leave so rich a prize as this.
Theridamas, Techelles, and the rest,
Who think you now is King of Persia?
 *All.*   Tamburlaine! Tamburlaine!
 *Tamb.*   Though Mars himself, the angry god of arms,
And all the earthly potentates conspire
To dispossess me of this diadem,
Yet will I wear it in despite of them,
As great commander of this eastern world,
If you but say that Tamburlaine shall reign.
 *All.*   Long live Tamburlaine and reign in Asia!
 *Tamb.*   So now it is more surer on my head,
Than if the gods had held a parliament,
And all pronounc'd me King of Persia.     [*Exeunt.*

*Finis Actus 2*

## *Actus 3.   Scæna 1.*

*Bajazeth, the Kings of Fez, Morocco, and Argier,*[7] *with others in great pomp*

 *Baj.*   Great Kings of Barbary and my portly bassoes,[8]
We hear the Tartars and the eastern thieves,
Under the conduct of one Tamburlaine,
Presume a bickering with your emperor,
And thinks to rouse us from our dreadful siege
Of the famous Grecian Constantinople.
You know our army is invincible:
As many circumcised Turks we have,
And warlike bands of Christians renied,[9]
As hath the ocean or the Terrene[1] sea
Small drops of water when the moon begins
To join in one her semicircled horns.
Yet would we not be brav'd with foreign power,
Nor raise our siege before the Grecians yield,
Or breathless lie before the city walls.

---

 [7] Algiers.      [8] Pashas.
 [9] Renegade.     [1] Mediterranean.

*Fez.*   Renowmed Emperor, and mighty general,
What, if you sent the bassoes of your guard
To charge him to remain in Asia,
Or else to threaten death and deadly arms
As from the mouth of mighty Bajazeth?

*Baj.*   Hie thee, my basso, fast to Persia.
Tell him thy Lord, the Turkish Emperor,
Dread Lord of Afric, Europe, and Asia,
Great King and conqueror of Græcia,
The ocean, Terrene, and the Coal-black sea,
The high and highest monarch of the world,
Wills and commands (for say not I entreat),
Not once to set his foot in Africa,
Or spread his colours in Græcia,
Lest he incur the fury of my wrath.
Tell him I am content to take a truce,
Because I hear he bears a valiant mind:
But if, presuming on his silly power,
He be so mad to manage arms with me,
Then stay thou with him; say, I bid thee so:
And if, before the sun have measur'd Heaven
With triple circuit, thou regreet us not,
We mean to take his morning's next arise
For messenger he will not be reclaim'd,
And mean to fetch thee in despite of him.

*Bas.*   Most great and puissant monarch of the earth,
Your basso will accomplish your behest,
And show your pleasure to the Persian,
As fits the legate of the stately Turk.          *Exit Bass.*

*Arg.*   They say he is the king of Persia;
But if he dare attempt to stir your siege,
'T were requisite he should be ten times more,
For all flesh quakes at your magnificence.

*Baj.*   True, Argier; and tremble at my looks.

*Mor.*   The spring is hind'red by your smothering host,
For neither rain can fall upon the earth,
Nor sun reflex his virtuous beams thereon, —
The ground is mantled with such multitudes.

*Baj.*   All this is true as holy Mahomet;
And all the trees are blasted with our breaths.

*Fez.*   What thinks your greatness best to be achiev'd
In pursuit of the city's overthrow?

*Baj.*   I will the captive pioners[2] of Argier

2 Engineers.

Cut off the water that by leaden pipes
Runs to the city from the mountain Carnon.
Two thousand horse shall forage up and down,
That no relief or succour come by land:
And all the sea my galleys countermand.[3]
Then shall our footmen lie within the trench,
And with their cannons, mouth'd like Orcus'[4] gulf,
Batter the walls, and we will enter in;
And thus the Grecians shall be conquered.                    *Exeunt*

## *Actus 3.  Scæna 2.*

### *Agydas, Zenocrate, Anippe, with others*

[*Agyd.*]    Madam Zenocrate, may I presume
To know the cause of these unquiet fits,
That work such trouble to your wonted rest?
'T is more than pity such a heavenly face
Should by heart's sorrow wax so wan and pale,
When your offensive rape[5] by Tamburlaine
(Which of your whole displeasures should be most)
Hath seem'd to be digested long ago.
    *Zeno.*    Although it be digested long ago,
As his exceeding favours have deserv'd,
And might content the Queen of Heaven as well
As it hath chang'd my first conceiv'd disdain,
Yet since a farther passion feeds my thoughts
With ceaseless and disconsolate conceits,
Which dyes my looks so lifeless as they are,
And might, if my extremes had full events,[6]
Make me the ghastly counterfeit[7] of death.
    *Agyd.*    Eternal heaven sooner be dissolv'd,
And all that pierceth Phoebe's silver eye,
Before such hap fall to Zenocrate!
    *Zeno.*    Ah, life and soul, still hover in his breast
And leave my body senseless as the earth;
Or else unite you to his life and soul,
That I may live and die with Tamburlaine!

### *Enter [behind] Tamburlaine, with Techelles, and others*

    *Agyd.*    With Tamburlaine!  Ah, fair Zenocrate,
Let not a man so vile and barbarous,

---

[3] Control.              [4] The underworld.              [5] Seizure.
[6] If the worst extremity should come to pass.            [7] Image.

That holds you from your father in despite,
And keeps you from the honours of a queen,
(Being suppos'd his worthless concubine,)
Be honour'd with your love but for necessity.
So, now the mighty Soldan hears of you,
Your highness needs not doubt but in short time
He will with Tamburlaine's destruction
Redeem you from this deadly servitude.

   *Zeno.*  Agydas, leave to wound me with these words,
And speak of Tamburlaine as he deserves.
The entertainment we have had of him
Is far from villainy or servitude,
And might in noble minds be counted princely.

   *Agyd.*  How can you fancy one that looks so fierce,
Only dispos'd to martial stratagems?
Who, when he shall embrace you in his arms,
Will tell how many thousand men he slew;
And when you look for amorous discourse,
Will rattle forth his facts of war and blood,
Too harsh a subject for your dainty ears.

   *Zeno.*  As looks the Sun through Nilus' flowing stream,
Or when the Morning holds him in her arms,
So looks my lordly love, fair Tamburlaine;
His talk much sweeter than the Muses' song
They sung for honour 'gainst Pierides;[8]
Or when Minerva did with Neptune strive:
And higher would I rear my estimate
Than Juno, sister to the highest god,
If I were match'd with mighty Tamburlaine.

   *Agyd.*  Yet be not so inconstant in your love;
But let the young Arabian live in hope
After your rescue to enjoy his choice.
You see, — though first the King of Persia,
Being a shepherd, seem'd to love you much, —
Now on his majesty he leaves those looks,
Those words of favour, and those comfortings,
And gives no more than common courtesies.

   *Zeno.*  Thence rise the tears that so distain my cheeks,
Fearing his love through my unworthiness. —

                *Tamburlaine goes to her and takes her
                    away lovingly by the hand, looking
                    wrathfully on Agydas, and says
                    nothing.* [Exeunt all but Agydas.]

---

[8] The nine daughters of Pierus, who entered into competition with
the Muses.

*Agyd.*   Betray'd by fortune and suspicious love,
Threat'ned with frowning wrath and jealousy,
Surpris'd with fear of hideous revenge,
I stand aghast; but most astonied
To see his choler shut in secret thoughts,
And wrapp'd in silence of his angry soul.
Upon his brows was portray'd ugly death;
And in his eyes the fury of his heart,
That shine as comets, menacing revenge,
And casts a pale complexion on his cheeks.
As when the seaman sees the Hyades[9]
Gather an army of Cimmerian[1] clouds,
(Auster and Aquilon[2] with winged steeds,
All sweating, tilt about the watery Heavens,
With shivering spears enforcing thunder claps,
And from their shields strike flames of lightening,)
All fearful folds his sails and sounds the main,
Lifting his prayers to the Heavens for aid
Against the terror of the winds and waves:
So fares Agydas for the late-felt frowns
That sent a tempest to my daunted thoughts,
And makes my soul divine her overthrow.

### *Enter Techelles with a naked dagger*

*Tech.*   See you, Agydas, how the king salutes you?
He bids you prophesy what it imports.                    *Exit.*
*Agyd.*   I prophesied before, and now I prove
The killing frowns of jealousy and love.
He needed not with words confirm my fear,
For words are vain where working tools present
The naked action of my threat'ned end.
It says: "Agydas, thou shalt surely die,
And of extremities elect the least;
More honour and less pain it may procure
To die by this resolved hand of thine,
Than stay the torments he and Heaven have sworn."
Then haste, Agydas, and prevent the plagues
Which thy prolonged fates may draw on thee.
Go, wander, free from fear of tyrant's rage,
Removed from the torments and the hell
Wherewith he may excruciate thy soul,

[9] A constellation of seven stars, supposed to bring rain.
[1] Dark.
[2] The southwest and north winds.

And let Agydas by Agydas die,
And with this stab slumber eternally. *Stabs himself.*

[*Re-enter Techelles with Usumcasane*]

*Tech.* Usumcasane, see, how right the man
Hath hit the meaning of my lord, the king.
*Usum.* Faith, and Techelles, it was manly done;
And since he was so wise and honourable,
Let us afford him now the bearing hence,
And crave his triple-worthy burial.
*Tech.* Agreed, Casane; we will honour him.

[*Exeunt bearing out the body.*]

## Actus 3. Scæna 3.

*Tamburlaine, Techelles, Usumcasane, Theridamas,
Basso, Zenocrate, [Anippe,] with others*

*Tamb.* Basso, by this thy lord and master knows
I mean to meet him in Bithynia:
See how he comes! Tush, Turks are full of brags,
And menace more than they can well perform.
He meet me in the field, and fetch thee hence!
Alas! poor Turk! his fortune is too weak
T' encounter with the strength of Tamburlaine.
View well my camp, and speak indifferently:[3]
Do not my captains and my soldiers look
As if they meant to conquer Africa?
*Bas.* Your men are valiant, but their number few,
And cannot terrify his mighty host.
My lord, the great commander of the world,
Besides fifteen contributory kings,
Hath now in arms ten thousand Janissaries,
Mounted on lusty Mauritanian steeds,
Brought to the war by men of Tripoli;
Two hundred thousand footmen that have serv'd
In two set battles fought in Græcia:
And for the expedition of this war,
If he think good, can from his garrisons
Withdraw as many more to follow him.
*Tech.* The more he brings the greater is the spoil,
For when they perish by our warlike hands,

[3] Impartially.

We mean to seat our footmen on their steeds,
And rifle[4] all those stately Janissars.
    *Tamb.*   But will those kings accompany your lord?
    *Bas.*   Such as his highness please; but some must stay
To rule the provinces he late subdu'd.
    *Tamb.* [*To his Officers.*] Then fight courageously: their
       crowns are yours;
This hand shall set them on your conquering heads,
That made me Emperor of Asia.
    *Usum.*   Let him bring millions infinite of men,
Unpeopling Western Africa and Greece,
Yet we assure us of the victory.
    *Ther.*   Even he that in a trice vanquish'd two kings,
More mighty than the Turkish emperor,
Shall rouse him out of Europe, and pursue
His scatter'd army till they yield or die.
    *Tamb.*   Well said, Theridamas; speak in that mood;
For *will* and *shall* best fitteth Tamburlaine,
Whose smiling stars gives him assured hope
Of martial triumph ere he meet his foes.
I that am term'd the scourge and wrath of God,
The only fear and terror of the world,
Will first subdue the Turk, and then enlarge
Those Christian captives, which you keep as slaves,
Burdening their bodies with your heavy chains,
And feeding them with thin and slender fare;
That naked row about the Terrene sea,
And when they chance to breathe and rest a space,
Are punish'd with bastones[5] so grievously,
That they lie panting on the galley's side,
And strive for life at every stroke they give.
These are the cruel pirates of Argier,
That damned train, the scum of Africa,
Inhabited with straggling runagates,[6]
That make quick havoc of the Christian blood;
But, as I live, that town shall curse the time
That Tamburlaine set foot in Africa.

    *Enter Bajazeth with his Bassoes, and contributory*
    *Kings* [*of Fez, Morocco, and Argier; Zabina and Ebea*]

    *Baj.*   Bassoes and Janissaries of my guard,
Attend upon the person of your lord,
The greatest potentate of Africa.

---

[4] Loot               [5] Cudgels.              [6] Runaways.

*Tamb.*   Techelles and the rest, prepare your swords;
I mean t' encounter with that Bajazeth.

*Baj.*   Kings of Fez, Moroccus, and Argier,
He calls me Bajazeth, whom you call Lord!
Note the presumption of this Scythian slave!
I tell thee, villain, those that lead my horse
Have to their names titles of dignity,
And dar'st thou bluntly call me Bajazeth?

*Tamb.*   And know thou, Turk, that those which lead my horse,
Shall lead thee captive thorough Africa;
And dar'st thou bluntly call me Tamburlaine?

*Baj.*   By Mahomet my kinsman's sepulchre,
And by the holy Alcoran I swear,
He shall be made a chaste and lustless eunuch,
And in my sarell[7] tend my concubines;
And all his captains that thus stoutly stand,
Shall draw the chariot of my emperess,
Whom I have brought to see their overthrow.

*Tamb.*   By this my sword, that conquer'd Persia,
Thy fall shall make me famous through the world.
I will not tell thee how I'll handle thee,
But every common soldier of my camp
Shall smile to see thy miserable state.

*Fez.*   What means the mighty Turkish emperor.
To talk with one so base as Tamburlaine?

*Mor.*   Ye Moors and valiant men of Barbary,
How can ye suffer these indignities?

*Arg.*   Leave words, and let them feel your lances' points
Which glided through the bowels of the Greeks.

*Baj.*   Well said, my stout contributory kings:
Your threefold army and my hugy host
Shall swallow up these base-born Persians.

*Tech.*   Puisant, renowm'd, and mighty Tamburlaine,
Why stay we thus prolonging all their lives?

*Ther.*   I long to see those crowns won by our swords,
That we may reign as kings of Africa.

*Usum.*   What coward would not fight for such a prize?

*Tamb.*   Fight all courageously, and be you kings;
I speak it, and my words are oracles.

*Baj.*   Zabina, mother of three braver boys
Than Hercules, that in his infancy
Did pash[8] the jaws of serpents venomous;
Whose hands are made to gripe a warlike lance,

[7] Seraglio.          [8] Crush.

Their shoulders broad for complete armour fit,
Their limbs more large, and of a bigger size,
Than all the brats ysprung from Typhon's[9] loins;
Who, when they come unto their father's age,
Will batter turrets with their manly fists: —
Sit here upon this royal chair of state,
And on thy head wear my imperial crown,
Until I bring this sturdy Tamburlaine
And all his captains bound in captive chains.

   *Zab.*   Such good success happen to Bajazeth!

   *Tamb.*   Zenocrate, the loveliest maid alive,
Fairer than rocks of pearl and precious stone,
The only paragon of Tamburlaine,
Whose eyes are brighter than the lamps of Heaven
And speech more pleasant than sweet harmony!
That with thy looks canst clear the darken'd sky,
And calm the rage of thund'ring Jupiter: —
Sit down by her, adorned with my crown,
As if thou wert the Empress of the world.
Stir not, Zenocrate, until thou see
Me march victoriously with all my men,
Triumphing over him and these his kings,
Which I will bring as vassals to thy feet.
Till then take thou my crown, vaunt of my worth,
And manage words with her, as we will arms.

   *Zeno.*   And may my love, the King of Persia,
Return with victory and free from wound!

   *Baj.*   Now shalt thou feel the force of Turkish arms,
Which lately made all Europe quake for fear.
I have of Turks, Arabians, Moors, and Jews,
Enough to cover all Bithynia.
Let thousands die; their slaughter'd carcases
Shall serve for walls and bulwarks to the rest,
And as the heads of Hydra, so my power,
Subdued, shall stand as mighty as before.
If they should yield their necks unto the sword,
Thy soldier's arms could not endure to strike
So many blows as I have heads for thee.
Thou know'st not, foolish-hardy Tamburlaine,
What 't is to meet me in the open field,
That leave no ground for thee to march upon.

   *Tamb.*   Our conquering swords shall marshal us **the way.**
We use to march upon the slaughter'd foe,

[9] Father of a brood of monsters.

Trampling their bowels with our horses' hoofs, —
Brave horses bred on the white Tartarian hills.
My camp is like to Julius Cæsar's host,
That never fought but had the victory;
Nor in Pharsalia[1] was there such hot war
As these, my followers, willingly would have.
Legions of spirits fleeting in the air
Direct our bullets and our weapons' points,
And make our strokes to wound the senseless air.
And when she sees our bloody colours spread,
Then Victory begins to take her flight,
Resting herself upon my milk-white tent. —
But come, my lords, to weapons let us fall;
The field is ours, the Turk, his wife, and all.

*Exit with his followers.*

*Baj.*   Come, kings and bassoes, let us glut our swords,
That thirst to drink the feeble Persians' blood.

*Exit with his followers.*

*Zab.*   Base concubine, must thou be plac'd by me,
That am the empress of the mighty Turk?

*Zeno.*   Disdainful Turkess and unrevered boss![2]
Call'st thou me concubine, that am betroth'd
Unto the great and mighty Tamburlaine?

*Zab.*   To Tamburlaine, the great Tartarian thief!

*Zeno.*   Thou wilt repent these lavish words of thine,
When thy great basso-master and thyself
Must plead for mercy at his kingly feet,
And sue to me to be your advocates.

*Zab.*   And sue to thee!  I tell thee, shameless girl,
Thou shalt be laundress to my waiting maid! —
How lik'st thou her, Ebea?  Will she serve?

*Ebea.*   Madam, she thinks, perhaps, she is too fine,
But I shall turn her into other weeds,[3]
And make her dainty fingers fall to work.

*Zeno.*   Hear'st thou, Anippe, how thy drudge doth talk?
And how my slave, her mistress, menaceth?
Both for their sauciness shall be employ'd
To dress the common soldiers' meat and drink,
For we will scorn they should come near ourselves.

*Anip.*   Yet sometimes let your highness send for them
To do the work my chambermaid disdains.

*They sound the battle within, and stay.*[4]

---

[1] Julius Caesar's famous victory over Pompey.
[2] Fat woman.          [3] Garments.          [4] Cease.

*Zeno.*   Ye gods and powers that govern Persia,
And made my lordly love her worthy king,
Now strengthen him against the Turkish Bajazeth,
And let his foes, like flocks of fearful roes
Pursu'd by hunters, fly his angry looks,
That I may see him issue conqueror!

*Zab.*   Now, Mahomet, solicit God himself,
And make him rain down murthering shot from Heaven
To dash the Scythians' brains, and strike them dead,
That dare to manage arms with him
That offer'd jewels to thy sacred shrine,
When first he warr'd against the Christians!

*To the battle again.*

*Zeno.*   By this the Turks lie welt'ring in their blood,
And Tamburlaine is Lord of Africa.

*Zab.*   Thou art deceiv'd. — I heard the trumpets sound
As when my emperor overthrew the Greeks,
And led them captive into Africa.
Straight will I use thee as thy pride deserves:
Prepare thyself to live and die my slave.

*Zeno.*   If Mahomet should come from Heaven and swear
My royal lord is slain or conquered,
Yet should he not persuade me otherwise
But that he lives and will be conqueror.

*Bajazeth flies and he pursues him. The battle short,
and they enter. Bajazeth is overcome*

*Tamb.*   Now, king of bassoes, who is conqueror?
*Baj.*   Thou, by the fortune of this damned foil.[5]
*Tamb.*   Where are your stout contributory kings?

*Enter Techelles, Theridamas, Usumcasane*

*Tech.*   We have their crowns, their bodies strow the field.
*Tamb.*   Each man a crown! Why, kingly fought, i' faith.
Deliver them into my treasury.

*Zeno.*   Now let me offer to my gracious lord
His royal crown again so highly won.

*Tamb.*   Nay, take the Turkish crown from her, Zenocrate,
And crown me Emperor of Africa.

*Zab.*   No, Tamburlaine: though now thou gat the best,
Thou shalt not yet be lord of Africa.

*Ther.*   Give her the crown, Turkess: you were best.

*He takes it from her, and gives it Zenocrate.*

*Zab.*   Injurious villains! thieves! runagates!

[5] Defeat.

How dare you thus abuse my majesty?

    *Ther.*   Here, madam, you are Empress; she is none.

    *Tamb.*   Not now, Theridamas; her time is past.

The pillars that have bolster'd up those terms,[6]

Are fallen in clusters at my conquering feet.

    *Zab.*   Though he be prisoner, he may be ransom'd.

    *Tamb.*   Not all the world shall ransom Bajazeth.

    *Baj.*   Ah, fair Zabina! we have lost the field;

And never had the Turkish emperor

So great a foil by any foreign foe.

Now will the Christian miscreants be glad,

Ringing with joy their superstitious bells,

And making bonfires for my overthrow.

But, ere I die, those foul idolators

Shall make me bonfires with their filthy bones.

For though the glory of this day be lost,

Afric and Greece have garrisons enough

To make me sovereign of the earth again.

    *Tamb.*   Those walled garrisons will I subdue,

And write myself great lord of Africa.

So from the East unto the furthest West

Shall Tamburlaine extend his puissant arm.

The galleys and those pilling brigandines,[7]

That yearly sail to the Venetian gulf,

And hover in the Straits for Christians' wrack,

Shall lie at anchor in the isle Asant,[8]

Until the Persian fleet and men of war,

Sailing along the oriental sea,

Have fetch'd about the Indian continent,

Even from Persepolis to Mexico,

And thence unto the straits of Jubalter;[9]

Where they shall meet and join their force in one,

Keeping in awe the bay of Portingale,

And all the ocean by the British shore;

And by this means I'll win the world at last.

    *Baj.*   Yet set a ransom on me, Tamburlaine.

    *Tamb.*   What, think'st thou Tamburlaine esteems thy gold?

I'll make the kings of India, ere I die,

Offer their mines to sue for peace to me,

And dig for treasure to appease my wrath.

Come, bind them both, and one lead in the Turk;

The Turkess let my love's maid lead away.

                             *They bind them.*

---

[6] Titles.         [7] Pillaging pirate ships.

[8] The island of Zante.        [9] Gibraltar.

*Baj.*   Ah, villains! — dare ye touch my sacred arms?
O Mahomet! — O sleepy Mahomet!
*Zab.*   O cursed Mahomet, that makest us thus
The slaves to Scythians rude and barbarous!
*Tamb.*   Come, bring them in; and for this happy conquest,
Triumph and solemnise a martial feast.          *Exeunt.*

### *Finis Actus Tertii*

### *Actus 4.   Scæna 1.*

*Soldan of Egypt, with three or four Lords,*
*Capolin [and a Messenger]*

*Sold.*   Awake, ye men of Memphis![1]  Hear the clang
Of Scythian trumpets!  Hear the basilisks
That, roaring, shake Damascus' turrets down!
The rogue of Volga holds Zenocrate,
The Soldan's daughter, for his concubine,
And with a troop of thieves and vagabonds,
Hath spread his colours to our high disgrace,
While you, faint-hearted, base Egyptians,
Lie slumbering on the flowery banks of Nile,
As crocodiles that unaffrighted rest
While thund'ring cannons rattle on their skins.
*Mess.*   Nay, mighty Soldan, did your greatness see
The frowning looks of fiery Tamburlaine,
That with his terror and imperious eyes
Commands the hearts of his associates,
It might amaze your royal majesty.
*Sold.*   Villain, I tell thee, were that Tamburlaine
As monsterous as Gorgon,[2] prince of hell,
The Soldan would not start a foot from him.
But speak, what power hath he?
*Mess.*                                  Mighty lord,
Three hundred thousand men in armour clad,
Upon their prancing steeds disdainfully
With wanton paces trampling on the ground:
Five hundred thousand footmen threat'ning shot,
Shaking their swords, their spears, and iron bills,
Environing their standard round, that stood
As bristle-pointed as a thorny wood:
Their warlike engines and munition

---

[1] City of ancient Egypt.                    [2] Demogorgon.

Exceed the forces of their martial men.

*Sold.*   Nay, could their numbers countervail[3] the stars,
Or ever-drizzling drops of April showers,
Or wither'd leaves that Autumn shaketh down
Yet would the Soldan by his conquering power,
So scatter and consume them in his rage,
That not a man should live to rue their fall.

*Capo.*   So might your highness, had you time to sort
Your fighting men, and raise your royal host.
But Tamburlaine, by expedition,
Advantage takes of your unreadiness.

*Sold.*   Let him take all th' advantages he can.
Were all the world conspir'd to fight for him,
Nay, were he devil, as he is no man,
Yet in revenge of fair Zenocrate,
Whom he detaineth in despite of us,
This arm should send him down to Erebus,[4]
To shroud his shame in darkness of the night.

*Mess.*   Pleaseth your mightiness to understand,
His resolution far exceedeth all.
The first day when he pitcheth down his tents,
White is their hue, and on his silver crest,
A snowy feather spangled white he bears,
To signify the mildness of his mind,
That, satiate with spoil, refuseth blood.
But when Aurora mounts the second time
As red as scarlet is his furniture;[5]
Then must his kindled wrath be quench'd with blood,
Not sparing any that can manage arms.
But if these threats move not submission,
Black are his colours, black pavilion;
His spear, his shield, his horse, his armour, plumes,
And jetty feathers menace death and hell!
Without respect of sex, degree, or age,
He razeth all his foes with fire and sword.

*Sold.*   Merciless villain! Peasant, ignorant
Of lawful arms or martial discipline!
Pillage and murder are his usual trades;
The slave usurps the glorious name of war.
See, Capolin, the fair Arabian king,
That hath been disappointed by this slave
Of my fair daughter and his princely love,
May have fresh warning to go war with us,
And be reveng'd for her disparagement.

[*Exeunt.*]

---

[3] Equal.          [4] Hell.          [5] Equipment.

### Actus 4.    Scæna 2.

*Tamburlaine, Techelles, Theridamas, Usumcasane,*
*Zenocrate, Anippe, two Moors drawing Bajazeth in his*
*cage, and his wife [Zabina] following him*

*Tamb.*    Bring out my footstool.

*They take him out of the cage.*

*Baj.*    Ye holy priests of heavenly Mahomet,
That, sacrificing, slice and cut your flesh,
Staining his altars with your purple blood!
Make Heaven to frown and every fixed star
To suck up poison from the moorish fens,
And pour it in this glorious[6] tyrant's throat.

*Tamb.*    The chiefest God, first mover of that sphere,
Enchas'd with thousands ever-shining lamps,
Will sooner burn the glorious frame of Heaven,
Than it should so conspire my overthrow.
But, villain! thou that wishest this to me,
Fall prostrate on the low disdainful earth,
And be the footstool of great Tamburlaine,
That I may rise into my royal throne.

*Baj.*    First shalt thou rip my bowels with thy sword,
And sacrifice my heart to death and hell,
Before I yield to such a slavery.

*Tamb.*    Base villain, vassal, slave to Tamburlaine!
Unworthy to embrace or touch the ground,
That bears the honour of my royal weight;
Stoop, villain, stoop! — Stoop! for so he bids
That may command thee piecemeal to be torn,
Or scatter'd like the lofty cedar trees
Struck with the voice of thund'ring Jupiter.

*Baj.*    Then, as I look down to the damned fiends,
Fiends, look on me! and thou, dread god of hell,
With ebon sceptre strike this hateful earth,
And make it swallow both of us at once!

*He gets up upon him to his chair.*

*Tamb.*    Now clear the triple region of the air,
And let the majesty of Heaven behold
Their scourge and terror tread on emperors.
Smile stars, that reign'd at my nativity,
And dim the brightness of their neighbour lamps!

---

[6] Boastful.

Disdain to borrow light of Cynthia!
For I, the chiefest lamp of all the earth,
First rising in the East with mild aspect,
But fixed now in the meridian line,
Will send up fire to your turning spheres,
And cause the sun to borrow light of you.
My sword struck fire from his coat of steel,
Even in Bithynia, when I took this Turk;
As when a fiery exhalation,
Wrapp'd in the bowels of a freezing cloud,
Fighting for passage, makes the welkin crack,
And casts a flash of lightning to the earth:
But ere I march to wealthy Persia,
Or leave Damascus and th' Egyptian fields,
As was the fame of Clymen's brain-sick son,[7]
That almost brent[8] the axle-tree of Heaven,
So shall our swords, our lances, and our shot
Fill all the air with fiery meteors.
Then, when the sky shall wax as red as blood,
It shall be said I made it red myself,
To make me think of naught but blood and war.

    *Zab.*   Unworthy king, that by thy cruelty
Unlawfully unsurp'st the Persian seat,
Dar'st thou, that never saw an emperor
Before thou met my husband in the field,
Being thy captive, thus abuse his state?
Keeping his kingly body in a cage,
That roofs of gold and sun-bright palaces
Should have prepar'd to entertain his grace?
And treading him beneath thy loathsome feet,
Whose feet the kings of Africa have kiss'd?

    *Tech.*   You must devise some torment worse, my lord,
To make these captives rein their lavish tongues.

    *Tamb.*   Zenocrate, look better to your slave.

    *Zeno.*   She is my handmaid's slave, and she shall look
That these abuses flow not from her tongue:
Chide her, Anippe.

    *Anip.*   Let these be warnings for you then, my slave,
How you abuse the person of the king;
Or else I swear to have you whipp'd, stark nak'd.

    *Baj.*   Great Tamburlaine, great in my overthrow,
Ambitious pride shall make thee fall as low,
For treading on the back of Bajazeth,

---

[7] Phaethon.          [8] Burnt.

That should be horsed on four mighty kings.
   *Tamb.*   Thy names and titles and thy dignities
Are fled from Bajazeth and remain with me,
That will maintain 't against a world of kings.
Put him in again.          [*They put him into the cage.*]
   *Baj.*   Is this a place for mighty Bajazeth?
Confusion light on him that helps thee thus!
   *Tamb.*   There, whiles he lives, shall Bajazeth be kept;
And, where I go, be thus in triumph drawn.
And thou, his wife, shalt feed him with the scraps
My servitors shall bring thee from my board;
For he that gives him other food than this
Shall sit by him and starve to death himself.
This is my mind and I will have it so.
Not all the kings and emperors of the earth,
If they would lay their crowns before my feet,
Shall ransom him or take him from his cage.
The ages that shall talk of Tamburlaine,
Even from this day to Plato's wondrous year,
Shall talk how I have handled Bajazeth.
These Moors, that drew him from Bithynia
To fair Damascus, where we now remain,
Shall lead him with us wheresoe'er we go.
Techelles, and my loving followers,
Now may we see Damascus' lofty towers,
Like to the shadows of Pyramides,
That with their beauties grac'd the Memphian fields.
The golden stature[9] of their feather'd bird[1]
That spreads her wings upon the city walls
Shall not defend it from our battering shot.
The townsmen mask in silk and cloth of gold,
And every house is as a treasury:
The men, the treasure, and the town is ours.
   *Ther.*   Your tents of white now pitch'd before the gates,
And gentle flags of amity display'd,
I doubt not but the governor will yield,
Offering Damascus to your majesty.
   *Tamb.*   So shall he have his life and all the rest.
But if he stay until the bloody flag
Be once advanc'd on my vermilion tent.
He dies, and those that kept us out so long.
And when they see me march in black array,
With mournful streamers hanging down their heads,

---

[9] Statue.          [1] Ibis.

Were in that city all the world contain'd,
Not one should scape, but perish by our swords.
   *Zeno.*    Yet would you have some pity for my sake,
Because it is my country's, and my father's.
   *Tamb.*    Not for the world, Zenocrate, if I have sworn.
Come; bring in the Turk.                   *Exeunt.*

### *Actus 4. Scæna 3.*

*Soldan, [the King of] Arabia, Capolin, with streaming*
*colours, and Soldiers*

   *Sold.*    Methinks we march as Meleager[2] did,
Environed with brave Argolian knights,
To chase the savage Calydonian boar,
Or Cephalus[3] with lusty Theban youths
Against the wolf that angry Themis sent
To waste and spoil the sweet Aonian fields.
A monster of five hundred thousand heads,
Compact of rapine, piracy, and spoil,
The scum of men, the hate and scourge of God,
Raves in Egyptia and annoyeth us.
My lord, it is the bloody Tamburlaine,
A sturdy felon and a base-bred thief,
By murder raised to the Persian crown,
That dares control us in our territories.
To tame the pride of this presumptuous beast,
Join your Arabians with the Soldan's power:
Let us unite our royal bands in one,
And hasten to remove Damascus' siege.
It is a blemish to the majesty
And high estate of mighty emperors,
That such a base usurping vagabond
Should brave a king, or wear a princely crown.
   *Arab.*    Renowmed Soldan, have ye lately heard
The overthrow of mighty Bajazeth
About the confines of Bithynia?
The slavery wherewith he persecutes
The noble Turk and his great emperess?
   *Sold.*    I have, and sorrow for his bad success;
But, noble lord of great Arabia,

   [2] Famous hunter who slew the Calydonian boar.
   [3] The exploit of Cephalus is related in the following lines.

Be so persuaded that the Soldan is
No more dismay'd with tidings of his fall
Than in the haven when the pilot stands
And views a stranger's ship rent in the winds,
And shivered against a craggy rock.
Yet in compassion of his wretched state,
A sacred vow to Heaven and him I make,
Confirming it with Ibis' holy name,
That Tamburlaine shall rue the day, the hour,
Wherein he wrought such ignominious wrong
Unto the hallow'd person of a prince,
Or kept the fair Zenocrate so long
As concubine, I fear, to feed his lust.

   *Arab.*    Let grief and fury hasten on revenge;
Let Tamburlaine for his offences feel
Such plagues as Heaven and we can pour on him.
I long to break my spear upon his crest,
And prove the weight of his victorious arm;
For Fame, I fear, hath been too prodigal
In sounding through the world his partial[4] praise.

   *Sold.*    Capolin, hast thou survey'd our powers?

   *Capol.*    Great Emperors of Egypt and Arabia,
The number of your hosts united is
A hundred and fifty thousand horse;
Two hundred thousand foot, brave men-at-arms,
Courageous, and full of hardiness,
As frolic as the hunters in the chase
Of savage beasts amid the desert woods.

   *Arab.*    My mind presageth fortunate success;
And, Tamburlaine, my spirit doth foresee
The utter ruin of thy men and thee.

   *Sold.*    Then rear your standards; let your sounding drums
Direct our soldiers to Damascus' walls.
Now, Tamburlaine, the mighty Soldan comes,
And leads with him the great Arabian king,
To dim thy baseness and obscurity,
Famous for nothing but for theft and spoil;
To raze and scatter thy inglorious crew
Of Scythians and slavish Persians.        *Exeunt.*

---

[4] Biased.

## *Actus 4. Scæna 4.*

*The Banquet; and to it cometh Tamburlaine, all in scarlet, [Zenocrate,] Theridamas, Techelles, Usumcasane, the Turk [Bajazeth in his cage, Zabina,] with others*

*Tamb.* Now hang our bloody colours by Damascus,
Reflexing hues of blood upon their heads,
While they walk quivering on their city walls,
Half dead for fear before they feel my wrath:
Then let us freely banquet and carouse
Full bowls of wine unto the god of war,
That means to fill your helmets full of gold,
And make Damascus spoils as rich to you
As was to Jason Colchos' golden fleece. —
And now, Bajazeth, hast thou any stomach?

*Baj.* Ay, such a stomach, cruel Tamburlaine, as I could willingly feed upon thy blood-raw heart.

*Tamb.* Nay, thine own is easier to come by; pluck out that, and 't will serve thee and thy wife. Well, Zenocrate, Techelles, and the rest, fall to your victuals.

*Baj.* Fall to, and never may your meat digest!
Ye Furies, that can mask invisible,
Dive to the bottom of Avernus' pool,
And in your hands bring hellish poison up
And squeeze it in the cup of Tamburlaine!
Or, winged snakes of Lerna, cast your stings,
And leave your venoms in this tyrant's dish!

*Zab.* And may this banquet prove as ominous
As Progne's to th' adulterous Thracian king,
That fed upon the substance of his child.

*Zeno.* My lord, how can you suffer these
Outrageous curses by these slaves of yours?

*Tamb.* To let them see, divine Zenocrate,
I glory in the curses of my foes,
Having the power from the imperial Heaven
To turn them all upon their proper[5] heads.

*Tech.* I pray you give them leave, madam; this speech is a goodly refreshing to them.

*Ther.* But if his highness would let them be fed, it would do them more good.

*Tamb.* Sirrah, why fall you not to? Are you so daintily

[5] Own.

brought up, you cannot eat your own flesh?

*Baj.*   First, legions of devils shall tear thee in pieces.

*Usum.*   Villain, knowest thou to whom thou speakest?

*Tamb.*   O, let him alone. Here; eat, sir; take it from my sword's point, or I'll thrust it to thy heart. *He takes it and stamps upon it.*

*Ther.*   He stamps it under his feet, my lord.

*Tamb.*   Take it up, villain, and eat it; or I will make thee slice the brawns of thy arms into carbonadoes[6] and eat them.

*Usum.*   Nay, 't were better he kill'd his wife, and then she shall be sure not to be starv'd, and he be provided for a month's victual beforehand.

*Tamb.*   Here is my dagger: despatch her while she is fat; for if she live but a while longer, she will fall into a consumption with fretting, and then she will not be worth the eating.

*Ther.*   Dost thou think that Mahomet will suffer this?

*Tech.*   'T is like he will when he cannot let it.

*Tamb.*   Go to; fall to your meat. — What, not a bit! Belike he hath not been watered today; give him some drink.

> *They give him water to drink, and*
> *he flings it on the ground.*

*Tamb.*   Fast, and welcome, sir, while hunger make you eat. How now, Zenocrate, doth not the Turk and his wife make a goodly show at a banquet?

*Zeno.*   Yes, my lord.

*Ther.*   Methinks, 't is a great deal better than a consort of music.[7]

*Tamb.*   Yet music would do well to cheer up Zenocrate. Pray thee, tell, why art thou so sad? If thou wilt have a song, the Turk shall strain his voice. But why is it?

*Zeno.*   My lord, to see my father's town besieg'd,
The country wasted where myself was born,
How can it but afflict my very soul?
If any love remain in you, my lord,
Or if my love unto your majesty
May merit favour at your highness' hands,
Then raise your siege from fair Damascus' walls,
And with my father take a friendly truce.

*Tamb.*   Zenocrate, were Egypt Jove's own land,
Yet would I with my sword make Jove to stoop.
I will confute those blind geographers
That make a triple region in the world,
Excluding regions which I mean to trace,
And with this pen[8] reduce them to a map,

---

[6] Steaks.          [7] Concert.          [8] I.e., his sword.

Calling the provinces, cities, and towns,
After my name and thine, Zenocrate.
Here at Damascus will I make the point
That shall begin the perpendicular;[9]
And would'st thou have me buy thy father's love
With such a loss? — Tell me, Zenocrate.

*Zeno.*   Honour still wait on happy Tamburlaine!
Yet give me leave to plead for him, my lord.

*Tamb.*   Content thyself: his person shall be safe,
And all the friends of fair Zenocrate,
If with their lives they will be pleas'd to yield,
Or may be forc'd to make me Emperor;
For Egypt and Arabia must be mine. —
Feed, you slave! Thou may'st think thyself happy to be fed from
my trencher.

*Baj.*   My empty stomach, full of idle heat,
Draws bloody humours from my feeble parts,
Preserving life by hasting cruel death.
My veins are pale, my sinews hard and dry,
My joints benumb'd: unless I eat, I die.

*Zab.*   Eat, Bajazeth. Let us live in spite of them, looking some
happy power will pity and enlarge us.

*Tamb.*   Here, Turk; wilt thou have a clean trencher?

*Baj.*   Ay, tyrant, and more meat.

*Tamb.*   Soft, sir; you must be dieted; too much eating will make
you surfeit.

*Ther.*   So it would, my lord, specially having so small a walk
and so little exercise.

### Enter a second course, of crowns

*Tamb.*   Theridamas, Techelles, and Casane, here are the cates[1]
you desire to finger, are they not?

*Ther.*   Ay, my lord; but none save kings must feed with these.

*Tech.*   'T is enough for us to see them, and for Tamburlaine
only to enjoy them.

*Tamb.*   Well; here is now to the Soldan of Egypt, the King of
Arabia, and the Governor of Damascus. Now take these three
crowns, and pledge me, my contributory kings. I crown you here,
Theridamas, King of Argier; Techelles, King of Fez; and Usumcasane, King of Moroccus. How say you to this, Turk? These are
not your contributory kings.

[9] He means that he will establish at Damascus the zero meridian, from
which longitude is reckoned.
[1] Viands.

*Baj.*   Nor shall they long be thine, I warrant them.

*Tamb.*   Kings of Argier, Moroccus, and of Fez,
You that have march'd with happy Tamburlaine
As far as from the frozen plage[2] of Heaven
Unto the watery morning's ruddy bower,
And thence by land unto the torrid zone:
Deserve these titles I endow you with
By valour and by magnanimity.
Your births shall be no blemish to your fame,
For virtue is the fount whence honour springs,
And they are worthy she[3] investeth kings.

*Ther.*   And since your highness hath so well vouchsaf'd,
If we deserve them not with higher meeds[4]
Than erst our states and actions have retain'd,
Take them away again and make us slaves.

*Tamb.*   Well said, Theridamas; when holy fates
Shall 'stablish me in strong Egyptia,
We mean to travel to th' antarctic pole,
Conquering the people underneath our feet,
And be renowm'd as never emperors were.
Zenocrate, I will not crown thee yet,
Until with greater honours I be grac'd.            [*Exeunt.*]

### *Finis Actus quarti*

## *Actus 5.   Scæna 1.*

*The Governor of Damascus, with three or four Citi-
zens, and four Virgins, with branches of laurel in their
hands*

*Gov.*   Still doth this man, or rather god, of war
Batter our walls and beat our turrets down;
And to resist with longer stubbornness
Or hope of rescue from the Soldan's power,
Were but to bring our wilful overthrow,
And make us desperate of our threat'ned lives.
We see his tents have now been altered
With terrors to the last and cruel'st hue.
His coal-black colours everywhere advanc'd
Threaten our city with a general spoil;

---

[2] Region.            [3] I.e., whom she.            [4] Deserts.

And if we should with common rites[5] of arms
Offer our safeties to his clemency,
I fear the custom, proper to his sword, —
Which he observes as parcel[6] of his fame,
Intending so to terrify the world, —
By any innovation or remorse
Will never be dispens'd with till our deaths.
Therefore, for these our harmless virgins' sakes,
Whose honours and whose lives rely on him,
Let us have hope that their unspotted prayers,
Their blubber'd cheeks, and hearty, humble moans,
Will melt his fury into some remorse,
And use us like a loving conqueror.

   *Virg.*   If humble suits or imprecations,[7]
(Utter'd with tears of wretchedness and blood
Shed from the heads and hearts of all our sex,
Some made your wives and some your children)
Might have entreated your obdurate breasts
To entertain some care of our securities
Whiles only danger beat upon our walls,
These more than dangerous warrants of our death[8]
Had never been erected as they be,
Nor you depend on such weak helps as we.

   *Gov.*   Well, lovely virgins, think our country's care,
Our love of honour, loath to be inthrall'd
To foreign powers and rough imperious yokes,
Would not with too much cowardice or fear,
(Before all hope of rescue were denied)
Submit yourselves and us to servitude.
Therefore in that your safeties and our own,
Your honours, liberties, and lives were weigh'd
In equal care and balance with our own,
Endure as we the malice of our stars,
The wrath of Tamburlaine, and power of wars;
Or be the means the overweighing heavens
Have kept to qualify these hot extremes,
And bring us pardon in your cheerful looks.

   2 *Virg.*   Then here before the majesty of Heaven
And holy patrons of Egyptia,
With knees and hearts submissive we entreat
Grace to our words and pity to our looks,
That this device may prove propitious,

---

[5] Established usages.      [6] Part.
[7] Prayers.        [8] I.e., the black tents.

And through the eyes and ears of Tamburlaine
Convey events of mercy to his heart.
Grant that these signs of victory we yield
May bind the temples of his conquering head,
To hide the folded furrows of his brows,
And shadow his displeased countenance
With happy looks of ruth and lenity.
Leave us, my lord, and loving countrymen;
What simple virgins may persuade, we will.

    *Gov.*   Farewell, sweet virgins, on whose safe return
Depends our city, liberty, and lives.   *Exeunt* [*all but the Virgins*].


## Actus 5. Scæna 2.

*Tamburlaine, Techelles, Theridamas, Usumcasane, with*
   *others. Tamburlaine all in black and very melancholy*

    *Tamb.*   What, are the turtles fray'd[9] out of their nests?
Alas, poor fools! must you be first shall feel
The sworn destruction of Damascus?
They know my custom; could they not as well
Have sent ye out when first my milk-white flags,
Through which sweet Mercy threw her gentle beams,
Reflexing them on your disdainful eyes,
As now, when fury and incensed hate
Flings slaughtering terror from my coal-black tents,
And tells for truth submissions comes too late?

    1 *Virg.*   Most happy King and Emperor of the earth,
Image of honour and nobility,
For whom the powers divine have made the world,
And on whose throne the holy Graces sit;
In whose sweet person is compris'd the sum
Of Nature's skill and heavenly majesty;
Pity our plights!  O pity poor Damascus!
Pity old age, within whose silver hairs
Honour and reverence evermore have reign'd!
Pity the marriage bed, where many a lord,
In prime and glory of his loving joy,
Embraceth now with tears of ruth and blood
The jealous body of his fearful wife,
Whose cheeks and hearts, so punish'd with conceit
To think thy puissant, never-stayed arm
Will part their bodies, and prevent their souls

    [9] Turtledoves frightened.

From heavens of comfort yet their age might bear,
Now wax all pale and withered to the death,
As well for grief our ruthless governor
Have thus refus'd the mercy of thy hand,
(Whose sceptre angels kiss and furies dread,)
As for their liberties, their loves, or lives.
O then for these, and such as we ourselves,
For us, for infants, and for all our bloods,
That never nourish'd thought against thy rule,
Pity, O pity, sacred Emperor,
The prostrate service of this wretched town,
And take in sign thereof this gilded wreath;
Whereto each man of rule hath given his hand,
And wish'd, as worthy subjects, happy means
To be investers of thy royal brows
Even with the true Egyptian diadem!
   *Tamb.*   Virgins, in vain ye labour to prevent
That which mine honour swears shall be perform'd.
Behold my sword! what see you at the point?
   *Virg.*   Nothing but fear and fatal steel, my lord.
   *Tamb.*   Your fearful minds are thick and misty then;
For there sits Death, there sits imperious Death,
Keeping his circuit by the slicing edge.
But I am pleas'd you shall not see him there;
He now is seated on my horsemen's spears,
And on their points his fleshless body feeds.
Techelles, straight go charge a few of them
To charge these dames, and show my servant, Death,
Sitting in scarlet on their armed spears.
   *Omnes.*   O pity us!
   *Tamb.*   Away with them, I say, and show them Death.
                             *They take them away.*

I will not spare these proud Egyptians,
Nor change my martial observations[1]
For all the wealth of Gihon's[2] golden waves,
Or for the love of Venus, would she leave
The angry god of arms and lie with me.
They have refus'd the offer of their lives,
And know my customs are as peremptory
As wrathful planets, death, or destiny.

*Enter Techelles*

What, have your horsemen shown the virgins Death?
   *Tech.*   They have, my lord, and on Damascus' walls

---

[1] Observances.                  [2] One of the rivers of Eden.

Have hoisted up their slaughter'd carcases.

    *Tamb.*   A sight as baneful to their souls, I think,
As are Thessalian drugs or mithridate:[3]
But go, my lords, put the rest to the sword.

              *Exeunt [all except Tamburlaine].*

Ah, fair Zenocrate! divine Zenocrate!
Fair is too foul an epithet for thee,
That in thy passion for thy country's love,
And fear to see thy kingly father's harm,
With hair dishevell'd wip'st thy watery cheeks;
And, like to Flora in her morning's pride
Shaking her silver tresses in the air,
Rain'st on the earth resolved pearl in showers,
And sprinklest sapphires on thy shining face,
Where Beauty, mother to the Muses, sits
And comments volumes with her ivory pen,
Taking instructions from thy flowing eyes;
Eyes when that Ebena[4] steps to Heaven,
In silence of thy solemn evening's walk,
Making the mantle of the richest night,
The moon, the planets, and the meteors, light.
There angels in their crystal armours fight
A doubtful battle with my tempted thoughts
For Egypt's freedom, and the Soldan's life;
His life that so consumes Zenocrate,
Whose sorrows lay more siege unto my soul,
Than all my army to Damascus' walls:
And neither Persia's sovereign, nor the Turk
Troubled my senses with conceit of foil[5]
So much by much as doth Zenocrate.
What is beauty, saith my sufferings, then?
If all the pens that ever poets held
Had fed the feeling of their masters' thoughts,
And every sweetness that inspir'd their hearts,
Their minds, and muses on admired themes;
If all the heavenly quintessence they still[6]
From their immortal flowers of poesy,
Wherein, as in a mirror, we perceive
The highest reaches of a human wit:
If these had made one poem's period,
And all combin'd in beauty's worthiness,

    [3] Poison.
    [4] Obscure; no such figure is known in classical mythology.
    [5] Thought of defeat.        [6] Distil.

Yet should there hover in their restless heads
One thought, one grace, one wonder, at the least,
Which into words no virtue can digest.
But how unseemly is it for my sex,
My discipline of arms and chivalry,
My nature, and the terror of my name,
To harbour thoughts effeminate and faint!
Save only that in beauty's just applause,
With whose instinct the soul of man is touch'd; —
And every warrior that is rapt with love
Of fame, of valour, and of victory,
Must needs have beauty beat on his conceits:
I thus conceiving and subduing both
That which hath stoop'd the tempest of the gods,
Even from the fiery-spangled veil of Heaven,
To feel the lovely warmth of shepherds' flames,
And mask in cottages of strowed weeds,
Shall give the world to note, for all my birth,
That virtue[7] solely is the sum of glory,
And fashions men with true nobility. —
Who 's within there?

*Enter two or three*

Hath Bajazeth been fed to-day?
  *Atten.*  Ay, my lord.
  *Tamb.*  Bring him forth; and let us know if the town be
ransack'd.                                         [*Exeunt Attendants.*]

*Enter Techelles, Theridamas, Usumcasane, and others*

  *Tech.*  The town is ours, my lord, and fresh supply
Of conquest and of spoil is offer'd us.
  *Tamb.*  That 's well, Techelles; what 's the news?
  *Tech.*  The Soldan and the Arabian king together,
March on us with such eager violence
As if there were no way but one with us.
  *Tamb.*  No more there is not, I warrant thee, Techelles.
                              *They bring in the Turk* [*and Zabina*].
  *Ther.*  We know the victory is ours, my lord;
But let us save the reverend Soldan's life,
For fair Zenocrate that so laments his state.
  *Tamb.*  That will we chiefly see unto, Theridamas,
For sweet Zenocrate, whose worthiness
Deserves a conquest over every heart.

  [7] Valor.

And now, my footstool, if I lose the field,
You hope of liberty and restitution?
Here let him stay, my masters, from the tents,
Till we have made us ready for the field.
Pray for us, Bajazeth; we are going.

                              *Exeunt [all except Bajazeth and Zabina]*.

  *Baj.*   Go, never to return with victory!
Millions of men encompass thee about,
And gore thy body with as many wounds!
Sharp, forked arrows light upon thy horse!
Furies from the black Cocytus lake[8]
Break up the earth, and with their firebrands
Enforce thee run upon the baneful pikes!
Volleys of shot pierce through thy charmed skin,
And every bullet dipp'd in poison'd drugs!
Or roaring cannons sever all thy joints,
Making thee mount as high as eagles soar!
  *Zab.*   Let all the swords and lances in the field
Stick in his breast as in their proper rooms!
At every pore let blood come dropping forth,
That ling'ring pains may massacre his heart,
And madness send his damned soul to hell!
  *Baj.*   Ah, fair Zabina! we may curse his power,
The heavens may frown, the earth for anger quake,
But such a star hath influence in his sword,
As rules the skies and countermands the gods
More than Cimmerian Styx or Destiny;
And then shall we in this detested guise, —
With shame, with hunger, and with horror aye
Griping our bowels with retorqued[9] thoughts, —
And have no hope to end our ecstasies.[1]
  *Zab.*   Then is there left no Mahomet, no God,
No Fiend, no Fortune, nor no hope of end
To our infamous, monstrous slaveries?
Gape, earth, and let the fiends infernal view
A hell as hopeless and as full of fear
As are the blasted banks of Erebus,
Where shaking ghosts with ever-howling groans
Hover about the ugly ferryman,
To get a passage to Elysium!
Why should we live? O, wretches, beggars, slaves!
Why live we, Bajazeth, and build up nests
So high within the region of the air

    [8] In the underworld.        [9] Twisted inwards.        [1] Sorrows.

By living long in this oppression,
That all the world will see and laugh to scorn
The former triumphs of our mightiness
In this obscure infernal servitude?
 *Baj.* O life, more loathsome to my vexed thoughts
Than noisome parbreak[2] of the Stygian snakes,
Which fills the nooks of hell with standing air,
Infecting all the ghosts with cureless griefs!
O dreary engines of my loathed sight,
That sees my crown, my honour, and my name
Thrust under yoke and thraldom of a thief,
Why feed ye still on day's accursed beams
And sink not quite into my tortur'd soul?
You see my wife, my queen and emperess,
Brought up and propped by the hand of fame,
Queen of fifteen contributory queens,
Now thrown to rooms of black abjection,
Smear'd with blots of basest drudgery,
And villeiness[3] to shame, disdain, and misery.
Accursed Bajazeth, whose words of ruth
(That would with pity cheer Zabina's heart,
And make our souls resolve[4] in ceaseless tears)
Sharp hunger bites upon, and gripes the root
From whence the issues of my thoughts do break.
O poor Zabina! O my queen! my queen!
Fetch me some water for my burning breast,
To cool and comfort me with longer date,
That in the short'ned sequel of my life
I may pour forth my soul into thine arms
With words of love, whose moaning intercourse
Hath hitherto been stay'd with wrath and hate
Of our expressless bann'd[5] inflictions.
 *Zab.* Sweet Bajazeth, I will prolong thy life,
As long as any blood or spark of breath
Can quench or cool the torments of my grief.  *She goes out.*
 *Baj.* Now, Bajazeth, abridge thy baneful days,
And beat thy brains out of thy conquer'd head,
Since other means are all forbidden me
That may be ministers of my decay.
O, highest lamp of ever-living Jove,
Accursed day! infected with my griefs,
Hide now thy stained face in endless night,

---

[2] Vomit.    [3] Servant woman.
[4] Dissolve.   [5] Cursed.

And shut the windows of the lightsome heavens!
Let ugly Darkness with her rusty coach,
Engirt with tempests, wrapp'd in pitchy clouds,
Smother the earth with never-fading mists,
And let her horses from their nostrils breathe
Rebellious winds and dreadful thunder-claps,
That in this terror Tamburlaine may live,
And my pin'd[6] soul, resolv'd in liquid air,
May still excruciate his tormented thoughts!
Then let the stony dart of senseless cold
Pierce through the centre of my wither'd heart,
And make a passage for my loathed life!

*He brains himself against the cage.*

### *Enter Zabina*

*Zab.*    What do mine eyes behold?  My husband dead!
His skull all riven in twain!  His brains dash'd out!
The brains of Bajazeth, my lord and sovereign!
O Bajazeth, my husband and my lord!
O Bajazeth!  O Turk!  O Emperor!
Give him his liquor?  Not I.  Bring milk and fire, and my blood
I bring him again. — Tear me in pieces!  Give me the sword with
a ball of wildfire upon it. — Down with him!  Down with him!
— Go to my child!  Away!  Away!  Away!  Ah, save that infant!
save him, save him! — I, even I, speak to her. — The sun was
down; streamers white, red, black, here, here, here! — Fling the
meat in his face — Tamburlaine, Tamburlaine! — Let the soldiers
be buried. — Hell!  Death!  Tamburlaine!  Hell! — Make ready
my coach, my chair, my jewels.  I come!  I come!  I come!

*She runs against the cage and brains herself.*

### [*Enter*] *Zenocrate with Anippe*

*Zeno.*    Wretched Zenocrate! that liv'st to see
Damascus' walls dy'd with Egyptian blood,
Thy father's subjects and thy countrymen;
Thy streets strow'd with dissevered joints of men
And wounded bodies gasping yet for life:
But most accurst, to see the sun-bright troop
Of heavenly virgins and unspotted maids
(Whose looks might make the angry god of arms
To break his sword and mildly treat of love)
On horsemen's lances to be hoisted up
And guiltlessly endure a cruel death:

6 Worn away.

For every fell[7] and stout Tartarian steed,
That stamp'd on others with their thundering hoofs,
When all their riders charg'd their quivering spears,
Began to check the ground and rein themselves,
Gazing upon the beauty of their looks.
Ah Tamburlaine! wert thou the cause of this,
That term'st Zenocrate thy dearest love?
Whose lives were dearer to Zenocrate
Than her own life, or aught save thine own love.
But see another bloody spectacle!
Ah, wretched eyes, the enemies of my heart,
How are ye glutted with these grievous objects,
And tell my soul more tales of bleeding ruth!
See, see, Anippe, if they breathe or no.
   *Anippe.*   No breath, nor sense, nor motion in them both.
Ah, madam! this their slavery hath enforc'd,
And ruthless cruelty of Tamburlaine.
   *Zeno.*   Earth, cast up fountains from thy entrails,
And wet thy cheeks for their untimely deaths!
Shake with their weight in sign of fear and grief!
Blush, Heaven, that gave them honour at their birth
And let them die a death so barbarous!
Those that are proud of fickle empery
And place their chiefest good in earthly pomp,
Behold the Turk and his great Emperess!
Ah, Tamburlaine! my love! sweet Tamburlaine!
That fight'st for sceptres and for slippery crowns,
Behold the Turk and his great Emperess!
Thou, that in conduct of thy happy stars
Sleep'st every night with conquest on thy brows,
And yet would'st shun the wavering turns of war,
In fear and feeling of the like distress
Behold the Turk and his great Emperess!
Ah, mighty Jove and holy Mahomet,
Pardon my love! — O, pardon his contempt
Of earthly fortune and respect of pity,
And let not conquest, ruthlessly pursu'd,
Be equally against his life incens'd
In this great Turk and hapless Emperess!
And pardon me that was not mov'd with ruth
To see them live so long in misery!
Ah, what may chance to thee, Zenocrate?
   *Anippe.*   Madam, content yourself, and be resolv'd.
   [7] Cruel.

Your love hath Fortune so at his command,
That she shall stay and turn her wheel no more,
As long as life maintains his mighty arm
That fights for honour to adorn your head.

*Enter [Philemus,] a Messenger*

*Zeno.*   What other heavy news now brings Philemus?
*Phil.*   Madam, your father, and th' Arabian king,
The first affecter of your excellence,
Comes now, as Turnus 'gainst Æneas did,
Armed with lance into the Egyptian fields,
Ready for battle 'gainst my lord, the king.
*Zeno.*   Now shame and duty, love and fear, presents
A thousand sorrows to my martyr'd soul.
Whom should I wish the fatal victory,
When my poor pleasures are divided thus
And rack'd by duty from my cursed heart?
My father and my first-betrothed love
Must fight against my life and present love;
Wherein the change I use condemns my faith,
And makes my deeds infamous through the world.
But as the gods, to end the Trojans' toil,
Prevented Turnus of[8] Lavinia
And fatally enrich'd Æneas' love,
So, for a final issue to my griefs,
To pacify my country and my love
Must Tamburlaine by their resistless powers,
With virtue of a gentle victory,
Conclude a league of honour to my hope;
Then, as the Powers divine have pre-ordain'd,
With happy safety of my father's life
Send like defence of fair Arabia.

*They sound to the battle [within]: and Tamburlaine enjoys
the victory. After, [the King of] Arabia enters wounded.*

*Arab.*   What cursed power guides the murthering hands
Of this infamous tyrant's soldiers,
That no escape may save their enemies,
Nor fortune keep themselves from victory?
Lie down, Arabia, wounded to the death,
And let Zenocrate's fair eyes behold
That, as for her thou bear'st these wretched arms,
Even so for her thou diest in these arms,

---

[8] From obtaining. In the *Aeneid*, Lavinia, though betrothed to Turnus,
became the wife of Aeneas.

Leaving thy blood for witness of thy love.
   *Zeno.*   Too dear a witness for such love, my lord.
Behold Zenocrate! the cursed object,
Whose fortunes never mastered her griefs;
Behold her wounded, in conceit, for thee,
As much as thy fair body is for me.
   *Arab.*   Then shall I die with full contented heart,
Having beheld divine Zenocrate,
Whose sight with joy would take away my life —
As now it bringeth sweetness to my wound —
If I had not been wounded as I am.
Ah! that the deadly pangs I suffer now
Would lend an hour's license to my tongue,
To make discourse of some sweet accidents
Have chanc'd thy merits in this worthless bondage;
And that I might be privy to the state
Of thy deserv'd contentment, and thy love.
But, making now a virtue of thy sight
To drive all sorrow from my fainting soul,
Since death denies me further cause of joy,
Depriv'd of care, my heart with comfort dies,
Since thy desired hand shall close mine eyes.     *[He dies.]*

   *Enter Tamburlaine, leading the Soldan, Techelles,*
      *Theridamas, Usumcasane, with others*

   *Tamb.*   Come, happy father of Zenocrate,
A title higher than thy Soldan's name;
Though my right hand have thus enthralled thee,
Thy princely daughter here shall set thee free;
She that hath calm'd the fury of my sword,
Which had ere this been bath'd in streams of blood
As vast and deep as Euphrates or Nile.
   *Zeno.*   O sight thrice welcome to my joyful soul,
To see the king, my father, issue safe
From dangerous battle of my conquering love!
   *Sold.*   Well met, my only dear Zenocrate,
Though with the loss of Egypt and my crown.
   *Tamb.*   'T was I, my lord, that gat the victory,
And therefore grieve not at your overthrow,
Since I shall render all into your hands,
And add more strength to your dominions
Than ever yet confirm'd th' Egyptian crown.
The god of war resigns his room to me,
Meaning to make me general of the world.

Jove, viewing me in arms, looks pale and wan,
Fearing my power should pull him from his throne.
Where'er I come the Fatal Sisters sweat,
And grisly Death, by running to and fro,
To do their ceaseless homage to my sword.
And here in Afric, where it seldom rains,
Since I arriv'd with my triumphant host,
Have swelling clouds, drawn from wide-gasping wounds,
Been oft resolv'd in bloody purple showers,
A meteor that might terrify the earth,
And make it quake at every drop it drinks.
Millions of souls sit on the banks of Styx,
Waiting the back return of Charon's boat;
Hell and Elysium swarm with ghosts of men
That I have sent from sundry foughten fields,
To spread my fame through hell and up to Heaven.
And see, my lord, a sight of strange import,
Emperors and kings lie breathless at my feet.
The Turk and his great Empress, as it seems,
Left to themselves while we were at the fight,
Have desperately despatch'd their slavish lives;
With them Arabia, too, hath left his life:
All sights of power to grace my victory.
And such are objects fit for Tamburlaine;
Wherein, as in a mirror, may be seen
His honour that consists in shedding blood,
When men presume to manage arms with him.
  *Sold.*  Mighty hath God and Mahomet made thy hand,
Renowmed Tamburlaine! to whom all kings
Of force must yield their crowns and emperies;
And I am pleas'd with this my overthrow,
If, as beseems a person of thy state,
Thou hast with honour us'd Zenocrate.
  *Tamb.*  Her state and person wants no pomp, you see;
And for all blot of foul inchastity
I record[9] Heaven her heavenly self is clear.
Then let me find no further time to grace
Her princely temples with the Persian crown.
But here these kings that on my fortunes wait,
And have been crown'd for proved worthiness
Even by this hand that shall establish them,
Shall now, adjoining all their hands with mine,
Invest her here my Queen of Persia.

  [9] Bear witness before.

What saith the noble Soldan and Zenocrate!

    *Sold.*    I yield with thanks and protestations
Of endless honour to thee for her love.

    *Tamb.*    Then doubt I not but fair Zenocrate
Will soon consent to satisfy us both.

    *Zeno.*    Else should I much forget myself, my lord.

    *Ther.*    Then let us set the crown upon her head,
That long hath ling'red for so high a seat.

    *Tech.*    My hand is ready to perform the deed;
For now her marriage-time shall work us rest.

    *Usum.*    And here's the crown, my lord; help set it on.

    *Tamb.*    Then sit thou down, divine Zenocrate;
And here we crown thee Queen of Persia,
And all the kingdoms and dominions
That late the power of Tamburlaine subdu'd.
As Juno, when the giants[1] were suppress'd,
That darted mountains at her brother Jove,
So looks my love, shadowing in her brows
Triumphs and trophies for my victories;
Or as Latona's daughter,[2] bent to arms,
Adding more courage to my conquering mind.
To gratify the sweet Zenocrate,
Egyptians, Moors, and men of Asia,
From Barbary unto the western Indie,
Shall pay a yearly tribute to thy sire;
And from the bounds of Afric to the banks
Of Ganges shall his mighty arm extend.
And now, my lords and loving followers,
That purchas'd kingdoms by your martial deeds,
Cast off your armour, put on scarlet robes,
Mount up your royal places of estate,
Environed with troops of noblemen,
And there make laws to rule your provinces.
Hang up your weapons on Alcides' post,[3]
For Tamburlaine takes truce with all the world.
Thy first-betrothed love, Arabia,
Shall we with honour, as beseems, entomb,
With this great Turk and his fair Emperess.
Then, after all these solemn exequies,
We will our rites of marriage solemnise.      [*Exeunt.*]

*Finis Actus quinti et ultimi huius primæ partis.*

[1] The Titans.          [2] Artemis, or Diana.

[3] On the doorpost of the temple of Hercules, as an offering to the god.

# THE
# SHOMAKERS
## Holiday.

O R

## *The Gentle Craft.*

## With the humorous life of Simon
## Eyre, shoomaker, and Lord Maior
## of London.

As it was acted before the Queenes most excellent Ma-
iestie on New-yeares day at night last, by the right
honourable the Earle of Notingham, Lord high Admirall
of England, his seruants.

Printed by Valentine Sims dwelling at the foote of Adling
hill, neere Bainards Castle, at the signe of the White
Swanne, and are there to be sold.
## 1 6 0 0 .

# The Shoemakers' Holiday

### ❧ THOMAS DEKKER

was London born and bred. The name Dekker is Dutch, and the dramatist was probably the son of immigrants from the Low Countries — a fact which helps to explain Lacy's disguise as Hans in *The Shoemakers' Holiday*. Dekker was born in 1572; nothing else is known of him until he appears as a dramatist in 1598. In that year he was mentioned by Francis Meres in *Palladis Tamia* along with Shakespeare, Chapman, and Jonson as a "tragedian," and he also appears as a playwright in Henslowe's accounts. Between 1598 and 1600 Dekker wrote or had a share in twenty-three plays written for the Admiral's Men. Between 1601 and 1603 Dekker and Marston attacked Ben Jonson on the stage in what was known as the Poetomachia or War of the Theatres; Dekker's principal contribution to this dispute was his *Satiromastix*. While the theatres were closed on account of the plague during 1603 and 1604, Dekker turned to pamphleteering and wrote some of his most vivid pieces, but he returned to the theatres as soon as they reopened. Between 1613 and 1619 Dekker was in the King's Bench Prison for debt, but he kept on writing with all his accustomed fluency. During his later years he collaborated a good deal with such dramatists as Rowley, Webster, and Ford. He died in 1632.

*The Shoemakers' Holiday* is one of Dekker's earlier plays. It was published in 1600 and the title page bore the statement that it had been acted before the Queen "on New-yeares day at night last" by the Admiral's company. The play was popular, and was republished in 1610, 1618, 1624, 1637, and 1657. No author's name appeared on the title page, but both the authorship and the date of the play are authenticated by Henslowe, who recorded that on 15 July 1599 he advanced £3 to the Admiral's Men "to bye a boocke called the gentle Craft of Thomas Dickers."

The source of the play is to be found in a prose work by the popular balladist and pamphleteer Thomas Deloney entitled *The Gentle Craft* which was first published in 1598. This is a collection of several tales about shoemakers clearly intended for reading by citizens with a minimum of literary pretensions, and one of these stories tells of the rise to success and fame of Sir Simon

69

Eyre. Dekker's dramatization of this tale seems to have been popular from the first, and the play has been successfully revived more than once in the twentieth century.

Books. The best modern edition of Dekker is *The Dramatic Works*, 4 vols., edited by Fredson Bowers, Cambridge, 1953–61. There are only two studies of Dekker's life and works: M. T. Jones-Davies, *Un peintre de la vie londonienne, Thomas Dekker*, 2 vols., Paris, 1958, and M. L. Hunt, *Thomas Dekker, a study*, New York, 1911.

[*Dramatis Personae*

THE KING (Henry V?)
EARL OF LINCOLN (Sir Hugh Lacy)
EARL OF CORNWALL
ROWLAND LACY, Lincoln's nephew
ASKEW, another relative
LOVELL, a courtier
DODGER, servant to Lincoln

SIR ROGER OTLEY, Lord Mayor of London
Master HAMMON,
Master WARNER, } Citizens of London
Master SCOTT,

SIMON EYRE, the Shoemaker
ROGER (known as HODGE),
FIRK, } EYRE's workmen
RAFE DAMPORT,

ROSE, daughter of OTLEY
SYBIL, her maid
MARGERY, wife of EYRE
JANE, wife of RAFE

A Dutch Skipper, a Boy, Officers, Soldiers, Shoemakers, and
Apprentices

SCENE: The City of London and the adjacent village of Old Ford.]

## The Prologue

*As it was pronounced before the Queen's Majesty*

As wretches in a storm, expecting day,
With trembling hands and eyes cast up to heaven,
Make prayers the anchor of their conquer'd hopes,
So we, dear goddess, wonder of all eyes,
Your meanest vassals, through mistrust and fear
To sink into the bottom of disgrace
By our imperfect pastimes, prostrate thus
On bended knees, our sails of hope do strike,
Dreading the bitter storms of your dislike.
Since then, unhappy men, our hap is such
That to ourselves ourselves no help can bring,
But needs must perish, if your saint-like ears,
Locking the temple where all mercy sits,
Refuse the tribute of our begging tongues;
Oh, grant, bright mirror of true chastity,
From those life-breathing stars, your sun-like eyes,
One gracious smile; for your celestial breath
Must send us life, or sentence us to death.

## [*Act I, Scene I*]

### *Enter Lord Mayor,* [*and the Earl of*] *Lincoln*

*Linc.*  My lord mayor, you have sundry times
Feasted myself and many courtiers more;
Seldom or never can we be so kind
To make requital of your courtesy.
But, leaving this, I hear my cousin[1] Lacy
Is much affected to your daughter Rose.
   *L. Mayor.*  True, my good lord, and she loves him so well
That I mislike her boldness in the chase.
   *Linc.*  Why, my lord, think you it then a shame,
To join a Lacy with an Otley's name?
   *L. Mayor.*  Too mean is my poor girl for his high birth;
Poor citizens must not with courtiers wed,
Who will in silks and gay apparel spend
More in one year than I am worth, by far:
Therefore your honour need not doubt my girl.
   *Linc.*  Take heed, my lord; advise you what you do!
A verier unthrift lives not in the world,
Than is my cousin; for I 'll tell you what:
'T is now almost a year since he requested
To travel countries for experience.
I furnish'd him with coin, bills of exchange,
Letters of credit, men to wait on him,
Solicited my friends in Italy
Well to respect him. But, to see the end!
Scant had he journey'd through half Germany,
But all his coin was spent, his men cast off,
His bills embezzl'd[2] and my jolly coz,
Asham'd to show his bankrupt presence here,
Became a shoemaker in Wittenberg.
A goodly science for a gentleman
Of such descent! Now judge the rest by this.
Suppose your daughter have a thousand pound,
He did consume me more in one half year:
And make him heir to all the wealth you have,
One twelvemonth's rioting will waste it all.
Then seek, my lord, some honest citizen
To wed your daughter to.

---

   [1] Kinsman.               [2] Used up.

*L. Mayor.* I thank your lordship.
[*Aside.*] Well, fox, I understand your subtlety. —
As for your nephew, let your lordship's eye
But watch his actions, and you need not fear,
For I have sent my daughter far enough.
And yet your cousin Rowland might do well,
Now he hath learn'd an occupation:
And yet I scorn to call him son-in-law.
 *Linc.* Ay, but I have a better trade for him.
I thank his grace, he hath appointed him
Chief colonel of all those companies
Must'red in London and the shires about,
To serve his highness in those wars of France.
See where he comes! —

    *Enter Lovell, Lacy, and Askew*

          Lovell, what news with you?
 *Lovell.* My Lord of Lincoln, 't is his highness' will,
That presently your cousin ship for France
With all his powers;[3] he would not for a million,
But they should land at Dieppe within four days.
 *Linc.* Go certify his grace, it shall be done.  *Exit Lovell.*
Now, cousin Lacy, in what forwardness
Are all your companies?
 *Lacy.*     All well prepar'd.
The men of Hertfordshire lie at Mile-end;
Suffolk and Essex train in Tothill-fields;
The Londoners and those of Middlesex,
All gallantly prepar'd in Finsbury,
With frolic spirits long for their parting hour.
 *L. Mayor.* They have their imprest,[4] coats, and furniture;[5]
And, if it please your cousin Lacy come
To the Guildhall, he shall receive his pay;
And twenty pounds besides my bretheren
Will freely give him, to approve[6] our loves
We bear unto my lord, your uncle here.
 *Lacy.* I thank your honour.
 *Linc.*  Thanks, my good lord mayor.
 *L. Mayor.* At the Guildhall we will expect your coming. *Exit.*
 *Linc.* To approve your loves to me! No subtlety!
Nephew, that twenty pound he doth bestow
For joy to rid you from his daughter Rose.

[3] Forces.    [4] Advance pay.
[5] Equipment.   [6] Demonstrate.

But, cousins both, now here are none but friends,
I would not have you cast an amorous eye
Upon so mean a project as the love
Of a gay, wanton, painted citizen.
I know, this churl even in the height of scorn
Doth hate the mixture of his blood with thine.
I pray thee, do thou so! Remember, coz,
What honourable fortunes wait on thee.
Increase the king's love, which so brightly shines,
And gilds thy hopes. I have no heir but thee, —
And yet not thee, if with a wayward spirit
Thou start from the true bias of my love.

 *Lacy.* My lord, I will for honour, not desire
Of land or livings, or to be your heir,
So guide my actions in pursuit of France,
As shall add glory to the Lacies' name.

 *Linc.* Coz, for those words here 's thirty portagues,[7]
And, nephew Askew, there's a few for you.
Fair Honour, in her loftiest eminence,
Stays in France for you, till you fetch her thence.
Then, nephews, clap swift wings on your designs.
Begone, begone, make haste to the Guildhall;
There presently I 'll meet you. Do not stay:
Where honour beckons, shame attends delay.    **Exit.**

 *Askew.* How gladly would your uncle have you gone!

 *Lacy.* True, coz, but I 'll o'erreach his policies.
I have some serious business for three days,
Which nothing but my presence can dispatch.
You, therefore, cousin, with the companies,
Shall haste to Dover; there I 'll meet with you:
Or, if I stay past my prefixed time,
Away for France; we 'll meet in Normandy.
The twenty pounds my lord mayor gives to me
You shall receive, and these ten portagues,
Part of mine uncle's thirty. Gentle coz,
Have care to our great charge; I know your wisdom
Hath tried itself in higher consequence.

 *Askew.* Coz, all myself am yours: yet have this care,
To lodge in London with all secrecy.
Our uncle Lincoln hath, besides his own,
Many a jealous eye, that in your face
Stares only to watch means for your disgrace.

 *Lacy.* Stay, cousin, who be these?

 [7] Large gold coins.

*Enter Simon Eyre, [Margery] his wife, Hodge, Firk,*
*Jane, and Rafe with a piece.*[8]

*Eyre.* Leave whining, leave whining! Away with this whimp'-
ring, this puling, these blubb'ring tears, and these wet eyes! I 'll
get thy husband discharg'd, I warrant thee, sweet Jane. Go to!

*Hodge.* Master, here be the captains.

*Eyre.* Peace, Hodge; husht, ye knave, husht!

*Firk.* Here be the cavaliers and the coronels,[9] master.

*Eyre.* Peace, Firk; peace, my fine Firk! Stand by with your
pishery-pashery; away! I am a man of the best presence; I 'll
speak to them, and they were Popes. — Gentlemen, captains,
colonels, commanders! Brave men, brave leaders, may it please you
to give me audience. I am Simon Eyre, the mad shoemaker of
Tower Street; this wench, with the mealy mouth that will never
tire, is my wife, I can tell you; here 's Hodge, my man and my foreman; here 's Firk, my fine firking journeyman, and this is blubbered
Jane. All we come to be suitors for this honest Rafe. Keep him at
home, and as I am a true shoemaker and a gentleman of the gentle
craft, buy spurs yourself, and I 'll find ye boots these seven years.

*Wife.* Seven years, husband?

*Eyre.* Peace, midriff, peace! I know what I do. Peace!

*Firk.* Truly, master cormorant,[1] you shall do God good service
to let Rafe and his wife stay together. She 's a young new-married
woman; if you take her husband away from her a-night, you undo
her. She may beg in the daytime, for he 's as good a workman at
a prick and an awl as any is in our trade.

*Jane.* O let him stay, else I shall be undone.

*Firk.* Ay, truly, she shall be laid at one side like a pair of old
shoes else, and be occupied for no use.

*Lacy.* Truly, my friends, it lies not in my power:
The Londoners are press'd,[2] paid, and set forth
By the lord mayor; I cannot change a man.

*Hodge.* Why, then you were as good be a corporal as a colonel,
if you cannot discharge one good fellow; and I tell you true, I
think you do more than you can answer, to press a man within a
year and a day of his marriage.

*Eyre.* Well said, melancholy Hodge; gramercy, my fine foreman.

*Wife.* Truly, gentleman, it were ill done for such as you, to
stand so stiffly against a poor young wife, considering her case,
she is new-married; but let that pass. I pray, deal not roughly
with her; her husband is a young man, and but newly ent'red; but
let that pass.

---

[8] Musket.          [9] Colonels.
[1] Malaprop for "coronel."          [2] Drafted.

*Eyre.* Away with your pishery-pashery, your pols and your edipols![3] Peace, midriff; silence, Cicely Bumtrinket! Let your head speak.

*Firk.* Yea, and the horns too, master.

*Eyre.* Too soon, my fine Firk, too soon! Peace, scoundrels! See you this man? Captains, you will not release him? Well, let him go; he 's a proper shot;[4] let him vanish! Peace, Jane, dry up thy tears, they 'll make his powder dankish.[5] Take him, brave men! Hector of Troy was an hackney[6] to him, Hercules and Termagant[7] scoundrels, Prince Arthur's Round-table — by the Lord of Ludgate — ne'er fed such a tall, such a dapper swordman; by the life of Pharaoh, a brave resolute swordman! Peace, Jane! I say no more, mad knaves.

*Firk.* See, see, Hodge, how my master raves in commendation of Rafe!

*Hodge.* Rafe, th' art a gull,[8] by this hand, and thou goest not.

*Askew.* I am glad, good Master Eyre, it is my hap
To meet so resolute a soldier.
Trust me, for your report and love to him,
A common slight regard shall not respect him.

*Lacy.* Is thy name Rafe?

*Rafe.*                                    Yes, sir.

*Lacy.*                                              Give me thy hand;
Thou shalt not want, as I am a gentleman.
Woman, be patient. God, no doubt, will send
Thy husband safe again; but he must go,
His country's quarrel says it shall be so.

*Hodge.* Th' art a gull, by my stirrup,[9] if thou dost not go.
I will not have thee strike thy gimlet into these weak vessels; prick thine enemies, Rafe.

*Enter Dodger.*

*Dodger.* My lord your uncle on the Towerhill
Stays with the lord mayor and the aldermen,
And doth request you, with all speed you may,
To hasten thither.

*Askew.*            Cousin, let 's go.

*Lacy.* Dodger, run you before, tell them we come. —

*Exit Dodger.*

This Dodger is mine uncle's parasite,
The arrant'st varlet that e'er breath'd on earth.
He sets more discord in a noble house

---

[3] Exclamations.                     [4] He must bear his share.
[5] Damp.                 [6] An old cab horse.
[7] A supposed Mohammedan deity, boisterous and boastful.
[8] Fool.              [9] Strap on shoemaker's bench to hold his work in place.

By one day's broaching of his pickthank[1] tales,
Than can be salv'd again in twenty years;
And he, I fear, shall go with us to France,
To pry into our actions.

   *Askew.*                Therefore, coz,
It shall behoove you to be circumspect.

   *Lacy.*   Fear not, good cousin. — Rafe, hie to your colours.

                                       *[Exit Lacy and Askew.]*

   *Rafe.*   I must, because there 's no remedy;
But, gentle master and my loving dame,
As you have always been a friend to me,
So in mine absence think upon my wife.

   *Jane.*   Alas, my Rafe!

   *Wife.*   She cannot speak for weeping.

   *Eyre.*   Peace, you crack'd groats,[2] you mustard tokens,[3] disquiet not the brave soldier. Go thy ways, Rafe!

   *Jane.*   Ay, ay, you bid him go! what shall I do
When he is gone?

   *Firk.*   Why, be doing with me or my fellow Hodge; be not idle.

   *Eyre.*   Let me see thy hand, Jane. This fine hand, this white hand, these pretty fingers must spin, must card, must work; work, you bombast cotton-candle-quean; work for your living, with a pox to you. — Hold thee, Rafe, here 's five sixpences for thee; fight for the honour of the gentle craft, for the gentlemen shoemakers, the courageous cordwainers, the flower of St. Martin's, the mad knaves of Bedlam, Fleet Street, Tower Street and Whitechapel; crack me the crowns of the French knaves; a pox on them, crack them; fight, by the Lord of Ludgate; fight, my fine boy!

   *Firk.*   Here, Rafe, here 's three twopences; two carry into France, the third shall wash our souls at parting, for sorrow is dry. For my sake, firk the *Basa mon cues.*[4]

   *Hodge.*   Rafe, I am heavy at parting; but here 's a shilling for thee. God send thee to cram thy slops with French crowns, and thy enemies' bellies with bullets.

   *Rafe.*   I thank you, master, and I shall thank you all.
Now, gentle wife, my loving lovely Jane,
Rich men, at parting, give their wives rich gifts,
Jewels and rings, to grace their lily hands.
Thou know'st our trade makes rings for women's heels:
Here take this pair of shoes, cut out by Hodge,
Stitch'd by my fellow Firk, seam'd by myself,

---

[1] Told to curry favor.                [2] Coins worth 4*d.*
[3] Currency issued by shopkeepers.         [4] Trounce the French.

Made up and pink'd with letters for thy name.
Wear them, my dear Jane, for thy husband's sake,
And every morning when thou pull'st them on,
Remember me, and pray for my return.
Make much of them; for I have made them so
That I can know them from a thousand mo.[5]

> *Sound drum. Enter Lord Mayor, Lincoln, Lacy, As-
> kew, Dodger, and Soldiers. They pass over the stage;
> Rafe falls in amongst them; Firk and the rest cry
> "Farewell," etc., and so exeunt.*

## [*Act II, Scene I*]

### *Enter Rose, alone, making a garland*

Here sit thou down upon this flow'ry bank
And make a garland for thy Lacy's head.
These pinks, these roses, and these violets,
These blushing gilliflowers, these marigolds,
The fair embroidery of his coronet,
Carry not half such beauty in their cheeks,
As the sweet count'nance of my Lacy doth.
O my most unkind father! O my stars,
Why lower'd[6] you so at my nativity,
To make me love, yet live robb'd of my love?
Here as a thief am I imprisoned
For my dear Lacy's sake within those walls,
Which by my father's cost were builded up
For better purposes. Here must I languish
For him that doth as much lament, I know,
Mine absence, as for him I pine in woe.

### *Enter Sybil*

*Sybil.* Good morrow, young mistress. I am sure you make that garland for me, against I shall be Lady of the Harvest.

*Rose.* Sybil, what news at London?

*Sybil.* None but good: my lord mayor, your father, and master Philpot, your uncle, and Master Scott, your cousin, and Mistress Frigbottom by Doctors' Commons, do all, by my troth, send you most hearty commendations.

*Rose.* Did Lacy send kind greetings to his love?

*Sybil.* O yes, out of cry,[7] by my troth. I scant knew him; here

---

[5] More.         [6] Looked unfavorably.         [7] Beyond description.

'a wore a scarf; and here a scarf, here a bunch of feathers, and here precious stones and jewels, and a pair of garters, — O, monstrous! like one of our yellow silk curtains at home here in Old Ford House here, in Master Bellymount's chamber. I stood at our door in Cornhill, look'd at him, he at me indeed, spake to him, but he not to me, not a word. Marry gup,[8] thought I, with a wanion![9] He pass'd by me as proud — Marry foh! are you grown humorous,[1] thought I; and so shut the door, and in I came.

*Rose.*    O Sybil, how dost thou my Lacy wrong!
My Rowland is as gentle as a lamb,
No dove was ever half so mild as he.

*Sybil.*    Mild? yea, as a bushel of stamp'd crabs.[2] He look'd upon me as sour as verjuice.[3] Go thy ways, thought I, thou may'st be much in my gaskins,[4] but nothing in my netherstocks.[5] This is your fault, mistress, to love him that loves not you; he thinks scorn to do as he 's done to; but if I were as you, I 'd cry, "Go by, Jeronimo, go by!"[6]

> I'd set mine old debts against my new driblets,
> And the hare's foot against the goose giblets,
> For if ever I sigh, when sleep I should take,
> Pray God I may lose my maidenhead when I wake.

*Rose.*    Will my love leave me then, and go to France?

*Sybil.*    I know not that, but I am sure I see him stalk before the soldiers. By my troth, he is a proper man; but he is proper[7] that proper doth. Let him go snick-up,[8] young mistress.

*Rose.*    Get thee to London, and learn perfectly
Whether my Lacy go to France, or no.
Do this, and I will give thee for thy pains
My cambric apron and my Romish gloves,
My purple stockings and a stomacher.[9]
Say, wilt thou do this, Sybil, for my sake?

*Sybil.*    Will I, quoth 'a? At whose suit? By my troth, yes, I 'll go. A cambric apron, gloves, a pair of purple stockings, and a stomacher! I 'll sweat in purple, mistress, for you; I 'll take anything that comes a' God's name. O rich! a cambric apron! Faith, then have at 'up tails all.'[1] I 'll go jiggy-joggy to London, and be here in a trice, young mistress.                                    *Exit.*

---

[8] Go up.                       [9] Vengeance.
[1] Moody.                       [2] Crushed crabapples.
[3] Sour juice.          [4] Breeches.                  [5] Stockings.
[6] A quotation from Kyd's play *The Spanish Tragedy.*
[7] Handsome.                   [8] Go hang.
[9] Ornamental front pinned on to the upper part of a woman's gown.
[1] A card game.

*Rose.* Do so, good Sybil. Meantime wretched I
Will sit and sigh for his lost company.       *Exit.*


## [Scene II]

### *Enter Rowland Lacy, like a Dutch Shoemaker*

*Lacy.* How many shapes have gods and kings devis'd,
Thereby to compass their desired loves!
It is no shame for Rowland Lacy, then,
To clothe his cunning with the gentle craft,
That, thus disguis'd, I may unknown possess
The only happy presence of my Rose.
For her have I forsook my charge in France,
Incurr'd the king's displeasure, and stirr'd up
Rough hatred in mine uncle Lincoln's breast.
O love, how powerful art thou, that canst change
High birth to baseness, and a noble mind
To the mean semblance of a shoemaker!
But thus it must be; for her cruel father,
Hating the single union of our souls,
Hath secretly convey'd my Rose from London,
To bar me of her presence; but I trust,
Fortune and this disguise will further me
Once more to view her beauty, gain her sight.
Here in Tower Street with Eyre the shoemaker
Mean I a while to work. I know the trade,
I learnt it when I was in Wittenberg.
Then cheer thy hoping sprites, be not dismay'd,
Thou canst not want: do Fortune what she can,
The gentle craft is living for a man.       *Exit.*


## [Scene III]

### *Enter Eyre, making himself ready.*[2]

*Eyre.* Where be these boys, these girls, these drabs, these
scoundrels? They wallow in the fat brewess[3] of my bounty, and
lick up the crumbs of my table, yet will not rise to see my walks
cleansed. Come out, you powder-beef[4] queans! What, Nan! what,
Madge Mumble-crust! Come out, you fat midriff, swag-belly-

---

[2] Getting dressed.       [3] Broth.       [4] Corned beef.

whores, and sweep me these kennels[5] that the noisome stench offend not the noses of my neighbours. What, Firk, I say; what, Hodge! Open my shop windows! What, Firk, I say!

### Enter Firk

*Firk.* O master, is 't you that speak bandog[6] and Bedlam this morning? I was in a dream, and mused what madman was got into the street so early. Have you drunk this morning that your throat is so clear?

*Eyre.* Ah, well said, Firk; well said, Firk. To work, my fine knave, to work! Wash thy face, and thou 't be more blest.

*Firk.* Let them wash my face that will eat it. Good master, send for a souse-wife,[7] if you 'll have my face cleaner.

### Enter Hodge

*Eyre.* Away, sloven! avaunt, scoundrel! — Good-morrow, Hodge; good-morrow, my fine foreman.

*Hodge.* O master, good-morrow; y' are an early stirrer. Here 's a fair morning. — Good-morrow, Firk, I could have slept this hour. Here 's a brave day towards.

*Eyre.* Oh, haste to work, my fine foreman, haste to work.

*Firk.* Master, I am dry as dust to hear my fellow Roger talk of fair weather; let us pray for good leather, and let clowns and ploughboys and those that work in the fields pray for brave days. We work in a dry shop; what care I if it rain?

### Enter Eyre's wife

*Eyre.* How now, Dame Margery, can you see to rise? Trip and go, call up the drabs, your maids.

*Marg.* See to rise? I hope 't is time enough! 't is early enough for any woman to be seen abroad. I marvel how many wives in Tower Street are up so soon. Gods me, 't is not noon, — here 's a yawling![8]

*Eyre.* Peace, Margery, peace! Where 's Cicely Bumtrinket, your maid? She has a privy fault, she farts in her sleep. Call the quean up; if my men want[9] shoe-thread, I 'll swinge[1] her in a stirrup.

*Firk.* Yet, that 's but a dry beating; here 's still a sign of drought.

### Enter Lacy [disguised], singing

*Lacy.*   *Der was een bore van Gelderland*
   *Frolick si byen;*

---

[5] Gutters.                 [6] Fiercely (like a watch dog).
[7] Seller of pickled pork.            [8] Howling.
[9] Are without.            [1] Beat.

*He was als dronck he cold nyet stand,*
  *Upsolce si byen.*
*Tap eens de canneken,*
*Drincke, schone mannekin.*[2]

*Firk.*  Master, for my life, yonder 's a brother of the gentle craft; if he bear not Saint Hugh's bones,[3] I 'll forfeit my bones. He 's some uplandish[4] workman: hire him, good master, that I may learn some gibble-gabble; 't will make us work the faster.

*Eyre.*  Peace, Firk! A hard world! Let him pass, let him vanish; we have journeymen enow. Peace, my fine Firk!

*Wife.*  Nay, nay, y' are best follow your man's counsel; you shall see what will come on 't. We have not men enow, but we must entertain every butter-box; but let that pass.

*Hodge.*  Dame, 'fore God, if my master follow your counsel, he 'll consume little beef. He shall be glad of men, and he can catch them.

*Firk.*  Ay, that he shall.

*Hodge.*  'Fore God, a proper man, and I warrant, a fine work-man. Master, farewell; dame, adieu; if such a man as he cannot find work, Hodge is not for you.               *Offers to go.*

*Eyre.*  Stay, my fine Hodge.

*Firk.*  Faith, and your foreman go, dame, you must take a jour-ney to seek a new journeyman; if Roger remove, Firk follows. If Saint Hugh's bones shall not be set a-work, I may prick mine awl in the walls, and go play. Fare ye well, master; good-bye, dame.

*Eyre.*  Tarry, my fine Hodge, my brisk foreman! Stay, Firk! Peace, pudding-broth! By the Lord of Ludgate, I love my men as my life. Peace, you gallimaufry![5] Hodge, if he want work, I 'll hire him. One of you to him; stay, — he comes to us.

*Lacy.*  *Goeden dach, meester, ende u vro oak.*[6]

*Firk.*  Nails! if I should speak after him without drinking, I should choke. And you, friend Oake, are you of the gentle craft?

*Lacy.*  *Yaw, yaw, ik bin den skomawker.*[7]

*Firk.*  "Den skomaker," quoth 'a! And hark you, "skomaker," have you all your tools, a good rubbing-pin, a good stopper, a good dresser, your four sorts of awls, and your two balls of wax, your paring knife, your hand-and-thumb-leathers, and good St. Hugh's bones to smooth up your work?

---

[2] There was a farmer of Gelderland, / Jolly they be; / He was so drunk he could not stand, / Tipsy (?) they be. / Tap once with the can, / Drink, pretty little man.

[3] Name for the shoemaker's tools.          [4] Foreign.

[5] Hodgepodge.          [6] Good day, master, and you too, Lady.

[7] Yes, yes, I am a shoemaker.

*Lacy.   Yaw, yaw; be niet vorveard. Ik hab all de dingen voour mack skooes groot and cleane.*[8]

*Firk.*   Ha, ha!  Good master, hire him; he 'll make me laugh so that I shall work more in mirth than I can in earnest.

*Eyre.*   Hear ye, friend, have ye any skill in the mystery of cordwainers?[9]

*Lacy.   Ik weet niet wat yow seg; ich verstaw you niet.*[1]

*Firk.*   Why, thus, man: [*Imitating by gesture a shoemaker at work.*]  "Ich verste u niet," quoth 'a.

*Lacy.   Yaw, yaw, yaw; ick can dat wel doen.*[2]

*Firk.   Yaw, yaw!*  He speaks yawing like a jackdaw that gapes to be fed with cheesecurds.  Oh, he 'll give a villainous pull at a can of double-beer; but Hodge and I have the vantage, we must drink first, because we are the eldest journeymen.

*Eyre.*   What is thy name?

*Lacy.*   Hans — Hans Meulter.

*Eyre.*   Give me thy hand; th' art welcome. — Hodge, entertain him; Firk, bid him welcome; come, Hans.  Run, wife, bid your maids, your trullibubs, make ready my fine men's breakfasts.  To him, Hodge!

*Hodge.*   Hans, th' art welcome; use thyself friendly, for we are good fellows; if not, thou shalt be fought with, wert thou bigger than a giant.

*Firk.*   Yea, and drunk with, wert thou Gargantua.  My master keeps no cowards, I tell thee. — Ho, boy, bring him an heel-block, here 's a new journeyman.

### Enter Boy

*Lacy.   O' ich wersto you; ich moet een halve dossen cans betaelen; here, boy, nempt dis skilling, tap eens freelicke.*[3]  *Exit Boy.*

*Eyre.*   Quick, snipper-snapper, away!  Firk, scour thy throat; thou shalt wash it with Castilian liquor.

### Enter Boy

Come, my last of the fives,[4] give me a can.  Have to thee, Hans; here, Hodge; here, Firk; drink, you mad Greeks, and work like true Trojans, and pray for Simon Eyre, the shoemaker. — Here, Hans, and th' art welcome.

[8] Yes, yes, don't be afraid.  I have all the things for making shoes great and small.

[9] Trade of leather-workers, or shoemakers.

[1] I don't know what you say; I don't understand you.

[2] Yes, yes, yes; I can do that well.

[3] O, I understand you; I must pay for a half dozen cans; here, boy, take this shilling; draw (from the cask) once freely.

[4] Your turn last.

*Firk.* Lo, dame, you would have lost a good fellow that will teach us to laugh. This beer came hopping in well.

*Wife.* Simon, it is almost seven.

*Eyre.* Is 't so, Dame Clapper-dudgeon? Is 't seven o'clock, and my men's breakfast not ready? Trip and go, you sous'd conger away! Come, you mad hyperboreans; follow me, Hodge; follow me, Hans; come after, my fine Firk; to work, to work a while, and then to breakfast.                                                  *Exit.*

*Firk.* Soft! *Yaw, yaw,* good Hans, though my master have no more wit but to call you afore me, I am not so foolish to go behind you, I being the elder journeyman.                      *Exeunt.*


[SCENE IV]

*Halloaing within. Enter Warner and Hammon, like Hunters*

*Ham.* Cousin, beat every brake, the game 's not far.
This way with winged feet he fled from death,
Whilst the pursuing hounds, scenting his steps,
Find out his highway to destruction.
Besides, the miller's boy told me even now,
He saw him take soil,[5] and he halloaed him,
Affirming him so emboss'd[6]
That long he could not hold.

*Warn.*                          If it be so,
'T is best we trace these meadows by Old Ford.

*A noise of Hunters within. Enter a Boy*

*Ham.* How now, boy? Where 's the deer? speak saw'st thou him?

*Boy.* O yea; I saw him leap through a hedge, and then over a ditch, then at my lord mayor's pale:[7] over he skipp'd me, and in he went me, and "Holla" the hunters cried, and "There, boy; there, boy!" But there he is, o' mine honesty.

*Ham.* Boy, Godamercy.[8] Cousin, let 's away; I hope we shall find better sport to-day.                                    *Exeunt.*


[SCENE V]

*Hunting within. Enter Rose and Sybil*

*Rose.* Why, Sybil, wilt thou prove a forester?

*Sybil.* Upon some, no. Forester? Go by; no, faith, mistress.

---

[5] Take refuge.                   [6] Foaming.
[7] Fence.                          [8] Thanks.

The deer came running into the barn through the orchard and over the pale; I wot well, I look'd as pale as a new cheese to see him. But whip, says Goodman Pinclose, up with his flail, and our Nick with a prong,[9] and down he fell, and they upon him, and I upon them. By my troth, we had such sport; and in the end we ended him; his throat cut, flay'd him, unhorn'd him, and my lord mayor shall eat of him anon, when he comes.

*Horns sound within.*

*Rose.*   Hark, hark, the hunters come; y' are best take heed,
They 'll have a saying to you[1] for this deed.

*Enter Hammon, Warner, Huntsmen, and Boy*

*Ham.*   God save you, fair ladies.
*Sybil.*                         Ladies! O gross!
*Warn.*   Came not a buck this way?
*Rose.*                         No, but two does.
*Ham.*   And which way went they? Faith, we 'll hunt at those.
*Sybil.*   At those? Upon some, no. When, can you tell?
*Warn.*   Upon some, ay.
*Sybil.*               Good Lord!
*Warn.*                         Wounds! Then farewell!
*Ham.*   Boy, which way went he?
*Boy.*                         This way, sir, he ran.
*Ham.*   This way he ran indeed, fair Mistress Rose;
Our game was lately in your orchard seen.
*Warn.*   Can you advise, which way he took his flight?
*Sybil.*   Follow your nose; his horns will guide you right.
*Warn.*   Th' art a mad wench.
*Sybil.*               O, rich!
*Rose.*                         Trust me, not I.
It is not like that the wild forest-deer
Would come so near to places of resort;
You are deceiv'd, he fled some other way.
*Warn.*   Which way, my sugar-candy, can you shew?
*Sybil.*   Come up, good honeysops! upon some, no.
*Rose.*   Why do you stay, and not pursue your game?
*Sybil.*   I 'll hold[2] my life, their hunting-nags be lame.
*Ham.*   A deer more  dear is found within this place.
*Rose.*   But not the deer, sir, which you had in chase.
*Ham.*   I chas'd the deer, but this dear chaseth me.
*Rose.*   The strangest hunting that ever I see.
But where's your park?            *She offers to go away.*
*Ham.*               'T is here: O stay!

---

[9] Hayfork.            [1] A word with you.            [2] Bet.

*Rose.*    Impale me,[3] and then I will not stray.
*Warn.*    They wrangle, wench; we are more kind than they.
*Sybil.*    What kind of hart is that dear heart you seek?
*Warn.*    A hart, dear heart.
*Sybil.*                    Who ever saw the like?
*Rose.*    To lose your hart, is 't possible you can?
*Ham.*    My heart is lost.
*Rose.*                    Alack, good gentleman!
*Ham.*    This poor lost heart would I wish you might find.
*Rose.*    You, by such luck, might prove your hart[4] a hind.[5]
*Ham.*    Why Luck had horns, so have I heard some say.
*Rose.*    Now, God, and 't be his will, send Luck into your way.

*Enter Lord Mayor and Servants*

*L. Mayor.*    What, Master Hammon?  Welcome to Old Ford!
*Sybil.*    Gods pittikins, hands off, sir!  Here 's my lord.
*L. Mayor.*    I hear you had ill luck, and lost your game.
*Ham.*    'T is true, my lord.
*L. Mayor.*                    I am sorry for the same.
What gentleman is this?
*Ham.*                    My brother-in-law.
*L. Mayor.*    Y' are welcome both; sith Fortune offers you
Into my hands, you shall not part from hence,
Until you have refresh'd your wearied limbs.
Go, Sybil, cover the board!  You shall be guest
To no good cheer, but even a hunter's feast.
*Ham.*    I thank your lordship. — Cousin, on my life,
For our lost venison I shall find a wife.
*L. Mayor.*    In, gentlemen; I 'll not be absent long. —

                                *Exeunt [all but Mayor].*

    This Hammon is a proper gentleman,
A citizen by birth, fairly allied;
How fit an husband were he for my girl!
Well, I will in, and do the best I can,
To match my daughter to this gentleman.          *Exit.*


## [Act III, Scene I]

*Enter Lacy [as Hans], Skipper, Hodge, and Firk*

    *Skip.*    *Ick sal yow wat seggen, Hans;[6] dis skip dat comen from
Candy, is all vol,[7] by Got 's sacrament, van sugar, civet, almonds,*

---

[3] Make me captive.          [4] Male deer.          [5] Female deer.
[6] I'll tell you something, Hans.          [7] Full.

*cambrick, end alle dingen, towsand towsand ding. Nempt[8] it,
Hans, nempt it vor u meester. Daer be de bils van laden. Your
meester Simon Eyre sal hae good copen.[9] Wat seggen yow, Hans?*

*Firk.    Wat seggen de reggen de copen, slopen* — laugh, Hodge,
laugh!

*Hans.    Mine liever broder Firk, bringt Meester Eyre tot den
signe un Swannekin; daer sal yow finde dis skipper end me. Wat
seggen yow, broder Firk? Doot it, Hodge.* Come, skipper.

*Exeunt.*

*Firk.*    Bring him, quod you? Here 's no knavery, to bring my
master to buy a ship worth the lading of two or three hundred
thousand pounds. Alas, that 's nothing; a trifle, a bauble, Hodge.

*Hodge.*    The truth is, Firk, that the merchant owner of the ship
dares not shew his head, and therefore this skipper that deals for
him, for the love he bears to Hans, offers my master Eyre a bargain in the commodities. He shall have a reasonable day of payment; he may sell the wares by that time, and be an huge gainer
himself.

*Firk.*    Yea, but can my fellow Hans lend my master twenty
porpentines as an earnest penny?

*Hodge.*    Portagues, thou wouldst say; here they be, Firk; hark,
they jingle in my pocket like St. Mary Overy's bells.[1]

*Enter Eyre and his Wife*

*Firk.*    Mum! here comes my dame and my master. She 'll scold,
on my life, for loitering this Monday; but all 's one. Let them all
say what they can, Monday 's our holiday.

*Wife.*

> You sing, Sir Sauce, but I beshrew your heart.
> I fear, for this your singing we shall smart.

*Firk.*    Smart for me, dame; why, dame, why?

*Hodge.*    Master, I hope you 'll not suffer my dame to take
down your journeymen.

*Firk.*    If she take me down, I 'll take her up.
Yea, and take her down too, a button-hole lower.

*Eyre.*    Peace, Firk; not I, Hodge; by the life of Pharaoh, by the
Lord of Ludgate, by this beard, every hair whereof I value at a
king's ransom, she shall not meddle with you. — Peace, you
bombast-cotton-candle-quean; away, queen of clubs; quarrel not
with me and my men, with me and my fine Firk; I 'll firk you, if
you do.

---

[8] Take.                [9] Bargain.
[1] A church on the south bank of the Thames, now Southwark Cathedral.

*Wife.* Yea, yea, man, you may use me as you please; but let that pass.

*Eyre.* Let it pass, let it vanish away; peace! Am I not Simon Eyre? Are not these my brave men, brave shoemakers, all gentlemen of the gentle craft? Prince am I none, yet am I nobly born, as being the sole son of a shoemaker. Away, rubbish! vanish, melt; melt like kitchen-stuff.[2]

*Wife.* Yea, yea, 't is well; I must be call'd rubbish, kitchen-stuff, for a sort[3] of knaves.

*Firk.* Nay, dame, you shall not weep and wail in woe for me. Master, I 'll stay no longer; here 's a vennentory[4] of my shop-tools. Adieu, master; Hodge, farewell.

*Hodge.* Nay, stay, Firk; thou shalt not go alone.

*Wife.* I pray, let them go; there be mo maids than Mawkin, more men than Hodge, and more fools than Firk.

*Firk.* Fools? Nails! if I tarry now, I would my guts might be turn'd to shoe-thread.

*Hodge.* And if I stay, I pray God I may be turn'd to a Turk, and set in Finsbury[5] for boys to shoot at. — Come, Firk.

*Eyre.* Stay, my fine knaves, you arms of my trade, you pillars of my profession. What, shall a tittle-tattle's words make you forsake Simon Eyre? — Avaunt, kitchen-stuff! Rip, you brown-bread Tannikin; out of my sight! Move me not! Have not I ta'en you from selling tripes in Eastcheap, and set you in my shop, and made you hail-fellow with Simon Eyre, the shoemaker? And now do you deal thus with my journeymen? Look, you powder-beef-quean, on the face of Hodge: here 's a face for a lord.

*Firk.* And here 's a face for any lady in Christendom.

*Eyre.* Rip, you chitterling,[6] avaunt! Boy, bid the tapster of the Boar's Head fill me a dozen cans of beer for my journeymen.

*Firk.* A dozen cans? O, brave! Hodge, now I 'll stay.

*Eyre.* [*Aside to Boy.*] And the knave fills any more than two, he pays for them. [*Exit Boy. Aloud.*] — A dozen cans of beer for my journeymen. [*Re-enter Boy.*] Here, you mad Mesopotamians, wash your livers with this liquor. Where be the odd ten? — No more, Madge, no more. — Well said. Drink and to work! — What work dost thou, Hodge? What work?

*Hodge.* I am a-making a pair of shoes for my lord mayor's daughter, Mistress Rose.

*Firk.* And I a pair of shoes for Sybil, my lord's maid. I deal with her.

*Eyre.* Sybil? Fie, defile not thy fine workmanly fingers with

---

[2] Grease.  [3] Crew.  [4] Inventory.
[5] Archey fields close to London.  [6] Pig's intestine.

the feet of kitchenstuff and basting-ladles. Ladies of the court, fine
ladies, my lads, commit their feet to our apparelling; put gross
work to Hans. Yark[7] and seam, yark and seam!

*Firk.*   For yarking and seaming let me alone, and I come to 't.

*Hodge.*   Well, master, all this is from the bias.[8] Do you remember the ship my fellow Hans told you of? The skipper and he are
both drinking at the Swan. Here be the portagues to give earnest.
If you go through with it, you cannot choose but be a lord at least.

*Firk.*   Nay, dame, if my master prove not a lord, and you a lady,
hang me.

*Wife.*   Yea, like enough, if you may loiter and tipple thus.

*Firk.*   Tipple, dame? No, we have been bargaining with Skel-
lum-Skanderbag-can-you-Dutch-spreaken for a ship of silk cypress,[9] laden with sugar-candy.

*Enter the Boy with a velvet coat and an Alderman's gown.
Eyre puts it on.*

*Eyre.*   Peace, Firk; silence, Tittle-tattle! Hodge, I 'll go through
with it. Here 's a seal-ring, and I have sent for a guarded[1] gown
and a damask cassock. See where it comes! look here, Maggy; help
me, Firk; apparel me, Hodge: silk and satin, you mad Philistines,
silk and satin!

*Firk.*   Ha, ha! my master will be as proud as a dog in a doublet,
all in beaten[2] damask and velvet.

*Eyre.*   Softly, Firk, for rearing of the nap, and wearing threadbare my garments. How dost thou like me, Firk? How do I look,
my fine Hodge?

*Hodge.*   Why, now you look like yourself, master. I warrant
you, there 's few in the city but will give you the wall, and come
upon you with the "right worshipful."

*Firk.*   Nails, my master looks like a threadbare cloak new turn'd
and dress'd. Lord, Lord, to see what good raiment doth! Dame,
dame, are you not enamoured?

*Eyre.*   How say'st thou, Maggy, am I not brisk? Am I not fine?

*Wife.*   Fine? By my troth, sweetheart, very fine! By my troth,
I never lik'd thee so well in my life, sweetheart; but let that pass.
I warrant, there be many women in the city have not such hand-
some husbands, but only for their apparel; but let that pass too.

*Enter Hans and Skipper*

*Hans.*   *Godden day, mester. Dis be de skipper dat heb de skip
van marchandice; de commodity ben good; nempt it, mester,
nempt it.*

---

[7] Tug.          [8] Beside the point.          [9] A light, fine fabric, like crape.
[1] Trimmed.          [2] Embroidered.

*Eyre.* Godamercy, Hans; welcome, skipper. Where lies this ship of merchandise?

*Skip.* *De skip ben in revere; dor be van sugar, civet, almonds, cambrick, and a towsand, towsand tings, gotz sacrament; nempt it, mester: ye sal heb good copen.*

*Firk.* To him, master! O sweet master! O sweet wares! Prunes, almonds, sugar-candy, carrot-roots, turnips, O brave fatting meat! Let not a man buy a nutmeg but yourself.

*Eyre.* Peace, Firk! Come, skipper, I 'll go aboard with you. — Hans, have you made him drink?

*Skip.* *Yaw, yaw, ic heb veale[3] gedrunck.*

*Eyre.* Come, Hans, follow me. Skipper, thou shalt have my countenance in the city. *Exeunt.*

*Firk.* "Yaw, heb veale gedrunck," quoth 'a. They may well be called butter-boxes, when they drink fat veal and thick beer too. But come, dame, I hope you 'll chide us no more.

*Wife.* No, faith, Firk; no, perdy, Hodge. I do feel honour creep upon me, and, which is more, a certain rising in my flesh; but let that pass.

*Firk.* Rising in your flesh do you feel, say you? Ay, you may be with child, but why should not my master feel a rising in his flesh, having a gown and a gold ring on? But you are such a shrew, you 'll soon pull him down.

*Wife.* Ha, ha! prithee, peace! Thou mak'st my worship laugh; but let that pass. Come, I 'll go in. Hodge, prithee, go before me; Firk, follow me.

*Firk.* Firk doth follow: Hodge, pass out in state. *Exeunt.*

[SCENE II]

*Enter Lincoln and Dodger*

*Linc.* How now, good Dodger, what 's the news in France?

*Dodger.* My lord, upon the eighteenth day of May
The French and English were prepar'd to fight;
Each side with eager fury gave the sign
Of a most hot encounter. Five long hours
Both armies fought together; at the length
The lot of victory fell on our sides.
Twelve thousand of the Frenchmen that day died,
Four thousand English, and no man of name
But Captain Hyam and young Ardington,

[3] Much.

Two gallant gentlemen, I knew them well.

  *Linc.*  But Dodger, prithee, tell me, in this fight
How did my cousin Lacy bear himself?

  *Dodger.*  My lord, your cousin Lacy was not there.

  *Linc.*  Not there?

  *Dodger.*          No, my good lord.

  *Linc.*                Sure, thou mistakest.
I saw him shipp'd, and a thousand eyes beside
Were witnesses of the farewells which he gave,
When I, with weeping eyes, bid him adieu.
Dodger, take heed.

  *Dodger.*        My lord, I am advis'd[4]
That what I spake is true: to prove it so,
His cousin Askew, that supplied his place,
Sent me for him from France, that secretly
He might convey himself hither.

  *Linc.*             Is 't even so?
Dares he so carelessly venture his life
Upon the indignation of a king?
Has he despis'd my love, and spurn'd those favours
Which I with prodigal hand pour'd on his head?
He shall repent his rashness with his soul.
Since of my love he makes no estimate,
I 'll make him wish he had not known my hate.
Thou hast no other news?

  *Dodger.*          None else, my lord.

  *Linc.*  None worse I know thou hast. — Procure the king
To crown his giddy brows with ample honours,
Send him chief colonel, and all my hope
Thus to be dash'd! But 't is in vain to grieve:
One evil cannot a worse relieve.
Upon my life, I have found out his plot;
That old dog, Love, that fawn'd upon him so,
Love to that puling girl, his fair-cheek'd Rose,
The lord mayor's daughter, hath distracted him,
And in the fire of that love's lunacy
Hath he burnt up himself, consum'd his credit,
Lost the king's love, yea, and, I fear, his life,
Only to get a wanton to his wife,
Dodger, it is so.

  *Dodger.*    I fear so, my good lord.

  *Linc.*  It is so — nay, sure it cannot be!
I am at my wits' end. — Dodger!

  [4] Assured.

*Dodger.*                  Yea, my lord.

*Linc.*   Thou art acquainted with my nephew's haunts.
Spend this gold for thy pains; go seek him out.
Watch at my lord mayor's — there, if he live,
Dodger, thou shalt be sure to meet with him.
Prithee, be diligent. — Lacy, thy name
Liv'd once in honour, now dead in shame. —
Be circumspect.                             *Exit.*

*Dodger.*   I warrant you, my lord.            *Exit.*


### [SCENE III]

*Enter L. Mayor and Master Scott*

*L. Mayor.*    Good Master Scott, I have been bold with you,
To be a witness to a wedding-knot
Betwixt young Master Hammon and my daughter.
O, stand aside; see where the lovers come.

*Enter Hammon and Rose*

*Rose.*   Can it be possible you love me so?
No, no, within those eyeballs I espy
Apparent likelihoods of flattery.
Pray now, let go my hand.

*Ham.*                Sweet Mistress Rose,
Misconstrue not my words, nor misconceive
Of my affection, whose devoted soul
Swears that I love thee dearer than my heart.

*Rose.*   As dear as your own heart? I judge it right,
Men love their hearts best when th' are out of sight.

*Ham.*   I love you, by this hand.

*Rose.*              Yet hands off now!
If flesh be frail, how weak and frail 's your vow!

*Ham.*   Then by my life I swear.

*Rose.*               Then do not brawl;
One quarrel loseth wife and life and all.
Is not your meaning thus?

*Ham.*            In faith, you jest.

*Rose.*   Love loves to sport; therefore leave love, y' are best.

*L. Mayor.*   What? square they,[5] Master Scott?

*Scott.*   Sir, never doubt.
Lovers are quickly in, and quickly out.

[5] Are they quarreling?

*Ham.*   Sweet Rose, be not so strange in fancying me.
Nay, never turn aside, shun not my sight:
I am not grown so fond, to fond[6] my love
On any that shall quit it with disdain;
If you will love me, so; — if not, farewell.
  *L. Mayor.*   Why, how now, lovers, are you both agreed?
  *Ham.*   Yes, faith, my lord.
  *L. Mayor.*                     'T is well, give me your hand.
Give me yours, daughter. — How now, both pull back!
What means this, girl?
  *Rose.*            I mean to live a maid.
  *Ham.* [*Aside.*] But not to die one; pause, ere that be said.
  *L. Mayor.*   Will you still cross me, still be obstinate?
  *Ham.*   Nay, chide her not, my lord, for doing well;
If she can live an happy virgin's life,
'T is far more blessed than to be a wife.
  *Rose.*   Say, sir, I cannot, I have made a vow:
Whoever be my husband, 't is not you.
  *L. Mayor.*   Your tongue is quick; but Master Hammon, know,
I bade you welcome to another end.
  *Ham.*   What, would you have me pule and pine and pray,
With "lovely lady," "mistress of my heart,"
"Pardon your servant," and the rhymer play,
Railing on Cupid and his tyrant's-dart;
Or shall I undertake some martial spoil,[7]
Wearing your glove at tourney and at tilt,
And tell how many gallants I unhors'd —
Sweet, will this pleasure you?
  *Rose.*                  Yea, when wilt begin?
What, love rhymes, man? Fie on that deadly sin!
  *L. Mayor.*   If you will have her, I 'll make her agree.
  *Ham.*   Enforced love is worse than hate to me.
[*Aside.*] There is a wench keeps shop in the Old Change,[8]
To her will I — it is not wealth I seek.
I have enough — and will prefer her love
Before the world. — [*Aloud.*] My good lord mayor, adieu.
Old love for me, I have no luck with new.          *Exit.*
  *L. Mayor.*   Now, mammet,[9] you have well behav'd yourself,
But you shall curse your coyness if I live. —
Who 's within there? See you convey your mistress

---

  [6] Fix.          [7] Exploit.
  [8] Near St. Paul's; "Old" because recently supplanted by Sir Thomas
Gresham's New Exchange.
  [9] Puppet.

Straight to th' Old Ford! I 'll keep you straight enough.
Fore God, I would have sworn the puling girl
Would willingly accepted Hammon's love;
But banish him, my thoughts! — Go, minion, in!        *Exit Rose.*
Now tell me, Master Scott, would you have thought
That Master Simon Eyre, the shoemaker,
Had been of wealth to buy such merchandise?
   *Scott.*    'T was well, my lord, your honour and myself
Grew partners with him; for your bills of lading
Shew that Eyre's gains in one commodity
Rise at the least to full three thousand pound,
Besides like gain in other merchandise.
   *L. Mayor.*    Well, he shall spend some of his thousands now,
For I have sent for him to the Guildhall.

### Enter Eyre

See, where he comes. — Good morrow, Master Eyre.
   *Eyre.*    Poor Simon Eyre, my lord, your shoemaker.
   *L. Mayor.*    Well, well, it likes[1] yourself to term you so.

### Enter Dodger

Now Master Dodger, what 's the news with you?
   *Dodger.*    I 'd gladly speak in private to your honour.
   *L. Mayor.*    You shall, you shall. — Master Eyre and Master
    Scott,
I have some business with this gentleman;
I pray, let me entreat you to walk before
To the Guildhall; I 'll follow presently.
Master Eyre, I hope ere noon to call you sheriff.
   *Eyre.*    I would not care, my lord, if you might call me
King of Spain. — Come, Master Scott.    *Exeunt* [*Eyre and Scott*].
   *L. Mayor.*    Now, Master Dodger, what 's the news you bring?
   *Dodger.*    The Earl of Lincoln by me greets your lordship,
And earnestly requests you, if you can,
Inform him where his nephew Lacy keeps.[2]
   *L. Mayor.*    Is not his nephew Lacy now in France?
   *Dodger.*    No, I assure your Lordship, but disguis'd
Lurks here in London.
   *L. Mayor.*                London? Is 't even so?
It may be; but upon my faith and soul,
I know not where he lives, or whether he lives:
So tell my Lord of Lincoln. — Lurch[3] in London?
Well, Master Dodger, you perhaps may start[4] him;

---

[1] Pleases.        [2] Lives.        [3] Lurk.        [4] Rouse.

Be but the means to rid him into France,
I 'll give you a dozen angels for your pains:
So much I love his honour, hate his nephew.
And, prithee, so inform thy lord from me.

 *Dodger.* I take my leave.      *Exit Dodger.*
 *L. Mayor.* Farewell, good Master Dodger.
Lacy in London? I dare pawn my life,
My daughter knows thereof, and for that cause
Denied young Master Hammon in his love.
Well, I am glad I sent her to Old Ford.
Gods Lord, 't is late! to Guildhall I must hie;
I know my brethren stay my company.     *Exit*


[SCENE IV]

*Enter Firk, Eyre's wife, [Lacy as] Hans, Roger*

 *Wife.* Thou goest too fast for me, Roger. O, Firk.
 *Firk.* Ay, forsooth.
 *Wife.* I pray thee, run — do you hear? — run to Guildhall,
and learn if my husband, Master Eyre, will take that worshipful
vocation of Master Sheriff upon him. Hie thee, good Firk.
 *Firk.* Take it? Well, I go; and he should not take it, Firk
swears to forswear him. Yes, forsooth, I go to Guildhall.
 *Wife.* Nay, when? Thou art too compendious[5] and tedious.
 *Firk.* O rare, your excellence is full of eloquence. How like a
new cart-wheel my dame speaks, and she looks like an old musty
ale-bottle going to scalding.
 *Wife.* Nay, when? Thou wilt make me melancholy.
 *Firk.* God forbid your worship should fall into that humour;
— I run.                   *Exit.*
 *Wife.* Let me see now, Roger and Hans.
 *Hodge.* Ay, forsooth, dame — mistress, I should say, but the
old term so sticks to the roof of my mouth, I can hardly lick it
off.
 *Wife.* Even what thou wilt, good Roger; dame is a fair name
for any honest Christian; but let that pass. How dost thou, Hans?
 *Hans.* *Mee tanck you, vro.*
 *Wife.* Well, Hans and Roger, you see, God hath bless'd your
master, and, perdy, if ever he comes to be Master Sheriff of London — as we are all mortal — you shall see, I will have some odd
thing or other in a corner for you: I will not be your back-
friend;[6] but let that pass. Hans, pray thee, tie my shoe.

---

[5] She means "long-winded."
[6] False friend.

*Hans.*    *Yaw, ic sal, vro.*

*Wife.*    Roger, thou know'st the length of my foot; as it is none of the biggest, so I thank God, it is handsome enough; prithee, let me have a pair of shoes made: cork, good Roger, wooden heel too.

*Hodge.*    You shall.

*Wife.*    Art thou acquainted with never a fardingale-maker, nor a French hood-maker? I must enlarge my bum,[7] ha, ha! How shall I look in a hood, I wonder! Perdy, oddly, I think.

*Hodge.* [*Aside.*] As a cat out of a pillory. — Very well, I warrant you, mistress.

*Wife.*    Indeed, all flesh is grass; and, Roger, canst thou tell where I may buy a good hair?[8]

*Hodge.*    Yes, forsooth, at the poulterer's in Gracious[9] Street.

*Wife.*    Thou art an ungracious wag: perdy, I mean a false hair for my periwig.

*Hodge.*    Why, mistress, the next time I cut my beard, you shall have the shavings of it; but they are all true hairs.

*Wife.*    It is very hot. I must get me a fan or else a mask.

*Hodge.* [*Aside.*] So you had need, to hide your wicked face.

*Wife.*    Fie upon it, how costly this world's calling is; perdy, but that it is one of the wonderful works of God, I would not deal with it. — Is not Firk come yet? Hans, be not so sad, let it pass and vanish, as my husband's worship says.

*Hans.*    *Ick bin vrolicke,*[1] *lot see yow soo.*

*Hodge.*    Mistress, will you drink[2] a pipe of tobacco?

*Wife.*    Oh, fie upon it, Roger, perdy! These filthy tobacco-pipes are the most idle slavering baubles that ever I felt. Out upon it! God bless us, men look not like men that use them.

### Enter Rafe, being lame

*Hodge.*    What, fellow Rafe? Mistress, look here, Jane's husband! Why, how now, lame? Hans, make much of him, he 's a brother of our trade, a good workman, and a tall soldier.

*Hans.*    You be welcome, broder.

*Wife.*    Perdy, I knew him not. How dost thou, good Rafe? I am glad to see thee well.

*Rafe.*    I would God you saw me, dame, as well
As when I went from London into France.

*Wife.*    Trust me, I am sorry, Rafe, to see thee impotent. Lord, how the wars have made him sunburnt! The left leg is not well; 't was a fair gift of God the infirmity took not hold a little higher, considering thou camest from France; but let that pass.

*Rafe.*    I am glad to see you well, and I rejoice

---

[7] Wire framework of shirt.      [8] Wig.
[9] I.e., Gracechurch.      [1] Merry.      [2] Smoke.

To hear that God hath bless'd my master so
Since my departure.

*Wife.*   Yea, truly, Rafe. I thank my Maker; but let that pass.

*Hodge.*   And, sirrah Rafe, what news, what news in France?

*Rafe.*   Tell me, good Roger, first, what news in England?
How does my Jane? When didst thou see my wife?
Where lives my poor heart? She 'll be poor indeed,
Now I want limbs to get whereon to feed.

*Hodge.*   Limbs? Hast thou not hands, man? Thou shalt never see a shoemaker want bread, though he have but three fingers on a hand.

*Rafe.*   Yet all this while I hear not of my Jane.

*Wife.*   O Rafe, your wife, — perdy, we know not what 's become of her. She was here a while, and because she was married, grew more stately than became her; I check'd her, and so forth; away she flung, never returned, nor said bye nor bah; and, Rafe, you know, "ka me, ka thee."[3] And so, as I tell ye —— Roger, is not Firk come yet?

*Hodge.*   No, forsooth.

*Wife.*   And so, indeed, we heard not of her, but I hear she lives in London; but let that pass. If she had wanted, she might have opened her case to me or my husband, or to any of my men. I am sure, there 's not any of them, perdy, but would have done her good to his power. Hans, look if Firk be come.

*Hans.*   *Yaw, ik sal, vro.*                              *Exit Hans.*

*Wife.*   And so, as I said — but, Rafe, why dost thou weep? Thou knowest that naked we came out of our mother's womb, and naked we must return; and, therefore, thank God for all things.

*Hodge.*   No, faith, Jane is a stranger here; but, Rafe, pull up a good heart. I know thou hast one. Thy wife, man, is in London; one told me, he saw her a while ago very brave and neat; we 'll ferret her out, and London hold her.

*Wife.*   Alas, poor soul, he 's overcome with sorrow; he does but as I do, weep for the loss of any good thing. But, Rafe, get thee in, call for some meat and drink: thou shalt find me worshipful towards thee.

*Rafe.*   I thank you, dame; since I want limbs and lands,
I 'll to God, my good friends, and to these my hands.

*Enter Hans and Firk running*

*Firk.*   Run, good Hans! O Hodge, O mistress! Hodge, heave up thine ears; mistress, smug up your looks; on with your best apparel; my master is chosen, my master is called, nay, condemn'd

---

[3] Tit for tat.

by the cry of the country to be sheriff of the city for this famous
year now to come. And, time now being, a great many men in
black gowns were ask'd for their voices and their hands, and my
master had all their fists about his ears presently, and they cried
"Ay, ay, ay, ay," — and so I came away —
Wherefore without all other grieve
I do salute you, Mistress Shrieve.

*Hans.* Yaw, *my mester is de groot man, de shrieve.*

*Hodge.* Did I not tell you, mistress? Now I may boldly say:
Good-morrow to your worship.

*Wife.* Good-morrow, good Roger. I thank you, my good people all. — Firk, hold up thy hand: here 's a three-penny piece for
thy tidings.

*Firk.* 'T is but three-half-pence, I think.
Yes, 't is three-pence, I small the rose.[4]

*Hodge.* But, mistress, be rul'd by me, and do not speak so
pulingly.

*Firk.* 'T is her worship speaks so, and not she. No, faith, mistress, speak me in the old key: "To it, Firk;" "there, good Firk;"
"ply your business, Hodge;" "Hodge; with a full mouth;" "I 'll fill
your bellies with good cheer, till they cry twang."

*Enter Simon Eyre wearing a gold chain*

*Hans.* See, *myn liever broder, heer compt my meester.*

*Wife.* Welcome home, Master Shrieve; I pray God continue
you in health and wealth.

*Eyre.* See here, my Maggy, a chain, a gold chain for Simon
Eyre. I shall make thee a lady; here 's a French hood for thee; on
with it, on with it! dress thy brows with this flap of a shoulder of
mutton,[5] to make thee look lovely. Where be my fine men?
Roger, I 'll make over my shop and tools to thee; Firk, thou shalt
be the foreman; Hans, thou shalt have an hundred for twenty.[6]
Be as mad knaves as your master Sim Eyre hath been, and you
shall live to be sheriffs of London. — How dost thou like me,
Margery? Prince am I none, yet am I princely born. Firk, Hodge,
and Hans!

*All Three.* Ay, forsooth, what says your worship, Master
Sheriff?

*Eyre.* Worship and honour, you Babylonian knaves, for the
gentle craft. But I forgot myself. I am bidden by my lord mayor
to dinner to Old Ford; he 's gone before, I must after. Come,

---

[4] The Tudor rose appeared on a number of Elizabethan coins.
[5] Sheep's wool.
[6] Viz., the twenty portagues mentioned in III.i.

Madge, on with your trinkets! Now, my true Trojans, my fine Firk, my dapper Hodge, my honest Hans, some device, some odd crotchets, some morris, or such like, for the honour of the gentle shoemakers. Meet me at Old Ford; you know my mind. Come, Madge, away. Shut up the shop, knaves, and make holiday.

*Exeunt.*

*Firk.*   O rare! O brave! Come, Hodge; follow me, Hans;
We 'll be with them for a morris-dance.          *Exeunt.*

[SCENE V]

*Enter Lord Mayor, [Rose,] Eyre, his wife in a French
hood, Sybil, and other Servants.*

*L. Mayor.*   Trust me, you are as welcome to Old Ford
As I myself.
*Wife.*      Truly, I thank your lordship.
*L. Mayor.*   Would our bad cheer were worth the thanks you
   give.
*Eyre.*   Good cheer, my lord mayor, fine cheer!
A fine house, fine walls, all fine and neat.
*L. Mayor.*   Now, by my troth, I 'll tell thee, Master Eyre,
It does me good, and all my brethren,
That such a madcap fellow as thyself
Is ent'red into our society.
*Wife.*   Ay, but, my lord, he must learn now to put on gravity.
*Eyre.*   Peace, Maggy, a fig for gravity! When I go to Guildhall
in my scarlet gown, I 'll look as demurely as a saint, and speak as
gravely as a justice of peace; but now I am here at Old Ford, at
my good lord mayor's house, let it go by, vanish, Maggy, I 'll be
merry; away with flip-flap, these fooleries, these gulleries. What,
honey? Prince am I none, yet am I princely born. What says my
lord mayor?
*L. Mayor.*   Ha, ha, ha! I had rather than a thousand pound I
had an heart but half so light as yours.
*Eyre.*   Why, what should I do, my lord? A pound of care pays
not a dram of debt. Hum, let 's be merry, whiles we are young;
old age, sack and sugar will steal upon us ere we be aware.

THE FIRST THREE-MAN'S SONG[7]

O the month of May, the merry month of May,
   So frolic, so gay, and so green, so green, so green!

[7] In the original editions this and the song in V.iv are printed at the
beginning of the play; editors have transferred them to their present
positions.

O, and then did I unto my true love say:
  "Sweet Peg, thou shalt be my summer's queen!

"Now the nightingale, the pretty nightingale,
  The sweetest singer in all the forest's choir,
Entreats thee, sweet Peggy, to hear thy true love's tale;
  Lo, yonder she sitteth, her breast against a brier.

"But O, I spy the cuckoo, the cuckoo, the cuckoo;
  See where she sitteth: come away, my joy;
Come away, I prithee: I do not like the cuckoo
  Should sing where my Peggy and I kiss and toy."

O the month of May, the merry month of May,
  So frolic, so gay, and so green, so green, so green!
And then did I unto my true love say:
  "Sweet Peg, thou shalt be my summer's queen!"

*L. Mayor.*  It 's well done.  Mistress Eyre, pray, give good coun-
  sel
To my daughter.
  *Wife.*  I hope, Mistress Rose will have the grace to take nothing
that 's bad.
  *L. Mayor.*  Pray God she do; for i' faith, Mistress Eyre,
I would bestow upon that peevish girl
A thousand marks more than I mean to give her
Upon condition she 'd be rul'd by me.
The ape still crosseth me.  There came of late
A proper[8] gentleman of fair revénues,
Whom gladly I would call son-in-law:
But my fine cockney[9] would have none of him.
You 'll prove a coxcomb[1] for it, ere you die:
A courtier, or no man, must please your eye.
  *Eyre.*  Be rul'd, sweet Rose: th' art ripe for a man.  Marry not
with a boy that has no more hair on his face than thou hast on thy
cheeks.  A courtier! wash, go by, stand not upon pishery-pashery:
those silken fellows are but painted images, outsides, outsides, Rose;
their inner linings are torn.  No, my fine mouse, marry me with a
gentleman grocer like my lord mayor, your father; a grocer is a
sweet trade: plums, plums.  Had I a son or daughter should marry
out of the generation and blood of the shoemakers, he should pack.
What, the gentle trade is a living for a man through Europe,
through the world.

                    *A noise within of a tabor*[2] *and a pipe.*
  *L. Mayor.*  What noise is this?

---

[8] Handsome.              [9] Squeamish one.
[1] Fool.                  [2] Small drum.

*Eyre.*  O my lord mayor, a crew of good fellows that for love to your honour are come hither with a morris-dance. Come in, my Mesopotamians, cheerily.

> *Enter Hodge, Hans, Rafe, Firk, and other Shoemakers,*
> *in a morris; after a little dancing, the Lord Mayor speaks.*

*L. Mayor.*  Master Eyre, are all these shoemakers?

*Eyre.*  All cordwainers, my good lord mayor.

*Rose.* [*Aside.*]  How like my Lacy looks yond shoemaker!

*Hans.* [*Aside.*]  O that I durst but speak unto my love!

*L. Mayor.*  Sybil, go fetch some wine to make these drink. You are all welcome.

*All.*  We thank your lordship.

> *Rose takes a cup of wine and goes to Hans.*

*Rose.*  For his sake whose fair shape thou represent'st,
Good friend, I drink to thee.

*Hans.*  *Ic bedancke, good frister.*[3]

*Wife.*  I see, Mistress Rose, you do not want judgment; you have drunk to the properest man I keep.

*Firk.*  Here be some have done their parts to be as proper as he.

*L. Mayor.*  Well, urgent business calls me back to London.
Good fellows, first go in and taste our cheer;
And to make merry as you homeward go,
Spend these two angels in beer at Stratford-Bow.

*Eyre.*  To these two, my mad lads, Sim Eyre adds another; then cheerily, Firk; tickle it, Hans, and all for the honour of shoemakers.    *All go dancing out.*

*L. Mayor.*  Come, Master Eyre, let 's have your company.

> *Exeunt.*

*Rose.*  Sybil, what shall I do?

*Sybil.*  Why, what 's the matter?

*Rose.*  That Hans the shoemaker is my love Lacy.
Disguis'd in that attire to find me out.
How should I find the means to speak with him?

*Sybil.*  What, mistress, never fear; I dare venture my maidenhead to nothing, and that 's great odds, that Hans the Dutchman, when we come to London, shall not only see and speak with you, but in spite of all your father's policies steal you away and marry you. Will not this please you?

*Rose.*  Do this, and ever be assured of my love.

*Sybil.*  Away, then, and follow your father to London, lest your absence cause him to suspect something:
To-morrow, if my counsel be obey'd,
I 'll bind you prentice to the gentle trade.    [*Exeunt.*]

---

[3] Young lady.

## [Act IV, Scene I]

*Enter Jane in a Sempster's shop, working; and Hammon,*
*muffled, at another door. He stands aloof.*

*Ham.*   Yonder 's the shop, and there my fair love sits.
She 's fair and lovely, but she is not mine.
O, would she were! Thrice have I courted her,
Thrice hath my hand been moist'ned with her hand,
Whilst my poor famish'd eyes do feed on that
Which made them famish. I am infortunate:
I still love one, yet nobody loves me.
I muse in other men what women see
That I so want! Fine Mistress Rose was coy,
And this too curious![4] Oh, no, she is chaste,
And for she thinks me wanton, she denies
To cheer my cold heart with her sunny eyes.
How prettily she works! Oh pretty hand!
Oh happy work! It doth me good to stand
Unseen to see her. Thus I oft have stood
In frosty evenings, a light burning by her,
Enduring biting cold, only to eye her.
One only look hath seem'd as rich to me
As a king's crown; such is love's lunacy.
Muffled I 'll pass along, and by that try
Whether she know me.
*Jane.*                    Sir, what is 't you buy?
What is 't you lack, sir? calico, or lawn,
Fine cambric shirts, or bands?[5] what will you buy?
*Ham.* [*Aside.*]   That which thou wilt not sell. Faith, yet I 'll
   try: —
How do you sell this handkercher?
*Jane.*                    Good cheap.[6]
*Ham.*   And how these ruffs?
*Jane.*                    Cheap too.
*Ham.*                         And how this band?
*Jane.*   Cheap too.
*Ham.*          All cheap; how sell you then this hand?
*Jane.*   My hands are not to be sold.
*Ham.*                         To be given then!
Nay, faith, I come to buy.
*Jane.*               But none knows when.
*Ham.*   Good sweet, leave work a little while; let 's play.
*Jane.*   I cannot live by keeping holiday.

---

[4] Fastidious.              [5] Collars.              [6] Bargain.

*Ham.*     I 'll pay you for the time which shall be lost.

*Jane.*     With me you shall not be at so much cost.

*Ham.*     Look, how you wound this cloth, so you wound me.

*Jane.*     It may be so.

*Ham.*                         'T is so.

*Jane.*                                             What remedy?

*Ham.*     Nay, faith, you are too coy.

*Jane.*                                             Let go my hand.

*Ham.*     I will do any task at your command.

I would let go this beauty, were I not

In mind to disobey you by a power

That controls kings: I love you!

    *Jane.*                                   So, now part.

    *Ham.*     With hands I may, but never with my heart.

In faith, I love you.

    *Jane.*                         I believe you do.

    *Ham.*     Shall a true love in me breed hate in you?

    *Jane.*     I hate you not.

    *Ham.*                         Then you must love?

    *Jane.*                                             I do.

What are you better now?  I love not you.

    *Ham.*     All this, I hope, is but a woman's fray,

That means, "Come to me," when she cries, "Away!"

In earnest, mistress, I do not jest,

A true chaste love hath ent'red in my breast.

I love you dearly, as I love my life,

I love you as a husband loves a wife;

That, and no other love, my love requires.

Thy wealth, I know, is little; my desires

Thirst not for gold.  Sweet, beauteous Jane, what 's mine

Shall, if thou make myself thine, all be thine.

Say, judge, what is thy sentence, life or death?

Mercy or cruelty lies in thy breath.

    *Jane.*     Good sir, I do believe you love me well;

For 't is a silly conquest, silly pride,

For one like you — I mean a gentleman —

To boast that by his love-tricks he hath brought

Such and such women to his amorous lure;

I think you do not so, yet many do,

And make it even a very trade to woo.

I could be coy, as many women be,

Feed you with sunshine smiles and wanton looks,

But I detest witchcraft; say that I

Do constantly believe you, constant have ——

*Ham.*    Why dost thou not believe me?

*Jane.*                                    I believe you;
But yet, good sir, because I will not grieve you
With hopes to taste fruit which will never fall,
In simple truth this is the sum of all:
My husband lives, — at least, I hope he lives.
Press'd was he to these bitter wars in France;
Bitter they are to me by wanting him.
I have but one heart, and that heart 's his due.
How can I then bestow the same on you?
Whilst he lives, his I live, be it ne'er so poor,
And rather be his wife than a king's whore.

*Ham.*    Chaste and dear woman, I will not abuse thee,
Although it cost my life, if thou refuse me.
Thy husband, press'd for France, what was his name?

*Jane.*    Rafe Damport.

*Ham.*                    Damport? — Here 's a letter sent
From France to me, from a dear friend of mine,
A gentleman of place; here he doth write
Their names that have been slain in every fight.

*Jane.*    I hope death's scroll contains not my love's name.

*Ham.*    Cannot you read?

*Jane.*                    I can.

*Ham.*                        Peruse the same.
To my remembrance such a name I read
Amongst the rest. See here.

*Jane.*                    Ay me, he 's dead!
He 's dead! If this be true, my dear heart 's slain!

*Ham.*    Have patience, dear love.

*Jane.*                    Hence, hence!

*Ham.*                                    Nay, sweet Jane,
Make not poor sorrow proud with these rich tears.
I mourn thy husband's death, because thou mourn'st.

*Jane.*    That bill is forg'd; 't is sign'd by forgery.

*Ham.*    I 'll bring thee letters sent besides to many,
Carrying the like report; Jane, 't is too true.
Come, weep not: mourning, though it rise from love,
Helps not the mourned, yet hurts them that mourn.

*Jane.*    For God's sake, leave me.

*Ham.*                    Whither dost thou turn?
Forget the dead, love them that are alive;
His love is faded, try how mine will thrive.

*Jane.*    'T is now no time for me to think on love.

*Ham.*    'T is now best time for you to think on love,

Because your love lives not.

*Jane.*                    Though he be dead,
My love to him shall not be buried;
For God's sake, leave me to myself alone.

*Ham.*   'T would kill my soul, to leave thee drown'd in moan.
Answer me to my suit, and I am gone;
Say to me yea or no.

*Jane.*             No.

*Ham.*                   Then farewell!
One farewell will not serve, I come again.
Come, dry these wet cheeks; tell me, faith, sweet Jane,
Yea, or no, once more.

*Jane.*                 Once more I say no;
Once more be gone, I pray; else will I go.

*Ham.*   Nay, then I will grow rude, by this white hand,
Until you change that cold "no"; here I 'll stand
Till by your hard heart ——

*Jane.*                    Nay, for God's love, peace!
My sorrows by your presence more increase.
Not that you thus are present, but all grief
Desires to be alone; therefore in brief
Thus much I say, and saying bid adieu:
If ever I wed man, it shall be you.

*Ham.*   O blessed voice! Dear Jane, I 'll urge no more;
Thy breath hath made me rich.

*Jane.*                    Death makes me poor.     *Exeunt.*


[SCENE II]

*Enter Hodge, at his shop-board, Rafe, Firk, Hans, and a
Boy at work*

*All.*   Hey, down a down, down derry.

*Hodge.*   Well said, my hearts; ply your work to-day, we loit'red
yesterday; to it pell-mell, that we may live to be lord mayors, or
aldermen at least.

*Firk.*   Hey, down a down, derry.

Hodge.   Well said, i' faith! How say'st thou, Hans, doth not
Firk tickle it?

*Hans.*   *Yaw, mester.*

*Firk.*   Not so neither; my organ-pipe squeaks this morning for
want of liquoring.  Hey, down a down, derry!

*Hans.*   *Forward, Firk, tow best un jolly yongster.  Hort,[7] I,*

[7] Listen.

*mester, ic bid yo, cut me un pair vampres*[8] *vor Mester Jeffre's boots.*

*Hodge.* Thou shalt, Hans.

*Firk.* Master!

*Hodge.* How now, boy?

*Firk.* Pray, now you are in the cutting vein, cut me out a pair of counterfeits,[9] or else my work will not pass current; hey, down a down!

*Hodge.* Tell me, sirs, are my cousin Mrs. Priscilla's shoes done?

*Firk.* Your cousin? No, master; one of your aunts,[1] hang her; let them alone.

*Rafe.* I am in hand with them; she gave charge that none but I should do them for her.

*Firk.* Thou do for her? Then 't will be a lame doing, and that she loves not. Rafe, thou might'st have sent her to me, in faith, I would have yarked and firked your Priscilla. Hey, down a down, derry. This gear will not hold.

*Hodge.* How say'st thou, Firk, were we not merry at Old Ford?

*Firk.* How, merry! Why, our buttocks went jiggy-joggy like a quagmire. Well, Sir Roger Oatmeal, if I thought all meal of that nature, I would eat nothing but bagpuddings.

*Rafe.* Of all good fortunes my fellow Hans had the best.

*Firk.* 'T is true, because Mistress Rose drank to him.

*Hodge.* Well, well, work apace. They say, seven of the aldermen be dead, or very sick.

*Firk.* I care not, I 'll be none.

*Rafe.* No, nor I; but then my Master Eyre will come quickly to be lord mayor.

*Enter Sybil*

*Firk.* Whoop, yonder comes Sybil.

*Hodge.* Sybil, welcome, i' faith; and how dost thou, mad wench?

*Firk.* Sib-whore, welcome to London.

*Sybil.* Godamercy, sweet Firk; good lord, Hodge, what a delicious shop you have got! You tickle it, i' faith.

*Rafe.* Godamercy, Sybil, for our good cheer at Old Ford.

*Sybil.* That you shall have, Rafe.

*Firk.* Nay, by the mass, we had tickling cheer, Sybil; and how the plague dost thou and Mistress Rose and my lord mayor? I put the women in first.

[8] Vamps.          [9] Patterns.          [1] Slang for "harlots."

*Sybil.* Well, Godamercy; but God's me, I forget myself, where 's Hans the Fleming?

*Firk.* Hark, butter-box, now you must yelp out some *spreken.*

*Hans.* *Wat begaie[2] you? Vat vod you, Frister?*

*Sybil.* Marry, you must come to my young mistress, to pull on her shoes you made last.

*Hans.* *Vare ben your egle fro,[3] vare ben your mistris?*

*Sybil.* Marry, here at our London house in Cornhill.

*Firk.* Will nobody serve her turn but Hans?

*Sybil.* No, sir. Come, Hans, I stand upon needles.

*Hodge.* Why then, Sybil, take heed of pricking.

*Sybil.* For that let me alone. I have a trick in my budget.[4] Come, Hans.

*Hans.* *Yaw, yaw, ic sall meete yo gane.[5]*

*Exit Hans and Sybil.*

*Hodge.* Go, Hans, make haste again.[6] Come, who lacks work?

*Firk.* I, master, for I lack my breakfast; 't is munching-time, and past.

*Hodge.* Is 't so? Why, then, leave work, Rafe. To breakfast! Boy, look to the tools. Come, Rafe; come, Firk. *Exeunt.*

[Scene III]

*Enter a Serving-man*

*Serv.* Let me see now! the sign of the Last in Tower Street. Mass, yonder 's the house. What, ho! Who 's within?

*Enter Rafe*

*Rafe.* Who calls there? What want you, sir?

*Serv.* Marry, I would have a pair of shoes made for a gentlewoman against to-morrow morning. What, can you do them?

*Rafe.* Yes, sir, you shall have them. But what length 's her foot?

*Serv.* Why you must make them in all parts like this shoe; but, at any hand, fail not to do them, for the gentlewoman is to be married very early in the morning.

*Rafe.* How? by this shoe must it be made? By this? Are you sure, sir, by this?

*Serv.* How, by this? Am I sure, by this? Art thou in thy wits? I tell thee, I must have a pair of shoes, — dost thou mark me? A

---

[2] Desire.  [3] Noble lady.  [4] Wallet.
[5] Yes, yes, I shall go with you.  [6] Back.

pair of shoes, two shoes, made by this very shoe, this same shoe, against to-morrow morning by four o'clock. Dost understand me? Canst thou do 't?

*Rafe.*　Yes, sir, yes — I — I — I can do 't. By this shoe, you say? I should know this shoe. Yes, sir, yes, by this shoe. I can do 't. Four o' clock, well. Whither shall I bring them?

*Serv.*　To the sign of the Golden Ball in Watling Street; enquire for one Master Hammon, a gentleman, my master.

*Rafe.*　Yea, sir; by this shoe, you say?

*Serv.*　I say, Master Hammon at the Golden Ball; he 's the bridgegroom, and those shoes are for his bride.

*Rafe.*　They shall be done by this shoe. Well, well, Master Hammon at the Golden Shoe — I would say, the Golden Ball; very well, very well. But I pray you, sir, where must Master Hammond be married?

*Serv.*　At Saint Faith's Church, under Paul's.[7] But what 's that to thee? Prithee, dispatch those shoes, and so farewell.　　***Exit.***

*Rafe.*　By this shoe, said he. How am I amaz'd
At this strange accident! Upon my life,
This was the very shoe I gave my wife,
When I was press'd for France; since when, alas!
I never could hear of her. It is the same,
And Hammon's bride no other but my Jane.

### Enter Firk

*Firk.*　'Snails, Rafe, thou hast lost thy part of three pots a countryman of mine gave me to breakfast.

*Rafe.*　I care not; I have found a better thing.

*Firk.*　A thing? Away! Is it a man's thing, or a woman's thing?

*Rafe.*　Firk, dost thou know this shoe?

*Firk.*　No, by my troth; neither doth that know me! I have no acquaintance with it, 't is a mere stranger to me.

*Rafe.*　Why, then, I do; this shoe, I durst be sworn,
Once covered the instep of my Jane.
This is her size, her breadth, thus trod my love;
These true-love knots I prick'd. I hold my life,
By this old shoe I shall find out my wife.

*Firk.*　Ha, ha! Old shoe, that wert new!
How a murrain[8] came this ague-fit of foolishness upon thee?

*Rafe.*　Thus, Firk: even now here came a serving-man.
By this shoe would he have a new pair made

---

[7] The east end of the crypt of St. Paul's was used as a parish church; this was St. Faith's.

[8] Plague.

Against to-morrow morning for his mistress,
That 's to be married to a gentleman.
And why may not this be my sweet Jane?
   *Firk.*   And why may'st not thou be my sweet ass?
Ha, ha!
   *Rafe.*   Well, laugh and spare not! But the truth is this:
Against to-morrow morning I 'll provide
A lusty crew of honest shoemakers,
To watch the going of the bride to church.
If she prove Jane, I 'll take her in despite
From Hammon and the devil, were he by.
If it be not my Jane, what remedy?
Hereof am I sure, I shall live till I die,
Although I never with a woman lie.       *Exit.*
   *Firk.*   Thou lie with a woman to build nothing but Cripple-gates![9] Well, God sends fools fortune, and it may be, he may light upon his matrimony[1] by such a device; for wedding and hanging goes by destiny.[2]       *Exit.*


[SCENE IV]

*Enter [Lacy as] Hans and Rose, arm in arm*

   *Hans.*   How happy am I by embracing thee!
Oh, I did fear such cross mishaps did reign
That I should never see my Rose again.
   *Rose.*   Sweet Lacy, since fair opportunity
Offers herself to further our escape,
Let not too over-fond esteem of me
Hinder that happy hour. Invent the means,
And Rose will follow thee through all the world.
   *Hans.*   Oh, how I surfeit with excess of joy,
Made happy by thy rich perfection!
But since thou pay'st sweet interest to my hopes,
Redoubling love on love, let me once more
Like to a bold-fac'd debtor crave of thee
This night to steal abroad, and at Eyre's house,
Who now by death of certain aldermen
Is mayor of London, and my master once,
Meet thou thy Lacy, where in spite of change,

[9] A pun; Cripplegate was the name of one of the gates in the old wall surrounding London.
   [1] Wife.         [2] A proverb.

Your father's anger, and mine uncle's hate,
Our happy nuptials will we consummate.

### Enter Sybil

*Sybil.*   Oh God, what will you do, mistress? Shift for yourself, your father is at hand! He 's coming, he 's coming! Master
Lacy, hide yourself in my mistress! For God's sake, shift for
yourselves!

*Hans.*   Your father come! Sweet Rose, what shall I do?
Where shall I hide me? How shall I escape?

*Rose.*   A man, and want wit in extremity?
Come, come, be Hans still, play the shoemaker, Pull on my shoe.

### Enter Sir Roger Otley

*Hans.*   Mass, and that 's well rememb'red.

*Sybil.*   Here comes your father.

*Hans.*   *Forware, metresse, 't is un good skow, it sal vel dute, or
ye sal neit betallen.*[3]

*Rose.*   Oh God, it pincheth me; what will you do?

*Hans. [Aside].*   Your father's presence pincheth, not the shoe.

*Otley.*   Well done; fit my daughter well, and she shall please
thee well.

*Hans.*   *Yaw, yaw, ick weit dat well; forware, 't is un good skoo,
't is gimait van neits leither: se ever, mine here.*

### Enter a Prentice

*Otley.*   I do believe it. — What 's the news with you?

*Prentice.*   Please you, the Earl of Lincoln at the gate
Is newly lighted, and would speak with you.

*Otley.*   The Earl of Lincoln come to speak with me?
Well, well, I know his errand. Daughter Rose,
Send hence your shoemaker, dispatch, have done!
Syb, make things handsome! Sir boy, follow me.          *Exit.*

*Hans.*   Mine uncle come! Oh, what may this portend?
Sweet Rose, this of our love threatens an end.

*Rose.*   Be not dismay'd at this; what'er befall,
Rose is thine own. To witness I speak truth,
Where thou appoints the place, I 'll meet with thee.
I will not fix a day to follow thee,
But presently[4] steal hence. Do not reply:
Love which gave strength to bear my father's hate,
Shall now add wings to further our escape.          *Exeunt.*

---

[3] Truly, mistress, 'tis a good shoe; it shall fit well, or you shall not pay.
[4] At once.

### [Scene V]

*Enter Sir Roger Otley and Lincoln*

*Otley.*   Believe me, on my credit, I speak truth:
Since first your nephew Lacy went to France,
I have not seen him.  It seem'd strange to me,
When Dodger told me that he stay'd behind,
Neglecting the high charge the king imposed.
   *Lincoln.*   Trust me, Sir Roger Otley, I did think
Your counsel had given head to this attempt,
Drawn to it by the love he bears your child.
Here I did hope to find him in your house;
But now I see mine error, and confess,
My judgment wrong'd you by conceiving so.
   *Otley.*   Lodge in my house, say you?  Trust me, my lord,
I love your nephew Lacy too too dearly,
So much to wrong his honour; and he hath done so,
That first gave him advice to stay from France.
To witness I speak truth, I let you know
How careful I have been to keep my daughter
Free from all conference or speech of him;
Not that I scorn your nephew, but in love
I bear your honour, lest your noble blood
Should by my mean worth be dishonoured.
   *Lincoln.* [*Aside.*]   How far the churl's tongue wanders from
his heart! —
Well, well, Sir Roger Otley, I believe you,
With more than many thanks for the kind love
So much you seem to bear me.  But, my lord,
Let me request your help to seek my nephew,
Whom, if I find, I 'll straight embark for France.
So shall your Rose be free, my thoughts at rest,
And much care die which now lies in my breast.

*Enter Sybil*

*Sybil.*   Oh Lord!  Help, for God's sake!  My mistress; oh, my
young mistress!
   *Otley.*   Where is thy mistress?  What 's become of her?
   *Sybil.*   She 's gone, she 's fled!
   *Otley.*   Gone!  Whither is she fled?
   *Sybil.*   I know not, forsooth; she 's fled out of doors with
Hans the shoemaker; I saw them scud, scud, scud, apace, apace!

*Otley.* Which way? What, John! Where be my men? Which way?

*Sybil.* I know not, and it please your worship.

*Otley.* Fled with a shoemaker? Can this be true?

*Sybil.* Oh Lord, sir, as true as God 's in Heaven.

*Lincoln.* Her love turn'd shoemaker? I am glad of this.

*Otley.* A Fleming butter-box, a shoemaker!
Will she forget her birth, requite my care
With such ingratitude? Scorn'd she young Hammon
To love a honnikin,[5] a needy knave?
Well, let her fly, I 'll not fly after her;
Let her starve, if she will: she 's none of mine.

*Lincoln.* Be not so cruel, sir.

    *Enter Firk with shoes*

*Sybil.*         I am glad, she 's scap'd.

*Otley.* I 'll not account of her as of my child.
Was there no better object for her eyes,
But a foul drunken lubber, swill-belly,
A shoemaker? That 's brave!

*Firk.* Yea, forsooth; 't is a very brave shoe, and as fit as a pudding.

*Otley.* How now, what knave is this? From whence comest thou?

*Firk.* No knave, sir. I am Firk the shoemaker, lusty Roger's chief lusty journeyman, and I come hither to take up the pretty leg of sweet Mistress Rose, and thus hoping your worship is in as good health, as I was at the making hereof, I bid you farewell, yours, Firk.

*Otley.* Stay, stay, Sir Knave!

*Lincoln.* Come hither, shoemaker!

*Firk.* 'T is happy the knave is put before the shoemaker, or else I would not have vouchsafed to come back to you. I am moved, for I stir.

*Otley.* My lord, this villain calls us knaves by craft.

*Firk.* Then 't is by the gentle craft, and to call one knave gently is no harm. Sit your worship merry! Syb, your young mistress — I 'll so bob[6] them, now my master, Master Eyre, is lord mayor of London.

*Otley.* Tell me, sirrah, whose man are you?

*Firk.* I am glad to see your worship so merry. I have no maw to this gear, no stomach as yet to a red petticoat. *Pointing to Sybil.*

---

[5] Contemptible fellow.
[6] Play tricks on.

*Lincoln.*   He means not, sir, to woo you to his maid,
But only doth demand whose man you are.

*Firk.*   I sing now to the tune of Rogero. Roger, my fellow,
is now my master.

*Lincoln.*   Sirrah, know'st thou one Hans, a shoemaker?

*Firk.*   Hans, shoemaker? Oh yes, stay, yes, I have him. I tell
you what, I speak it in secret: Mistress Rose and he are by this
time — no, not so, but shortly are to come over one another with
"Can you dance the shaking of the sheets?"[7] It is that Hans —
[*Aside.*] I 'll so gull these diggers![8]

*Otley.*   Know'st thou, then, where he is?

*Firk.*   Yes, forsooth; yea, marry!

*Lincoln.*   Canst thou, in sadness ——

*Firk.*   No, forsooth, no, marry!

*Otley.*   Tell me, good honest fellow, where he is,
And thou shalt see what I 'll bestow of thee.

*Firk.*   Honest fellow? No, sir; not so, sir; my profession is
the gentle craft; I care not for seeing, I love feeling; let me feel
it here; *aurium tenus,*[9] ten pieces of gold; *genuum tenus,*[1] ten
pieces of silver; and then Firk is your man — [*Aside.*] in a new
pair of stretchers.[2]

*Otley.*   Here is an angel, part of thy reward,
Which I will give thee; tell me where he is.

*Firk.*   No point! Shall I betray my brother? No! Shall I prove
Judas to Hans? No! Shall I cry treason to my corporation? No,
I shall be firk'd and yerk'd then. But give me your angel; your
angel shall tell you.

*Lincoln.*   Do so, good fellow; 't is no hurt to thee.

*Firk.*   Send simpering Syb away.

*Otley.*   Huswife, get you in.                          *Exit Sybil.*

*Firk.*   Pitchers have ears, and maids have wide mouths; but for
Hans Prauns, upon my word, to-morrow morning he and young
Mistress Rose go to this gear:[3] they shall be married together,
by this rush, or else turn Firk to a firkin of butter, to tan leather
withal.

*Otley.*   But art thou sure of this?

*Firk.*   Am I sure that Paul's steeple is a handful higher than
London Stone,[4] or that the Pissing-Conduit[5] leaks nothing but

---

[7] A rather ribald popular song.          [8] Questioners.
[9] Actually means "Up to the ears."
[1] Means "Up to the knees."
[2] Quibbles.                    [3] Business.
[4] Stone in central London from which distances were measured, and
by which other milestones were regulated.
[5] Conduit near the Royal Exchange.

pure Mother Bunch?[6] Am I sure I am lusty Firk? God's nails, do you think I am so base to gull you?

*Lincoln.* Where are they married? Dost thou know the church?

*Firk.* I never go to church, but I know the name of it; it is a swearing church — stay a while, 't is — ay, by the mass, no, no, — 't is — ay, by my troth, no, nor that; 't is — ay, by my faith, that, that, 't is, ay, by my Faith's Church under Paul's Cross. There they shall be knit like a pair of stockings in matrimony; there they 'll be inconie.[7]

*Lincoln.* Upon my life, my nephew Lacy walks
In the disguise of this Dutch shoemaker.

*Firk.* Yes, forsooth.

*Lincoln.* Doth he not, honest fellow?

*Firk.* No, forsooth; I think Hans is nobody but Hans, no spirit.

*Otley.* My mind misgives me now, 't is so, indeed.

*Lincoln.* My cousin speaks the language, knows the trade.

*Otley.* Let me request your company, my lord;
Your honourable presence may, no doubt,
Refrain their headstrong rashness, when myself
Going alone perchance may be o'erborne.
Shall I request this favour?

*Lincoln.* This, or what else.

*Firk.* Then you must rise betimes,[8] for they mean to fall to their hey-pass and repass, pindy-pandy, which hand will you have,[9] very early.

*Otley.* My care shall every way equal their haste.
This night accept your lodging in my house.
The earlier shall we stir, and at Saint Faith's
Prevent this giddy hare-brain'd nuptial.
This traffic of hot love shall yield cold gains:
They ban our loves, and we 'll forbid their banns. *Exit.*

*Lincoln.* At Saint Faith's Church, thou say'st?

*Firk.* Yes, by their troth.

*Lincoln.* Be secret, on thy life. *Exit.*

*Firk.* Yes, when I kiss your wife! Ha, ha, here 's no craft in the gentle craft. I came hither of purpose with shoes to Sir Roger's worship, whilst Rose, his daughter, be conycatch'd[1] by Hans. Soft now; these two gulls will be at Saint Faith's Church to-morrow morning, to take Master Bridegroom and Mistress Bride napping,

---

[6] Water.    [7] A fine sight.    [8] Early.
[9] Conjuror's patter; Firk apparently means that they will exchange vows and give their hands to one another.
[1] Deceived.

and they, in the mean time, shall chop up the matter at the Savoy.[2]
But the best sport is, Sir Roger Otley will find my fellow lame
Rafe's wife going to marry a gentleman, and then he 'll stop her
instead of his daughter. Oh brave! there will be fine tickling
sport. Soft now, what have I to do? Oh, I know; now a mess[3]
of shoemakers meet at the Woolsack in Ivy Lane, to cozen my
gentleman of lame Rafe's wife: that 's true.

> Alack, alack!
> Girls, hold out tack![4]
> For now smocks for this jumbling
> Shall go to wrack.

## [Act V, Scene I]

### Enter Eyre, his wife, [Lacy as] Hans, and Rose

*Eyre.* This is the morning, then; say, my bully, my honest
Hans, is it not?

*Hans.* This is the morning that must make us two happy or
miserable; therefore, if you ——

*Eyre.* Away with these ifs and ans, Hans, and these et ceteras!
By mine honour, Rowland Lacy, none but the king shall wrong
thee. Come, fear nothing, am not I Sim Eyre? Is not Sim Eyre
lord mayor of London? Fear nothing, Rose: let them all say what
they can; dainty, come thou to me — laughest thou?

*Wife.* Good my lord, stand her friend in what thing you may.

*Eyre.* Why, my sweet Lady Madgy, think you Simon Eyre
can forget his fine Dutch journeyman? No, vah! Fie, I scorn it.
It shall never be cast in my teeth, that I was unthankful. Lady
Madgy, thou had'st never cover'd thy Saracen's head with this
French flap, nor loaden thy bum with this farthingale,[5] ('t is trash,
trumpery, vanity); Simon Eyre had never walk'd in a red petticoat, nor wore a chain of gold, but for my fine journeyman's portagues. — And shall I leave him? No! Prince am I none, yet bear
a princely mind.

*Hans.* My lord, t' is time for us to part from hence.

*Eyre.* Lady Madgy, Lady Madgy, take two or three of my
pie-crust-eaters, my buff-jerkin varlets, that do walk in black gowns
at Simon Eyre's heels; take them, good Lady Madgy; trip and go,

---

[2] A chapel outside ordinary ecclesiastical jurisdiction where surrepti-
tious marriages were often celebrated.

[3] Group of four.          [4] Make good resistance.

[5] Hooped skirt.

my brown queen of periwigs, with my delicate Rose and my jolly
Rowland to the Savoy; see them link'd, countenance the marriage;
and when it is done, cling, cling together, you Hamborow[6] turtledoves. I 'll bear you out: come to Simon Eyre; come, dwell with
me, Hans, thou shalt eat minc'd-pies and marchpane.[7] Rose, away,
cricket; trip and go, my Lady Madgy, to the Savoy; Hans, wed,
and to bed; kiss, and away! Go, vanish!

*Wife.*  Farewell, my lord.

*Rose.*  Make haste, sweet love.

*Wife.*                    She 'd fain the deed were done.

*Hans.*  Come, my sweet Rose; faster than deer we 'll run.

                                             *They go out.*

*Eyre.*  Go, vanish, vanish! Avaunt, I say! By the Lord of Ludgate, it 's a mad life to be a lord mayor; it 's a stirring life, a fine
life, a velvet life, a careful life. Well, Simon Eyre, yet set a good
face on it, in the honour of Saint Hugh. Soft, the king this day
comes to dine with me, to see my new buildings; his majesty is
welcome, he shall have good cheer, delicate cheer, princely cheer.
This day, my fellow prentices of London come to dine with me
too; they shall have fine cheer, gentlemanlike cheer. I promised
the mad Cappadocians, when we all served at the Conduit together, that if ever I came to be mayor of London, I would feast
them all, and I 'll do 't, I 'll do 't, by the life of Pharaoh; by this
beard, Sim Eyre will be no flincher. Besides, I have procur'd that
upon every Shrove-Tuesday,[8] at the sound of the pancake bell, my
fine dapper Assyrian lads shall clap up their shop windows, and
away. This is the day, and this day they shall do 't, they shall
do 't.

> Boys, that day are you free; let masters care,
> And prentices shall pray for Simon Eyre.

## [SCENE II]

*Enter Hodge, Firk, Rafe, and five or six Shoemakers,*
*all with cudgels or such weapons*

*Hodge.*  Come, Rafe; stand to it, Firk. My masters, as we are
the brave bloods of the shoemakers, heirs apparent to Saint Hugh,
and perpetual benefactors to all good fellows, thou shalt have no
wrong: were Hammon a king of spades, he should not delve in thy
close without thy sufferance. But tell me, Rafe, art thou sure 't is
thy wife?

---

[6] Hamburg, German.                    [7] Marzipan.

[8] Day before the beginning of Lent, celebrated with pancake feasts.

*Rafe.* Am I sure this is Firk? This morning, when I strok'd on her shoes, I look'd upon her, and she upon me, and sighed, ask'd me if ever I knew one Rafe. Yes, said I. For his sake, said she — tears standing in her eyes — and for thou art somewhat like him, spend this piece of gold. I took it; my lame leg and my travel beyond sea made me unknown. All is one for that: I know she 's mine.

*Firk.* Did she give thee this gold? O glorious glittering gold! She's thine own, 't is thy wife, and she loves thee; for I 'll stand to 't, there's no woman will give gold to any man, but she thinks better of him that she thinks of them she gives silver to. And for Hammon, neither Hammon nor hangman shall wrong thee in London! Is not our old master Eyre lord mayor? Speak, my hearts.

*All.* Yes, and Hammon shall know it to his cost.

### *Enter Hammon, his man, Jane, and others*

*Hodge.* Peace, my bullies; yonder they come.

*Rafe.* Stand to 't, my hearts. Firk, let me speak first.

*Hodge.* No, Rafe, let me. — Hammon, whither away so early?

*Ham.* Unmannerly, rude slave, what 's that to thee?

*Firk.* To him, sir? Yes, sir, and to me, and others. Good-morrow, Jane, how dost thou? Good Lord, how the world is changed with you! God be thanked!

*Ham.* Villains, hands off! How dare you touch my love?

*All.* Villains? Down with them! Cry clubs for prentices!

*Hodge.* Hold, my hearts! Touch her, Hammon? Yea, and more than that: we 'll carry her away with us. My masters and gentlemen, never draw your bird-spits;[9] shoemakers are steel to the back, men every inch of them, all spirit.

*All of Hammon's side.* Well, and what of all this?

*Hodge.* I 'll show you. — Jane, dost thou know this man? 'T is Rafe, I can tell thee; nay, 't is he in faith, though he be lam'd by the wars. Yet look not strange, but run to him, fold him about the neck and kiss him.

*Jane.* Lives then my husband? Oh God, let me go,
Let me embrace my Rafe.

*Ham.*                    What means my Jane?

*Jane.* Nay, what meant you, to tell me he was slain?

*Ham.* Pardon me, dear love, for being misled.
[*To Rafe.*] 'T was rumour'd here in London, thou wert dead.

*Firk.* Thou seest he lives. Lass, go, pack home with him.
Now, Master Hammon, where 's your mistress, your wife?

*Serv.* 'Swounds, master, fight for her! Will you thus lose her?

9 Rapiers.

*All.*  Down with that creature! Clubs! Down with him!

*Hodge.*  Hold, hold!

*Ham.*  Hold, fool! Sirs, he shall do no wrong. Will my Jane leave me thus, and break her faith?

*Firk.*  Yea, sir! She must, sir! She shall, sir! What then? Mend it!

*Hodge.*  Hark, fellow Rafe, follow my counsel: set the wench in the midst, and let her choose her man, and let her be his woman.

*Jane.*  Whom should I choose? Whom should my thoughts affect
But him whom Heaven hath made to be my love?
Thou art my husband, and these humble weeds
Makes thee more beautiful than all his wealth.
Therefore, I will but put off his attire,
Returning it into the owner's hand,
And after ever be thy constant wife.

*Hodge.*  Not a rag! The law's on our side: he that sows in another man's ground, forfeits his harvest. Get thee home, Rafe; follow him, Jane; he shall not have so much as a busk-point¹ from thee.

*Firk.*  Stand to that, Rafe; the appurtenances are thine own. Hammon, look not at her!

*Serv.*  O, 'swounds, no!

*Firk.*  Blue coat² be quiet, we 'll give you a new livery else; we 'll make Shrove Tuesday Saint George's Day³ for you. Look not, Hammon, leer not! I 'll firk you! For thy head now, one glance, one sheep's eye, anything, at her! Touch not a rag, lest I and my brethren beat you to clouts.

*Serv.*  Come, Master Hammon, there 's no striving here.

*Ham.*  Good fellows, hear me speak; and, honest Rafe,
Whom I have injur'd most by loving Jane,
Mark what I offer thee: here in fair gold
Is twenty pound, I 'll give it for thy Jane;
If this content thee not, thou shalt have more.

*Hodge.*  Sell not thy wife, Rafe; make her not a whore.

*Ham.*  Say, wilt thou freely cease thy claim in her,
And let her be my wife?

*All.*             No, do not, Rafe.

*Rafe.*  Sirrah Hammon, Hammon, dost thou think a shoemaker is so base to be a bawd to his own wife for commodity?⁴ Take thy gold, choke with it! Were I not lame, I would make thee eat thy words.

---

¹ Corset string.          ² Servant.

³ April 23, the servingman's holiday.          ⁴ Merchandise.

*Firk.*   A shoemaker sell his flesh and blood?  Oh indignity!

*Hodge.*   Sirrah, take up your pelf, and be packing.

*Ham.*   I will not touch one penny, but in lieu
Of that great wrong I offered thy Jane,
To Jane and thee I give that twenty pound.
Since I have fail'd of her, during my life,
I vow, no woman else shall be my wife.
Farewell, good fellows of the gentle trade:
Your morning mirth my mourning day hath made.          *Exit.*

*Firk* [*To the Serving-man.*]   Touch the gold, creature, if you
dare!  Y' are best be trudging.  Here, Jane, take thou it.  Now let 's
home, my hearts.

*Hodge.*   Stay!  Who comes here?  Jane, on again with thy
mask!

*Enter Lincoln, Otley, and Servants*

*Lincoln.*   Yonder 's the lying varlet mock'd us so.

*Otley.*   Come hither, sirrah!

*Firk.*   I, sir?  I am sirrah?  You mean me, do you not?

*Lincoln.*   Where is my nephew married?

*Firk.*   Is he married?  God give him joy, I am glad of it.  They
have a fair day, and the sign is in a good planet, Mars in Venus.

*Otley.*   Villain, thou toldst me that my daughter Rose
This morning should be married at Saint Faith's.
We have watch'd there these three hours at the least,
Yet we see no such thing.

*Firk.*   Truly, I am sorry for 't; a bride 's a pretty thing.

*Hodge.*   Come to the purpose.  Yonder 's the bride and bridegroom you look for, I hope.  Though you be lords, you are not to
bar by your authority men from women, are you?

*Otley.*   See, see, my daughter 's masked.

*Lincoln.*                                              True, and my nephew,
To hide his guilt, counterfeits him lame.

*Firk.*   Yea, truly; God help the poor couple, they are lame and
blind.

*Otley.*   I 'll ease her blindness.

*Lincoln.*                               I 'll his lameness cure.

*Firk.*   Lie down, sirs, and laugh!  My fellow Rafe is taken for
Rowland Lacy, and Jane for Mistress Damask Rose.  This is all my
knavery.

*Otley.*   What, have I found you, minion?

*Lincoln.*                                          O base wretch!
Nay, hide thy face; the horror of thy guilt
Can hardly be wash'd off.  Where are thy powers?

What battles have you made?  O yes, I see.
Thou fought'st with Shame, and Shame hath conquer'd thee.
This lameness will not serve.

*Otley.*                    Unmask yourself.

*Lincoln.*   Lead home your daughter.

*Otley.*                         Take your nephew hence.

*Rafe.*   Hence!  'Swounds, what mean you?  Are you mad?  I
hope you cannot enforce my wife from me.  Where 's Hammon?

*Otley.*   Your wife?

*Lincoln.*   What, Hammon?

*Rafe.*   Yea, my wife; and, therefore, the proudest of you that
lay hands on her first, I 'll lay my crutch 'cross his pate.

*Firk.*   To him, lame Rafe!  Here 's brave sport!

*Rafe.*   Rose you call her?  Why, her name is Jane.  Look here
else; do you know her now?                    [*Unmasking Jane.*]

*Lincoln.*   Is this your daughter?

*Otley.*                    No, nor this your nephew.
My Lord of Lincoln, we are both abus'd
By this base, crafty varlet.

*Firk.*   Yea, forsooth, no varlet; forsooth, no base; forsooth, I
am but mean;[5] no crafty neither, but of the gentle craft.

*Otley.*   Where is my daughter Rose?  Where is my child?

*Lincoln.*   Where is my nephew Lacy married?

*Firk.*   Why, here is good lac'd mutton,[6] as I promis'd you.

*Lincoln.*   Villain, I 'll have thee punish'd for this wrong.

*Firk.*   Punish the journeyman villain, but not the journeyman
shoemaker.

### *Enter Dodger*

*Dodger.*   My lord, I come to bring unwelcome news.
Your nephew Lacy and your daughter Rose
Early this morning wedded at the Savoy,
None being present but the lady mayoress.
Besides, I learnt among the officers,
The lord mayor vows to stand in their defence
'Gainst any that shall seek to cross the match.

*Lincoln.*   Dares Eyre the shoemaker uphold the deed?

*Firk.*   Yes, sir, shoemakers dare stand in a woman's quarrel, I
warrant you, as deep as another, and deeper too.

*Dodger.*   Besides, his grace to-day dines with the mayor,
Who on his knees humbly intends to fall
And beg a pardon for your nephew's fault.

*Lincoln.*   But I 'll prevent him!  Come, Sir Roger Otley;

[5] Middle (or tenor).                    [6] Strumpet.

The king will do us justice in this cause.
Howe'er their hands have made them man and wife.
I will disjoin the match, or lose my life.                    *Exeunt.*

*Firk.*  Adieu, Monsieur Dodger! Farewell, fools! Ha, ha! Oh,
if they had stay'd, I would have so lamm'd them with flouts![7]
O heart, my codpiece-point is ready to fly in pieces every time I
think upon Mistress Rose. But let that pass, as my lady mayoress
says.

*Hodge.*  This matter is answer'd. Come, Rafe; home with thy
wife. Come, my fine shoemakers, let 's to our master's the new
lord mayor, and there swagger this Shrove Tuesday. I 'll promise
you wine enough, for Madge keeps the cellar.

*All.*  O rare! Madge is a good wench.

*Firk.*  And I 'll promise you meat enough, for simp'ring Susan
keeps the larder. I 'll lead you to victuals, my brave soldiers;
follow your captain. O brave! Hark, hark! *Bell rings.*

*All.*  The pancake-bell rings, the pancake-bell! Trilill, my
hearts!

*Firk.*  Oh brave! Oh sweet bell! O delicate pancakes! Open
the doors, my hearts, and shut up the windows! keep in the house,
let out the pancakes! Oh rare, my hearts! Let 's march together
for the honour of Saint Hugh to the great new hall[8] in Gracious
Street corner, which our master, the new lord mayor, hath built.

*Rafe.*  O the crew of good fellows that will dine at my lord
mayor's cost to-day!

*Hodge.*  By the Lord, my lord mayor is a most brave man.
How shall prentices be bound to pray for him and the honour
of the gentlemen shoemakers! Let 's feed and be fat with my lord's
bounty.

*Firk.*  O musical bell, still! O Hodge, O my brethren! There 's
cheer for the heavens: venison-pasties walk up and down piping
hot, like sergeants; beef and brewess[9] comes marching in dry-fats,[1]
fritters and pancakes comes trowling[2] in in wheel-barrows; hens
and oranges hopping in porters' baskets, collops and eggs in scuttles,
and tarts and custards comes quavering in in malt-shovels.

*Enter more Prentices*

*All.*  Whoop, look here, look here!

*Hodge.*  How now, mad lads, whither away so fast?

*1 Pren.*  Whither? Why, to the great new hall, know you not
why? The lord mayor hath bidden all the prentices in London to
breakfast this morning.

---

[7] Battered them with insults.                    [8] Leadenhall.
[9] Broth.                    [1] Casks.                    [2] Trundling.

*All.* Oh brave shoemaker, oh brave lord of incomprehensible good-fellowship! Whoo! Hark you! The pancake-bell rings.

*Cast up caps.*

*Firk.* Nay, more, my hearts! Every Shrove-Tuesday is our year of jubilee; and when the pancake-bell rings, we are as free as my lord mayor; we may shut up our shops, and make holiday; I 'll have it call'd Saint Hugh's Holiday.

*All.* Agreed, agreed! Saint Hugh's Holiday.

*Hodge.* And this shall continue for ever.

*All.* Oh brave! Come, come, my hearts! Away, away!

*Firk.* O eternal credit to us of the gentle craft! March fair, my hearts! Oh rare!       *Exeunt.*


[SCENE III]

*Enter King and his Train over the stage*

*King.* Is our lord mayor of London such a gallant?

*Nobleman.* One of the merriest madcaps in your land.
Your grace will think, when you behold the man,
He 's rather a wild ruffian than a mayor.
Yet thus much I 'll ensure your majesty:
In all his actions that concern his state
He is as serious, provident, and wise,
As full of gravity amongst the grave,
As any mayor hath been these many years.

*King.* I am with child[3] till I behold this huffcap.
But all my doubt is, when we come in presence,
His madness will be dash'd clean out of countenance.

*Nobleman.* It may be so, my liege.

*King.*            Which to prevent,
Let some one give him notice, 't is our pleasure
That he put on his wonted merriment.
Set forward!

*All.*     On afore!          *Exeunt.*


[SCENE IV]

*Enter Eyre, Hodge, Firk, Rafe, and other
Shoemakers, all with napkins on their shoulders*

*Eyre.* Come, my fine Hodge, my jolly gentlemen shoemakers! soft, where be these cannibals, these varlets, my officers? Let them

[3] Full of longing.

all walk and wait upon my brethren; for my meaning is, that none but shoemakers, none but the livery[4] of my company shall in their satin hoods wait upon the trencher of my sovereign.

*Firk.*   O my lord, it will be rare!

*Eyre.*   No more, Firk; come, lively! Let your fellow-prentices want no cheer; let wine be plentiful as beer, and beer as water. Hang these penny-pinching fathers, that cram wealth in innocent lamb-skins.[5] Rip, knaves, avaunt! Look to my guests!

*Hodge.*   My lord, we are at our wits' end for room; those hundred tables will not feast the fourth part of them.

*Eyre.*   Then cover me those hundred tables again, and again, till all my jolly prentices be feasted. Avoid, Hodge! Run, Rafe! Frisk about, my nimble Firk! Carouse me fadom-healths[6] to the honour of the shoemakers. Do they drink lively, Hodge? Do they tickle it, Firk?

*Firk.*   Tickle it? Some of them have taken their liquor standing so long that they can stand no longer; but for meat, they would eat it and they had it.

*Eyre.*   Want they meat? Where 's this swagbelly, this greasy kitchen-stuff cook? Call the varlet to me! Want meat? Firk, Hodge, lame Rafe, run, my tall men, beleaguer the shambles, beggar all Eastcheap, serve me whole oxen in chargers, and let sheep whine upon the tables like pigs for want of good fellows to eat them. Want meat Vanish, Firk! Avaunt, Hodge!

*Hodge.*   Your lordship mistakes my man Firk; he means, their bellies want meat, not the boards; for they have drunk so much, they can eat nothing.

THE SECOND THREE-MAN'S SONG

Cold 's the wind, and wet 's the rain,
  Saint Hugh be our good speed:
Ill is the weather that bringeth no gain,
  Nor helps good hearts in need.

Trowl[7] the bowl, the jolly nut-brown bowl,
  And here, kind mate, to thee:
Let's sing a dirge for Saint Hugh's soul,
  And down it merrily.

Down a down, hey down a down,
  (*Close with the tenor boy*)
Hey derry derry, down a down!
Ho, well done; to me let come!
Ring, compass gentle joy.

[4] Membership.          [5] Parchments.
[6] Healths a fathom deep.          [7] Pass around.

> Trowl the bowl, the nut-brown bowl,
>     And here, kind mate, to thee: etc.
> [*Repeat*] *as often as there be men to drink.*
> *At last when all have drunk, this verse:*
> Cold 's the wind, and wet 's the rain,
>     Saint Hugh be our good speed:
> Ill is the weather that bringeth no gain,
>     Nor helps good hearts in need.

*Enter Hans, Rose, and Wife*

*Wife.* Where is my lord?

*Eyre.* How now, Lady Madgy?

*Wife.* The king's most excellent majesty is now come; he sends me for thy honour; one of his most worshipful peers bade me tell thou must be merry, and so forth; but let that pass.

*Eyre.* Is my sovereign come? Vanish, my tall shoemakers, my nimble brethren; look to my guests, the prentices. Yet stay a little! How now, Hans? How looks my little Rose?

*Hans.* Let me request you to remember me.
I know, your honour easily may obtain
Free pardon of the king for me and Rose,
And reconcile me to my uncle's grace.

*Eyre.* Have done, my good Hans, my honest journeyman; look cheerily! I 'll fall upon both my knees, till they be as hard as horn, but I 'll get thy pardon.

*Wife.* Good my lord, have a care what you speak to his grace.

*Eyre.* Away, you Islington whitepot![8] hence, you hopperarse![9] hence, you barley-pudding, full of maggots! you broiled carbonado! avaunt, avaunt, avoid, Mephistophilus! Shall Sim Eyre learn to speak of you, Lady Madgy? Vanish, Mother Minivercap;[1] vanish, go, trip and go; meddle with your partlets[2] and your pishery-pashery, your flewes[3] and your whirligigs; go, rub,[4] out of mine alley! Sim Eyre knows how to speak to a Pope, to Sultan Soliman, to Tamburlaine, an he were here, and shall I melt, shall I droop before my sovereign? No, come, my Lady Madgy! Follow me, Hans! About your business, my frolic free-booters! Firk, frisk about, and about, and about, for the honour of mad Simon Eyre, lord mayor of London.

*Firk.* Hey, for the honour of the shoemakers!       *Exeunt.*

---

[8] A dish made of milk, eggs, sugar, etc.
[9] With hips shaped like the hopper of a mill.
[1] Fur cap.
[2] Neckbands.
[3] Flapping skirts.
[4] Obstruction.

[SCENE V]

*A long flourish, or two. Enter King, Nobles, Eyre, his Wife, Lacy, Rose. Lacy and Rose kneel.*

*King.*  Well, Lacy, though the fact was very foul
Of your revolting from our kingly love
And your own duty, yet we pardon you.
Rise both, and, Mistress Lacy, thank my lord mayor
For your young bridegroom here.

*Eyre.*  So, my dear liege, Sim Eyre and my brethren, the gentlemen shoemakers, shall set your sweet majesty's image cheek by jowl by Saint Hugh for this honour you have done poor Simon Eyre. I beseech your grace, pardon my rude behavior; I am a handicraftsman, yet my heart is without craft; I would be sorry at my soul that my boldness should offend my king.

*King.*  Nay, I pray thee, good lord mayor, be even as merry
As if thou wert among thy shoemakers;
It does me good to see thee in this humour.

*Eyre.*  Say'st thou me so, my sweet Dioclesian? Then, hump! Prince am I none, yet am I princely born. By the Lord of Ludgate, my liege, I 'll be as merry as a pie.[5]

*King.*  Tell me, in faith, mad Eyre, how old thou art.

*Eyre.*  My liege, a very boy, a stripling, a younker; you see not a white hair on my head, not a gray in this beard. Every hair, I assure thy majesty, that sticks in this beard, Sim Eyre values at the King of Babylon's ransom. Tamar Cham's beard was a rubbing brush to 't: yet I 'll shave it off, and stuff tennis-balls with it, to please my bully[6] king.

*King.*  But all this while I do not know your age.

*Eyre.*  My liege, I am six-and-fifty year old, yet I can cry hump! with a sound heart for the honour of Saint Hugh. Mark this old wench, my king: I danc'd the shaking of the sheets with her six and thirty years ago, and yet I hope to get two or three young lord mayors, ere I die. I am lusty still, Sim Eyre still. Care and cold lodging brings white hairs. My sweet Majesty, let care vanish, cast it upon thy nobles: it will make thee look always young like Apollo, and cry hump! Prince am I none, yet am I princely born.

*King.*  Ha, ha!
Say, Cornwall, didst thou ever see his like?

*Nobleman.*  Not I, my lord.

*Enter Lincoln and Sir Roger Otley*

*King.*          Lincoln, what news with you?

*Lincoln.*  My gracious lord, have care unto yourself,
For there are traitors here.

---

[5] Magpie.          [6] Gallant.

*All.*                    Traitors? Where? Who?

*Eyre.* Traitors in my house? God forbid! Where be my officers? I 'll spend my soul, ere my king feel harm.

*King.* Where is the traitor, Lincoln?

*Lincoln.*                    Here he stands.

*King.* Cornwall, lay hold on Lacy! — Lincoln, speak,
What canst thou lay unto thy nephew's charge?

*Lincoln.* This, my dear liege: your Grace, to do me honour,
Heap'd on the head of this degenerous[7] boy
Desertless favours; you made choice of him
To be commander over powers in France.
But he ——

*King.* Good Lincoln, prithee, pause a while!
Even in thine eyes I read what thou wouldst speak.
I know how Lacy did neglect our love,
Ran himself deeply, in the highest degree,
Into vile treason ——

*Lincoln.*                Is he not a traitor?

*King.* Lincoln, he was; now have we pardon'd him.
'T was not a base want of true valour's fire,
That held him out of France, but love's desire.

*Lincoln.* I will not bear his shame upon my back.

*King.* Nor shalt thou, Lincoln; I forgive you both.

*Lincoln.* Then, good my liege, forbid the boy to wed
One whose mean birth will much disgrace his bed.

*King.* Are they not married?

*Lincoln.*                    No, my liege.

*Both.*                              We are.

*King.* Shall I divorce them then? O be it far
That any hand on earth should dare untie
The sacred knot, knit by God's majesty;
I would not for my crown disjoin their hands
That are conjoin'd in holy nuptial bands.
How say'st thou, Lacy, wouldst thou lose thy Rose?

*Lacy.* Not for all India's wealth, my sovereign.

*King.* But Rose, I am sure, her Lacy would forgo?

*Rose.* If Rose were ask'd that question, she'd say no.

*King.* You hear them, Lincoln?

*Lincoln.*                    Yea, my liege, I do.

*King.* Yet canst thou find i' th' heart to part these two?
Who seeks, besides you, to divorce these lovers?

*Otley.* I do, my gracious lord. I am her father.

*King.* Sir Roger Otley, our last mayor, I think?

*Nobleman.* The same, my liege.

7 Degenerate.

*King.*                    Would you offend Love's laws?
Well, you shall have your wills. You sue to me
To prohibit the match. Soft, let me see —
You both are married, Lacy, art thou not?
I charge thee, not to call this woman wife.

*Lacy.* I am, dread sovereign.

*King.*                      Then, upon thy life,

*Otley.* I thank your grace.

*Rose.*                  O my most gracious lord!    *Kneel.*

*King.* Nay, Rose, never woo me; I tell you true,
Although as yet I am a bachelor,
Yet I believe I shall not marry you.

*Rose.* Can you divide the body from the soul,
Yet make the body live?

*King.*              Yea, so profound?
I cannot, Rose, but you I must divide.
This fair maid, bridegroom, cannot be your bride.
Are you pleas'd, Lincoln? Otley, are you pleas'd?

*Both.* Yes, my lord.

*King.*            Then must my heart be eas'd;
For, credit me, my conscience lives in pain,
Till these whom I divorc'd, be join'd again.
Lacy, give me thy hand; Rose, lend me thine!
Be what you would be! Kiss now! So, that's fine.
At night, lovers, to bed! — Now, let me see,
Which of you all mislikes this harmony.

*Otley.* Will you then take from me my child perforce?

*King.* Why tell me, Otley: shines not Lacy's name
As bright in the world's eye as the gay beams
Of any citizen?

*Lincoln.*            Yea, but, my gracious lord,
I do mislike the match far more than he;
Her blood is too too base.

*King.*                Lincoln, no more.
Dost thou not know that love respects no blood,
Cares not for difference of birth or state?
The maid is young, well born, fair, virtuous,
A worthy bride for any gentleman.
Besides, your nephew for her sake did stoop
To bare necessity, and, as I hear,
Forgetting honours and all courtly pleasures,
To gain her love, became a shoemaker.
As for the honour which he lost in France,
Thus I redeem it: Lacy, kneel thee down! —

Arise, Sir Rowland Lacy!  Tell me now,
Tell me in earnest, Otley, canst thou chide,
Seeing thy Rose a lady and a bride?

*Otley.*  I am content with what your grace hath done.

*Lincoln.*  And I, my liege, since there 's no remedy.

*King.*  Come on, then, all shake hands: I 'll have you friends;
Where there is much love, all discord ends.
What says my mad lord mayor to all this love?

*Eyre.*  O my liege, this honour you have done to my fine
journeyman here, Rowland Lacy, and all these favours which you
have shown to me this day in my poor house, will make Simon
Eyre live longer by one dozen of warm summers more than he
should.

*King.*  Nay, my mad lord mayor, that shall be thy name;
If any grace of mine can length thy life,
One honour more I 'll do thee: that new building,
Which at thy cost in Cornhill is erected,
Shall take a name from us; we 'll have it call'd
The Leadenhall, because in digging it
You found the lead that covereth the same.

*Eyre.*  I thank your majesty.

*Wife.*                     God bless your grace!

*King.*  Lincoln, a word with you!

*Enter Hodge, Firk, Rafe, and more Shoemakers*

*Eyre.*  How now, my mad knaves?  Peace, speak softly; yonder
is the king.

*King.*  With the old troop, which there we keep in pay,
We will incorporate a new supply.
Before one summer more pass o'er my head,
France shall repent, England was injured.
What are all those?

*Lacy.*            All shoemakers, my liege,
Sometimes[8] my fellows; in their companies
I liv'd as merry as an emperor.

*King.*  My mad lord mayor, are all these shoemakers?

*Eyre.*  All shoemakers, my liege; all gentlemen of the gentle
craft, true Trojans, courageous cordwainers; they all kneel to the
shrine of holy Saint Hugh.

*All.*  God save your majesty, all shoemakers!

*King.*  Mad Simon, would they anything with us?

*Eyre.*  Mum, mad knaves!  Not a word!  I 'll do 't; I warrant
you.  They are all beggars, my liege; all for themselves, and I for

8 Formerly.

them all on both my knees do entreat, that for the honour of poor Simon Eyre and the good of his brethren, these mad knaves, your grace would vouchsafe some privilege to my new Leaden-hall, that it may be lawful for us to buy and sell leather there two days a week.

*King.*   Mad Sim, I grant your suit, you shall have patent
To hold two market-days in Leadenhall.
Mondays and Fridays, those shall be the times.
Will this content you?

*All.*                    Jesus bless your grace!

*Eyre.*   In the name of these my poor brethren shoemakers, I most humbly thank your grace. But before I rise, seeing you are in the giving vein and we in the begging, grant Sim Eyre one boon more.

*King.*   What is it, my lord mayor?

*Eyre.*   Vouchsafe to taste of a poor banquet that stands sweetly waiting for your sweet presence.

*King.*   I shall undo thee, Eyre, only with feasts;
Already have I been too troublesome;
Say, have I not?

*Eyre.*   O my dear king, Sim Eyre was taken unawares upon a day of shroving,[9] which I promis'd long ago to the prentices of London.
For, an 't please your highness, in time past,
I bare the water-tankard,[1] and my coat
Sits not a whit the worse upon my back;
And then, upon a morning, some mad boys
(It was Shrove Tuesday, even as 't is now)
gave me my breakfast, and I swore then by the stopple of my tankard, if ever I came to be lord mayor of London, I would feast all the prentices. This day, my liege, I did it, and the slaves had an hundred tables five times covered.
They are gone home and vanish'd.
Yet add more honour to the gentle trade:
Taste of Eyre's banquet, Simon 's happy made.

*King.*   Eyre, I will taste of thy banquet, and will say,
I have not met more pleasure on a day.
Friends of the gentle craft, thanks to you all.
Thanks, my kind lady mayoress, for our cheer. —
Come, lords, a while let 's revel it at home!
When all our sports and banquetings are done,
Wars must right wrongs which Frenchmen have begun.

                                                  *Exeunt.*

FINIS

[9] Celebration.                    [1] I was an apprentice.

# THE
# KNIGHT OF
# the Burning Pestle.

—— *Quod si*
*Iudicium subtile, videndis artibus illud*
*Ad libros et ad hæc Musarum dona vocares:*
*Bœotum in crasso iurares aere natos.*
Horat. in Epist. ad Oct. Aug.[1]

**LONDON,**
Printed for Walter Burre, and are to be sold at the
signe of the Crane in Paules Church-yard.
1 6 1 3 .

[1] But if you were to call that judgment a subtle one which he exercised on the arts and towards books and the gifts of the Muses, you would swear they had been born in the leaden air of the Boeotians.

# The Knight of the Burning Pestle

❧ FRANCIS BEAUMONT and JOHN FLETCHER were both of better birth than most of their fellow dramatists. Beaumont (born 1584) was the son of a judge and Fletcher (born 1579) the son of a bishop. Beaumont was educated at Oxford and Fletcher at Cambridge. They seem to have met and begun writing plays together about 1606; they were close friends, shared lodgings, and knew one another more intimately than other collaborators usually did. There was, according to an early writer, "a wonderful consimility of fancy" between them. Their earliest plays were not very successful, but about 1609–10 they scored three resounding successes with *Philaster*, *The Maid's Tragedy*, and *King and No King*. Beaumont married in 1613 and seems to have retired from the stage; he died in 1616 at the early age of thirty-two. After his retirement Fletcher collaborated for a while with Shakespeare in such plays as *Henry VIII* and *The Two Noble Kinsmen* and then succeeded Shakespeare as the principal dramatist to the King's Men. Fletcher wrote fluently, often composing as many as four plays in a year. His most frequent collaborator during the later part of his career was Philip Massinger. He died of the plague in 1625.

It was for a long time thought impossible to divide the work of Beaumont from that of Fletcher in the plays in which they collaborated, but eventually a set of stylistic and metrical tests was worked out which made it possible to distinguish their work. These tests, however, are not of much value for *The Knight of the Burning Pestle*, since they can only be applied to verse, and much of *The Knight of the Burning Pestle* is in prose; further, what verse it contains is parody and not typical of the natural styles of the authors. The majority of critics, however, believe that the greater part of the play is by Beaumont.

*The Knight of the Burning Pestle* was published in 1613, and again in 1635. There was no author's name on the title page of the first edition, but Beaumont and Fletcher appeared as the authors in the second and subsequent editions. The publisher in an introductory epistle in the first edition stated that the play was "in eight daies . . . begot and borne" and "exposed to the wide world, who . . . utterly rejected it." He goes on to say that the manuscript had been sent to him by the producer, and that he had "cherished it these two yeares." He adds: "Perhaps it will be thought to bee of the race of Don Quixote: we both may confidently swear, it is his elder by above a yeare." If this is taken to refer to the first English translation of Cervantes, published in 1612, we get a date of 1611 for the play, which agrees with the publisher's statement that he had had the manuscript for two years. The text, however, makes it clear that the play was acted by one of the boy companies which came to an end in 1610, so 1610 or earlier is the most likely date for the play.

Books. The complete plays of Beaumont and Fletcher are available in the *Works*, 10 vols., Cambridge, 1905–10. A brief selection of studies of the plays would include: W. W. Appleton, *Beaumont and Fletcher, a critical study*, London, 1956; E. H. C. Oliphant, *The Plays of Beaumont and Fletcher*, New Haven, 1927; L. B. Wallis, *Beaumont and Fletcher and Company, entertainers to the Jacobean gentry*, New York, 1947.

## The Actors' Names

THE PROLOGUE [a boy actor]

Then a CITIZEN [George, a Grocer]

The Citizen's WIFE [Nell], and RALPH, her man,
sitting below amidst the Spectators

A rich Merchant [VENTUREWELL]

JASPER [MERRYTHOUGHT], his Apprentice

Master HUMPHREY, a Friend to the Merchant

MICHAEL, a second Son of Mistress Merrythought

Old Master MERRYTHOUGHT

[TIM] A Squire,  ⎱[Apprentices to the Grocer,
[GEORGE] A Dwarf,⎰serving Ralph]

LUCE, the Merchant's Daughter

Mistress MERRYTHOUGHT, Jasper's Mother

[POMPIONA, Daughter of the King of Moldavia]

A Tapster; A Boy that danceth and singeth; An Host; A Barber;
Two Knights [*i.e.*, Travellers, also a Man and Woman, all Prisoners
to the Barber]; A Captain; A Sergeant [and] Soldiers [in a militia
company]

[SCENE: Various parts of London, Waltham and Waltham
Forest; Moldavia]

## [*Induction*

*Several Gentlemen sitting on Stools upon the Stage.*
*The Citizen, his Wife, and Ralph sitting below among*
*the Audience*]

*Enter Prologue*

*Prol.* "From all that's near the court, from all that's great,
Within the compass of the city-walls,
We now have brought our scene —— "

### *Citizen* [*leaps on the stage.*]

*Cit.* Hold your peace, goodman boy!

*Prol.* What do you mean, sir?

*Cit.* That you have no good meaning: this seven years there hath been plays at this house, I have observed it, you have still girds at citizens; and now you call your play "The London Merchant." Down with your title, boy! down with your title!

*Prol.* Are you a member of the noble city?

*Cit.* I am.

*Prol.* And a freeman?

*Cit.* Yea, and a grocer.

*Prol.* So, grocer, then, by your sweet favour, we intend no abuse to the city.

*Cit.* No, sir! yes, sir. If you were not resolv'd to play the jacks,[2] what need you study for new subjects, purposely to abuse your betters? Why could not you be contented, as well as others, with "The legend of Whittington,"[3] or "The Life and Death of Sir Thomas Gresham with the building of the Royal Exchange,"[4] or "The story of Queen Eleanor, with the rearing of London woolsacks?"[5]

*Prol.* You seem to be an understanding man: what would you have us do, sir?

*Cit.* Why, present something notably in honour of the commons of the city.

---

[2] Knaves; cf. "Jack of Clubs."

[3] Sir Richard Whittington, famous Lord Mayor of London. No play about him is known.

[4] Sub-title of Thomas Heywood's play, *If You Know not Me*, Part II.

[5] These events are part of the plot of George Peele's *Edward I*.

136

*Prol.*  Why, what do you say to "The Life and Death of fat Drake,[6] or the Repairing of Fleet-privies?"

*Cit.*  I do not like that; but I will have a citizen, and he shall be of my own trade.

*Prol.*  Oh, you should have told us your mind a month since; our play is ready to begin now.

*Cit.*  'T is all one for that; I will have a grocer, and he shall do admirable things.

*Prol.*  What will you have him do?

*Cit.*  Marry, I will have him ——

*Wife. below.*  Husband, husband!

*Ralph. below.*  Peace, mistress.

*Wife.* [*below.*]  Hold thy peace, Ralph;[7]  I know what I do, I warrant ye. — Husband, husband!

*Cit.*  What sayst thou, cony?

*Wife.* [*below.*]  Let him kill a lion with a pestle, husband!  Let him kill a lion with a pestle!

*Cit.*  So he shall.  I 'll have him kill a lion with a pestle.

*Wife.* [*below.*]  Husband! shall I come up, husband?

*Cit.*  Ay, cony. — Ralph, help your mistress this way. — Pray, gentlemen, make her a little room. — I pray you, sir, lend me your hand to help up my wife: I thank you, sir. — So.

*[Wife comes on the stage.]*

*Wife.*  By your leave, gentlemen all; I 'm something trouble-some.  I 'm a stranger here; I was ne'er at one of these plays, as they say, before; but I should have seen "Jane Shore"[8] once; and my husband hath promised me, any time this twelvemonth, to carry me to "The Bold Beauchamps,"[9] but in truth he did not.  I pray you, bear with me.

*Cit.*  Boy, let my wife and I have a couple of stools and then begin; and let the grocer do rare things.    [*Stools are brought.*]

*Prol.*  But, sir, we have never a boy to play him; every one hath a part already.

*Wife.*  Husband, husband, for God's sake, let Ralph play him!  Beshrew me, if I do not think he will go beyond them all.

*Cit.*  Well remem'bred, wife. — Come up, Ralph. — I 'll tell you, gentlemen; let them but lend him a suit of reparel[1] and neces-

[6] Perhaps a scavenger.

[7] Spelt "Rafe" or "Raph" in the original editions, and pronounced accordingly, as the name still is in England.

[8] Mistress of King Edward IV, and a character in Heywood's *Edward IV*.

[9] This play has not survived.

[1] Malaprop for "apparel."

saries, and, by gad, if any of them all blow wind in the tail on him,[2] I 'll be hang'd.

[*Ralph comes on the stage.*]

*Wife.* I pray you, youth, let him have a suit of reparel! — I 'll be sworn, gentlemen, my husband tells you true. He will act you sometimes at our house, that all the neighbours cry out on him; he will fetch you up[3] a couraging[4] part so in the garret, that we are all as fear'd, I warrant you, that we quake again: we 'll fear[5] our children with him; if they be never so unruly, do but cry, "Ralph comes, Ralph comes!" to them, and they 'll be as quiet as lambs. — Hold up thy head, Ralph; show the gentlemen what thou canst do; speak a huffing[6] part; I warrant you, the gentlemen will accept of it.

*Cit.* Do, Ralph, do.

*Ralph.* "By Heaven, methinks, it were an easy leap
To pluck bright honour from the pale-fac'd moon;
Or dive into the bottom of the sea,
Where never fathom-line touch'd any ground,
And pluck up drowned honour from the lake of hell." [7]

*Cit.* How say you, gentlemen, is it not as I told you?

*Wife.* Nay, gentlemen, he hath play'd before, my husband says, "Mucedorus,"[8] before the wardens of our company.

*Cit.* Ay, and he should have play'd Jeronimo[9] with a shoemaker for a wager.

*Prol.* He shall have a suit of apparel, if he will go in.

*Cit.* In, Ralph, in, Ralph; and set out the grocery in their kind,[1] if thou lov'st me.                    [*Exit Ralph.*]

*Wife.* I warrant, our Ralph will look finely when he 's dress'd.

*Prol.* But what will you have it call'd?

*Cit.* "The Grocer's Honour."

*Prol.* Methinks "The Knight of the Burning Pestle" were better.

*Wife.* I 'll be sworn, husband, that 's as good a name as can be.

*Cit.* Let it be so. — Begin, begin; my wife and I will sit down.

*Prol.* I pray you, do.

*Cit.* What stately music have you? You have shawms?[2]

*Prol.* Shawms? No.

*Cit.* No! I 'm a thief if my mind did not give[3] me so. Ralph

[2] Approach him.    [3] Assume.    [4] Violent.
[5] Frighten.    [6] Swaggering.
[7] Cf. Shakespeare's *1 Henry IV*, I.iii.201–5.
[8] An old, but extremely popular, play.
[9] Hero of Kyd's play, *The Spanish Tragedy*.
[1] Portray the grocers as they really are.
[2] An instrument like an oboe.
[3] Misgive.

plays a stately part, and he must needs have shawms. I 'll be at the charge of them myself, rather than we 'll be without them.

*Prol.*  So you are like to be.

*Cit.*  Why, and so I will be: there 's two shillings; — [*gives money.*] — let 's have the waits of Southwark; they are as rare fellows as any are in England; and that will fetch them all o'er the water with a vengeance, as if they were mad.

*Prol.*  You shall have them. Will you sit down then?

*Cit.*  Ay. — Come, wife.

*Wife.*  Sit you merry all, gentlemen; I 'm bold to sit amongst you for my ease.    [*Citizen and Wife sit down.*]

*Prol.*  "From all that 's near the court, from all that 's great,
Within the compass of the city-walls,
We now have brought our scene. Fly far from hence
All private taxes,[4] immodest phrases,
Whatever may but show like vicious!
For wicked mirth never true pleasure brings,
But honest minds are pleas'd with honest things." —
Thus much for that we do; but for Ralph's part you must answer for yourself.

*Cit.*  Take you no care for Ralph; he 'll discharge himself, I warrant you.    [*Exit Prologue.*]

*Wife.*  I' faith, gentlemen, I 'll give my word for Ralph.


## Actus Primus.    Scæna Prima.

*Enter Merchant [Venturewell] and Jasper, his Prentice*

*Vent.*  Sirrah, I 'll make you know you are my prentice,
And whom my charitable love redeem'd
Even from the fall of fortune; gave thee heat
And growth, to be what now thou art; new-cast thee,
Adding the trust of all I have, at home,
In foreign staples,[5] or upon the sea,
To thy direction; tied the good opinions
Both of myself and friends to thy endeavours,
So fair were thy beginnings. But with these,
As I remember, you had never charge
To love your master's daughter, and even[6] then
When I had found a wealthy husband for her.
I take it, sir, you had not; but, however,
I 'll break the neck of that commission,

----

[4] Personal attacks.
[5] Trading posts.              [6] Especially.

And make you know you are but a merchant's factor.[7]

*Jasp.*   Sir, I do liberally confess I am yours,
Bound both by love and duty to your service,
In which my labour hath been all your profit:
I have not lost in bargain, nor delighted
To wear your honest gains upon my back;
Nor have I given a pension to my blood,[8]
Or lavishly in play consum'd your stock.
These, and the miseries that do attend them,
I dare with innocence proclaim are strangers
To all my temperate actions.  For your daughter,
If there be any love to my deservings
Borne by her virtuous self, I cannot stop it;
Nor am I able to refrain[9] her wishes.
She 's private to herself, and best of knowledge
Whom she will make so happy as to sigh for:
Besides, I cannot think you mean to match her
Unto a fellow of so lame a presence,[1]
One that hath little left of nature in him.

*Vent.*   'T is very well, sir: I can tell your wisdom
How all this shall be cur'd.

*Jasp.*                        Your care becomes you.

*Vent.*   And thus it must be, sir: I here discharge you
My house and service; take your liberty;
And when I want a son, I 'll send for you.          *Exit.*

*Jasp.*   These be the fair rewards of them that love!
Oh, you that live in freedom, never prove[2]
The travail of a mind led by desire!

### Enter Luce

*Luce.*   Why, how now, friend?  Struck with my father's thunder!

*Jasp.*   Struck, and struck dead, unless the remedy
Be full of speed and virtue; I am now,
What I expected long, no more your father's.

*Luce.*   But mine.

*Jasp.*             But yours, and only yours, I am;
That 's all I have to keep me from the statute.[3]
You dare be constant still?

*Luce.*                      Oh, fear me not!
In this I dare be better than a woman:

---

[7] Agent.                    [8] Allowed my blood to run riot.
[9] Restrain.                 [1] Such uncouth behavior.
[2] Make trial of.            [3] From being arrested as a vagrant.

Nor shall his anger nor his offers move me,
Were they both equal to a prince's power.
  *Jasp.*  You know my rival!
  *Luce.*                  Yes, and love him dearly,
Even as I love an ague or foul weather.
I prithee, Jasper, fear him not.
  *Jasp.*            Oh, no!
I do not mean to do him so much kindness.
But to our own desires: you know the plot
We both agreed on?
  *Luce.*            Yes, and will perform
My part exactly.
  *Jasp.*       I desire no more.
Farewell, and keep my heart; 't is yours.
  *Luce.*                I take it;
He must do miracles makes me forsake it.

                         *Exeunt* [*severally*].

  *Cit.*  Fie upon 'em, little infidels! what a matter 's here now! Well, I 'll be hang'd for a halfpenny, if there be not some abomination knavery in this play. Well; let 'em look to 't; Ralph must come, and if there be any tricks a-brewing ——
  *Wife.*  Let 'em brew and bake too, husband, a' God's name; Ralph will find all out, I warrant you, and they were older than they are. — [*Enter Boy.*] — I pray, my pretty youth, is Ralph ready?
  *Boy.*  He will be presently.
  *Wife.*  Now, I pray you, make my commendations unto him, and withal carry him this stick of liquorice. Tell him his mistress sent it him; and bid him bite a piece; 't will open his pipes the better, say.               [*Exit Boy.*]


[SCENE II]

*Enter Merchant* [*Venturewell*] *and Master Humphrey*

  *Vent.*  Come, sir, she 's yours; upon my faith, she 's yours;
You have my hand: for other idle lets[4]
Between your hopes and her, thus with a wind
They are scatter'd and no more. My wanton prentice,
That like a bladder blew himself with love,
I have let out, and sent him to discover

---

4 Impediments.

New masters yet unknown.

*Hum.*                    I thank you, sir,
Indeed, I thank you, sir; and, ere I stir,
It shall be known, however you do deem,
I am of gentle blood and gentle seem.[5]

*Vent.*   Oh, sir, I know it certain.

*Hum.*                         Sir, my friend,
Although, as writers say, all things have end,
And that we call a pudding hath his two,[6]
Oh, let it not seem strange, I pray, to you,
If in this bloody simile I put
My love, more endless than frail things or gut!

*Wife.*   Husband, I prithee, sweet lamb, tell me one thing; but tell me truly. — Stay, youths, I beseech you, till I question my husband.

*Cit.*   What is it, mouse?

*Wife.*   Sirrah, didst thou ever see a prettier child? how it behaves itself, I warrant ye, and speaks and looks, and perts[7] up the head! — I pray you, brother, with your favour, were you never none of Master Moncaster's[8] scholars?

*Cit.*   Chicken, I prithee heartily, contain thyself: the childer[9] are pretty childer; but when Ralph comes, lamb ——

*Wife.*   Ay, when Ralph comes, cony! — Well, my youth, you may proceed.

*Vent.*   Well, sir, you know my love, and rest, I hope,
Assur'd of my consent; get but my daughter's,
And wed her when you please. You must be bold,
And clap in[1] close unto her: come, I know
You have language good enough to win a wench.

*Wife.*   A whoreson tyrant! h'as been an old stringer[2] in 's days, I warrant him.

*Hum.*   I take your gentle offer, and withal
Yield love again for love reciprocal.

*Vent.*   What, Luce! within there!

*Enter Luce.*

*Luce.*                    Call'd you, sir?
*Vent.*                                   I did:
Give entertainment to this gentleman;

---

[5] Appearance.          [6] I.e., ends.          [7] Tosses.
[8] Richard Mulcaster, Headmaster of St. Paul's school, 1596–1608.
[9] Children.          [1] Approach briskly.          [2] Wencher.

And see you be not froward.[3] — To her, sir:

My presence will but be an eye-sore to you.                    *Exit.*

    *Hum.*   Fair Mistress Luce, how do you?  Are you well?

Give me your hand, and then I pray you tell

How doth your little sister and your brother;

And whether you love me or any other.

    *Luce.*   Sir, these are quickly answer'd.

    *Hum.*                              So they are,

Where women are not cruel.  But how far

Is it now distant, from the place we are in.

Unto that blessed place, your father's warren?[4]

    *Luce.*   What makes you think of that, sir?

    *Hum.*                                    Even that face;

For, stealing rabbits whilom in that place,

God Cupid, or the keeper, I know not whether,[5]

Unto my cost and charges brought you thither,

And there began ——

    *Luce.*              Your game, sir.

    *Hum.*                            Let no game,

Or anything that tendeth to the same,

Be evermore rememb'red, thou fair killer,

For whom I sat me down, and brake my tiller.[6]

    *Wife.*   There 's a kind gentleman, I warrant you; when will you do as much for me, George?

    *Luce.*   Beshrew me, sir, I am sorry for your losses,

But, as the proverb says, I cannot cry.

I would you had not seen me!

    *Hum.*                            So would I,

Unless you had more maw[7] to do me good.

    *Luce.*   Why, cannot this strange passion be withstood?

Send for a constable, and raise the town.

    *Hum.*   Oh, no! my valiant love will batter down

Millions of constables, and put to flight

Even that great watch of Midsummer-day at night.[8]

    *Luce.*   Beshrew me, sir, 't were good I yielded, then;

Weak women cannot hope, where valiant men

Have no resistance.

    *Hum.*              Yield, then; I am full

Of pity, though I can say it, and can pull

Out of my pocket thus a pair of gloves.

---

[3] Forward.       [4] Rabbit warren.       [5] Which of the two.
[6] Part of crossbow.              [7] Desire.
[8] Annual gathering of the London militia.

Look, Lucy, look; the dog's tooth nor the dove's
Are not so white as these; and sweet they be,
And whipp'd about with silk, as you may see.
If you desire the price, shoot from your eye
A beam to this place, and you shall espy
*F S*,[9] which is to say, my sweetest honey,
They cost me three and twopence, or no money.

 *Luce.* Well, sir, I take them kindly, and I thank you:
What would you more?
  *Hum.*      Nothing.
  *Luce.*        Why, then, farewell.
  *Hum.* Nor so, nor so; for, lady, I must tell,
Before we part, for what we met together:
God grant me time and patience and fair weather!
 *Luce.* Speak, and declare your mind in terms so brief.
 *Hum.* I shall: then, first and foremost, for relief
I call to you, if that you can afford it;
I care not at what price, for, on my word, it
Shall be repaid again, although it cost me
More than I 'll speak of now; for love hath tost me
In furious blanket like a tennis-ball,
And now I rise aloft, and now I fall.
 *Luce.* Alas, good gentleman, alas the day!
 *Hum.* I thank you heartily; and, as I say,
Thus do I still continue without rest,
I' th' morning like a man, at night a beast,
Roaring and bellowing mine own disquiet,
That much I fear, forsaking of my diet
Will bring me presently to that quandary,
I shall bid all adieu.
 *Luce.*      Now, by St. Mary,
That were great pity!
 *Hum.*     So it were, beshrew me!
Then, ease me, lusty Luce, and pity show me.
 *Luce.* Why, sir, you know my will is nothing worth
Without my father's grant; get his consent,
And then you may with assurance try me.
 *Hum.* The worshipful your sire will not deny me;
For I have ask'd him, and he hath replied,
"Sweet Master Humphrey, Luce shall be thy bride."
 *Luce.* Sweet Master Humphrey, then I am content.
 *Hum.* And so am I, in truth.
 *Luce.*      Yet take me with you;

 [9] Dealer's code mark for the price.

There is another clause must be annex'd,
And this it is: I swore, and will perform it,
No man shall ever enjoy me as his wife
But he that stole me hence. If you dare venture,
I am yours (you need not fear; my father loves you);
If not, farewell for ever!

 *Hum.*     Stay, nymph, stay:
I have a double gelding, colour'd bay,
Sprung by his father from Barbarian kind;
Another for myself, though somewhat blind,
Yet true as trusty tree.

 *Luce.*    I am satisfied;
And so I give my hand. Our course must lie
Through Waltham Forest, where I have a friend
Will entertain us. So, farewell, sir Humphrey,
And think upon your business.     *Exit.*

 *Hum.*    Though I die,
I am resolv'd to venture life and limb
For one so young, so fair, so kind, so trim.  *Exit.*

 *Wife.* By my faith and troth, George, and as I am virtuous, it is e'en the kindest young man that ever trod on shoe-leather. — Well, go thy ways; if thou hast her not, 't is not thy fault, 'faith.

 *Cit.* I prithee, mouse, be patient; 'a shall have her, or I 'll make some of 'em smoke[1] for 't.

 *Wife.* That's my good lamb, George. — Fie, this stinking tobacco kills me! would there were none in England! — Now, I pray, gentlemen, what good does this stinking tobacco do you? Nothing, I warrant you: make chimneys o' your faces! — Oh, husband, husband, now, now! there 's Ralph, there 's Ralph.

## [SCENE III]

*Enter Ralph, like a Grocer in 's shop with two prentices*
*[Tim and George], reading "Palmerin of England."*[2]

 *Cit.* Peace, fool! let Ralph alone. — Hark you, Ralph; do not strain yourself too much at the first. — Peace! — Begin, Ralph.

 *Ralph.* [*reads.*] Then Palmerin and Trineus, snatching their lances from their dwarfs, and clasping their helmets, gallop'd

---

[1] Give some of them a warm time.
[2] A popular romance of knightly adventure; however, scholars have pointed out that the passage quoted comes from *Palmerin de Oliva.*

amain after the giant; and Palmerin, having gotten a sight of him, came posting amain, caying, "Stay, traitorous thief! for thou mayst not so carry away her, that is worth the greatest lord in the world;" and, with these words, gave him a blow on the shoulder, that he struck him besides[3] his elephant. And Trineus, coming to the knight that had Agricola[4] behind him, set him soon besides his horse, with his neck broken in the fall; so that the princess, getting out of the throng, between joy and grief, said, "All happy knight, the mirror of all such as follow arms, now may I be well assured of the love thou bearest me." I wonder why the kings do not raise an army of fourteen or fifteen hundred thousand men, as big as the army that the Prince of Portigo brought against Rosicleer, and destroy these giants; they do much hurt to wandering damsels, that go in quest of their knights.

*Wife.* Faith, husband, and Ralph says true; for they say the King of Portugal cannot sit at his meat, but the giants and the ettins[5] will come and snatch it from him.

*Cit.* Hold thy tongue. — On, Ralph!

*Ralph.* And certainly those knights are much to be commended, who, neglecting their possessions, wander with a squire and a dwarf through the deserts to relieve poor ladies.

*Wife.* Ay, but my faith, are they, Ralph; let 'em say what they will, they are indeed. Our knights neglect their possessions well enough, but they do not the rest.

*Ralph.* There are no such courteous and fair well-spoken knights in this age: they will call one the son of a whore, that Palmerin of England would have called "fair sir;" and one that Rosicleer would have call'd "right beauteous damsel," they will call "damn'd bitch."

*Wife.* I 'll be sworn will they, Ralph; they have call'd me so an hundred times about a scurvy pipe of tobacco.

*Ralph.* But what brave spirit could be content to sit in his shop, with a flappet[6] of wood, and a blue apron before him, selling mithridatum[7] and dragon's-water[8] to visited houses, that might pursue feats of arms, and, through his noble achievements, procure such a famous history to be written of his heroic prowess?

---

[3] Down from.
[4] A captive princess.
[5] A race of giants.
[6] A small flap to keep away flies.
[7] Antidote for poisons.
[8] Name of a remedy against the plague.

*Cit.* Well said, Ralph; some more of those words, Ralph!

*Wife.* They go finely, by my troth.

*Ralph.* Why should not I, then, pursue this course, both for the credit of myself and our company? for amongst all the worthy books of achievements, I do not call to mind that I yet read of a grocer-errant. I will be the said knight. — Have you heard of any that hath wandered unfurnished of his squire and dwarf? My elder prentice Tim shall be my trusty squire, and little George my dwarf. Hence, my blue apron! Yet, in remembrance of my former trade, upon my shield shall be portray'd a Burning Pestle, and I will be call'd the Knight of the Burning Pestle.

*Wife.* Nay, I dare swear thou wilt not forget thy old trade; thou wert ever meek.

*Ralph.* Tim!

*Tim.* Anon.

*Ralph.* My beloved squire, and George, my dwarf, I charge you that from henceforth you never call me by any other name but "the right courteous and valiant Knight of the Burning Pestle;" and that you never call any female by the name of a woman or wench, but "fair lady," if she have her desires, if not, "distressed damsel;" that you call all forests and heaths "deserts," and all horses "palfreys."

*Wife.* This is very fine, faith. — Do the gentlemen like Ralph, think you, husband?

*Cit.* Ay, I warrant thee; the players would give all the shoes in their shop for him.

*Ralph.* My beloved squire Tim, stand out. Admit this were a desert, and over it a knight-errant pricking, and I should bid you inquire of his intents: what would you say?

*Tim.* Sir, my master sent me to know whither you are riding?

*Ralph.* No, thus: "Fair sir, the right courteous and valiant Knight of the Burning Pestle commanded me to inquire upon what adventure you are bound, whether to relieve some distressed damsel, or otherwise."

*Cit.* Whoreson blockhead, cannot remember!

*Wife.* I' faith, and Ralph told him on 't before: all the gentlemen heard him. — Did he not, gentlemen? Did not Ralph tell him on 't?

*George.* Right courteous and valiant Knight of the Burning Pestle, here is a distressed damsel to have a halfpenny-worth of pepper.

*Wife.* That 's a good boy! See, the little boy can hit it; by my troth, it 's a fine child.

*Ralph.* Relieve her, with all courteous language. Now shut up shop; no more my prentice, but my trusty squire and dwarf. I must bespeak[9] my shield and arming[1] pestle.

[*Exeunt Tim and George.*]

*Cit.* Go thy ways, Ralph! As I 'm a true man, thou art the best on 'em all.

*Wife.* Ralph, Ralph!

*Rilph.* What say you, mistress?

*Wife.* I prithee, come again quickly, sweet Ralph.

*Ralph.* By and by.                                          *Exit.*


## [Scene IV]

### *Enter Jasper and his mother, Mistress Merrythought*

*Mist. Mer.* Give thee my blessing? No, I 'll ne'er give thee my blessing; I 'll see thee hang'd first; it shall ne'er be said I gave thee my blessing. Th' are thy father's own son, of the right blood of the Merrythoughts. I may curse the time that e'er I knew thy father; he hath spent all his own and mine too; and when I tell him of it, he laughs, and dances, and sings, and cries, "A merry heart lives long-a." And thou art a wastethrift, and art run away from thy master that lov'd thee well, and art come to me; and I have laid up a little for my younger son Michael, and thou think'st to bezzle[2] that, but thou shalt never be able to do it. — Come hither, Michael!

### *Enter Michael*

Come, Michael, down on thy knees: thou shalt have my blessing.

*Mich.* [*kneels.*] I pray you, mother, pray to God to bless me.

*Mist. Mer.* God bless thee! but Jasper shall never have my blessing; he shall be hang'd first; shall he not, Michael? How sayst thou?

*Mich.* Yes, forsooth, mother, and grace of God.

*Mist. Mer.* That 's a good boy!

*Wife.* I' faith, it 's a fine spoken child.

*Jasp.* Mother, though you forget a parent's love,
I must preserve the duty of a child.

---

[9] Order.                          [1] Armorial, i.e., painted on the shield.
[2] Tipple away.

I ran not from my master, nor return
To have your stock maintain my idleness.

*Wife.* Ungracious child. I warrant him; hark, how he chops logic with his mother! — Thou hadst best tell her she lies; do, tell her she lies.

*Cit.* If he were my son, I would hang him up by the heels, and flay him, and salt him, whoreson haltersack.[3]

*Jasp.* My coming only is to beg your love,
Which I must ever, though I never gain it;
And, howsoever you esteem of me,
There is no drop of blood hid in these veins
But, I remember well, belongs to you
That brought me forth, and would be glad for you
To rip them all again, and let it out.

*Mist. Mer.* I' faith, I had sorrow enough for thee, God knows; but I 'll hamper thee well enough. Get thee in, thou vagabond, get thee in, and learn of thy brother Michael.

*[Exeunt Jasper and Michael.]*

*Old Mer. within.*

> Nose, nose, jolly red nose,
> And what gave thee this jolly red nose?

*Mist. Mer.* Hark, my husband! he 's singing and hoiting;[4] and I 'm fain to cark and care, and all little enough. — Husband! Charles! Charles Merrythought!

*Enter old Merrythought*

*Mer.* [*sings.*]

> Nutmegs and ginger, cinnamon and cloves;
> And they gave me this jolly red nose.

*Mist. Mer.* If you would consider your estate, you would have list[5] to sing, i-wis.[6]

*Mer.* It should never be considered, while it were an estate, if I thought it would spoil my singing.

*Mist. Mer.* But how wilt thou do, Charles? Thou art an old man, and thou canst not work, and thou hast not forty shillings left, and thou eatest good meat, and drinkest good drink, and laughest.

*Mer.* And will do.

*Mist. Mer.* But how wilt thou come by it, Charles?

[3] Gallows bird.     [4] Roistering.
[5] Desire.     [6] Assuredly.

*Mer.*  How! why, how have I done hitherto this forty years? I never came into my dining room, but, at eleven and six o'clock, I found excellent meat and drink o' th' table; my clothes were never worn out, but next morning a tailor brought me a new suit: and without question it will be so ever; use makes perfectness. If all should fail, it is but a little straining myself extraordinary, and laugh myself to death.

*Wife.*  It 's a foolish old man this; is not he, George?
*Cit.*  Yes, cony.
*Wife.*  Give me a penny i' th' purse while I live, George.
*Cit.*  Ay, by lady, cony, hold thee there.

*Mist. Mer.*  Well, Charles, you promis'd to provide for Jasper, and I have laid up for Michael. I pray you, pay Jasper his portion: he 's come home, and he shall not consume Michael's stock. He says his master turn'd him away, but, I promise you truly, I think he ran away.

*Wife.*  No, indeed, Mistress Merrythought; though he be a notable gallows,[7] yet I 'll assure you his master did turn him away, even in this place. 'T was, i' faith, within this half-hour, about his daughter; my husband was by.
*Cit.*  Hang him, rogue! he serv'd him well enough: love his master's daughter! By my troth, cony, if there were a thousand boys, thou wouldst spoil them all with taking their parts; let his mother alone with him.
*Wife.*  Ay, George; but yet truth is truth.

*Mer.*  Where is Jasper? He 's welcome, however. Call him in; he shall have his portion. Is he merry?
*Mist. Mer.*  Ah, foul chive[8] him, he is too merry! — Jasper! Michael!

### Enter Jasper and Michael

*Mer.*  Welcome, Jasper! though thou run'st away, welcome! God bless thee! 'T is thy mother's mind thou shouldst receive thy portion; thou hast been abroad,[9] and I hope hast learn'd experience enough to govern it; thou art of sufficient years. Hold thy hand: — one, two, three, four, five, six, seven, eight, nine, there 's ten shillings for thee. [*Gives money.*] Thrust thyself into the world with that, and take some settled course. If fortune cross thee, thou hast a retiring place; come home to me; I have twenty shillings left. Be a good husband;[1] that is, wear ordinary

---

[7] Gallows bird.          [8] Befall.
[9] Away from home.          [1] Manager.

clothes, eat the best meat, and drink the best drink; be merry, and give to the poor, and, believe me, thou hast no end of thy goods.

*Jasp.*  Long may you live free from all thought of ill,
And long have cause to be thus merry still!
But, father ——

*Mer.*  No more words, Jasper; get thee gone. Thou hast my blessing; thy father's spirit upon thee!
Farewell, Jasper!                                                      [*Sings.*]

> But yet, or ere you part (oh cruel?)
> Kiss me, kiss me, sweeting, mine own dear jewel!

So, now begone; no words.                                    *Exit Jasper.*

*Mist. Mer.*  So, Michael, now get thee gone too.

*Mich.*  Yes, forsooth, mother; but I 'll have my father's blessing first.

*Mist. Mer.*  No, Michael; 't is no matter for his blessing. Thou hast my blessing; begone. I 'll fetch my money and jewels, and follow thee; I 'll stay no longer with him, I warrant thee [*Exit Michael.*] — Truly, Charles, I 'll be gone too.

*Mer.*  What! you will not?

*Mist. Mer.*  Yes, indeed will I.

*Mer.*  [*sings.*]

> Heigh-ho, farewell, Nan!
> I'll never trust wench more again, if I can.

*Mist. Mer.*  You shall not think, when all your own is gone, to spend that I have been scraping up for Michael.

*Mer.*  Farewell, good wife; I expect it not: all I have to do in this world is to be merry; which I shall, if the ground be not taken from me; and if it be,                                    [*Sings.*]

> When earth and seas from me are reft,
> The skies aloft for me are left.

*Exeunt* [*severally*].

*Boy danceth. Music*
*Finis Actus Primi*

*Wife.*  I 'll be sworn he 's a merry old gentleman for all that. Hark, hark, husband, hark! fiddles, fiddles! now surely they go finely. They say 't is present death for these fiddlers to tune their rebecks[2] before the great Turk's grace;[3] is 't not, George? But, look, look! here 's a youth dances! — Now, good youth, do

[2] Early form of the violin.
[3] His majesty the Sultan of Turkey.

a turn o' th' toe. — Sweetheart, i' faith, I 'll have Ralph come and
do some of his gambols. — He 'll ride the wild mare,[4] gentlemen,
't would do your hearts good to see him. — I thank you, kind
youth; pray, bid Ralph come.

*Cit.* Peace, cony! — Sirrah, you scurvy boy, bid the players
send Ralph; or, by God's —— and they do not, I 'll tear some of
their periwigs beside their heads: this is all riff-raff.   [*Exit Boy.*]

## *Actus Secundus. Scæna Prima.*

### *Enter Merchant [Venturewell] and Humphrey*

*Vent.* And how, faith, how goes it now, son Humphrey?
*Hum.* Right worshipful, and my beloved friend,
And father dear, this matter 's at an end.
*Vent.* 'T is well; it should be so. I 'm glad the girl
Is found so tractable.
*Hum.*            Nay, she must whirl
From hence (and you must wink; for so, I say,
The story tells,) to-morrow before day.

*Wife.* George, dost thou think in thy conscience now 't will
be a match? Tell me but what thou think'st, sweet rogue. Thou
seest the poor gentleman, dear heart, how it labours and throbs,
I warrant you, to be at rest! I 'll go move the father for 't.
*Cit.* No, no; I prithee, sit still, honeysuckle; thou 'lt spoil all.
If he deny him, I 'll bring half-a-dozen good fellows myself, and
in the shutting[5] of an evening, knock 't up, and there 's an end.
*Wife.* I 'll buss thee for that, i' faith, boy. Well, George, well,
you have been a wag in your days, I warrant you; but God forgive
you, and I do with all my heart.

*Vent.* How was it, son? You told me that to-morrow
Before day break, you must convey her hence.
*Hum.* I must, I must; and thus it is agreed:
Your daughter rides upon a brown-bay steed,
I on a sorrel,[6] which I bought of Brian,
The honest host of the Red roaring Lion,
In Waltham[7] situate. Then, if you may,
Consent in seemly sort; lest, by delay,
The Fatal Sisters come, and do the office,
And then you 'll sing another song.
*Vent.*            Alas,

---

[4] Seesaw.          [5] Twilight.
[6] A horse of reddish-brown color.
[7] Village a few miles north of London.

Why should you be thus full of grief to me,
That do as willing as yourself agree
To anything, so it be good and fair?
Then, steal her when you will, if such a pleasure
Content you both; I 'll sleep and never see it,
To make your joys more full. But tell me why
You may not here perform your marriage?

*Wife.* God's blessing o' thy soul, old man! I' faith, thou art
loath to part true hearts. I see 'a has her, George; and I 'm as
glad on 't — Well, go thy ways, Humphrey, for a fair-spoken man;
I believe thou hast not thy fellow within the walls of London;
and I should say the suburbs too, I should not lie. — Why dost
not rejoice with me, George?

*Cit.* If I could but see Ralph again, I were as merry as mine
host, i' faith.

*Hum.* The cause you seem to ask, I thus declare —
Help me, O Muses nine! Your daughter sware
A foolish oath, the more it was the pity;
Yet none but myself within this city
Shall dare to say so, but a bold defiance
Shall meet him, were he of the noble science;[8]
And yet she sware, and yet why did she swear?
Truly, I cannot tell, unless it were
For her own ease; for, sure, sometimes an oath,
Being sworn, thereafter is like cordial broth;
And this it was she swore, never to marry
But such a one whose mighty arm could carry
(As meaning me, for I am such a one)
Her bodily away, through stick and stone,
Till both of us arrive, at her request,
Some ten miles off, in the wild Waltham Forest.

*Vent.* If this be all, you shall not need to fear
Any denial in your love: proceed;
I 'll neither follow, nor repent the deed.

*Hum.* Good night, twenty good nights, and twenty more,
And twenty more good nights, — that makes three-score!

*Exeunt [severally].*

[Scene II]

*Enter Mistress Merrythought and her son Michael*

*Mist. Mer.* Come, Michael; art thou not weary, boy?
*Mich.* No, forsooth, mother, not I.

[8] A fencing-master.

*Mist. Mer.* Where be we now, child?

*Mich.* Indeed, forsooth, mother, I cannot tell, unless we be at Mile-End.[9] Is not all the world Mile-End, mother?

*Mist. Mer.* No, Michael, not all the world, boy; but I can assure thee, Michael, Mile-End is a goodly matter: there has been a pitchfield,[1] my child, between the naughty Spaniels[2] and the Englishmen; and the Spaniels ran away, Michael, and the Englishmen followed. My neighbour Coxstone was there, boy, and kill'd them all with a birding-piece.

*Mich.* Mother, forsooth —

*Mist. Mer.* What says my white[3] boy?

*Mich.* Shall not my father go with us too?

*Mist. Mer.* No, Michael, let thy father go snick-up;[4] he shall never come between a pair of sheets with me again while he lives; let him stay at home, and sing for his supper, boy. Come, child, sit down, and I 'll show my boy fine knacks indeed. [*They sit down: and she takes out a casket.*] Look here, Michael; here 's a ring, and here 's a brooch, and here 's a bracelet, and here 's two rings more, and here 's money and gold by th' eye,[5] my boy.

*Mich.* Shall I have all this, mother?

*Mist. Mer.* Ay, Michael, thou shalt have all, Michael.

*Cit.* How lik'st thou this, wench?

*Wife.* I cannot tell; I would have Ralph, George; I 'll see no more else, indeed, la; and I pray you, let the youths understand so much by word of mouth; for, I tell you truly, I 'm afraid o' my boy. Come, come, George, let 's be merry and wise: the child 's a fatherless child; and say they should put him into a strait pair of gaskins,[6] 't were worse than knot-grass;[7] he would never grow after it.

*Enter Ralph, Squire [Tim], and Dwarf [George]*

*Cit.* Here 's Ralph, here 's Ralph!

*Wife.* How do you, Ralph? you are welcome, Ralph, as I may say. It 's a good boy, hold up thy head, and be not afraid; we are thy friends, Ralph; the gentlemen will praise thee, Ralph, if thou play'st thy part with audacity. Begin, Ralph, o' God's name!

*Ralph.* My trusty squire, unlace my helm; give me my hat. Where are we, or what desert may this be?

---

9 A suburban district, one mile from the old city walls.
1 Sham military manoeuvres?    2 Spaniards.
3 Sweet.        4 Hang.    5 In crowds.
6 A tight pair of breeches.
7 A herb supposed to check growth.

*George.*  Mirror of knighthood, this is, as I take it, the perilous
Waltham-down, in whose bottom stands the enchanted valley.

*Mist. Mer.*  Oh, Michael, we are betray'd, we are betray'd!
Here be giants! Fly, boy! fly, boy, fly!

>            *Exeunt Mother and Michael [leaving the casket]*

*Ralph.*  Lace on my helm again. What noise is this?
A gentle lady, flying the embrace
Of some uncourteous knight! I will relieve her.
Go, squire, and say, the Knight that wears this Pestle
In honour of all ladies, swears revenge
Upon that recreant coward that pursues her.
Go, comfort her, and that same gentle squire
That bears her company.

*Tim.*              I go, brave knight.              [*Exit.*]

*Ralph.*  My trusty dwarf and friend, reach me my shield,
And hold it while I swear. First, by my knighthood;
Then by the soul of Amadis de Gaul,[8]
My famous ancestor; then by my sword
The beauteous Brionella[9] girt about me;
By this bright burning Pestle, of mine honour
The living trophy; and by all respect
Due to distressed damsels: here I vow
Never to end the quest of this fair lady
And that forsaken squire till by my valour
I gain their liberty!

*George.*          Heaven bless the knight
That thus relieves poor errant gentlewomen!              *Exeunt.*

*Wife.*  Ay, marry, Ralph, this has some savour in 't; I would
see the proudest of them all offer to carry his books after him.
But, George, I will not have him go away so soon; I shall be sick
if he go away, that I shall. Call Ralph again, George, call Ralph
again; I prithee, sweetheart, let him come fight before me, and
let 's ha' some drums and some trumpets, and let him kill all that
comes near him, and thou lov'st me, George!

*Cit.*  Peace a little, bird: he shall kill them all, and[1] they were
twenty more on 'em than there are.

> *Enter Jasper*

*Jasp.*  Now, Fortune, if thou be'st not only ill,
Show me thy better face, and bring about
Thy desperate wheel, that I may climb at length,

---

[8] Hero of a famous romance of knight-errantry.
[9] A lady in *Palmerin de Oliva.*                    [1] If.

And stand. This is our place of meeting,
If love have any constancy. Oh age,
Where only wealthy men are counted happy!
How shall I please thee, how deserve thy smiles,
When I am only rich in misery?
My father's blessing and this little coin
Is my inheritance, a strong revénue!
From earth thou art, and to the earth I give thee:

                                       [*Throws away the money.*]

There grow and multiply, whilst fresher air
Breeds me a fresher fortune. — How! illusion?   *Spies the casket.*
What, hath the devil coin'd himself before me?
'T is metal good, it rings well; I am waking,
And taking too, I hope. Now, God's dear blessing
Upon his heart that left it here! 'T is mine;
These pearls, I take it, were not left for swine.

                                              *Exit* [*with the casket*].

   *Wife.* I do not like that this unthrifty youth should embezzle away the money; the poor gentlewoman his mother will have a heavy heart for it, God knows.

   *Cit.* And reason good, sweetheart.

   *Wife.* But let him go; I 'll tell Ralph a tale in 's ear shall fetch him again with a wanion;[2] I warrant him, if he be above ground; and besides, George, here are a number of sufficient gentlemen can witness, and myself, and yourself, and the musicians, if we be call'd in question. But here comes Ralph, George; thou shalt hear him speak as he were an emperal.[3]

### [SCENE III]

#### *Enter Ralph and Dwarf* [*George*]

   *Ralph.* Comes not sir squire again?

   *George.*                          Right courteous knight,
Your squire doth come, and with him comes the lady,

#### *Enter Mistress Merrythought, Michael, and Squire* [*Tim*]

For and[4] the Squire of Damsels, as I take it.

   *Ralph.* Madam, if any service or devoir
Of a poor errant knight may right your wrongs,
Command it; I am prest[5] to give you succour,
For to that holy end I bear my armour.

---

  2 Vengeance.                         3 Emperor.
  4 As well as.                       5 Ready.

*Mist. Mer.*     Alas, sir, I am a poor gentlewoman, and I have lost
my money in this forest!

*Ralph.*     Desert, you would say, lady; and not lost
Whilst I have sword and lance. Dry up your tears,
Which ill befits the beauty of that face,
And tell the story, if I may request it,
Of your disastrous fortune.

*Mist. Mer.*     Out, alas! I left a thousand pound, a thousand
pound, e'en all the money I had laid up for this youth, upon the
sight of your mastership, you look'd so grim, and, as I may say
it, saving your presence, more like a giant than a mortal man.

*Ralph.*     I am as you are, lady; so are they;
All mortal. But why weeps this gentle squire?

*Mist. Mer.*     Has he not cause to weep, do you think, when he
hath lost his inheritance?

*Ralph.*     Young hope of valour, weep not; I am here
That will confound thy foe, and pay it dear
Upon his coward head, that dares deny
Distressed squires and ladies equity.
I have but one horse, on which shall ride
This fair lady behind me, and before,
This courteous squire: fortune will give us more
Upon our next adventure. Fairly speed
Beside us, squire and dwarf, to do us need!          *Exeunt.*

*Cit.*     Did not I tell you, Nell, what your man would do? By
the faith of my body, wench, for clean action and good delivery,
they may all cast their caps at him.[6]

*Wife.*     And so they may, i' faith; for I dare speak it boldly, the
twelve companies of London[7] cannot match him, timber for timber. Well, George, and he be not inveigled by some of these
paltry players, I ha' much marvel: but, George, we ha' done our
parts, if the boy have any grace to be thankful.

*Cit.*     Yes, I warrant thee, duckling.

## [SCENE IV]

### *Enter Humphrey and Luce*

*Hum.*     Good Mistress Luce, however I in fault am
For your lame horse, you 're welcome unto Waltham;

---

[6] Despair of rivaling.

[7] The twelve major livery companies, or guilds, of London, from
whose membership the Mayor and sheriffs were elected.

But which way now to go, or what to say,
I know not truly, till it be broad day.

   *Luce.*   Oh, fear not, Master Humphrey; I am guide
For this place good enough.

   *Hum.*            Then, up and ride;
Or, if it please you, walk, for your repose;
Or sit, or, if you will, go pluck a rose;[8]
Either of which shall be indifferent
To your good friend and Humphrey, whose consent
Is so entangled ever to your will,
As the poor harmless horse is to the mill.

   *Luce.*   Faith, and you say the word, we 'll e'en sit down,
And take a nap.

   *Hum.*       'T is better in the town,
Where we may nap together; for, believe me,
To sleep without a snatch[9] would mickle grieve me.

   *Luce.*   You 're merry, Master Humphrey.

   *Hum.*            So I am,
And have been ever merry from my dam.

   *Luce.*   Your nurse had the less labour.

   *Hum.*          Faith, it may be,
Unless it were by chance I did beray[1] me.

*Enter Jasper*

   *Jasp.*   Luce! dear friend Luce!

   *Luce.*        Here, Jasper.

   *Jasp.*          You are mine.

   *Hum.*   If it be so, my friend, you use me fine.
What do you think I am?

   *Jasp.*       An arrant noddy.

   *Hum.*   A word of obloquy! Now, by God's body,
I 'll tell thy master; for I know thee well.

   *Jasp.*   Nay, and you be so forward for to tell,
Take that, and that; and tell him, sir, I gave it:
And say, I paid you well.          **[Beats him.]**

   *Hum.*      Oh, sir, I have it,
And do confess the payment! Pray, be quiet.

   *Jasp.*   Go, get you to your night-cap and the diet,
To cure your beaten bones.

   *Luce.*      Alas, poor Humphrey;
Get thee some wholesome broth, with sage and comfrey;[2]

---

[8] Relieve yourself.      [9] Snack.
[1] Befoul.      [2] A herb.

A little oil of roses and a feather
To 'noint thy back withal.

*Hum.*                         When I came hither,
Would I had gone to Paris with John Dory![3]

*Luce.*  Farewell, my pretty Nump;[4] I am very sorry
I cannot bear thee company.

*Hum.*                         Farewell:
The devil's dam was ne'er so bang'd in hell.

> *Exeunt Luce and Jasper.*
> *Manet Humphrey.*

*Wife.*  This young Jasper will prove me another thing, o' my conscience, and he may be suffered. George, dost not see, George, how 'a swaggers, and flies at the very heads o' folks, as he were a dragon? Well, if I do his lesson[5] for wronging the poor gentleman, I am no true woman. His friends that brought him up might have been better occupied, i-wis, than ha' taught him these fegaries:[6] he 's e'en in the high way to the gallows, God bless him!

*Cit.*  You 're too bitter, cony; the young man may do well enough for all this.

*Wife.*  Come hither, Master Humphrey; has he hurt you? Now, beshrew[7] his fingers for 't! Here, sweetheart, here 's some green ginger for thee. Now, beshrew my heart, but 'a has peppernel[8] in 's head, as big as a pullet's egg! Alas, sweet lamb, how thy temples beat! Take the peace on him, sweetheart, take the peace on him.

*Cit.*  No, no; you talk like a foolish woman: I 'll ha' Ralph fight with him, and swinge him up well-favour'dly.[9]  *Enter a Boy.*
— Sirrah boy, come hither. Let Ralph come in and fight with Jasper.

*Wife.*  Ay, and beat him well; he 's an unhappy boy.

*Boy.*  Sir, you must pardon us; the plot of our play lies contrary; and 't will hazard the spoiling of our play.

*Cit.*  Plot me no plots! I 'll ha' Ralph come out; I 'll make your house too hot for you else.

*Boy.*  Why, sir, he shall; but if anything fall out of order, the gentlemen must pardon us.

*Cit.*  Go your ways, goodman boy! [*Exit Boy.*] I 'll hold him a penny, he shall have his bellyful of fighting now. Ho, here comes Ralph! No more!

---

[3] The central figure of a popular song; he was captain of a French privateer who undertook to take English prisoners to Paris, but was himself captured in the attempt.

[4] Pet name for Humphrey.   [5] Teach him.   [6] Vagaries.

[7] Curse.   [8] A swelling.   [9] Beat him soundly.

*Enter Ralph, Mistress Merrythought, Michael,*
*Squire [Tim], and Dwarf [George]*

*Ralph.*    What knight is that, squire?  Ask him if he keep
The passage, bound by love of lady fair,
Or else but prickant.[1]
   *Hum.*        Sir, I am no knight,
But a poor gentleman, that this same night
Had stol'n from me, on yonder green,
My lovely wife, and suffer'd (to be seen
Yet extant on my shoulders) such a greeting,
That whilst I live I shall think of that meeting.

*Wife.*   Ay, Ralph, he beat him unmercifully, Ralph; and thou
spar'st him, Ralph, I would thou wert hang'd.
   *Cit.*   No more, wife, no more.

*Ralph.*   Where is the caitiff-wretch hath done this deed?
Lady, your pardon, that I may proceed
Upon the quest of this injurious knight. —
And thou, fair squire, repute me not the worse,
In leaving the great venture of the purse
And the rich casket, till some better leisure.

### Enter Jasper and Luce

*Hum.*   Here comes the broker hath purloin'd my treasure.
   *Ralph.*   Go, squire, and tell him I am here,
An errant knight-at-arms, to crave delivery
Of that fair lady to her own knight's arms.
If he deny, bid him take choice of ground,
And so defy him.
   *Tim.*       From the Knight that bears
The Golden Pestle, I defy thee, knight,
Unless thou make fair restitution
Of that bright lady.
   *Jasp.*       Tell the knight that sent thee,
He is an ass; and I will keep the wench,
And knock his head-piece.
   *Ralph.*          Knight, thou art but dead
If thou recall not thy uncourteous terms.

*Wife.*   Break 's pate, Ralph; break 's pate, Ralph, soundly!

*Jasp.*   Come knight; I am ready for you. Now your Pestle
                            *(Snatches away his pestle.)*

---

[1] Riding by.

Shall try what temper, sir, your mortar 's of.
"With that he stood upright in his stirrups, and gave the Knight of
the calf-skin such a knock [*knocks Ralph down.*] that he forsook
his horse, and down he fell; and then he leaped upon him, and
plucking off his helmet —— "

*Hum.*   Nay, and my noble knight be down so soon,
Though I can scarcely go, I needs must run.

*Exeunt Humphrey and Ralph.*

*Wife.*   Run, Ralph, run, Ralph; run for thy life, boy!
Jasper comes, Jasper comes!

*Jasp.*   Come Luce, we must have other arms for you:
Humphrey, and Golden Pestle, both adieu!   *Exeunt.*

*Wife.*   Sure the devil (God bless us!) is in this springald![2] Why,
George, didst ever see such a fire-drake?[3] I am afraid my boy 's
miscarried:[4] if he be, though he were Master Merrythought's son
a thousand times, if there be any law in England, I 'll make some
of them smart for 't.

*Cit.*   No, no; I have found out the matter, sweetheart; Jasper
is enchanted; as sure as we are here, he is enchanted: he could no
more have stood in Ralph's hands than I can stand in my lord
mayor's. I 'll have a ring to discover all enchantments, and Ralph
shall beat him yet. Be no more vex'd, for it shall be so.

## [SCENE V]

### *Enter Ralph, Squire [Tim], Dwarf [George],*
### *Mistress Merrythought, and Michael*

*Wife.*   Oh, husband, here 's Ralph again! — Stay, Ralph, let
me speak with thee. How dost thou, Ralph? Art thou not shrewdly
hurt? — The foul great lungies[5] laid unmercifully on thee: there 's
some sugar-candy for thee. Proceed; thou shalt have another bout
with him.

*Cit.*   If Ralph had him at the fencing-school, if he did not make
a puppy of him, and drive him up and down the school, he should
ne'er come in my shop more.

*Mist. Mer.*   Truly, Master Knight of the Burning Pestle, I am
weary.

*Mich.*   Indeed, la, mother, and I am very hungry.

<hr>

[2] Youth.            [3] Dragon.
[4] Failed.           [5] Tall fellow.

*Ralph.*   Take comfort, gentle dame, and you, fair squire;
For in this desert there must needs be plac'd
Many strong castles held by courteous knights;
And till I bring you safe to one of those,
I swear by this my order ne'er to leave you.

*Wife.*   Well said, Ralph! — George, Ralph was ever comfortable,[6] was he not?

*Cit.*   Yes, duck.

*Wife.*   I shall ne'er forget him. When we had lost our child, (you know it was stray'd almost, alone, to Puddle-Wharf, and the criers were abroad for it, and there it had drown'd itself but for a sculler,) Ralph was the most comfortablest to me: "Peace, mistress," says he, "let it go; I 'll get you another as good." Did he not, George, did he not say so?

*Cit.*   Yes, indeed did he, mouse.

*George.*   I would we had a mess of pottage and a pot of drink, squire, and were going to bed!

*Tim.*   Why, we are at Waltham town's end, and that 's the Bell Inn.

*George.*   Take courage, valiant knight, damsel, and squire!
I have discovered, not a stone cast off,
An ancient castle, held by the old knight
Of the most holy order of the Bell,
Who gives to all knights-errant entertain.[7]
There plenty is of food, and all prepar'd
By the white hands of his own lady dear.
He hath three squires that welcome all his guests:
The first, hight Chamberlino, who will see
Our beds prepar'd, and bring us snowy sheets,
Where never footman[8] stretch'd his butter'd hams;
The second, hight Tapstero, who will see
Our pots full filled, and no froth therein;
The third, a gentle squire, Ostlero hight,
Who will our palfreys slick[9] with wisps of straw,
And in the manger put them oats enough,
And never grease their teeth with candle-snuff.[1]

*Wife.*   That same dwarf 's a pretty boy, but the squire 's a groutnol.[2]

*Ralph.*   Knock at the gates, my squire, with stately lance.

                              [*Tim knocks at the door.*]

[6] Helpful.                [7] A kind reception.
[8] Runner.                [9] Groom.
[1] In order to stop them from eating.              [2] Blockhead.

*Enter Tapster*

*Tap.*  Who 's there? — You 're welcome, gentlemen: will you see a room?

*George.*  Right courteous and valiant Knight of the Burning Pestle, this is the Squire Tapstero.

*Ralph.*  Fair Squire Tapstero, I a wandering knight,
Hight of the Burning Pestle, in the quest
Of this fair lady's casket and wrought purse,
Losing myself in this vast wilderness,
Am to this castle well by fortune brought;
Where, hearing of the goodly entertain
Your knight of holy order of the Bell
Gives to all damsels and all errant knights,
I thought to knock, and now am bold to enter.

*Tap.*  An 't please you see a chamber, you are very welcome.

*Exeunt.*

*Wife.*  George, I would have something done, and I cannot tell what it is.

*Cit.*  What is it, Nell?

*Wife.*  Why, George, shall Ralph beat nobody again? Prithee, sweetheart, let him.

*Cit.*  So he shall, Nell; and if I join with him, we' ll knock them all.

[Scene VI]

*Enter Humphrey and Merchant [Venturewell]*

*Wife.*  Oh, George, here 's Master Humphrey again now, that lost Mistress Luce, and Mistress Luce's father. Master Humphrey will do somebody's errand, I warrant him.

*Hum.*  Father, it 's true in arms I ne'er shall clasp her;
For she is stol'n away by your man Jasper.

*Wife.*  I thought he would tell him.

*Vent.*  Unhappy that I am, to lose my child!
Now I begin to think on Jasper's words,
Who oft hath urg'd to me thy foolishness.
Why didst thou let her go? Thou lov'st her not,
That wouldst bring home thy life, and not bring her.

*Hum.*  Father, forgive me. Shall I tell you true?
Look on my shoulders, they are black and blue.

Whilst to and fro fair Luce and I were winding,
He came and basted me with a hedge-binding.[3]

*Vent.*   Get men and horses straight: we will be there
Within this hour. You know the place again?

*Hum.*   I know the place where he my loins did swaddle;[4]
I 'll get six horses, and to each a saddle.

*Vent.*   Meantime I 'll go talk with Jasper's father.

*Exeunt* [*severally*].

*Wife.*   George, what wilt thou lay with me now, that Master Humphrey has not Mistress Luce yet? Speak, George, what wilt thou lay with me?

*Cit.*   No, Nell; I warrant thee Jasper is at Puckeridge[5] with her by this.

*Wife.*   Nay, George, you must consider Mistress Luce's feet are tender; and besides 't is dark; and, I promise you truly, I do not see how he should get out of Waltham Forest with her yet.

*Cit.*   Nay, cony, what wilt thou lay with me, that Ralph has her not yet?

*Wife.*   I will not lay against Ralph, honey, because I have not spoken with him. But look, George, peace! here comes the merry old gentleman again.


## [Scene VII]

### *Enter old Merrythought*

*Mer.* [*sings.*]

> When it was grown to dark midnight,
>      And all were fast asleep,
> In came Margaret's grimly ghost,
>      And stood at William's feet.

I have money, and meat, and drink beforehand, till to-morrow at noon; why should I be sad? Methinks I have half-a-dozen jovial spirits within me!                                    [*Sings.*]

> I am three merry men, and three merry men!

To what end should any man be sad in this world? Give me a man who when he goes to hanging cries,

> Trowl[6] the black bowl to me!

and a woman that will sing a catch in her travail! I have seen a man come by my door with a serious face, in a black cloak, without

---

[3] Beat me with a cane.                    [4] Beat.
[5] Village twenty-five miles north of London.                    [6] Pass round.

a hatband, carrying his head as if he look'd for pins in the street;
I have look'd out of my window half a year after, and have spied
that man's head upon London-bridge.[7] 'T is vile: never trust a
tailor that does not sing at his work; his mind is of nothing but
filching.

*Wife.* Mark this, George; 't is worth noting: Godfrey my
tailor, you know, never sings, and he had fourteen yards to make
this gown: and I 'll be sworn, Mistress Pennistone, the draper's
wife, had one made with twelve.

*Mer.* [*sings.*]

> 'T is mirth that fills the veins with blood,
> More than wine, or sleep, or food;
> Let each man keep his heart at ease,
> No man dies of that disease.
> He that would his body keep
> From diseases, must not weep;
> But whoever laughs and sings,
> Never he his body brings
> Into fevers, gouts, or rheums,
> Or ling'ringly his lungs consumes,
> Or meets with achés in the bone.
> Or catarrhs or griping stone;
> But contented lives for aye:
> The more he laughs, the more he may.

*Wife.* Look, George; how saist thou by this, George? Is 't not
a fine old man? — Now, God's blessing o' thy sweet lips! — When
wilt thou be so merry, George? Faith, thou art the frowning'st
little thing, when thou art angry, in a country.

*Enter Merchant [Venturewell]*

*Cit.* Peace, cony; thou shalt see him taken down too, I warrant
thee. Here 's Luce's father come now.

*Mer.* [*sings.*]

> As you came from Walsingham,
>     From that holy land,
> There met you not with my true love
>     By the way as you came?

*Vent.* Oh, Master Merrythought, my daughter 's gone!
This mirth becomes you not; my daughter 's gone!

*Mer.* [*sings.*]

> Why, an if she be, what care I?
> Or let her come, or go, or tarry.

[7] The heads of executed traitors were displayed on London Bridge.

*Vent.*   Mock not my misery; it is your son
(Whom I have made my own, when all forsook him)
Has stol'n my only joy, my child away.
   *Mer.* [*sings.*]

> He set her on a milk-white steed,
>    And himself upon a grey;
> He never turn'd his face again,
>    But he bore her quite away.

*Vent.*   Unworthy of the kindness I have shown
To thee and thine! too late I well perceive
Thou art consenting to my daughter's loss.
   *Mer.*   Your daughter! what a stir 's here wi' your daughter?
Let her go, think no more on her, but sing loud. If both my sons
were on the gallows, I would sing,

> Down, down, down they fall;
> Down, and arise they never shall.

*Vent.*   Oh, might I behold her once again,
And she once more embrace her aged sire!
   *Mer.*   Fie, how scurvily this goes! "And she once more embrace
her aged sire"? You 'll make a dog on her, will ye? She cares much
for her aged sire, I warrant you.          [*Sings.*]

> She cares not for her daddy, nor
> She cares not for her mammy,
> For she is, she is, she is, she is
> My lord of Lowgave's lassy.

*Vent.*   For this thy scorn I will pursue that son
Of thine to death.
   *Mer.*          Do; and when you ha' kill'd him,        [*Sings.*]

> Give him flowers enow, palmer, give him flowers enow;
> Give him red, and white, and blue, green, and yellow.

*Vent.*   I 'll fetch my daughter ——
   *Mer.*   I 'll hear no more o' your daughter; it spoils my mirth.
*Vent.*   I say, I 'll fetch my daughter.
   *Mer.* [*sings.*]

> Was never man for lady's sake.
>    Down, down,
> Tormented as I, poor Sir Guy,
>    De derry down,
> For Lucy's sake, that lady bright,
>    Down, down,
> As ever men beheld with eye
>    De derry down.

*Vent.*  I 'll be reveng'd, by Heaven!              *Exeunt* [*severally*].
            *Music. Finis Actus secundi*

*Wife.*  How dost thou like this, George?
*Cit.*  Why, this is well, cony; but if Ralph were hot once, thou
shouldst see more.
*Wife.*  The fiddlers go again, husband.
*Cit.*  Ay, Nell; but this is scurvy music. I gave the whoreson
gallows[8] money, and I think he has not got me the waits of South-
wark. If I hear 'em not anon, I 'll twinge him by the ears. — You
musicians, play *Baloo!*[9]
*Wife.*  No, good George, let 's ha' *Lachrymæ!*[9]
*Cit.*  Why, this is it, cony.
*Wife.*  It 's all the better, George. Now, sweet lamb, what
story is that painted upon the cloth? The Confutation[1] of St.
Paul?
*Cit.*  No, lamb; that 's Ralph and Lucrece.[2]
*Wife.*  Ralph and Lucrece! Which Ralph? Our Ralph?
*Cit.*  No, mouse; that was a Tartarian.[3]
*Wife.*  A Tartarian! Well, I would the fiddlers had done, that
we might see out Ralph again!


### *Actus Tertius. Scæna Prima.*

#### *Enter Jasper and Luce*

*Jasp.*  Come, my dear dear; though we have lost our way,
We have not lost ourselves. Are you not weary
With this night's wand'ring, broken from your rest,
And frighted with the terror that attends
The darkness of this wild unpeopled place?
*Luce.*  No, my best friend; I cannot either fear,
Or entertain a weary thought, whilst you
(The end of all my full desires) stand by me.
Let them that lose their hopes, and live to languish
Amongst the number of forsaken lovers,
Tell the long weary steps, and number time,
Start at a shadow, and shrink up their blood,
Whilst I (possess'd with all content and quiet)
Thus take my pretty love, and thus embrace him.
*Jasp.*  You have caught me, Luce, so fast, that, whilst I live,

---

[8] Rogue.                    [9] Names of popular tunes.
[1] Conversion.              [2] The Rape of Lucrece.
[3] Presumably he means a Tarquin.

I shall become your faithful prisoner,
And wear these chains for ever. Come, sit down,
And rest your body, too, too delicate
For these disturbances. — [*They sit down.*] So: will you sleep?
Come, do not be more able[4] than you are;
I know you are not skilful in these watches,
For women are no soldiers. Be not nice,[5]
But take it; sleep, I say.

*Luce.*                I cannot sleep;
Indeed, I cannot, friend.

*Jasp.*                Why, then we 'll sing,
And try how that will work upon our senses.

*Luce.*  I 'll sing, or say, or anything but sleep.

*Jasp.*  Come, little mermaid, rob me of my heart
With that enchanting voice.

*Luce.*  You mock me, Jasper.                [*They sing.*]

### Song

*Jasp.*     Tell me, dearest, what is love?
*Luce.*     'T is a lightning from above;
            'T is an arrow, 't is a fire,
            'T is a boy they call Desire;
                'T is a smile
                Doth beguile
*Jasp.*     The poor hearts of men that prove.[6]

            Tell me more, are women true?
*Luce.*     Some love change, and so do you.
*Jasp.*     Are they fair and never kind?
*Luce.*     Yes, when men turn with the wind.
*Jasp.*        Are they froward?
*Luce.*        Ever toward
            Those that love, to love anew.

*Jasp.*  Dissemble it no more; I see the god
Of heavy sleep lay on his heavy mace
Upon your eyelids.

*Luce.*                I am very heavy. [*Sleeps.*]

*Jasp.*  Sleep, sleep; and quiet rest crown thy sweet thoughts!
Keep from her fair blood distempers, startings,
Horrors, and fearful shapes! Let all her dreams
Be joys, and chaste delights, embraces, wishes,
And such new pleasures as the ravish'd soul

---

[4] Active.            [5] Reluctant.            [6] Try it.

Gives to the senses! — So; my charms have took. —
Keep her, you powers divine, whilst I contemplate
Upon the wealth and beauty of her mind!
She is only fair and constant, only kind,
And only to thee, Jasper. Oh, my joys!
Whither will you transport me? Let not fulness
Of my poor buried hopes come up together
And overcharge my spirits! I am weak.
Some say (however ill) the sea and women
Are govern'd by the moon; both ebb and flow,
Both full of changes; yet to them that know,
And truly judge, these but opinions are,
And heresies, to bring on pleasing war
Between our tempers, that without these were
Both void of after-love and present fear;
Which are the best of Cupid. Oh, thou child
Bred from despair, I dare not entertain thee,
Having a love without the faults of women,
And greater in her perfect goods than men!
Which to make good, and please myself the stronger,
Though certainly I am certain of her love,
I 'll try her, that the world and memory
May sing to after-times her constancy. —         [*Draws his sword.*]
Luce! Luce! awake!

*Luce.*              Why do you fright me, friend,
With those distemper'd looks? What makes your sword
Drawn in your hand? Who hath offended you?
I prithee, Jasper, sleep; thou art wild with watching.

*Jasp.*  Come, make your way to Heaven, and bid the world,
With all the villainies that stick upon it,
Farewell; you 're for another life.

*Luce.*                Oh, Jasper,
How have my tender years committed evil,
(Especially against the man I love)
Thus to be cropp'd untimely?

*Jasp.*                Foolish girl,
Canst thou imagine I could love his daughter,
That flung me from my fortune into nothing?
Discharged me his service, shut the doors
Upon my poverty, and scorn'd my prayers,
Sending me, like a boat without a mast,
To sink or swim? Come; by this hand you die;
I must have life and blood, to satisfy
Your father's wrongs.

*Wife.* Away, George, away! raise the watch at Ludgate, and bring a mittimus⁷ from the justice for this desperate villain! — Now, I charge you, gentlemen, see the king's peace kept! — Oh, my heart, what a varlet 's this to offer manslaughter upon the harmless gentlewoman!

*Cit.* I warrant thee, sweetheart, we 'll have him hampered.

*Luce.* Oh, Jasper, be not cruel!
If thou wilt kill me, smile, and do it quickly,
And let not many deaths appear before me.
I am a woman, made of fear and love,
A weak, weak woman; kill not with thy eyes,
They shoot me through and through. Strike, I am ready;
And, dying, still I love thee.

*Enter Merchant* [*Venturewell*], *Humphrey, and his men*

*Vent.*                                           Whereabouts?
*Jasp.* No more of this; now to myself again.      [*Aside.*]
*Hum.* There, there he stands, with sword, like martial knight,
Drawn in his hand; therefore beware the fight,
You that be wise; for, were I good Sir Bevis,
I would not stay his coming, by your leavés.
*Vent.* Sirrah, restore my daughter!
*Jasp.*                                 Sirrah, no.
*Vent.* Upon him, then!
            [*They attack Jasper, and force Luce from him.*]

*Wife.* So; down with him, down with him, down with him!
Cut him i' th' leg, boys, cut him i' th' leg!

*Vent.* Come your ways, minion:⁸ I 'll provide a cage
For you, you 're grown so tame. — Horse her away.
*Hum.* Truly, I 'm glad your forces have the day.
                                    *Exeunt. Manet Jasper.*

*Jasp.* They are gone, and I am hurt; my love is lost,
Never to get again. Oh, me unhappy!
Bleed, bleed and die! I cannot. Oh, my folly,
Thou hast betray'd me! Hope, where art thou fled?
Tell me, if thou be'st anywhere remaining,
Shall I but see my love again? Oh, no!
She will not design to look upon her butcher,
Nor is it fit she should; yet I must venter.
Oh, Chance, or Fortune, or whate'er thou art,

⁷ A warrant of commitment to prison.
⁸ Hussy.

That men adore for powerful, hear my cry.
And let me loving live, or losing die!     *Exit.*

*Wife.*   Is 'a gone, George?

*Cit.*   Ay, cony.

*Wife.*   Marry, and let him go, sweetheart. By the faith o' my body, 'a has put me into such a fright, that I tremble (as they say) as 't were an aspen-leaf. Look o' my little finger, George, how it shakes. Now, i' truth, every member of my body is the worse for 't.

*Cit.*   Come, hug in mine arms, sweet mouse; he shall not fright thee any more. Alas, mine own dear heart, how it quivers!


### [Scene II]

*Enter Mistress Merrythought, Ralph, Michael, Squire*
*[Tim], Dwarf [George], Host, and a Tapster*

*Wife.*   Oh, Ralph! how dost thou, Ralph? How hast thou slept to-night?[9] Has the knight us'd thee well?

*Cit.*   Peace, Nell; let Ralph alone.

*Tap.*   Master, the reckoning is not paid.

*Ralph.*   Right courteous knight, who, for the order's sake
Which thou hast ta'en, hang'st out the holy Bell,
As I this flaming Pestle bear about,
We render thanks to your puissant self,
Your beauteous lady, and your gentle squires,
For thus refreshing of our wearied limbs,
Stiff'ned with hard achievements in wild desert.

*Tap.*   Sir, there is twelve shillings to pay.

*Ralph.*   Thou merry Squire Tapstero, thanks to thee
For comforting our souls with double jug:[1]
And, if advent'rous fortune prick thee forth,
Thou jovial squire, to follow feats of arms,
Take heed thou tender every lady's cause,
Every true knight, and every damsel fair;
But spill the blood of treacherous Saracens,
And false enchanters that with magic spells
Have done to death full many a noble knight.

*Host.*   Thou valiant Knight of the Burning Pestle, give ear to me; there is twelve shillings to pay, and, as I am a true knight, I will not bate[2] a penny.

*Wife.*   George, I prithee, tell me, must Ralph pay twelve shillings now?

---

[9] Last night.       [1] Strong beer.       [2] Deduct.

*Cit.*  No, Nell, no; nothing but the old knight is merry with Ralph.

*Wife.*  Oh, is 't nothing else?  Ralph will be as merry as he.

*Ralph.*  Sir Knight, this mirth of yours becomes you well;
But to requite this liberal courtesy,
If any of your squires will follow arms,
He shall receive from my heroic hand
A knighthood, by the virtue of this Pestle.

*Host.*  Fair knight, I thank you for your noble offer:
Therefore, gentle knight,
Twelve shillings you must pay, or I must cap³ you.

*Wife.*  Look, George! did not I tell thee as much?  The knight of the Bell is in earnest. Ralph shall not be beholding to him: give him his money, George, and let him go snick up.

*Cit.*  Cap Ralph?  No. — Hold your hand, Sir Knight of the Bell; there 's your money [*gives money*.]: have you anything to say to Ralph now?  Cap Ralph!

*Wife.*  I would you should know it, Ralph has friends that will not suffer him to be capp'd for ten times so much, and ten times to the end of that. — Now take thy course, Ralph.

*Mist. Mer.*  Come, Michael; thou and I will go home to thy father; he hath enough left to keep us a day or two, and we 'll set fellows abroad to cry our purse and our casket: shall we, Michael?

*Mich.*  Ay, I pray, mother; in truth my feet are full of chilblains with travelling.

*Wife.*  Faith, and those chilblains are a foul trouble. Mistress Merrythought, when your youth comes home, let him rub all the soles of his feet, and his heels, and his ankles, with a mouse-skin; or, if none of your people can catch a mouse, when he goes to bed, let him roll his feet in the warm embers, and, I warrant you, he shall be well; and you may make him put his fingers between his toes, and smell to them: it 's very sovereign for his head, if he be costive.⁴

*Mist. Mer.*  Master Knight of the Burning Pestle, my son Michael and I bid you farewell: I thank your worship heartily for your kindness.

*Ralph.*  Farewell, fair lady, and your tender squire.
If pricking⁵ through these deserts, I do hear
Of any traitorous knight, who through his guile
Hath light upon your casket and your purse,
I will despoil him of them, and restore them.

*Mist. Mer.*  I thank your worship.          *Exit with Michael.*

³ Arrest.          ⁴ Constipated.          ⁵ Riding.

*Ralph.*   Dwarf, bear my shield; squire, elevate my lance: —
And now farewell, you Knight of holy Bell.

*Cit.*   Ay, ay, Ralph, all is paid.

*Ralph.*   But yet, before I go, speak, worthy knight,
If aught you do of sad adventures know,
Where errant knight may through his prowess win
Eternal fame, and free some gentle souls
From endless bonds of steel and ling'ring pain.

*Host.*   Sirrah, go to Nick the barber, and bid him prepare himself, as I told you before, quickly.

*Tap.*   I am gone, sir.                                    *Exit.*

*Host.*   Sir Knight, this wilderness affordeth none
But the great venture, where full many a knight
Hath tried his prowess, and come off with shame;
And where I would not have you lose your life,
Against no man, but furious fiend of hell.

*Ralph.*   Speak on, Sir Knight; tell what he is and where:
For here I vow, upon my blazing badge,
Never to blaze[6] a day in quietness,
But bread and water will I only eat,
And the green herb and rock shall be my couch,
Till I have quell'd that man, or beast, or fiend,
That works such damage to all errant knights.

*Host.*   Not far from hence, near to a craggy cliff,
At the north end of this distressed town,
There doth stand a lowly house,
Ruggedly builded, and in it a cave
In which an ugly giant now doth won,[7]
Ycleped Barbaroso: in his hand
He shakes a naked lance of purest steel,
With sleeves turn'd up; and him before he wears
A motley garment, to preserve his clothes
From blood of those knights which he massacres,
And ladies gent:[8] without his door doth hang
A copper basin on a prickant[9] spear;
At which no sooner gentle knights can knock,
But the shrill sound fierce Barbaroso hears,
And rushing forth, brings in the errant knight
And sets him down in an enchanted chair;
Then with an engine, which he hath prepar'd,
With forty teeth, he claws his courtly crown;

---

[6] Celebrate.              [7] Dwell.
[8] Of gentle birth.                [9] Pointing upward.

Next makes him wink, and underneath his chin
He plants a brazen piece of mighty bord.[1]
And knocks his bullets[2] round about his cheeks;
Whilst with his fingers, and an instrument
With which he snaps his hair off, he doth fill
The wretch's ears with a most hideous noise.
Thus every knight-adventurer he doth trim,
And now no creature dares encounter him.

   *Ralph.* In God's name, I will fight him. Kind sir,
Go but before me to this dismal cave,
Where this huge giant Barbaroso dwells,
And, by that virtue that brave Rosicleer[3]
That damned brood of ugly giants slew,
And Palmerin Franarco[4] overthrew,
I doubt not but to curb this traitor foul,
And to the devil send his guilty soul.

   *Host.* Brave-sprighted knight, thus far I will perform
This your request: I 'll bring you within sight
Of this most loathsome place, inhabited
By a more loathsome man; but dare not stay,
For his main force swoops all he sees away.

   *Ralph.* Saint George, set on before! March, squire and page!
           *Exeunt.*

   *Wife.* George, dost think Ralph will confound the giant?

   *Cit.* I hold my cap to a farthing he does. Why, Nell, I saw him wrastle with the great Dutchman, and hurl him.

   *Wife.* Faith, and that Dutchman was a goodly man, if all things were answerable to his bigness. And yet they say there was a Scotchman higher than he, and that they two and a knight met, and saw one another for nothing. But of all the sights that ever were in London, since I was married, methinks the little child that was so fair grown about the members was the prettiest; that and the hermaphrodite.

   *Cit.* Nay, by your leave, Nell, Ninivie[5] was better.

   *Wife.* Ninivie! Oh, that was the story of Jone and the wall,[6] was it not, George?

   *Cit.* Yes, lamb.

*Enter Mistress Merrythought*

   *Wife.* Look, George, here comes Mistress Merrythought again! and I would have Ralph come and fight with the giant. I tell you true, I long to see 't.

[1] Rim.    [2] Soap pellets.    [3] Another hero of knightly romance.
[4] A giant.    [5] A puppet play.    [6] Jonah and the whale.

*Cit.* Good Mistress Merrythought, begone, I pray you, for my sake; I pray you, forbear a little; you shall have audience presently. I have a little business.

*Wife.* Mistress Merrythought, if it please you to refrain your passion a little, till Ralph have despatch'd the giant out of the way, we shall think ourselves much bound to you. I thank you, good Mistress Merrythought.          *Exit Mistress Merrythought.*

*Enter a Boy*

*Cit.* Boy, come hither. Send away Ralph and this whoreson giant quickly.

*Boy.* In good faith, sir, we cannot; you 'll utterly spoil our play, and make it to be hiss'd; and it cost money. You will not suffer us to go on with our plot. — I pray, gentlemen, rule him.

*Cit.* Let him come now and despatch this, and I 'll trouble you no more.

*Boy.* Will you give me your hand of that?

*Wife.* Give him thy hand, George, do; and I 'll kiss him. I warrant thee, the youth means plainly.[7]

*Boy.* I 'll send him to you presently.[8]

*Wife.* [*kissing him.*] I thank you, little youth. (*Exit Boy.*) Faith, the child hath a sweet breath, George; but I think it be troubled with the worms; *carduus benedictus*[9] and mare's milk were the only thing in the world for 't. Oh, Ralph 's here, George! — God send thee good luck, Ralph!

[SCENE III]

*Enter Ralph, Host, Squire [Tim], and Dwarf [George]*

*Host.* Puissant knight, yonder his mansion is.
Lo, where the spear and copper basin are!
Behold that string, on which hangs many a tooth.
Drawn from the gentle jaw of wand'ring knights!
I dare not stay to sound;[1] he will appear.          *Exit.*

*Ralph.* O faint not, heart! Susan, my lady dear,
The cobbler's maid in Milk-street, for whose sake
I take these arms, O, let the thought of thee
Carry thy knight through all adventurous deeds;
And, in the honour of thy beauteous self,
May I destroy this monster Barbaroso! —

[7] Honestly.          [8] Immediately.
[9] A species of thistle, used medicinally.          [1] Blow a trumpet.

Knock, squire, upon the basin, till it break
With the shrill strokes, or till the giant speak.

> [*Tim knocks upon the basin.*]

#### Enter Barber

*Wife.*   O, George, the giant, the giant! —
Now, Ralph for thy life!

*Bar.*   What fond,[2] unknowing wight is this, that dares
So rudely knock at Barbaroso's cell,
Where no man comes but leaves his fleece behind?

*Ralph.*   I, traitorous caitiff, who am sent by fate
To punish all the sad enormities
Thou hast committed against ladies gent
And errant knights.  Traitor to God and men,
Prepare thyself!  This is the dismal hour
Appointed for thee to give strict account
Of all thy beastly treacherous villainies.

*Bar.*   Fool-hardy knight, full soon thou shalt aby[3]
This fond reproach: thy body will I bang;

> *He takes down his pole.*

And, lo, upon that string thy teeth shall hang!
Prepare thyself, for dead soon shalt thou be.

*Ralph.*   Saint George for me!                    *They fight.*

*Bar.*   Gargantua for me!

*Wife.*   To him, Ralph, to him! hold up the giant; set out thy
leg before, Ralph!

*Cit.*   Falsify a blow, Ralph, falsify a blow![4]  The giant lies open
on the left side.

*Wife.*   Bear 't off, bear 't off still! there, boy! —
Oh, Ralph 's almost down, Ralph 's almost down!

*Ralph.*   Susan, inspire me!  Now have up again.

*Wife.*   Up, up, up, up, up! so, Ralph! down with him, down
with him, Ralph!

*Cit.*   Fetch him o'er the hip, boy!

> [*Ralph knocks down the Barber.*]

*Wife.*   There, boy! kill, kill, kill, kill, kill, Ralph!

*Cit.*   No, Ralph; get all out of him first.

*Ralph.*   Presumptuous man, see to what desperate end
Thy treachery hath brought thee!  The just gods,
Who never prosper those that do despise them,
For all the villainies which thou hast done

---

[2] Foolish.              [3] Atone for.              [4] Feint.

To knights and ladies, now have paid thee home
By my stiff arm, a knight adventurous.
But say, vile wretch, before I send thy soul
To sad Avernus, whither it must go,
What captives holdst thou in thy sable cave?
  *Bar.*   Go in, and free them all; thou hast the day.
  *Ralph.*   Go, squire and dwarf, search in this dreadful cave,
And free the wretched prisoners from their bonds.
                              *Exeunt Squire and Dwarf.*
  *Bar.*   I crave for mercy, as thou art a knight,
And scorn'st to spill the blood of those that beg.
  *Ralph.*   Thou show'd'st no mercy, nor shalt thou have any;
Prepare thyself, for thou shalt surely die.

    *Enter Squire [Tim], leading one winking, with a basin*
                  *under his chin*

  *Tim.*   Behold, brave knight, here is one prisoner,
Whom this wild man hath used as you see.

  *Wife.*   This is the first wise word I heard the squire speak.

  *Ralph.*   Speak what thou art, and how thou hast been us'd,
That I may give him condign punishment.
  *1 Kn.*   I am a knight that took my journey post.[5]
Northward from London; and in courteous wise
This giant train'd me to his loathsome den,
Under pretence of killing of the itch;
And all my body with a powder strew'd,
That smarts and stings; and cut away my beard,
And my curl'd locks wherein were ribands tied;
And with a water wash'd my tender eyes,
(Whilst up and down about me still he skipp'd,)
Whose virtue is, that, till mine eyes be wip'd
With a dry cloth, for this my foul disgrace,
I shall not dare to look a dog i' th' face.

  *Wife.*   Alas, poor knight! — Relieve him,
Ralph; relieve poor knights, whilst you live.

  *Ralph.*   My trusty squire, convey him to the town,
Where he may find relief. — Adieu, fair knight.   *Exit Knight.*

   *Enter Dwarf [George], leading one with a patch o'er his nose*

  *George.*   Puissant Knight, of the Burning Pestle hight,
See here another wretch, whom this foul beast

[5] With speed.

Hath scorch'd and scor'd in this inhuman wise.

    *Ralph.*  Speak me thy name, and eke thy place of birth,
And what hath been thy usage in this cave.

    *2 Kn.*  I am a knight, Sir Pockhole is my name,
And by my birth I am a Londoner,
Free by my copy,[6] but my ancestors
Were Frenchmen all; and riding hard this way
Upon a trotting horse, my bones did ache;
And I, faint knight, to ease my weary limbs,
Light at this cave; when straight this furious fiend,
With sharpest instrument of purest steel,
Did cut the gristle of my nose away,
And in the place this velvet plaster stands.
Relieve me, gentle knight, out of his hands!

    *Wife.*  Good Ralph, relieve Sir Pockhole, and send him away;
for in truth his breath stinks.

    *Ralph.*  Convey him straight after the other knight. —
Sir Pockhole, fare you well.

    *2 Kn.*              Kind sir, good night.        *Exit.*
    *Man.* [*within.*]  Deliver us!        *Cries within.*
    *Woman.* [*within.*]  Deliver us!

    *Wife.*  Hark, George, what a woeful cry there is!  I think some
woman lies in there.

    *Man.* [*within.*]  Deliver us!
    *Woman.* [*within.*]  Deliver us!
    *Ralph.*  What ghastly noise is this?  Speak, Barbaroso,
Or, by this blazing steel, thy head goes off!
    *Bar.*  Prisoners of mine, whom I in diet keep.
Send lower down into the cave,
And in a tub that's heated smoking hot,
There may they find them, and deliver them.
    *Ralph.*  Run, squire and dwarf; deliver them with speed.

                                *Exeunt Squire and Dwarf.*
    *Wife.*  But will not Ralph kill this giant?  Surely I am afeard,
if he let him go, he will do as much hurt as ever he did.
    *Cit.*  Not so, mouse, neither, if he could convert him.
    *Wife.*  Ay, George, if he could convert him; but a giant is not
so soon converted as one of us ordinary people.  There's a pretty
tale of a witch, that had the devil's mark about her, (God bless us!)
that had a giant to her son, that was call'd Lob-lie-by-the-fire;
didst never hear it, George?

    [6] Enrolled as a freeman.

*Enter Squire [Tim], leading a Man, with a glass of lotion in his hand, and Dwarf [George], leading a Woman, with diet-bread and drink*

*Cit.*   Peace, Nell, here comes the prisoners.

*George.*   Here be these pined[7] wretches, manful knight,
That for these six weeks have not seen a wight.
   *Ralph.*   Deliver what you are, and how you came
To this sad cave, and what your usage was?
   *Man.*   I am an errant knight that followed arms
With spear and shield; and in my tender years
I stricken was with Cupid's fiery shaft,
And fell in love with this my lady dear,
And stole her from her friends in Turnbull-street.[8]
And bore her up and down from town to town,
Where we did eat and drink, and music hear;
Till at the length at this unhappy town
We did arrive, and coming to this cave,
This beast us caught, and put us in a tub,
Where we this two months sweat, and should have done
Another month, if you had not reliev'd us.
   *Woman.*   This bread and water hath our diet been,
Together with a rib cut from a neck
Of burned mutton: hard hath been our fare.
Release us from this ugly giant's snare!
   *Man.*   This hath been all the food we have receiv'd;
But only twice a-day, for novelty,
He gave a spoonful of this hearty broth
To each of us, through this same slender quill.   *Pulls out a syringe.*
   *Ralph.*   From this infernal monster you shall go,
That useth knights and gentle ladies so! —
Convey them hence.                    *Exeunt Man and Woman.*

*Cit.*   Cony, I can tell thee, the gentlemen like Ralph.
   *Wife.*   Ay, George, I see it well enough. — Gentlemen, I thank you all heartily for gracing my man Ralph; and I promise you, you shall see him oft'ner.

*Bar.*   Mercy, great knight! I do recant my ill,
And henceforth never gentle blood will spill.
   *Ralph.*   I give thee mercy; but yet shalt thou swear
Upon my Burning Pestle, to perform
Thy promise utter'd.
   *Bar.*   I swear and kiss.                    *[Kisses the Pestle.]*

---

[7] Starved.                    [8] A street noted for its brothels.

*Ralph.*                    Depart, then, and amend. — [*Exit Barber.*]
Come, squire and dwarf; the sun grows towards his set,
And we have many more adventures yet.                    *Exeunt.*

*Cit.*  Now Ralph is in this humour, I know he would ha' beaten
all the boys in the house, if they had been set on him.

*Wife.*  Ay, George, but it is well as it is. I warrant you, the
gentlemen do consider what it is to overthrow a giant. But, look,
George; here comes Mistress Merrythought, and her son Michael.
— Now you are welcome, Mistress Merrythought; now Ralph has
done, you may go on.

## [Scene IV]

### *Enter Mistress Merrythought and Michael*

*Mist. Mer.*  Be merry, Mick; we are at home now; where, I
warrant you, you shall find the house flung out at the windows.
[*Music within.*] Hark! hey, dogs, hey! this is the old world, i' faith,
with my husband. If I get in among 'em I 'll play 'em such a lesson,
that they shall have little list[9] to come scraping hither again. —
Why, Master Merrythought! husband! Charles Merrythought!

*Mer. within* [*appearing above, and singing.*]

> If you will sing, and dance, and laugh,
>     And hollo, and laugh again,
> And then cry, "There, boys, there!" why, then,
>     One, two, three, and four,
>     We shall be merry within this hour.

*Mist. Mer.*  Why, Charles, do you not know your own natural
wife? I say, open the door, and turn me out those mangy companions; 't is more than time that they were fellow and fellow-like
with you. You are a gentleman, Charles, and an old man, and
father of two children; and I myself, (though I say it) by my
mother's side niece to a worshipful gentleman and a conductor;[1]
he has been three times in his majesty's service at Chester, and is
now the fourth time, God bless him and his charge, upon his
journey.

*Mer.* [*sings.*]

> Go from my window, love, go;
> Go from my window, my dear!
>     The wind and the rain
>     Will drive you back again;
> You cannot be lodged here.

___

[9] Desire.                    [1] Officer.

Hark you, Mistress Merrythought, you that walk upon adventures, and forsake your husband, because he sings with never a penny in his purse; what, shall I think myself the worse? Faith, no, I 'll be merry. You come not here; here 's none but lads of mettle, lives of a hundred years and upwards; care never drunk their bloods, nor want made 'em warble "Heigh-ho, my heart is heavy."

*Mist. Mer.* Why, Master Merrythought, what am I, that you should laugh me to scorn thus abruptly? Am I not your fellow-feeler, as we may say, in all our miseries? your comforter in health and sickness? Have I not brought you children? Are they not like you, Charles? look upon thine own image, hard-hearted man! and yet for all this ——

*Mer.* [*sings.*] *within.*

> Begone, begone, my juggy, my puggy,
> Begone, my love, my dear!
> The weather is warm,
> 'T will do thee no harm:
> Thou canst not be lodged here.——

Be merry, boys! some light music, and more wine!     [*Exit above.*]

*Wife.* He 's not in earnest, I hope, George, is he?

*Cit.* What if he be, sweetheart?

*Wife.* Marry, if he be, George, I 'll make bold to tell him he 's an ingrant[2] old man to use his bed-fellow so scurvily.

*Cit.* What! how does he use her, honey?

*Wife.* Marry, come up, sir saucebox! I think you 'll take his part, will you not? Lord, how hot you are grown! You are a fine man, an you had a fine dog; it becomes you sweetly!

*Cit.* Nay, prithee, Nell, chide not; for, as I am an honest man and a true Christian grocer, I do not like his doings.

*Wife.* I cry you mercy, then, George! you know we are all frail and full of infirmities. — D' ye hear, Master Merrythought? May I crave a word with you?

*Mer. within* [*appearing above.*]     Strike up lively, lads!

*Wife.* I had not thought, in truth, Master Merrythought, that a man of your age and discretion (as I may say) being a gentle-man, and therefore known by your gentle conditions, could have used so little respect to the weakness of his wife; for your wife is your own flesh, the staff of your age, your yoke-fellow, with whose help you draw through the mire of this transitory world. Nay, she 's your own rib: and again ——

*Mer.* [*sings.*]

---

2 Ignorant?

> I come not hither for thee to teach,
> I have no pulpit for thee to preach,
> I would thou hadst kiss'd me under the breech,
>     As thou art a lady gay.

*Wife.* Marry, with a vengeance! I am heartily sorry for the poor gentlewoman: but if I were thy wife, i' faith, greybeard, i' faith ——

*Cit.* I prithee, sweet honeysuckle, be content.

*Wife.* Give me such words, that am a gentlewoman born! Hang him, hoary rascal! Get me some drink, George; I am almost molten with fretting: now, beshrew his knave's heart for it!

[Exit Citizen.]

*Mer.* Play me a light lavolta.[3] Come, be frolic. Fill the good fellows wine.

*Mist. Mer.* Why, Master Merrythought, are you disposed to make me wait here? You 'll open, I hope; I 'll fetch them that shall open else.

*Mer.* Good woman, if you will sing, I 'll give you something; if not ——            [*Sings.*]

> You are no love for me, Margaret,
> I am no love for you.—

Come aloft, boys, aloft!          [*Exit above.*]

*Mist. Mer.* Now a churl's fart in your teeth, sir! — Come, Mick, we 'll not trouble him; 'a shall not ding us i' th' teeth[4] with his bread and his broth, that he shall not. Come, boy; I 'll provide for thee, I warrant thee. We 'll go to Master Venturewell's, the merchant: I 'll get his letter to mine host of the Bell in Waltham; there I 'll place thee with the tapster: will not that do well for thee, Mick? And let me alone for that old cuckoldly knave your father; I 'll use him in his kind,[5] I warrant ye.     [*Exeunt.*]

[Re-enter Citizen with Beer]

*Wife.* Come, George, where 's the beer?

*Cit.* Here, love.

*Wife.* This old fornicating fellow will not out of my mind yet. — Gentlemen, I 'll begin to you all; and I desire more of your acquaintance with all my heart. [*Drinks.*] Fill the gentlemen some beer, George.          *Music.*

Finis Actus tertii.

---

3 A lively dance.
4 Reproach us.
5 Suitably.

### *Actus Quartus.  Scæna Prima.*

*Wife.*  Look, George, the little boy 's come again: methinks he
looks something like the Prince of Orange in his long stocking, if
he had a little harness[6] about his neck. George, I will have him
dance *Fading*.[7] — *Fading* is a fine jig, I 'll assure you, gentlemen.
— Begin, brother. — Now 'a capers, sweetheart! — Now a turn
o' th' toe, and then tumble! cannot you tumble, youth?

*Boy.*  No, indeed, forsooth.

*Wife.*  Nor eat fire?

*Boy.*  Neither.

*Wife.*  Why, then, I thank you heartily; there 's twopence to
buy you points[8] withal.

#### *Enter Jasper and Boy*

*Jasp.*  There, boy, deliver this; but do it well.   [*Gives a letter.*]
Hast thou provided me four lusty fellows,
Able to carry me? and art thou perfect
In all thy business?

*Boy.*                Sir, you need not fear;
I have my lesson here, and cannot miss it:
The men are ready for you, and what else
Pertains to this employment.

*Jasp.*                    There, my boy;
Take it, but buy no land.                   [*Gives money.*]

*Boy.*                Faith, sir, 't were rare
To see so young a purchaser. I fly,
And on my wings carry your destiny.

*Jasp.*  Go and be happy! [*Exit Boy.*] Now, my latest hope,
Forsake me not, but fling thy anchor out,
And let it hold! Stand fix'd, thou rolling stone,
Till I enjoy my dearest! Hear me, all
You powers, that rule in men, celestial!                   *Exit.*

*Wife.*  Go thy ways; thou art as crooked a sprig as ever grew
in London. I warrant him, he 'll come to some naughty end or
other; for his looks say no less: besides, his father (you know,
George) is none of the best; you heard him take me up like a
flirt-gill,[9] and sing bawdy songs upon me; but i' faith, if I live,
George ——

*Cit.*  Let me alone, sweetheart: I have a trick in my head shall

---

[6] Armor.                    [7] A jig was a combination of dance and song.
[8] Laces for tying up breeches.         [9] Hussy.

lodge him in the Arches[1] for one year, and make him sing *peccavi* ere I leave him; and yet he shall never know who hurt him neither.

*Wife.*   Do, my good George, do!

*Cit.*   What shall we have Ralph do now, boy?

*Boy.*   You shall have what you will, sir.

*Cit.*   Why, so, sir; go and fetch me him then, and let the Sophy of Persia come and christen him a child.[2]

*Boy.*   Believe me, sir, that will not do so well; 't is stale; it has been had before at the Red Bull.[3]

*Wife.*   George, let Ralph travel over great hills, and let him be very weary, and come to the King of Cracovia's[4] house, covered with velvet; and there let the king's daughter stand in her window, all in beaten gold, combing her golden locks with a comb of ivory; and let her spy Ralph, and fall in love with him, and come down to him, and carry him into her father's house; and then let Ralph talk with her.

*Cit.*   Well said, Nell; it shall be so. — Boy, let 's ha 't done quickly.

*Boy.*   Sir, if you will imagine all this to be done already, you shall hear them talk together; but we cannot present a house covered with black velvet, and a lady in beaten gold.

*Cit.*   Sir boy, let 's ha 't as you can, then.

*Boy.*   Besides, it will show ill-favouredly to have a grocer's prentice to court a king's daughter.

*Cit.*   Will it so, sir? You are well read in histories! I pray you, what was Sir Dagonet?[5]   Was not he prentice to a grocer in London?   Read the play of "the Four Prentices of London,"[6] where they toss their pikes so. I pray you, fetch him in, sir, fetch him in.

*Boy.*   It shall be done. — It is not our fault, gentlemen.

*Wife.*   Now we shall see fine doings, I warrant 'ee, George.

## [SCENE II]

*Enter Ralph and the Lady [Pompiona], Squire, and Dwarf*

*Wife.*   Oh, here they come, how prettily the King of Cracovia's daughter is dress'd!

---

[1] Ecclesiastical court which had jurisdiction in matrimonial cases.

[2] I.e., christen a child for him. Such an incident occurs in the play *The Travels of the Three English Brothers.*

[3] A London theatre which catered to popular audiences.

[4] Poland. He is called King of Moldavia in the next scene.

[5] The jester at the court of King Arthur.

[6] By Thomas Heywood.

*Cit.*   Ay, Nell, it is the fashion of that country, I warrant 'ee.

*Lady.*   Welcome, Sir Knight, unto my father's court,
King of Moldavia:[7] unto me Pompiona,
His daughter dear! But, sure, you do not like
Your entertainment, that will stay with us
No longer but a night.
    *Ralph.*           Damsel right fair.
I am on many sad adventures bound,
That call me forth into the wilderness;
Besides, my horse's back is something gall'd,
Which will enforce me ride a sober pace.
But many thanks, fair lady, be to you
For using errant knight with courtesy!
    *Lady.*   But say, brave knight, what is your name and birth?
    *Ralph.*   My name is Ralph; I am an Englishman,
As true as steel, a hearty Englishman,
And prentice to a grocer in the Strand
By deed indent,[8] of which I have one part:
But fortune calling me to follow arms,
On me this holy order I did take
Of Burning Pestle, which in all men's eyes
I bear, confounding ladies' enemies.
    *Lady.*   Oft have I heard of your brave countrymen,
And fertile soil, and store of wholesome food.
My father oft will tell me of a drink
In England found, and nipitato[9] call'd,
Which driveth all the sorrow from your hearts.
    *Ralph.*   Lady, 't is true; you need not lay your lips
To better nipitato than there is.
    *Lady.*   And of a wild fowl he will often speak,
Which powd'red[1]-beef-and-mustard called is:
For there have been great wars 'twixt us and you;
But truly, Ralph, it was not 'long of me.
Tell me then, Ralph, could you contented be
To wear a lady's favour in your shield?
    *Ralph.*   I am a knight of religious order,
And will not wear a favour of a lady's
That trusts in Antichrist and false traditions.

*Cit.*   Well said, Ralph! convert her, if thou canst.

[7] Moldavia is a province of the modern Rumania.
[8] Indenture; made in two copies, of which each signatory kept one.
[9] Strong liquor.
[1] Salted, corned.

*Ralph.*    Besides, I have a lady of my own
In merry England, for whose virtuous sake
I took these arms; and Susan is her name.
A cobbler's maid in Milk-Street; whom I vow
Ne'er to forsake whilst life and Pestle last.
  *Lady.*    Happy that cobbling dame, whoe'er she be,
That for her own, dear Ralph, hath gotten thee!
Unhappy I, that ne'er shall see the day
To see thee more, that bear'st my heart away!
  *Ralph.*    Lady, farewell; I needs must take my leave.
  *Lady.*    Hard-hearted Ralph, that ladies dost deceive!

  *Cit.*    Hark thee, Ralph: there 's money for thee [*gives money*]:
give something in the King of Cracovia's house; be not beholding
to him.

  *Ralph.*    Lady, before I go, I must remember
Your father's officers, who truth to tell,
Have been about me very diligent.
Hold up thy snowy hand, thou princely maid!
There 's twelve-pence for your father's chamberlain;
And another shilling for his cook,
For, by my troth, the goose was roasted well;
And twelve-pence for your father's horsekeeper,
For 'nointing my horse' back, and for his butter
There is another shilling.  To the maid
That wash'd my boot-hose there 's an English groat,[2]
And two-pence to the boy that wip'd my boots;
And last, fair lady, there is for yourself
Three-pence, to buy you pins at Bumbo Fair.[3]
  *Lady.*    Full many thanks; and I will keep them safe
Till all the heads be off, for thy sake, Ralph.
  *Ralph.*    Advance, my squire and dwarf!  I cannot stay.
  *Lady.*    Thou kill'st my heart in parting thus away.    *Exeunt.*

  *Wife.*    I commend Ralph yet, that he will not stoop to a Craco-
vian; there 's properer[4] women in London than any are there, I-wis.
But here comes Master Humphrey and his love again now, George.
  *Cit.*    Ay, cony; peace.

---

[2] Four pence.
[3] No fair of this name is known.
[4] Handsomer.

[Scene III]

*Enter Merchant [Venturewell], Humphrey, Luce, and*
*a Boy*

*Vent.*  Go, get you up; I will not be entreated;
And, gossip mine, I 'll keep your sure hereafter
From gadding out again with boys and unthrifts.
Come, they are women's tears; I know your fashion, —
Go, sirrah, lock her in, and keep the key
Safe as love your life.                    *Exeunt Luce and Boy.*
                      Now, my son Humphrey,
You may both rest assured of my love
In this, and reap your own desire.
    *Hum.*  I see this love you speak of, through your daughter,
Although the hole be little; and hereafter
Will yield the like in all I may or can,
Fitting a Christian and a gentleman.
    *Vent.*  I do believe you, my good son, and thank you;
For 't were an impudence to think you flattered.
    *Hum.*  It were, indeed: but shall I tell you why
I have been beaten twice about the lie.
    *Vent.*  Well, son, no more of compliment. My daughter
Is yours again: appoint the time and take her.
We 'll have no stealing for it; I myself
And some few of our friends will see you married.
    *Hum.*  I would you would, i' faith! for, be it known,
I ever was afraid to lie alone.
    *Vent.*  Some three days hence, then.
    *Hum.*                    Three days! let me see:
'T is somewhat of the most;[5] yet I agree,
Because I mean against the appointed day
To visit all my friends in new array.

*Enter Servant*

    *Serv.*  Sir, there 's a gentlewoman without would speak with
your worship.
    *Vent.*  What is she?
    *Serv.*  Sir, I ask'd her not.
    *Vent.*  Bid her come in.                    [*Exit Servant.*]

*Enter Mistress Merrythought and Michael*

    *Mist. Mer.*  Peace be to your worship!  I come as a poor suitor
to you, sir, in the behalf of this child.

---

[5] Too much.

*Vent.*   Are you not wife to Merrythought?

*Mist. Mer.*   Yes, truly. Would I had ne'er seen his eyes! He has undone me and himself and his children; and there he lives at home, and sings and hoits and revels among his drunken companions! but, I warrant you, where to get a penny to put bread in his mouth he knows not: and therefore, if it like your worship, I would entreat your letter to the honest host of the Bell in Waltham, that I may place my child under the protection of his tapster, in some settled course of life.

*Vent.*   I 'm glad the heavens have heard my prayers.  Thy hus-
    band,
When I was ripe in sorrows, laugh'd at me;
Thy son, like an unthankful wretch, I having
Redeem'd him from his fall, and made him mine,
To show his love again, first stole my daughter,
Then wrong'd this gentleman, and, last of all,
Gave me that grief had almost brought me down
Unto my grave, had not a stronger hand
Reliev'd my sorrows.  Go, and weep as I did,
And be unpitied: for I here profess
An everlasting hate to all thy name.

*Mist. Mer.*   Will you so, sir? how say you by that? — Come, Mick; let him keep his wind to cool his porridge.  We 'll go to thy nurse's, Mick: she knits silk stockings, boy; and we 'll knit too, boy, and be beholding to none of them all.  *Exeunt Michael and Mother.*

### *Enter a Boy with a letter*

*Boy.*   Sir, I take it you are the master of this house.

*Vent.*   How then, boy?

*Boy.*   Then to yourself, sir, comes this letter.

*Vent.*   From whom, my pretty boy

*Boy.*   From him that was your servant; but no more
Shall that name ever be, for he is dead:
Grief of your purchas'd[6] anger broke his heart.
I saw him die, and from his hand receiv'd
This paper, with a charge to bring it hither:
Read it, and satisfy yourself in all.

### *Letter*

*Vent.* [reads.] *Sir, that I have wronged your love I must confess; in which I have purchas'd to myself, besides mine own undoing, the ill opinion of my friends. Let not your anger, good sir, outlive me, but suffer me to rest in peace with your forgiveness: let my body*

---

6 I.e., obtained from you.

*(if a dying man may so much prevail with you) be brought to your daughter, that she may truly know my hot flames are now buried, and withal receive a testimony of the zeal I bore her virtue. Farewell for ever, and be ever happy!*                    Jasper.

God's hand is great in this. I do forgive him;
Yet I am glad he 's quiet, where I hope
He will not bite again. — Boy, bring the body,
And let him have his will, if that be all.
   *Boy.*  'T is here without, sir.
   *Vent.*                    So, sir; if you please,
You may conduct it in; I do not fear it.
   *Hum.*  I 'll be your usher, boy; for, though I say it,
He ow'd me something once, and well did pay it.        *Exeunt.*


### [Scene IV]

*Enter Luce alone*

   *Luce.*  If there be any punishment inflicted
Upon the miserable, more than yet I feel,
Let it together seize me, and at once
Press down my soul! I cannot bear the pain
Of these delaying tortures. — Thou that art
The end of all, and the sweet rest of all,
Come, come, oh, Death! bring me to thy peace,
And blot out all the memory I nourish
Both of my father and my cruel friend! —
Oh, wretched maid, still living to be wretched,
To be a say[7] to Fortune in her changes,
And grow to number times and woes together!
How happy had I been, if, being born,
My grave had been my cradle!

*Enter Servant*

   *Serv.*                    By your leave,
Young mistress; here 's a boy hath brought a coffin:
What 'a would say, I know not; but your father
Charg'd me to give you notice. Here they come.        [*Exit.*]

*Enter two bearing a Coffin, Jasper in it*

   *Luce.*  For me I hope 't is come, and 't is most welcome.
   *Boy.*  Fair mistress, let me not add greater grief

---

⁷ Test.

To that great store you have already.  Jasper
(That whilst he liv'd was yours, now dead
And here enclos'd) commanded me to bring
His body hither, and to crave a tear
From those fair eyes, (though he deserv'd not pity,)
To deck his funeral; for so he bid me
Tell her for whom he died.

    *Luce.*               He shall have many. —
Good friends, depart a little, whilst I take
My leave of this dead man, that once I lov'd.

                            *Exeunt Coffin-carrier and Boy.*

Hold yet a little, life! and then I give thee
To thy first heavenly being.  Oh, my friend!
Hast thou deceiv'd me thus, and got before me?
I shall not long be after.  But, believe me,
Thou wert too cruel, Jasper, 'gainst thyself,
In punishing the fault I could have pardon'd
With so untimely death: thou didst not wrong me,
But ever wert most kind, most true, most loving;
And I most unkind, most false, most cruel!
Didst thou but ask a tear?  I 'll give thee all,
Even all my eyes can pour down, all my sighs,
And all myself, before thou goest from me.
These are but sparing rites; but if thy soul
Be yet about this place, and can behold
And see what I prepare to deck thee with,
It shall go up, borne on the wings of peace,
And satisfied.  First will I sing thy dirge,
Then kiss thy pale lips, and then die myself,
And fill one coffin and one grave together.

### Song

Come, you whose loves are dead,
    And, whiles I sing,
    Weep, and wring
Every hand, and every head
Bind with cypress and sad yew;
Ribands black and candles blue
For him that was of men most true!

Come with heavy moaning,
    And on his grave
    Let him have
Sacrifice of sighs and groaning;
Let him have fair flowers enow,

    White and purple, green and yellow,
    For him that was of most men was true!

Thou sable cloth, sad cover of my joys,
I lift thee up, and thus I meet with death.
        [*Removes the cloth, and Jasper rises out of the coffin.*]
   *Jasp.*    And thus you meet the living.
   *Luce.*                      Save me, Heaven!
   *Jasp.*    Nay, do not fly me, fair; I am no spirit:
Look better on me; do you know me yet?
   *Luce.*    Oh, thou dear shadow of my friend!
   *Jasp.*                    Dear substance!
I swear I am no shadow; feel my hand.
It is the same it was; I am your Jasper,
Your Jasper that 's yet living, and yet loving.
Pardon my rash attempt, my foolish proof
I put in practice of your constancy;
For sooner should my sword have drunk my blood,
And set my soul at liberty, than drawn
The least drop from that body: for which boldness
Doom me to anything; if death, I take it,
And willingly.
   *Luce.*       This death I 'll give you for it.       [*Kisses him.*]
So, now I am satisfied you are no spirit,
But my own truest, truest, truest friend.
Why do you come thus to me?
   *Jasp.*               First, to see you;
Then to convey you hence.
   *Luce.*             It cannot be;
For I am lock'd up here, and watch'd at all hours,
That 't is impossible for me to 'scape.
   *Jasp.*    Nothing more possible. Within this coffin
Do you convey yourself. Let me alone:
I have the wits of twenty men about me.
Only I crave the shelter of your closet
A little, and then fear me not. Creep in,
That they may presently convey you hence:
Fear nothing, dearest love; I 'll be your second;
       [*Luce lies down in the coffin, and Jasper covers her with
                  the cloth.*]
Lie close: so; all goes well yet. — Boy!

             [*Re-enter Boy and Man*]

   *Boy.*                            At hand, sir.
   *Jasp.*    Convey away the coffin, and be wary.

*Boy.* 'T is done already.                    [*Exeunt with the coffin.*]

*Jasp.* Now I must go conjure.                    Exit [*into a closet*].

#### Enter Merchant [Venturewell]

*Vent.* Boy, boy!

*Boy.* Your servant, sir.

*Vent.* Do me this kindness, boy: — (hold, here 's a crown:) —
Before thou bury the body of this fellow, carry it to his old merry
father, and salute him from me, and bid him sing. He hath cause.

*Boy.* I will, sir.

*Vent.* And then bring me word what tune he is in,
And have another crown; but do it truly.
I have fitted him a bargain now will vex him.

*Boy.* God bless your worship's health, sir!

*Vent.* Farewell, boy!                    Exeunt [*severally*].


#### [Scene V]

#### Enter Master Merrythought

*Wife.* Ah, old Merrythought, art thou there again? Let's hear
some of thy songs.

*Mer.* [*sings.*]

> Who can sing a merrier note
> Than he that cannot change a groat?

Not a denier[8] left, and yet my heart leaps. I do wonder yet, as old
as I am, that any man will follow a trade, or serve, that may sing
and laugh, and walk the streets. My wife and both my sons are I
know not where; I have nothing left, nor know I how to come by
meat to supper; yet am I merry still, for I know I shall find it upon
the table at six o'clock. Therefore, hang thought!    [*Sings.*]

> I would not be a serving-man
> To carry the cloak-bag still,
> Nor would I be a falconer
> The greedy hawks to fill;
> But I would be in a good house,
> And have a good master too;
> But I would eat and drink of the best,
> And no work would I do.

This is it that keeps life and soul together, — mirth; this is the
philosopher's stone that they write so much on, that keeps a man
ever young.

8 Penny.

*Enter a Boy*

*Boy*.  Sir, they say they know all your money is gone, and they will trust you for no more drink.

*Mer*.  Will they not? let 'em choose! The best is, I have mirth at home, and need not send abroad for that; let them keep their drink to themselves.  [*Sings*.]

> For Jillian of Berry, she dwells on a hill,
> And she hath good beer and ale to sell,
> And of good fellows she thinks no ill;
> And thither will we go now, now now,
> And thither will we go now.
>
> And when you have made a little stay,
> You need not ask what is to pay,
> But kiss your hostess, and go your way;
> And thither will we go now, now, now,
> And thither will we go now.

*2 Boy*.  Sir, I can get no bread for supper.

*Mer*.  Hang bread and supper! Let 's preserve our mirth, and we shall never feel hunger, I 'll warrant you. Let 's have a catch; boy, follow me, come sing this catch.

> Meat, nor drink, nor money ha' we none.
> Ho, ho, nobody at home!
> Fill the pot, Eedy,[9]
> Never more need I.

*Mer*.  So, boys; enough. Follow me: let 's change our place, and we shall laugh afresh.  *Exeunt*.

*Wife*.  Let him go, George: 'a shall not have any countenance from us, nor a good word from any i' the company, if I may strike stroke[1] in 't.

*Cit*.  No more 'a sha'not, love. But, Nell, I will have Ralph do a very notable matter now, to the eternal honour and glory of all grocers. — Sirrah! you there, boy! Can none of you hear?

[*Enter Boy*]

*Boy*.  Sir, your pleasure?

*Cit*.  Let Ralph come out on May-day in the morning, and speak upon a conduit, with all his scarfs about him, and his feathers, and his rings and his knacks.

*Boy*.  Why, sir, you do not think of our plot. What will become of that, then?

*Cit*.  Why, sir, I care not what become on 't: I 'll have him come

---

[9] Edith.  [1] Have any part.

out, or I 'll fetch him out myself; I 'll have something done in honour of the city. Besides, he hath been long enough upon adventures. Bring him out quickly; or, if I come amongst you ——

*Boy.* Well, sir, he shall come out, but if our play miscarry, sir, you are likely to pay for 't.

*Cit.* Bring him away then!                                    *Exit Boy.*

*Wife.* This will be brave, i' faith! George, shall not he dance the morris too, for the credit of the Strand?

*Cit.* No, sweetheart, it will be too much for the boy. Oh, there he is, Nell! he 's reasonable well in reparel: but he has not rings enough.

*Enter Ralph [dressed as a May-lord]*

*Ralph.* London, to thee I do present the merry month of May;
Let each true subject be content to hear me what I say:
For from the top of conduit-head, as plainly may appear,
I will both tell my name to you, and wherefore I came here.
My name is Ralph, by due descent though not ignoble I,
Yet far inferior to the flock of gracious grocery;
And by the common counsel of my fellows in the Strand,
With gilded staff and crossed scarf, the May-lord here I stand.
Rejoice, oh, English hearts, rejoice! rejoice, oh, lovers dear!
Rejoice, oh, city, town, and country! rejoice, eke every Shire!
For now the fragrant flowers do spring and sprout in seemly sort,
The little birds do sit and sing, the lambs do make fine sport;
And now the birchen-tree doth bud, that makes the schoolboy cry;
The morris rings, while hobby-horse doth foot it feateously;[2]
The lords and ladies now abroad, for their disport and play,
Do kiss sometimes upon the grass, and sometimes in the hay;
Now butter with a leaf of sage is good to purge the blood;
Fly Venus and phlebotomy,[3] for they are neither good.
Now little fish on tender stone begin to cast their bellies,[4]
And sluggish snails, that erst were mew'd,[5] do creep out of their
    shellies;
The rumbling rivers now do warm, for little boys to paddle;
The sturdy steed now goes to grass, and up they hang his saddle;
The heavy hart, the bellowing buck, the rascal,[6] and the pricket,[7]
Are now among the yeoman's peas, and leave the fearful thicket:
And be like them, oh, you, I say, of this same noble town,
And lift aloft your velvet heads, and slipping off your gown,
With bells on legs, and napkins clean unto your shoulders tied,
With scarfs and garters as you please, and "Hey for our town!"
    cried,

[2] Nimbly.                    [3] Blood letting.                    [4] Spawn.
[5] Shut up.          [6] Inferior deer of a herd.          [7] Two-year-old buck.

*March out, and show your willing minds, by twenty and by twenty,*
*To Hogsden or to Newington,[8] where ale and cakes are plenty;*
*And let it ne'er be said for shame, that we the youths of London*
*Lay thrumming of our caps at home, and left our custom undone.*
*Up, then, I say, both young and old, both man and maid a-maying,*
*With drums, and guns that bounce[9] aloud, and merry tabor playing!*
*Which to prolong, God save our king, and send his country peace,*
*And root out treason from the land! and so, my friends, I cease.*

                                                  *Exit.*

### Finis Act. 4

### Actus Quintus.   Scæna Prima.

#### Enter Merchant [Venturewell], solus

*Vent.*   I will have no great store of company at the wedding; a couple of neighbours and their wives; and we will have a capon in stewed broth, with marrow, and a good piece of beef stuck with rosemary.

#### Enter Jasper, his face mealed

*Jasp.*   Forbear thy pains, fond man! it is too late.
*Vent.*   Heaven bless me! Jasper!
*Jasp.*                                  Ay, I am his ghost,
Whom thou hast injur'd for his constant love,
Fond worldly wretch! who dost not understand
In death that true hearts cannot parted be.
First know, thy daughter is quite borne away
On wings of angels, through the liquid air,
To far out of thy reach, and never more
Shalt thou behold her face: but she and I
Will in another world enjoy our loves;
Where neither father's anger, poverty,
Nor any cross that troubles earthly men,
Shall make us sever our united hearts.
And never shalt thou sit or be alone
In any place, but I will visit thee
With ghastly looks, and put into thy mind
The great offences which thou didst to me.
When thou art at thy table with thy friends,
Merry in heart, and fill'd with swelling wine,
I'll come in midst of all thy pride and mirth,

[8] Villages outside London.
[9] Boom.

Invisible to all men but thyself,
And whisper such a sad tale in thine ear
Shall make thee let the cup fall from thy hand,
And stand as mute and pale as death itself.

*Vent.*   Forgive me, Jasper! Oh, what might I do,
Tell me, to satisfy thy troubled ghost?

*Jasp.*   There is no means; too late thou think'st of this.

*Vent.*   But tell me what were best for me to do?

*Jasp.*   Repent thy deed, and satisfy my father,
And beat fond Humphrey out of thy doors.              *Exit.*

*Wife.*   Look, George; his very ghost would have folks beaten.

#### *Enter Humphrey*

*Hum.*   Father, my bride is gone, fair Mistress Luce:
My soul 's the fount of vengeance, mischief's sluice.

*Vent.*   Hence, fool, out of my sight with thy fond passion!
Thou hast undone me.                                *[Beats him.]*

*Hum.*                        Hold, my father dear,
For Luce thy daughter's sake, that had no peer!

*Vent.*   Thy father, fool! There 's some blows more; begone. —
                                                   *[Beats him.]*

Jasper, I hope thy ghost be well appeas'd
To see thy will perform'd. Now will I go
To satisfy thy father for thy wrongs.              *Exit.*

*Hum.*   What shall I do? I have been beaten twice,
And Mistress Luce is gone. Help me, device!
Since my true love is gone, I never more,
Whilst I do live, upon the sky will pore;
But in the dark will wear out my shoe-soles
In passion in Saint Faith's church under Paul's.[1]    *Exit.*

*Wife.*   George, call Ralph hither; if you love me, call Ralph
hither: I have the bravest thing for him to do, George; prithee,
call him quickly.

*Cit.*   Ralph! why, Ralph, boy!

#### *Enter Ralph*

*Ralph.*   Here, sir.

*Cit.*   Come hither, Ralph; come to thy mistress, boy.

*Wife.*   Ralph, I would have thee call all the youths together in
battle-ray, with drums, and guns, and flags, and march to Mile-End
in pompous fashion, and there exhort your soldiers to be merry and
wise, and to keep their beards from burning, Ralph; and then skir-

---

[1] See note 7 on page 109.

mish, and let your flags fly, and cry, "Kill, kill, kill!" My husband shall lend you his jerkin, Ralph, and there 's a scarf; for the rest, the house shall furnish you, and we 'll pay for 't. Do it bravely, Ralph; and think before whom you perform, and what person you represent.

*Ralph.*   I warrant you, mistress; if I do it not for the honour of the city and the credit of my master, let me never hope for freedom![2]

*Wife.*   'T is well spoken, i' faith. Go thy ways; thou art a spark indeed.

*Cit.*   Ralph, Ralph, double your files bravely, Ralph!

*Ralph.*   I warrant you, sir.                                    *Exit.*

*Cit.*   Let him look narrowly to his service;[3] I shall take him[4] else. I was there myself a pikeman once, in the hottest of the day, wench; had my feather shot sheer away, the fringe of my pike burnt off with powder, my pate broken with a scouring-stick,[5] and yet, I thank God, I am here.                        *Drum wtihin.*

*Wife.*   Hark, George, the drums!

*Cit.*   Ran, tan, tan, tan; ran, tan! Oh, wench, an thou hadst but seen little Ned of Aldgate, Drum Ned, how he made it roar again, and laid on like a tyrant, and then struck softly till the ward[6] came up, and then thundr'red again, and together we go! "Sa, sa, sa, bounce!" quoth the guns; "Courage, my hearts!" quoth the captains; "Saint George!" quoth the pikemen; and withal, here they lay, and there they lay: and yet for all this I am here, wench.

*Wife.*   Be thankful for it, George; for indeed 't is wonderful.

## [SCENE II]

*Enter Ralph and his Company, with drums and colours*

*Ralph.*   March fair, my hearts! Lieutenant, beat the rear up. — Ancient,[7] let your colours fly; but have a great care of the butchers' hooks at Whitechapel; they have been the death of many a fair ancient. — Open your files, that I may take a view both of your persons and munition. — Sergeant, call a muster.

*Serg.*   A stand! — William Hammerton, pewterer!

*Ham.*   Here, captain!

*Ralph.*   A corselet and a Spanish pike: 't is well: can you shake it with a terror?

---

[2] Membership of the Grocers' Company at the expiration of his apprenticeship.
[3] Drill.        [4] Find him out.                [5] Baton.
[6] The troops from his ward.            [7] Ensign.

*Ham.*   I hope so, captain.

*Ralph.*   Charge upon me. [*He charges on Ralph.*] — 'T is with
the weakest: put more strength, William Hammerton, more
strength. As you were again! — Proceed, Sergeant.

*Serg.*   George Greengoose, poulterer!

*Green.*   Here!

*Ralph.*   Let me see your piece,[8] neighbour Greengoose: when
was she shot in?

*Green.*   An 't like you, master captain, I made a shot even now,
partly to scour her, and partly for audacity.

*Ralph.*   It should seem so certainly, for her breath is yet in-
flamed; besides, there is a main fault in the touch-hole, it runs and
stinketh; and I tell you moreover, and believe it, ten such touch-
holes would breed the pox in the army. Get you a feather, neighbour, get you a feather, sweet oil, and paper, and your piece may do
well enough yet. Where 's your powder?

*Green.*   Here.

*Ralph.*   What, in a paper! As I am a soldier and a gentleman, it
craves a martial court! You ought to die for 't. Where 's your
horn? Answer me to that.

*Green.*   An 't like you, sir, I was oblivious.

*Ralph.*   It likes me not you should be so; 't is a shame for you,
and a scandal to all our neighbours, being a man of worth and estimation, to leave your horn behind you: I am afraid 't will breed
example. But let me tell you no more on 't. — Stand, till I view you
all. What 's become o' th' nose of your flask?

*1 Sold.*   Indeed, la, captain, 't was blown away with powder.

*Ralph.*   Put on a new one at the city's charge. — Where 's the
stone[9] of this piece?

*2 Sold.*   The drummer took it out to light tobacco.

*Ralph.*   'T is a fault, my friend; put it in again. — You want a
nose, — and you a stone. — Sergeant, take a note on 't, for I mean
to stop it in the pay. — Remove, and march! [*They march.*] Soft
and fair, gentlemen, soft and fair! Double your files! As you were!
Faces about! Now, you with the sodden face, keep in there! Look
to your match, sirrah, it will be in your fellow's flask anon. So;
make a crescent now: advance your pikes: stand and give ear! —
Gentlemen, countrymen, friends, and my fellow-soldiers, I have
brought you this day, from the shops of security and the counters
of content, to measure out in these furious fields honour by the ell,
and prowess by the pound. Let it not, oh, let it not, I say, be told
hereafter, the noble issue of this city fainted; but bear yourselves in
this fair action like men, valiant men, and free men! Fear not the

---

[8] Musket.          [9] Flint.

face of the enemy, nor the noise of the guns, for, believe me, breth-
ren, the rude rumbling of a brewer's car is far more terrible, of
which you have a daily experience. Neither let the stink of powder
offend you, since a more valiant stink is nightly with you.
To a resolved mind his home is everywhere:
I speak not this to take away
The hope of your return; for you shall see
(I do not doubt it) and that very shortly
Your loving wives again and your sweet children,
Whose care doth bear you company in baskets.
Remember, then, whose cause you have in hand,
And, like a sort[1] of true-born scavengers,
Scour me this famous realm of enemies.
I have no more to say but this: stand to your tacklings,[2] lads, and
show to the world you can as well brandish a sword as shake an
apron. Saint George, and on, my hearts!

    *Omnes.* Saint George, Saint George!              *Exeunt.*

    *Wife.* 'T was well done, Ralph! I 'll send thee a cold capon a-
field and a bottle of March beer; and, it may be, come myself to see
thee.

    *Cit.* Nell, the boy has deceived me much; I did not think it had
been in him. He has performed such a matter, wench, that, if I live,
next year I 'll have him captain of the galley-foist[3] or I 'll want my
will.

### [Scene III]

#### *Enter Old Merrythought*

    *Mer.* Yet, I thank God, I break not a wrinkle more than I had.
Not a stoop, boys! Care, live with cats; I defy thee! My heart is as
sound as an oak; and though I want drink to wet my whistle, I can
sing;                                                 *[Sings.]*

        Come no more there, boys, come no more there;
        For we shall never whilst we live come any more there.

#### *Enter a Boy, [and two Men] with a Coffin*

    *Boy.* God save you, sir!
    *Mer.* It 's a brave boy. Canst thou sing?

---

[1] Company.
[2] Hold your ground.
[3] State barge used in Lord Mayor's procession.

*Boy.* Yes, sir, I can sing; but 't is not so necessary at this time.
*Mer.* [*sings.*]

> Sing we, and chant it;
> Whilst love doth grant it.

*Boy.* Sir, sir, if you knew what I have brought you, you would
have little list to sing.
*Mer.* [*sings.*]

> Oh, the Mimon round,
> Full long, long I have thee sought,
> And now I have thee found,
> And what has thou here brought?

*Boy.* A coffin, sir, and your dead son Jasper in it.

                                                  [*Exit with Men.*]
*Mer.* Dead!                                                   [*Sings.*]

> Why, farewell he!
> Thou wast a bonny boy,
> And I did love thee.

### Enter Jasper

*Jasp.* Then, I pray you, sir, do so still.
*Mer.* Jasper's ghost!                                           [*Sings.*]

> Thou art welcome from Stygian lake so soon;
> Declare to me what wondrous things in Pluto's court are done.

*Jasp.* By my troth, sir, I ne'er came there; 't is too hot for me,
sir.
*Mer.* A merry ghost, a very merry ghost!          [*Sings.*]

> And where is your true love? Oh, where is yours?

*Jasp.* Marry, look you, sir!          *Heaves up the coffin.*
*Mer.* Ah, ha! art thou good at that, i' faith?    [*Sings.*]

> With hey, trixy, terlery-whiskin,
> The world it runs on wheels:
> When the young man's ——,
> Up goes the maiden's heels.

### Mistress Merrythought and Michael within

*Mist. Mer.* [*within.*] What, Master Merrythought! will you not
let 's in? What do you think shall become of us?
*Mer.* [*sings.*]

> What voice is that, that calleth at our door?

*Mist. Mer.* [*within.*]  You know me well enough; I am sure I
have not been such a stranger to you.

*Mer.* [*sings.*]

> And some they whistled, and some they sung,
>> Hey, down, down!
>> And some did loudly say,
> Ever as the Lord Barnet's horn blew,
>> Away, Musgrave, away!

*Mist. Mer.* [*within.*]  You will not have us starve here, will you,
Master Merrythought?

*Jasp.*  Nay, good sir, be persuaded; she is my mother.
If her offences have been great against you,
Let your own love remember she is yours,
And so forgive her.

*Luce.*          Good Master Merrythought,
Let me entreat you; I will not be denied.

*Mist. Mer.* [*within.*]  Why, Master Merrythought, will you be a
vext thing still?

*Mer.*  Woman, I take you to my love again; but you shall sing
before you enter; therefore despatch your song and so come in.

*Mist. Mer.* [*within.*]  Well, you must have your will, when all 's
done. — Mick, what song canst thou sing, boy?

*Mich.* [*within.*]  I can sing none, forsooth, but *A Lady's Daughter, of Paris properly.*

*Mist. Mer.*               Song.

> It was a lady's daughter, &c.

[*Merrythought opens the door. Enter Mistress
Merrythought and Michael*]

*Mer.*  Come, you 're welcome home again.          [*Sings.*]

> If such danger be in playing,
>> And jest must to earnest turn,
>> You shall go no more a-maying —

*Vent. within.*  Are you within, sir?  Master Merrythought!

*Jasp.*  It is my master's voice!  Good sir, go hold him
In talk, whilst we convey ourselves into
Some inward room.                    [*Exit with Luce.*]

*Mer.*          What are you?  Are you merry?
You must be very merry, if you enter.

*Vent.* [*within.*]  I am, sir.

*Mer.*  Sing, then.

*Vent.* [*within.*]  Nay, good sir, open to me.

*Mer.*   Sing, I say, or, by the merry heart, you come not in!

*Vent.* [*within.*]   Well, sir, I 'll sing.                    [*Sings.*]

Fortune, my foe, &c.

[*Merrythought opens the door. Enter Venturewell*]

*Mer.*   You are welcome, sir, you are welcome: you see your entertainment; pray you, be merry.

*Vent.*   Oh, Master Merrythought, I am come to ask you
Forgiveness for the wrongs I offer'd you
And your most virtuous son!  They 're infinite;
Yet my contrition shall be more than they:
I do confess my hardness broke his heart,
For which just Heaven hath given me punishment
More than my age can carry.  His wand'ring spirit,
Not yet at rest, pursues me everywhere,
Crying, "I 'll haunt thee for thy cruelty."
My daughter, she is gone, I know not how,
Taken invisible, and whether living
Or in grave, 't is yet uncertain to me.
Oh, Master Merrythought, these are the weights
Will sink me to my grave!  Forgive me, sir.

*Mer.*   Why, sir, I do forgive you; and be merry.
And if the wag in 's lifetime play'd the knave,
Can you forgive him too?

*Vent.*                    With all my heart, sir.

*Mer.*   Speak it again, and heartily.

*Vent.*                         I do, sir;
Now, by my soul, I do.

*Enter Luce and Jasper*

*Mer.* [*sings.*]

> With that came out his paramour;
> She was as white as the lily flower:
>    Hey, troul, troly, loly!
> With that came out her own dear knight;
> He was as true as ever did fight, &c.

Sir, if you will forgive him, clap their hands together; there 's no more to be said i' th' matter.

*Vent.*   I do, I do.

*Cit.*   I do not like this.  Peace, boys!  Hear me, one of you!
Everybody's part is come to an end but Ralph's, and he 's left out.

*Boy.*   'T is 'long of yourself, sir; we have nothing to do with his part.

*Cit.*  Ralph, come away! — Make an end on him, as you have
done of the rest, boys; come.

*Wife.*  Now, good husband, let him come out and die.

*Cit.*  He shall, Nell. — Ralph, come away quickly, and die, boy!

*Boy.*  'T will be very unfit he should die, sir, upon no occasion,
and in a comedy too.

*Cit.*  Take you no care of that, sir boy; is not his part at an end,
think you, when he 's dead? — Come away, Ralph!

*Enter Ralph, with a forked arrow through his head*

*Ralph.*  When I was mortal, this my costive corpse
Did lap up figs and raisins in the Strand;
Where sitting, I espi'd a lovely dame,
Whose master wrought with lingel[4] and with awl,
And underground he vamped many a boot.
Straight did her love prick forth me, tender sprig,
To follow feats of arms in warlike wise
Through Waltham Desert; where I did perform
Many achievements, and did lay on ground
Huge Barbaroso, that insulting giant,
And all his captives soon set at liberty.
Then honour prick'd me from my native soil
Into Moldavia, where I gain'd the love
Of Pompiona, his beloved daughter;
But yet prov'd constant to the black thumb'd maid,
Susan, and scorned Pompiona's love.
Yet liberal I was, and gave her pins,
And money for her father's officers.
I then returned home, and thrust myself
In action, and by all men chosen was
Lord of the May, where I did flourish it,
With scarfs and rings, and posy in my hand.
After this action I preferred was,
And chosen city-captain at Mile-End,
With hat and feather, and with leading-staff,
And train'd my men, and brought them all off clear,
Save one man that beray'd[5] him with the noise.
But all these things I Ralph did undertake
Only for my beloved Susan's sake.
Then coming home, and sitting in my shop
With apron blue, Death came unto my stall
To cheapen[6] *aqua vitæ;* but ere I

[4] Shoemaker's waxed thread.                    [5] Befouled.
[6] Bargain for.

Could take the bottle down and fill a taste,
Death caught a pound of pepper in his hand,
And sprinkled all my face and body o'er,
And in an instant vanished away.

*Cit.*   'T is a pretty fiction, i' faith.

*Ralph.*   Then took I up my bow and shaft in hand,
And walk'd into Moorfields to cool myself;
But there grim cruel Death met me again,
And shot this forked arrow through my head;
And now I faint; therefore be warn'd by me,
My fellows every one, of forked heads!
Farewell, all you good boys in merry London!
Ne'er shall we more upon Shrove-Tuesday meet,
And pluck down house of iniquity; — [7]
My pain increaseth — I shall never more
Hold open, whilst another pumps both legs,
Nor daub a satin gown with rotten eggs;
Set up a stake, oh, never more I shall!
I die! fly, fly, my soul, to Grocers' Hall!
Oh, oh, oh, &c.

*Wife.*   Well said, Ralph! do your obeisance to the gentlemen,
and go your ways: well said, Ralph!            *Exit Ralph.*

*Mer.*   Methinks all we, thus kindly and unexpectedly reconciled,
should not depart without a song.

*Vent.*   A good motion.

*Mer.*   Strike up, then!

### Song

> Better music ne'er was known
> Than a choir of hearts in one.
> Let each other, that hath been
> Troubled with the gall or spleen,
> Learn of us to keep his brow
> Smooth and plain, as ours are now.
> Sing, though before the hour of dying;
> He shall rise, and then be crying,
> "Hey, ho, 't is nought but mirth
> That keeps the body from the earth!"

*Exeunt omnes.*

---

[7] On Shrove Tuesday, the apprentices' holiday, they used to band together and loot the brothels.

## Epilogus

*Cit.* Come, Nell, shall we go? The play 's done.

*Wife.* Nay, by my faith, George, I have more manners than so; I 'll speak to these gentlemen first. — I thank you all, gentlemen, for your patience and countenance to Ralph, a poor fatherless child; and if I might see you at my house, it should go hard but I would have a pottle of wine and a pipe of tobacco for you: for, truly, I hope you do like the youth, but I would be glad to know the truth. I refer it to your own discretions, whether you will applaud him or no; for I will wink, and whilst[8] you shall do what you will. I thank you with all my heart. God give you good night! — Come, George.                    [*Exeunt.*]

[8] Meanwhile.

Comedy to show the folly of deviating
from society's and nature's norms.

Morose: "All discourses but mine own
          afflict me."

# EPICOENE,

## OR

# The Silent Woman.

*A Comoedie.*

Acted in the Yeere 1609. By
the Children of her Maiesties
Revells.

## The Author B. I.

Horat.

*Vt sis tu similis Cæli, Byrrhique latronum,*
*Non ego sim Capri, neque Sulci. Cur metuas me?*[1]

LONDON,
Printed by William Stansby.
M . D . C . XVI.

---

[1] Though you may be like Caelius and Byrrhus, who are robbers, I
would not be like Caprius or Sulcus, so why should you fear me?

# Epicoene

### ❧ BENJAMIN JONSON

(born 1572) was the posthumous son of a minister. He was educated under the famous William Camden at Westminster School, but, instead of going on to the university, he was taken from school to learn his stepfather's trade of bricklayer. Then for a time he served with the English forces in the Low Countries. On returning to England he became an actor for a while and by 1597 he was working as a dramatist for Henslowe. In 1598 he killed a fellow actor, Gabriel Spencer, in a duel, and in the same year he achieved his first considerable dramatic success with the play *Every Man in his Humour*. This play was performed by the Chamberlain's Men at the insistence, it is said, of Shakespeare, who took one of the leading parts in it. In 1600 and 1601 Jonson was actively engaged in the Poetomachia or War of the Theatres, and attacked Dekker and Marston in *Cynthia's Revels* and *Poetaster*. These and a number of subsequent plays were written for the boy actors. Jonson's most brilliant comedies beside the present one were *Volpone* (1606), *The Alchemist* (1610), and *Bartholomew Fair* (1614). After the accession of James I in 1603 Jonson became more and more dependent on court patronage, and wrote over thirty masques for court performance. In 1616 he received a royal pension and became in effect poet laureate. His later years were marred by a series of failures on the popular stage and quarrels with some of his former associates (especially the architect and stage designer Inigo Jones), but he maintained his self-appointed position of dictator of English letters. He died in 1637, five years before the opening of the Civil War and five years before the closing of the theatres.

"A booke called Epicoene, or the Silent Woman by Ben. Johnson" was entered on the Stationers' Register on 20 September 1610, and a quarto edition of 1612 is said to have existed, though no copy is known to have survived. The play was next printed by Jonson in the collected folio edition of his *Workes*, 1616. There it is stated that "This Comoedie was first acted in the yeere 1609, by the Children of her Maiesties Revells," and the statement is followed by a list of the actors, including Nat Field, who afterwards became a dramatist, and a disciple of Jonson. The play is said to have received some harsh criticism at the time of the original performances, largely because of supposed personal allusions in it.

Dryden recorded a tradition that Jonson had known a man who served as the model for Morose; nevertheless the editors of the standard modern edition of Jonson remark that "The main plot is an adroit combination of two Greek jests or practical jokes; both variations on the stock comic motive of the man induced to marry by false pretences. In the one a quiet-loving recluse is led to marry an inexhaustibly loquacious woman under the pretence that she is 'silent'; in the other an old voluptuary is proxy-wedded to a boy." The duel between La-Foole and Sir John Daw is obviously modeled on the duel between Viola and Sir Andrew Aguecheek in *Twelfth Night*. The most interesting borrowings in the play are to be found in Truewit's speeches in II,ii; large portions of these are adaptations of passages from Juvenal's sixth Satire, against women.

BOOKS. Jonson's *Works* have been magnificently edited by C. H. Herford and Percy and Evelyn Simpson, 11 volumes, Oxford, 1925–52. There are many critical studies of Jonson, of which the following are a selection: J. B. Bamborough, *Ben Jonson*, London, 1959; J. A. Barish, *Ben Jonson and the Language of Prose Comedy*, Cambridge, Mass., 1960; Marchette Chute, *Ben Jonson of Westminster*, New York, 1953; L. C. Knights, *Drama and Society in the Age of Jonson*, London, 1937; E. B. Partridge, *The Broken Compass, a study of the major comedies of Ben Jonson*, New York, 1958; G. Gregory Smith, *Ben Jonson*, 1919.

## The Persons of the Play

MOROSE, a Gentleman that loves no noise
[SIR] DAUPHINE EUGENIE, a Knight, his nephew
[NED] CLERIMONT, a Gentleman, his friend
TRUEWIT, another friend
EPICOENE, a young gentleman, suppos'd the Silent Woman
[SIR] JOHN DAW, a Knight, her servant
[SIR] AMOROUS LA-FOOLE, a Knight also
THOMAS OTTER, a land and sea Captain
CUTBEARD, a Barber
MUTE, one of MOROSE his servants

MADAME HAUGHTY,
MADAME CENTAURE,   } Ladies Collegiates
MISTRESS [DOL.]
  MAVIS,

MISTRESS TRUSTY,
  the LADY HAUGHTY'S
  woman,            } Pretenders
MISTRESS OTTER, the
  Captain's wife,

Parson, Pages, Servants

THE SCENE: LONDON

211

## Prologue

Truth says, of old the art of making plays  
    Was to content the people; and their praise  
    Was to the poet money, wine, and bays.  
But in this age, a sect of writers are,  
    That, only, for particular likings care,  
    And will taste nothing that is populare.  
With such we mingle neither brains nor breasts;  
    Our wishes, like to those make[2] public feasts,  
    Are not to please the cook's taste but the guests'.  
Yet, if those cunning palates hither come,  
    They shall find guests' entreaty,[3] and good room;  
    And though all relish not, sure there will be some,  
That, when they leave their seats, shall make 'em say,  
    Who wrote that piece, could so have wrote a play,  
    But that he knew this was the better way.  
For, to present all custard, or all tart,  
    And have no other meats to bear a part,  
    Or to want bread, and salt, were but coarse art.  
The poet prays you then, with better thought  
    To sit; and, when his cates[4] are all in brought,  
    Though there be none far-fet,[5] there will dear-bought,[6]  
Be fit for ladies: some for lords, knights, squires;  
    Some for your waiting-wench, and city-wires;[7]  
    Some for your men, and daughters of Whitefriars.  
Nor is it, only, while you keep your seat  
    Here, that his feast will last; but you shall eat  
    A week at ord'naries,[8] on his broken meat:  
        If his muse be true,  
        Who commends her to you.

[2] Those who make.  
[3] Entertainment.  
[4] Dainties.  
[5] Fetched from abroad.  
[6] Costly.  
[7] Citizens' wives who aped the fashions.  
[8] Restaurants.

## Another

*Occasion'd by some person's impertinent exception*

The ends of all, who for the scene do write,
   Are, or should be, to profit and delight.
And still 't hath been the praise of all best times,
   So persons were not touch'd, to tax the crimes.[9]
Then, in this play, which we present tonight,
   And make the object of your ear and sight,
On forfeit of yourselves, think nothing true:
   Lest so you make the maker to judge you.
For he knows, poet never credit gain'd
   By writing truths, but things, like truths, well feign'd.
If any yet will, with particular sleight
   Of application, wrest what he doth write;
And that he meant, or him, or her, will say:
   They make a libel, which he made a play.

[9] Denounce abuses.

## Act I.  Scene I

### Clerimont, Boy, [later] Truewit

[*Cler.*]  Ha' you got the song yet perfect, I ga' you, boy?

*Boy.*  Yes, sir.                    *He comes out making himself ready.*

*Cler.*  Let me hear it.

*Boy.*  You shall, sir; but i' faith let nobody else.

*Cler.*  Why, I pray?

*Boy.*  It will get you the dangerous name of a poet in town, sir; besides me a perfect deal of ill-will at the mansion you wot of, whose lady is the argument[1] of it; where now I am the welcom'st thing under a man that comes there.

*Cler.*  I think; and above a man too, if the truth were rack'd out of you.

*Boy.*  No, faith, I 'll confess before, sir.  The gentlewomen play with me, and throw me o' the bed, and carry me in to my lady: and she kisses me with her oil'd face, and puts a peruke[2] o' my head; and asks me an I will wear her gown? and I say no: and then she hits me a blow o' the ear, and calls me innocent, and lets me go.

*Cler.*  No marvel if the door be kept shut against your master, when the entrance is so easy to you —— well, sir, you shall go there no more, lest I be fain to seek your voice in my lady's rushes,[3] a fortnight hence. Sing, sir.                    *Boy sings.*

### [Enter Truewit]

*True.*  Why, here 's the man that can melt away his time and never feels it! What between his mistress abroad and his ingle[4] at home, high fare, soft lodging, fine clothes, and his fiddle; he thinks the hours ha' no wings, or the day no post-horse. Well, sir gallant, were you struck with the plague this minute, or condemn'd to any capital punishment tomorrow, you would begin then to think, and value every article o' your time, esteem it at the true rate, and give all for 't.

*Cler.*  Why, what should a man do?

*True.*  Why, nothing; or that which, when 'tis done, is as idle. Hearken after the next horse-race, or hunting-match, lay wagers, praise Puppy, or Peppercorn, White-foot, Franklin;[5] swear upon Whitemane's party; spend aloud, that my lords may hear you; visit my ladies at night, and be able to give 'em the character of

---

[1] Subject.                    [2] Wig.                    [3] Strewn on the floor.
[4] Boy.                    [5] Names of race horses.

every bowler or better o' the green. These be the things wherein
your fashionable men exercise themselves, and I for company.

*Cler.* Nay, if I have thy authority, I 'll not leave[6] yet. Come,
the other are considerations, when we come to have gray heads and
weak hams, moist eyes and shrunk members. We 'll think on 'em
then; then we 'll pray and fast.

*True.* Ay, and destine only that time of age to goodness, which
our want of ability will not let us employ in evil!

*Cler.* Why, then 't is time enough.

*True.* Yes; as if a man should sleep all the term,[7] and think to
effect his business the last day. O' Clerimont, this time, because it
is an incorporeal thing, and not subject to sense, we mock ourselves
the fineliest out of it, with vanity and misery indeed! not seeking
an end of wretchedness, but only changing the matter still.

*Cler.* Nay, thou 'lt not leave now —

*True.* See but our common disease![8] with what justice can we
complain, that great men will not look upon us, nor be at leisure
to give our affairs such dispatch as we expect, when we will never
do it to ourselves? nor hear, nor regard ourselves?

*Cler.* Foh! thou hast read Plutarch's *Morals*, now, or some such
tedious fellow; and it shows so vilely with thee! 'fore God, 't will
spoil thy wit utterly. Talk me of pins, and feathers, and ladies,
and rushes, and such things: and leave this Stoicity[9] alone, till thou
mak'st sermons.

*True.* Well, sir; if it will not take, I have learn'd to lose as
little of my kindness as I can; I 'll do good to no man against his
will, certainly. When were you at the college?

*Cler.* What college?

*True.* As if you knew not!

*Cler.* No, faith, I came but from court yesterday.

*True.* Why, is it not arriv'd there yet, the news? A new
foundation, sir, here i' the town, of ladies, that call themselves the
Collegiates, an order between courtiers and countrymadams, that
live from their husbands; and give entertainment to all the wits,
and braveries[1] o' the time, as they call 'em: cry down, or up, what
they like or dislike in a brain or a fashion, with most masculine, or
rather hermaphroditical authority; and every day gain to their college some new probationer.

*Cler.* Who is the president?

*True.* The grave and youthful matron, the lady Haughty.

*Cler.* A pox of her autumnal face, her piec'd beauty! there 's
no man can be admitted till she be ready, now-a-days, till she has
painted, and perfum'd, and wash'd, and scour'd, but the boy, here;

---

[6] Leave off.              [7] Term during which the law courts sat.
[8] Fault.        [9] Stoicism.        [1] Gallants.

and him she wipes her oil'd lips upon, like a sponge. I have made a song (I pray thee hear it) o' the subject.    [*Boy sings.*]

### Song

Still to be neat, still to be dress'd,
As you were going to a feast;
Still to be powder'd, still perfum'd;
Lady, it is to be presumed,
Though art's hid causes are not found,
All is not sweet, all is not sound.

Give me a look, give me a face,
That makes simplicity a grace;
Robes loosely flowing, hair as free:
Such sweet neglect more taketh me,
Than all th' adulteries[2] of art;
They strike mine eyes, but not my heart.

*True.*    And I am clearly o' the other side: I love a good dressing before any beauty o' the world. O, a woman is then like a delicate garden; nor is there one kind of it; she may vary every hour; take often counsel of her glass, and choose the best. If she have good ears, show 'em; good hair, lay it out; good legs, wear short clothes; a good hand, discover it often: practise any art to mend breath, cleanse teeth, repair eye-brows; paint, and profess it.

*Cler.*    How! publicly?

*True.*    The doing of it, not the manner: that must be private. Many things that seem foul i' the doing, do please done. A lady should, indeed, study her face, when we think she sleeps; nor, when the doors are shut, should men be enquiring; all is sacred within, then. Is it for us to see their perukes put on, their false teeth, their complexion, their eyebrows, their nails? You see gilders will not work, but inclos'd.[3] They must not discover how little serves, with the help of art, to adorn a great deal. How long did the canvas hang afore Aldgate? Were the people suffer'd to see the city's Love and Charity,[4] while they were rude stone, before they were painted and burnish'd? No. No more should servants[5] approach their mistresses, but when they are complete and finish'd.

*Cler.*    Well said, my Truewit.

*True.*    And a wise lady will keep a guard always upon the place, that she may do things securely. I once followed a rude fellow into a chamber, where the poor madam, for haste, and troubled, snatch'd at her peruke to cover her baldness; and put it on the wrong way.

---

[2] Adulteration.                  [3] Unless shut up.
[4] Two statues decorating Aldgate, one of the gates in old London wall.
[5] Lovers.

*Cler.* O prodigy!

*True.* And the unconscionable knave held her in compliment an hour with that revers'd face, when I still[6] look'd when she should talk from the t'other side.

*Cler.* Why, thou shouldst ha' reliev'd her.

*True.* No, faith, I let her alone, as we 'll let this argument, if you please, and pass to another. When saw you Dauphine Eugenie?

*Cler.* Not these three days. Shall we go to him this morning? he is very melancholic, I hear.

*True.* Sick o' the uncle, is he? I met that stiff piece of formality, his uncle, yesterday, with a huge turban of night-caps on his head, buckled over his ears.

*Cler.* O, that 's his custom when he walks abroad. He can endure no noise, man.

*True.* So I have heard. But is the disease so ridiculous in him as it is made? They say he has been upon divers treaties with the fish-wives and orange-women;[7] and articles propounded between them: marry, the chimney-sweepers will not be drawn in.

*Cler.* No, nor the broom-men: they stand out stiffly. He cannot endure a costard-monger,[8] he swoons if he hear one.

*True.* Methinks a smith should be ominous.

*Cler.* Or any hammer-man. A brasier is not suffer'd to dwell in the parish, nor an armourer. He would have hang'd a pewterer's prentice once upon a Shrove-Tuesday's riot,[9] for being o' that trade, when the rest were quit.

*True.* A trumpet should fright him terribly, or the hautboys.

*Cler.* Out of his senses. The waits of the city[1] have a pension of him not to come near that ward. This youth practis'd on him one night like the bell-man;[2] and never left till he had brought him down to the door with a long sword; and there left him flourishing with the air.

*Boy.* Why, sir, he hath chosen a street to lie in so narrow at both ends, that it will receive no coaches, nor carts, nor any of these common noises: and therefore we that love him devise to bring him in such as we may, now and then, for his exercise, to breathe him. He would grow resty[3] else in his ease: his virtue would rust without action. I entreated a bearward,[4] one day, to come down with the dogs of some four parishes that way, and I thank him he did; and cried his games under master Morose's windore:[5] till he was sent crying away, with his head made a most bleeding spectacle to the multitude. And, another time, a

---

[6] All the time.                    [7] Who cried their wares through the streets.
[8] Seller of fruits.                [9] See note 7 on p. 204.
[1] Street musicians.                [2] Night watchman who carried a bell.
[3] Lazy.              [4] Keeper of a tame bear.              [5] Window.

fencer, marching to his prize,[6] had his drum most tragically run through, for taking that street in his way at my request.

*True.*    A good wag! How does he for the bells?[7]

*Cler.*    O, i' the Queen's time, he was wont to go out of town every Saturday at ten o'clock, or on holy day eves. But now, by reason of the sickness,[8] the perpetuity of ringing[9] has made him devise a room, with double walls and treble ceilings; the windores close shut and caulk'd: and there he lives by candlelight. He turn'd away a man, last week, for having a pair of new shoes that creak'd. And this fellow waits on him now in tennis-court socks, or slippers sol'd with wool: and they talk each to other in a trunk.[1] See, who comes here!

## Act I.  Scene II

### Dauphine, Truewit, Clerimont

[*Daup.*]    How now! what ail you, sirs? dumb?

*True.*    Struck into stone, almost, I am here, with tales o' thine uncle. There was never such a prodigy heard of.

*Daup.*    I would you would once lose this subject, my masters, for my sake. They are such as you are, that have brought me into that predicament I am with him.

*True.*    How is that?

*Daup.*    Marry, that he will disinherit me; no more. He thinks, I and my company are authors of all the ridiculous Acts and Monuments[2] are told of him.

*True.*    'Slid, I would be the author of more to vex him; that purpose deserves it: it gives thee law of plaguing him. I 'll tell thee what I would do. I would make a false almanack, get it printed; and then ha' him drawn out on a coronation day to the Tower-wharf,[3] and kill him with the noise of the ordnance. Disinherit thee! he cannot, man. Art not thou next of blood, and his sister's son?

*Daup.*    Ay, but he will thrust me out of it, he vows, and marry.

*True.*    How! that 's a more[4] portent. Can he endure no noise, and will venture on a wife?

*Cler.*    Yes: why thou art a stranger, it seems, to his best trick, yet. He has employ'd a fellow this half year all over England to

---

[6] Match, contest.            [7] Church bells.            [8] Plague.
[9] Tolling for the dead.            [1] Speaking tube.
[2] The actual title of John Fox's famous "Book of Martyrs."
[3] Where the artillery fired a salute.            [4] Greater, more serious.

hearken him out a dumb woman; be she of any form, or any quality, so she be able to bear children: her silence is dowry enough, he says.

*True.* But I trust to God he has found none.

*Cler.* No; but he has heard of one that 's lodg'd i' the next street to him, who is exceedingly soft-spoken; thrifty of her speech; that spends but six words a day. And her he 's about now, and shall have her.

*True.* Is 't possible! who is his agent i' the business?

*Cler.* Marry, a barber, one Cutbeard; an honest fellow, one that tells Dauphine all here.

*True.* Why you oppress me with wonder: a woman, and a barber, and love no noise!

*Cler.* Yes, faith. The fellow trims him silently, and has not the knack with his shears or his fingers: and that continence in a barber he thinks so eminent a virtue, as it has made him chief of his counsel.

*True.* Is the barber to be seen, or the wench?

*Cler.* Yes, that they are.

*True.* I prithee, Dauphine, let 's go thither.

*Daup.* I have some business now: I cannot, i' faith.

*True.* You shall have no business shall make you neglect this, sir: we 'll make her talk, believe it; or, if she will not, we can give out at least so much as shall interrupt the treaty; we will break it. Thou art bound in conscience, when he suspects thee without cause, to torment him.

*Daup.* Not I, by any means. I 'll give no suffrage to 't. He shall never ha' that plea against me, that I oppos'd the least phant'sy of his. Let it lie upon my stars[5] to be guilty, I 'll be innocent.

*True.* Yes, and be poor, and beg; do, innocent: when some groom of his has got him an heir, or this barber, if he himself cannot. Innocent! — I pray thee, Ned, where lies she? let him be innocent still.

*Cler.* Why, right over against the barber's; in the house where Sir John Daw lies.

*True.* You do not mean to confound me!

*Cler.* Why?

*True.* Does he that would marry her know so much?

*Cler.* I cannot tell.

*True.* 'T were enough of imputation to her[6] with him.

*Cler.* Why?

*True.* The only talking sir i' th' town! Jack Daw! and he

---

[5] Even though it is my fate.
[6] A sufficient accusation against her.

teach her not to speak! — God be wi' you. I have some business too.

*Cler.* Will you not go thither, then?

*True.* Not with the danger to meet Daw, for mine ears.

*Cler.* Why, I thought you two had been upon very good terms.

*True.* Yes, of keeping distance.

*Cler.* They say, he is a very good scholar.

*True.* Ay, and he says it first. A pox on him, a fellow that pretends only to learning, buys titles, and nothing else of books in him!

*Cler.* The world reports him to be very learned.

*True.* I am sorry the world should so conspire to belie him.

*Cler.* Good faith, I have heard very good things come from him.

*True.* You may; there 's none so desperately ignorant to deny that: would they were his own! God be wi' you, gentlemen.

[*Exit hastily.*]

*Cler.* This is very abrupt!

### Act I. Scene III
#### Dauphine, Clerimont, Boy

[*Daup.*] Come, you are a strange open man, to tell everything thus.

*Cler.* Why, believe it, Dauphine, Truewit 's a very honest fellow.

*Daup.* I think no other: but this frank nature of his is not for secrets.

*Cler.* Nay, then, you are mistaken, Dauphine: I know where he has been well trusted, and discharg'd the trust very truly, and heartily.

*Daup.* I contend not, Ned; but with the fewer a business is carried, it is ever the safer. Now we are alone, if you 'll go thither, I am for you.

*Cler.* When were you there?

*Daup.* Last night: and such a Decameron of sport fallen out! Boccace never thought of the like. Daw does nothing but court her; and the wrong way. He would lie with her, and praises her modesty; desires that she would talk and be free, and commends her silence in verses; which he reads, and swears are the best that ever man made. Then rails at his fortunes, stamps, and mutines,[7] why he is not made a counsellor, and call'd to affairs of state.

---

[7] Rebels.

*Cler.* I pray thee, let 's go. I would fain partake this. — Some water, boy.                                    [*Exit Boy.*]

*Daup.* We are invited to dinner together, he and I, by one that came thither to him, Sir La-Foole.

*Cler.* O, that 's a precious mannikin!

*Daup.* Do you know him?

*Cler.* Ay, and he will know you too, if e'er he saw you but once, though you should meet him at church in the midst of prayers. He is one of the braveries, though he be none o' the wits. He will salute a judge upon the bench, and a bishop in the pulpit, a lawyer when he is pleading at the bar, and a lady when she is dancing in a masque, and put her out. He does give plays, and suppers, and invites his guests to 'em, aloud, out of his windore, as they ride by in coaches. He has a lodging in the Strand for the purpose. Or to watch when ladies are gone to the china-houses,[8] or the Exchange, that he may meet 'em by chance, and give 'em presents, some two or three hundred pounds' worth of toys, to be laugh'd at. He is never without a spare banquet,[9] or sweet-meats in his chamber, for their women to alight at, and come up to for a bait.[1]

*Daup.* Excellent! he was a fine youth last night; but now he is much finer! what is his christen-name? I ha' forgot.

### [*Enter Boy*]

*Cler.* Sir Amorous La-Foole.

*Boy.* The gentleman is here below that owns that name.

*Cler.* 'Heart, he 's come to invite me to dinner, I hold my life.

*Daup.* Like enough: pray thee, let 's ha' him up.

*Cler.* Boy, marshal him.

*Boy.* With a truncheon,[2] sir?

*Cler.* Away, I beseech you. [*Exit Boy.*] — I 'll make him tell us his pedigree now; and what meat he has to dinner; and who are his guests; and the whole course of his fortunes; with a breath.

## *Act I.  Scene IIII*

### *La-Foole, Clerimont, Dauphine*

[*La-F.*] 'Save, dear Sir Dauphine! honour'd master Clerimont!

*Cler.* Sir Amorous! you have very much honested my lodging with your presence.

---

[8] Shops selling oriental wares.
[9] A course of sweetmeats, wine, and fruit.
[1] Refreshment.                    [2] Marshal's staff.

*La-F.* Good faith, it is a fine lodging: almost as delicate a lodging as mine.

*Cler.* Not so, sir.

*La-F.* Excuse me, sir, if it were i' the Strand, I assure you. I am come, master Clerimont, to entreat you wait upon two or three ladies, to dinner, to-day.

*Cler.* How, sir! wait upon 'em? did you ever see me carry dishes?

*La-F.* No, sir, dispense with[3] me; I meant, to bear 'em company.

*Cler.* O, that I will, sir: the doubtfulness o' your phrase, believe it, sir, would breed you a quarrel once an hour, with the terrible boys, if you should but keep 'em fellowship a day.

*La-F.* It should be extremely against my will, sir, if I contested with any man.

*Cler.* I believe it, sir. Where hold you your feast?

*La-F.* At Tom Otter's, sir.

*Daup.* Tom Otter! what 's he?

*La-F.* Captain Otter, sir; he is a kind of gamester, but he has had command both by sea and by land.

*Daup.* O, then he is *animal amphibium?*

*La-F.* Ay, sir: his wife was the rich china-woman, that the courtiers visited so often; that gave the rare entertainment. She commands all at home.

*Cler.* Then she is Captain Otter.

*La-F.* You say very well, sir; she is my kinswoman, a La-Foole by the mother-side, and will invite any great ladies for my sake.

*Daup.* Not of the La-Fooles of Essex?

*La-F.* No, sir, the La-Fooles of London.

*Cler.* [*Aside.*]  Now, h' is in.

*La-F.* They all come out of our house, the La-Fooles o' the north, the La-Fooles of the west, the La-Fooles of the east and south — we are as ancient a family as any is in Europe — but I myself am descended lineally of the French La-Fooles — and, we do bear for our coat[4] yellow, or *or*, checker'd *azure*, and *gules*,[5] and some three or four colours more, which is a very noted coat, and has, sometimes, been solemnly worn by divers nobility of our house — but let that go, antiquity is not respected now. — I had a brace of fat does sent me, gentlemen, and half a dozen of pheasants, a dozen or two of godwits,[6] and some other fowl, which I would have eaten, while they are good, and in good company: — there will be a great lady or two, my lady Haughty, my lady Centaure,

---

[3] Excuse.                    [4] Coat of arms.
[5] Red.                       [6] Marsh birds.

mistress Dol Mavis — and they come o' purpose to see the silent
gentlewoman, mistress Epicœne, that honest Sir John Daw has
promis'd to bring thither — and then, mistress Trusty, my lady's
woman, will be there too, and this honourable knight, Sir Dauphine, with yourself, master Clerimont — and we 'll be very merry,
and have fiddlers, and dance. — I have been a mad wag in my time,
and have spent some crowns since I was a page in court, to my
lord Lofty, and after, my lady's gentleman-usher, who got me
knighted in Ireland, since it pleas'd my elder brother to die. — I
had as fair a gold jerkin on that day, as any worn in the Island
Voyage,[7] or at Caliz,[8] none disprais'd: and I came over in it hither,
show'd myself to my friends in court, and after went down to my
tenants in the country, and survey'd my lands, let new leases, took
their money, spent it in the eye o' the land[9] here, upon ladies: —
and now I can take up[1] at my pleasure.

*Daup.*   Can you take up ladies, sir?

*Cler.*   O, let him breathe, he has not recover'd.

*Daup.*   Would I were your half in that commodity![2]

*La-F.*   No, sir, excuse me: I meant money, which can take up
anything. I have another guest or two, to invite, and say as much
to, gentlemen. I 'll take my leave abruptly, in hope you will not
fail —— Your servant.                                    [*Exit.*]

*Daup.*   We will not fail you, sir precious La-Foole; but she shall,
that your ladies come to see, if I have credit afore Sir Daw.

*Cler.*   Did you ever hear such a wind-sucker,[3] as this?

*Daup.*   Or such a rook as the other, that will betray his mistress
to be seen! Come, 't is time we prevented it.

*Cler.*   Go.                                           [*Exeunt.*]


### Act II.   Scene 1

#### Morose, Mute

[*Mor.*]   Cannot I, yet, find out a more compendious[4] method,
than by this trunk,[5] to save my servants the labour of speech, and
mine ears the discord of sounds?  Let me see: all discourses but mine
own afflict me; they seem harsh, impertinent, and irksome.  Is it not

---

[7] Against the Azores, in 1597.
[8] Cadiz, attacked and captured by the English fleet in 1596.
[9] London.         [1] Borrow.
[2] Would I were half as successful as you with the ladies!
[3] A species of hawk.              [4] Economical.
[5] Speaking tube.

possible, that thou should'st answer me by signs, and I apprehend
thee, fellow? Speak not, though I question you. You have taken
the ring off from the street door, as I bade you? Answer me not by
speech, but by silence; unless it be otherwise [*Mute makes a leg.*[6]]
— Very good. And you have fastened on a thick quilt, or flock-bed,
on the outside of the door; that if they knock with their daggers,
or with brick-bats, they can make no noise? — But[7] with your leg,
your answer, unless it be otherwise [*makes a leg.*] — Very good.
This is not only fit modesty in a servant, but good state and discretion in a master. And you have been with Cutbeard the barber,
to have him come to me? [*makes a leg.*] — Good. And, he will
come presently? Answer me not but with your leg, unless it be
otherwise; if it be otherwise, shake your head, or shrug [*makes a
leg.*] — So! Your Italian and Spaniard are wise in these: and it is a
frugal and comely gravity. How long will it be ere Cutbeard come?
Stay; if an hour, hold up your whole hand, if half an hour, two
fingers; if a quarter, one; [*holds up a finger bent.*] — Good: half a
quarter? 'tis well. And have you given him a key, to come in without knocking? [*makes a leg.*] — Good. And is the lock oil'd, and
the hinges, to-day? [*makes a leg.*] — Good. And the quilting of
the stairs nowhere worn out and bare? [*makes a leg.*] — Very
good. I see, by much doctrine, and impulsion,[8] it may be effected;
stand by. The Turk, in this divine discipline, is admirable, exceeding all the potentates of the earth; still waited on by mutes; and
all his commands so executed; yea, even in the war, as I have heard,
and in his marches, most of his charges and directions given by
signs, and with silence: an exquisite art! and I am heartily asham'd,
and angry oftentimes, that the princes of Christendom should suffer
a barbarian to transcend 'em in so high a point of felicity. I will
practise it hereafter. (*One winds a horn without.*) — How now?
oh! oh! what villain, what prodigy of mankind is that? look.    [*Exit
Mute.*] (*Again.*) — Oh! cut his throat, cut his throat! what mur-
derer, hell-hound, devil can this be?

[*Enter Mute*]

*Mute.* It is a post from the court —
*Mor.* Out, rogue! and must thou blow thy horn too?
*Mute.* Alas, it is a post from the court, sir, that says, he must
speak with you, pain of death —
*Mor.* Pain of thy life, be silent!

---

[6] Bow.
[7] Only.
[8] Instruction and compulsion.

## *Act II.  Scene II*

### *Truewit, Morose, [later] Cutbeard*

[*True.*]  By your leave, sir; — I am a stranger here: — Is your name master Morose? is your name master Morose? Fishes! Pythagoreans[9] all! This is strange. What say you, sir? nothing! Has Harpocrates[1] been here with his club, among you? Well, sir, I will believe you to be the man at this time. I will venture upon you, sir. Your friends at court commend 'em to you, sir —

*Mor.* [*Aside.*]  O men! O manners! was there ever such an impudence?

*True.*  And are extremely solicitous for you, sir.

*Mor.*  Whose knave[2] are you?

*True.*  Mine own knave, and your compeer, sir.

*Mor.*  Fetch me my sword —

*True.*  You shall taste the one half of my dagger, if you do, groom; and you the other, if you stir, sir: Be patient, I charge you, in the king's name, and hear me without insurrection. They say, you are to marry; to marry! do you mark, sir?

*Mor.*  How then, rude companion!

*True.*  Marry, your friends do wonder, sir, the Thames being so near, wherein you may drown so handsomely; or London-bridge, at a low fall,[3] with a fine leap, to hurry you down the stream; or, such a delicate steeple i' the town, as Bow,[4] to vault from; or a braver height, as Paul's. Or, if you affected to do it nearer home, and a shorter way, an excellent garret-windore into the street; or, a beam in the said garret, with this halter (*He shows him a halter.*) — which they have sent, and desire, that you would sooner commit your grave head to this knot, than to the wedlock noose; or, take a little sublimate,[5] and go out of the world like a rat; or a fly, as one said, with a straw i' your arse: any way, rather than to follow this goblin Matrimony. Alas, sir, do you ever think to find a chaste wife in these times? now? when there are so many masques, plays, Puritan preachings, mad folks, and other strange sights to be seen daily, private and public? If you had liv'd in King Etheldred's time, sir, or Edward the Confessor's,[6] you might perhaps have found in some cold country hamlet, then, a dull frosty

---

[9] Noted because they kept silence about their beliefs.
[1] Horus, Egyptian god of silence.
[2] Servant.
[3] Flow of the ebb tide under the bridge.
[4] The church of St. Mary-le-Bow.
[5] Arsenic.
[6] I.e., before the Norman Conquest.

wench, would have been contented with one man: now, they will as soon be pleas'd with one leg, or one eye. I'll tell you, sir, the monstrous hazards you shall run with a wife.

*Mor.* Good sir, have I ever cozen'd[7] any friends of yours of their land? bought their possessions? taken forfeit of their mortgage? begg'd a reversion[8] from[9] 'em? bastarded their issue? What have I done, that may deserve this

*True.* Nothing, sir, that I know, but your itch of marriage.

*Mor.* Why, if I had made an assassinate[1] upon your father, vitiated[2] your mother, ravished your sisters —

*True.* I would kill you, sir, I would kill you, if you had.

*Mor.* Why, you do more in this, sir: it were a vengeance centuple, for all facinorous[3] acts that could be nam'd, to do that[4] you do.

*True.* Alas, sir, I am but a messenger: I but tell you, what you must hear. It seems your friends are careful after your soul's health, sir, and would have you know the danger: (but you may do your pleasure for all them, I persuade not, sir.) If, after you are married, your wife do run away with a vaulter, or the Frenchman that walks upon ropes, or him that dances the jig, or a fencer for his skill at his weapon; why it is not their fault, they have discharged their consciences, when you know what may happen. Nay, suffer valiantly, sir, for I must tell you all the perils that you are obnoxious[5] to. If she be fair, young and vegetous,[6] no sweetmeats ever drew more flies; all the yellow doublets and great roses[7] i' the town will be there. If foul and crooked, she'll be with them, and buy those doublets and roses, sir. If rich, and that you marry her dowry, not her, she'll reign in your house as imperious as a widow. If noble, all her kindred will be your tyrants. If fruitful, as proud as May, and humorous[8] as April; she must have her doctors, her midwives, her nurses, her longings every hour; though it be for the dearest morsel of man. If learned, there was never such a parrot; all your patrimony will be too little for the guests that must be invited to hear her speak Latin and Greek; and you must lie with her in those languages too, if you will please her. If precise,[9] you must feast all the silenc'd brethren,[1] once in three days; salute the sisters; entertain the whole family, or wood[2] of 'em; and hear long-winded exercises, singings and catechizings, which you are not

---

[7] Cheated.    [8] Right of succession to an office.

[9] Away from.    [1] Murderous attack.    [2] Debauched.

[3] Criminal.    [4] What.    [5] Liable.

[6] Active.    [7] I.e., gallants. Roses were ornaments on shoes.

[8] Changeable.    [9] Puritanical.

[1] Puritan clergy who had been deprived of their licenses to preach.

[2] Crowd.

given to, and yet must give for; to please the zealous matron your wife, who for the holy cause, will cozen you over and above. You begin to sweat, sir! but this is not half, i' faith: you may do your pleasure, notwithstanding, as I said before: I come not to persuade you. (*The Mute is stealing away.*) — Upon my faith, master serving-man, if you do stir, I will beat you.

*Mor.* O, what is my sin! what is my sin!

*True.* Then, if you love your wife, or rather dote on her, sir; O, how she 'll torture you, and take pleasure i' your torments! you shall lie with her but when she lists; she will not hurt her beauty, her complexion; or it must be for that jewel, or that pearl, when she does: every half hour's pleasure must be bought anew, and with the same pain and charge you woo'd her at first. Then you must keep what servants she please; what company she will; that friend must not visit you without her license; and him she loves most, she will seem to hate eagerliest, to decline[3] your jealousy; or feign to be jealous of you first; and for that cause go live with her she-friend, or cousin at the college, that can instruct her in all the mysteries of writing letters, corrupting servants, taming spies; where she must have that rich gown for such a great day; a new one for the next; a richer for the third; be serv'd in silver;[4] have the chamber fill'd with a succession of grooms, footmen, ushers, and other messengers; besides embroiderers, jewellers, tire-women,[5] semp-sters, feathermen, perfumers; while she feels not how the land drops away, nor the acres melt; nor forsees the change when the mercer has your woods for her velvets; never weighs what her pride costs, sir; so she may kiss a page, or a smooth chin, that has the despair of a beard: be a stateswoman, know all the news, what was done at Salisbury, what at the Bath, what at court, what in progress;[6] or, so she may censure[7] poets and authors, and styles, and compare 'em; Daniel with Spenser, Jonson with the t' other youth, and so forth; or be thought cunning in controversies, or the very knots of divinity; and have often in her mouth the state of the question;[8] and then skip to the mathematics, and demonstration: and answer in religion to one, in state to another, in bawdry to a third.

*Mor.* O, O!

*True.* All this is very true, sir. And then her going in disguise to that conjurer, and this cunning woman:[9] where the first question is, how soon you shall die? next, if her present servant[1] love her? next that, if she shall have a new servant? and how many? which of

---

[3] Avert.  [4] I.e., silver dishes.  [5] Dressmakers.
[6] Official journey of the sovereign through the provinces.
[7] Pass judgment on.  [8] A cant phrase.
[9] Fortune teller.  [1] Lover.

her family would make the best bawd, male or female? what precedence she shall have by her next match? and sets down the answers, and believes 'em above the scriptures. Nay, perhaps she 'll study the art.

*Mor.*    Gentle sir, ha' you done? ha' you had your pleasure o' me? I 'll think of these things.

*True.*    Yes, sir: and then comes reeking home of vapour and sweat, with going afoot, and lies in a month of a new face, all oil and birdlime; and rinses in asses' milk, and is cleans'd with a new fucus:[2] God be wi' you, sir. One thing more, which I had almost forgot. This too, with whom you are to marry, may have made a conveyance of her virginity aforehand, as your wise widows do of their states, before they marry, in trust to some friend, sir. Who can tell? Or if she have not done it yet, she may do, upon the wedding-day, or the night before, and antedate you cuckold. The like has been heard of in nature. 'T is no devis'd, impossible thing, sir.   God be wi' you: I 'll be bold to leave this rope with you, sir, for a remembrance. — Farewell, Mute!                    [*Exit.*]

*Mor.*    Come, ha' me to my chamber: but first shut the door. (*The horn again.*)   O, shut the door, shut the door! is he come again?

### [*Enter Cutbeard*]

*Cut.*    'T is I, sir, your barber.

*Mor.*    O, Cutbeard, Cutbeard, Cutbeard! here has been a cut-throat with me: help me in to my bed, and give me physic with thy counsel.                    [*Exeunt.*]

## Act II.   Scene III
### *Daw, Clerimont, Dauphine, Epicœne*

[*Daw.*]   Nay, and she will, let her refuse at her own charges;[3] 't is nothing to me, gentlemen: but she will not be invited to the like feasts or guests every day.

*Cler.*    O, by no means, she may not refuse — to stay at home, if you love your reputation. 'Slight, you are invited thither o' purpose to be seen, and laugh'd at by the lady of the college, and her shadows.[4] This trumpeter hath proclaim'd you. (*They dissuade her privately.*)

*Daup.*    You shall not go; let him be laugh'd at in your stead, for

---

[2] Cosmetic.                    [3] And bear the expense.
[4] Friends brought along by a guest.

not bringing you: and put him to his extemporal faculty of fooling
and talking loud, to satisfy the company.          [*Aside to Epi.*]

*Cler.*   He will suspect us; talk aloud. — Pray, mistress Epicœne,
let 's see your verses; we have Sir John Daw's leave; do not conceal your servant's merit, and your own glories.

*Epi.*   They 'll prove my servant's glories, if you have his leave so
soon.

*Daup.*   His vain-glories, lady!

*Daw.*   Show 'em, show 'em, mistress; I dare own 'em.

*Epi.*   Judge you, what glories.

*Daw.*   Nay, I 'll read 'em myself too: an author must recite
his own works. It is a madrigal of Modesty.

> *Modest and fair, for fair and good are near Neigh-*
> *bours, howe'er. —*

*Daup.*   Very good.

*Cler.*   Ay, is 't not?

*Daw.*   *No noble virtue ever was alone,*
>            *But two in one.*

*Daup.*   Excellent!

*Cler.*   That again, I pray, Sir John.

*Daup.*   It has something in 't like rare wit and sense.

*Cler.*   Peace.

*Daw.*   *No noble virtue ever was alone,*
>            *But two in one.*
> *Then, when I praise sweet modesty, I praise*
>            *Bright beauty's rays:*
> *And having prais'd both beauty and modestee,*
>            *I have prais'd thee.*

*Daup.*   Admirable!

*Cler.*   How it chimes, and cries tink i' the close, divinely!

*Daup.*   Ay, 't is Seneca.

*Cler.*   No, I think 't is Plutarch.

*Daw.*   The dor on[5] Plutarch and Seneca! I hate it: they are mine
own imaginations, by that light. I wonder those fellows have such
credit with gentlemen.

*Cler.*   They are very grave authors.

*Daw.*   Grave asses! mere essayists: a few loose sentences, and
that 's all. A man would talk so his whole age: I do utter as good
things every hour, if they were collected and observ'd, as either of
'em.

*Daup.*   Indeed, Sir John!

*Cler.*   He must needs; living among the wits and braveries too.

*Daup.*   Ay, and being president of 'em, as he is.

---

[5] To hell with.

*Daw.* There 's Aristotle, a mere commonplace fellow; Plato, a discourser; Thucydides and Livy, tedious and dry; Tacitus, an entire knot; sometimes worth the untying, very seldom.

*Cler.* What do you think of the poets, Sir John?

*Daw.* Not worthy to be nam'd for authors. Homer, an old tedious prolix ass, talks of curriers[6] and chines[7] of beef; Vergil of dunging of land, and bees;[8] Horace, of I know not what.

*Cler.* I think so.

*Daw.* And so, Pindarus, Lycophron, Anacreon, Catullus, Seneca the tragedian, Lucan, Propertius, Tibullus, Martial, Juvenal, Ausonius, Statius, Politian, Valerius Flaccus, and the rest —

*Cler.* What a sackfull of their names he has got!

*Daup.* And how he pours 'em out! Politian with Valerius Flaccus!

*Cler.* Was not the character[9] right of him

*Daup.* As could be made, i' faith.

*Daw.* And Persius, a crabbed coxcomb, not to be endur'd.

*Daup.* Why, whom do you account for authors, Sir John Daw?

*Daw.* *Syntagma juris civilis; Corpus juris civilis; Corpus juris canonici;*[1] the King of Spain's Bible —

*Daup.* Is the king of Spain's Bible an author?

*Cler.* Yes, and Syntagma.

*Daup.* What was that Syntagma, sir?

*Daw.* A civil lawyer, a Spaniard.

*Daup.* Sure, Corpus was a Dutchman.

*Cler.* Ay, both the Corpuses, I knew 'em: they were very corpulent authors.

*Daw.* And then there 's Vatablus, Pomponatius, Symancha:[2] the other are not to be receiv'd, within the thought of a scholar.

*Daup.* 'Fore God, you have a simple learn'd servant, lady, — in titles.                                                    [*Aside.*]

*Cler.* I wonder that he is not called to the helm, and made a counsellor.

*Daup.* He is one extraordinary.

*Cler.* Nay, but in ordinary: to say truth, the state wants such.

*Daup.* Why, that will follow.

*Cler.* I muse a mistress can be so silent to the dotes[3] of such a servant.

*Daw.* 'T is her virtue, sir. I have written somewhat of her silence too.

*Daup.* In verse, Sir John?

---

[6] Leather dressers.                    [7] The cut along the backbone.
[8] In his *Georgics.*                    [9] Description.
[1] Compilation of civil law; corpus of civil law; corpus of canon law.
[2] Writers and scholars of the sixteenth century.
[3] Good qualities.

*Cler.* What else?

*Daup.* Why, how can you justify your own being of a poet, that so slight all the old poets?

*Daw.* Why, every man that writes in verse is not a poet; you have of the wits that write verses, and yet are no poets: they are poets that live by it, the poor fellows that live by it.

*Daup.* Why, would not you live by your verses, Sir John?

*Cler.* No, 't were pity he should. A knight live by his verses! he did not make 'em to that end, I hope.

*Daup.* And yet the noble Sidney lives by his, and the noble family not asham'd.

*Cler.* Ay, he profess'd[4] himself; but Sir John Daw has more caution: he 'll not hinder his own rising i' the state so much. Do you think he will? Your verses, good Sir John, and no poems.

*Daw.* Silence in women, is like speech in man;
　　　　Deny 't who can.

*Daup.* Not I, believe it: your reason, sir.

*Daw.* 　　Nor is 't a tale,
　　That female vice should be a virtue male,
　　Or masculine vice a female virtue be:
　　　　You shall it see
　　　　Prov'd with increase;
　　I know to speak, and she to hold her peace.
Do you conceive me, gentlemen

*Daup.* No, faith; how mean you "with increase," Sir John?

*Daw.* Why, with increase is, when I court her for the common cause of mankind, and she says nothing, but *consentire videtur*;[5] and in time is *gravida*.[6]

*Daup.* Then this is a ballad of procreation?

*Cler.* A madrigal of procreation; you mistake.

*Epi.* Pray give me my verses again, servant.

*Daw.* If you 'll ask 'em aloud, you shall.

*Cler.* See, here 's Truewit again!

　　　　　　　　　　[*Walks aside with the papers.*]


## Act II.　Scene IIII

*Clerimont, Truewit, Dauphine, [later] Cutbeard, Daw,*
*Epicœne*

[*Cler.*] Where hast thou been, in the name of madness, thus accoutred with thy horn?

*True.* Where the sound of it might have pierc'd your senses

---

[4] Openly acknowledged.　　[5] Seems to consent.　　[6] Pregnant.

with gladness, had you been in ear-reach of it. Dauphine, fall down and worship me; I have forbid the bans, lad: I have been with thy virtuous uncle, and have broke the match.

*Daup.*   You ha' not, I hope.

*True.*   Yes, faith; and thou shouldst hope otherwise, I should repent me: this horn got me entrance; kiss it. I had no other way to get in, but by feigning to be a post;[7] but when I got in once, I prov'd none, but rather the contrary, turn'd him into a post, or a stone, or what is stiffer, with thund'ring into him the incommodities of a wife, and the miseries of marriage. If ever Gorgon were seen in the shape of a woman, he hath seen her in my description: I have put him off o' that scent for ever. — Why do you not applaud and adore me, sirs? Why stand you mute? Are you stupid? You are not worthy o' the benefit.

*Daup.*   Did not I tell you? Mischief! —

*Cler.*   I would you had plac'd this benefit somewhere else.

*True.*   Why so?

*Cler.*   'Slight, you have done the most inconsiderate, rash, weak thing, that ever man did to his friend.

*Daup.*   Friend! if the most malicious enemy I have had studied to inflict an injury upon me, it could not be a greater.

*True.*   Wherein, for God's sake? Gentlemen, come to yourselves again.

*Daup.*   But I presag'd thus much afore to you.

*Cler.*   Would my lips had been solder'd when I spake on 't! 'Slight, what mov'd you to be thus impertinent?[8]

*True.*   My masters, do not put on this strange face to pay my courtesy; off with this vizor. Have good turns done you, and thank 'em this way!

*Daup.*   'Fore heaven, you have undone me. That which I have plotted for, and been maturing now these four months, you have blasted in a minute. Now I am lost, I may speak. This gentlewoman was lodg'd here by me o' purpose, and, to be put upon my uncle, hath profess'd this obstinate silence for my sake; being my entire friend, and one that for the requital of such a fortune as to marry him, would have made me very ample conditions; where now, all my hopes are utterly miscarried by this unlucky accident.

*Cler.*   'Thus 't is when a man will be ignorantly officious, do services, and not know his why; I wonder what courteous itch possess'd you. You never did[9] absurder part i' your life, nor a greater trespass to friendship, to humanity.

*Daup.*   Faith, you may forgive it best; 't was your cause principally.

*Cler.*   I know it; would it had not.

---

[7] Messenger.          [8] Behave so unsuitably.          [9] Played.

*[Enter Cutbeard]*

*Daup.*   How now, Cutbeard! what news?

*Cut.*   The best, the happiest that ever was, sir. There has been a mad gentleman with your uncle this morning, *[seeing Truewit.]* — I think this be the gentleman — that has almost talk'd him out of his wits, with threat'ning him from marriage —

*Daup.*   On, I pray thee.

*Cut.*   And your uncle, sir, he thinks 't was done by your procurement; therefore he will see the party you wot of presently;[1] and if he like her, he says, and that she be so inclining to dumb as I have told him, he swears he will marry her to-day, instantly, and not defer it a minute longer.

*Daup.*   Excellent! beyond our expectation!

*True.*   Beyond your expectation! By this light, I knew it would be thus.

*Dap.*   Nay, sweet Truewit, forgive me.

*True.*   No, I was "ignorantly officious, impertinent;" this was the "absurd, weak part."

*Cler.*   Wilt thou ascribe that to merit now, was mere fortune!

*True.*   Fortune! mere providence. Fortune had not a finger in 't. I saw it must necessarily in nature fall out so: my genius is never false to me in these things. Show me how it could be otherwise.

*Daup.*   Nay, gentlemen, contend not; 't is well now.

*True.*   Alas, I let him go on with "inconsiderate," and "rash," and what he pleas'd.

*Cler.*   Away, thou strange justifier of thyself, to be wiser than thou wert, by the event![2]

*True.*   Event! by this light, thou shalt never persuade me, but I foresaw it as well as the stars themselves.

*Daup.*   Nay, gentlemen, 't is well now. Do you two entertain Sir John Daw with discourse, while I send her away with instructions.

*True.*   I 'll be acquainted with her first, by your favour.

*Cler.*   Master Truewit, lady, a friend of ours.

*True.*   I am sorry I have not known you sooner, lady, to celebrate this rare virtue of your silence.

*[Exeunt Daup, Epi., and Cutbeard.]*

*Cler.*   Faith, an you had come sooner, you should ha' seen and heard her well celebrated in Sir John Daw's madrigals.

*True.*   *[Advances to Daw.]* Jack Daw, God save you! when saw you La-Foole?

*Daw.*   Not since last night, master Truewit.

---

[1] At once.                    [2] Result.

*True.*  That 's a miracle! I thought you two had been inseparable.

*Daw.*  He 's gone to invite his guests.

*True.*  Gods so! 't is true! What a false memory have I towards that man! I am one: I met him e'en now, upon that he calls his delicate, fine, black horse, rid into a foam, with posting from place to place, and person to person, to give 'em the cue —

*Cler.*  Lest they should forget?

*True.*  Yes: there was never poor captain took more pains at a muster[3] to show[4] men, than he, at this meal, to show friends.

*Daw.*  It is his quarter-feast, sir.

*Cler.*  What! do you say so, Sir John?

*True.*  Nay. Jack Daw will not be out, at the best friends he has, to the talent of his wit. Where 's his mistress, to hear and applaud him? Is she gone?

*Daw.*  Is mistress Epicœne gone?

*Cler.*  Gone afore, with Sir Dauphine, I warrant, to the place.

*True.*  Gone afore! That were a manifest injury, a disgrace and a half; to refuse him at such a festival-time as this, being a bravery, and a wit too!

*Cler.*  Tut, he 'll swallow it like cream: he 's better read in *Jure civili*, than to esteem anything a disgrace, is offer'd him from a mistress.

*Daw.*  Nay, let her e'en go; she shall sit alone, and be dumb in her chamber a week together, for John Daw, I warrant her. Does she refuse me?

*Cler.*  No, sir, do not take it so to heart; she does not refuse you, but a little neglect you. Good faith, Truewit, you were to blame, to put it into his head, that she does refuse him.

*True.*  She does refuse him, sir, palpably, however you mince it. An I were as he, I would swear to speak ne'er a word to her to-day for 't.

*Daw.*  By this light, no more I will not.

*True.*  Nor to anybody else, sir.

*Daw.*  Nay, I will not say so, gentlemen.

*Cler.* [*Aside.*]  It had been an excellent happy condition for the company, if you could have drawn him to it.

*Daw.*  I 'll be very melancholic, i' faith.

*Cler.*  As a dog, if I were as you, Sir John.

*True.*  Or a snail, or a hog-louse: I would roll myself up for this day; in troth, they should not unwind me.

*Daw.*  By this pick-tooth,[5] so I will.

*Cler.*  'T is well done. He begins already to be angry with his teeth.

---

[3] Parade.          [4] Show off.          [5] Toothpick.

*Daw.*  Will you go, gentlemen?

*Cler.*  Nay, you must walk alone, if you be right melancholic, Sir John.

*True.*  Yes, sir, we 'll dog you, we 'll follow you afar off.

[*Exit Daw.*]

*Cler.*  Was there ever such a two yards of knighthood measur'd out by time, to be sold to laughter?

*True.*  A mere talking mole, hang him! no mushroom was ever so fresh. A fellow so utterly nothing, as he knows not what he would be.

*Cler.*  Let 's follow him: but first let 's go to Dauphine, he 's hovering about the house to hear what news.

*True.*  Content.                    [*Exeunt.*]

## Act II.  Scene V

### *Morose, Epicœne, Cutbeard, Mute*

[*Mor.*]  Welcome, Cutbeard! draw near with your fair charge: and in her ear softly entreat her to unmask. [*Epi. takes off her mask.*] — So! Is the door shut? [*Mute makes a leg.*] — Enough. Now, Cutbeard, with the same discipline I use to my family, I will question you. As I conceive, Cutbeard, this gentlewoman is she you have provided, and brought, in hope she will fit me in the place and person of a wife? Answer me not but with your leg, unless it be otherwise. [*Cut. makes a leg.*] — Very well done, Cutbeard. I conceive, besides, Cutbeard, you have been pre-acquainted with her birth, education, and qualities, or else you would not prefer⁶ her to my acceptance, in the weighty consequence of marriage. This I conceive, Cutbeard. Answer me not but with your leg, unless it be otherwise. [*Cutbeard bows again.*] — Very well done, Cutbeard. Give aside now a little, and leave me to examine her condition, and aptitude to my affection. (*He goes about her and views her.*) — She is exceeding fair, and of a special good favour;⁷ a sweet composition or harmony of limbs; her temper of beauty has the true height of my blood. The knave hath exceedingly well fitted me without: I will now try her within. — Come near, fair gentlewoman; let not my behaviour seem rude, though unto you, being rare,⁸ it may haply appear strange. (*She curtsies.*) Nay, lady, you may speak, though Cutbeard and my man might not; for of all sounds, only the sweet voice of a fair

---

⁶ Offer.                    ⁷ Appearance.                    ⁸ Strange to it.

lady has the just length of[9] mine ears. I beseech you, say, lady;
out of the first fire of meeting eyes, they say, love is stricken: do
you feel any such motion suddenly shot into you, from any part
you see in me? ha, lady? (*Curtsy.*) — Alas, lady, these answers
by silent curtsies from you are too courtless[1] and simple. I have
ever had my breeding in court; and she that shall be my wife,
must be accomplished with courtly and audacious ornaments. Can
you speak, lady?

  *Epi.* Judge you, forsooth.             *She speaks softly.*

  *Mor.* What say you, lady? Speak out, I beseech you.

  *Epi.* Judge you, forsooth.

  *Mor.* O' my judgment, a divine softness! But can you naturally,
lady, as I enjoin these by doctrine and industry,[2] refer yourself to
the search of my judgment, and, not taking pleasure in your
tongue, which is a woman's chiefest pleasure, think it plausible to
answer me by silent gestures, so long as my speeches jump right
with[3] what you conceive? (*Curtsy.*) — Excellent! divine! if it
were possible she should hold out thus! — Peace, Cutbeard, thou
art made for ever, as thou hast made me, if this felicity have lasting: but I will try her further. Dear lady, I am courtly, I tell you,
and I must have mine ears banqueted with pleasant and witty con-
ferences, pretty girds,[4] scoffs, and dalliance in her that I mean to
choose for my bed-pheere.[5] The ladies in court think it a most
desperate impair[6] to their quickness of wit, and good carriage, if
they cannot give occasion for a man to court 'em; and when an
amorous discourse is set on foot, minister as good matter to continue it, as himself. And do you alone so much differ from all
them, that what they, with so much circumstance,[7] affect and toil
for, to seem learn'd, to seem judicious, to seem sharp and con-
ceited,[8] you can bury in yourself with silence, and rather trust your
graces to the fair conscience[9] of virtue, than to the world's or
your own proclamation?

  *Epi.* [*Softly.*] I should be sorry else.

  *Mor.* What say you, lady? good lady, speak out.

  *Epi.* I should be sorry else.

  *Mor.* That sorrow doth fill me with gladness. O Morose, thou
mayest contain thyself. I will only put her to it once more, and it
shall be with the utmost touch and test of their sex. But hear me,
fair lady; I do also love to see her whom I shall choose for my
heifer, to be the first and principal in all fashions, precede all the

---

[9] Is properly attuned to.         [1] Uncourtly.
[2] By instruction and practice.     [3] Agree with.
[4] Taunts.        [5] Bed-fellow.       [6] Impairment.
[7] Formality.        [8] Clever.       [9] Consciousness.

dames at court by a fortnight, have her council of tailors, lineners, lace-women, embroiderers: and sit with 'em sometimes twice a day upon French intelligences,[1] and then come forth varied like nature, or oftener than she, and better by the help of art, her emulous servant. This do I affect: and how will you be able, lady, with this frugality of speech, to give the manifold but necessary instructions, for that bodice, these sleeves, those skirts, this cut, that stitch, this embroidery, that lace, this wire, those knots, that ruff, those roses, this girdle, that fan, the t' other scarf, these gloves? Ha! what say you, lady?

*Epi.* [*Softly.*]  I 'll leave it to you, sir.

*Mor.*  How, lady? pray you, rise a note.

*Epi.*  I leave it to wisdom and you, sir.

*Mor.*  Admirable creature! I will trouble you no more: I will not sin against so sweet a simplicity. Let me now be bold to print on those divine lips the seal of being mine. — Cutbeard, I give thee the lease of thy house free; thank me not but with thy leg. [*Cutbeard makes a leg.*] — I know what thou wouldst say: she 's poor, and her friends deceased. She has brought a wealthy dowry in her silence, Cutbeard; and in respect of her poverty, Cutbeard, I shall have her more loving and obedient, Cutbeard. Go thy ways, and get me a minister presently, with a soft low voice, to marry us; and pray him he will not be impertinent,[2] but brief as he can; away: softly, Cutbeard. [*Exit Cut.*] — Sirrah, conduct your mistress into the dining-room, your now-mistress. [*Exit Mute, followed by Epi.*] — O my felicity! how I shall be reveng'd on mine insolent kinsman, and his plots to fright me from marrying! This night I will get an heir, and thrust him out of my blood, like a stranger. He would be knighted, forsooth, and thought by that means to reign over me; his title must do it: No, kinsman, I will now make you bring me the tenth lord's and the sixteenth lady's letter, kinsman; and it shall do you no good, kinsman. Your knighthood itself shall come on its knees, and it shall be rejected; it shall be sued for its fees to execution,[3] and not be redeem'd; it shall cheat at the twelvepenny ordinary,[4] it[5] knighthood, for its diet, all the term-time, and tell tales for it in the vacation to the hostess; or it knighthood shall do worse, take sanctuary in Coleharbour,[6] and fast. It shall fright all it friends with borrowing letters; and when one of the fourscore hath brought it knighthood

---

[1] News.                        [2] Irrelevant.

[3] Right up to the service of the writ of seizure.

[4] Restaurant where the table d'hote was twelve pence, or one shilling.

[5] Its.

[6] A sanctuary for debtors, where they were free from arrest.

ten shillings, it knighthood shall go to the Cranes, or the Bear at the Bridge-foot,[7] and be drunk in fear; it shall not have money to discharge one tavern-reckoning, to invite the old creditors to forbear it knighthood, or the new, that should be, to trust it knighthood. It shall be the tenth name in the bond to take up the commodity[8] of pipkins and stone-jugs: and the part thereof shall not furnish it knighthood forth for the attempting of a baker's widow, a brown baker's[9] widow. It shall give it knighthood's name for a stallion, to all gamesome citizens' wives, and be refus'd, when the master of a dancing-school, or How-do-you-call him, the worst reveller in the town, is taken: it shall want clothes, and by reason of that, wit, to fool to lawyers. It shall not have hope to repair itself by Constantinople, Ireland, or Virginia;[1] but the best and last fortune to it knighthood shall be to make Dol Tear-sheet, or Kate Common a lady, and so it knighthood may eat.    [*Exit.*]

## Act II.  Scene VI

### *Truewit, Dauphine, Clerimont, [later] Cutbeard*

[*True.*]    Are you sure he is not gone by?

*Daup.*  No, I stay'd in the shop ever since.

*Cler.*  But he may take the other end of the lane.

*Daup.*  No, I told him I would be here at this end: I appointed him[2] hither.

*True.*  What a barbarian it is to stay, then!

*Daup.*  Yonder he comes.

*Cler.*  And his charge left behind him, which is a very good sign, Dauphine.

### [*Enter Cutbeard*]

*Daup.*  How now, Cutbeard! succeeds it, or no?

*Cut.*  Past imagination, sir, *omnia secunda;*[3] you could not have pray'd to have had it so well. *Saltat senex,*[4] as it is i' the proverb; he does triumph in his felicity, admires the party! He has given me the lease of my house too! and I am now going for a silent minister to marry 'em, and away.

---

[7] Well-known London taverns.

[8] Goods forced on borrowers instead of a cash loan.

[9] Baker of cheap bread.

[1] Three places being opened up to trade or settlement by merchant companies.

[2] Arranged for him to come.

[3] Everything favorable.

[4] The old man jumps for joy.

*True.* 'Slight! get one o' the silenc'd ministers; a zealous brother would torment him purely.[5]

*Cut.* *Cum privilegio,*[6] sir.

*Daup.* O, by no means; let 's do nothing to hinder it now: when 't is done and finished, I am for you, for any device of vexation.

*Cut.* And that shall be within this half hour, upon my dexterity, gentlemen. Contrive what you can in the mean time, *bonis avibus.*[7]

[*Exit.*]

*Cler.* How the slave doth Latin it!

*True.* It would be made a jest to posterity, sirs, this day's mirth, if ye will.

*Cler.* Beshrew his heart that will not, I pronounce.

*Daup.* And for my part. What is 't?

*True.* To translate[8] all La-Foole's company, and his feast hither, to-day, to celebrate this bride-ale.[9]

*Daup.* Ay, marry; but how will 't be done?

*True.* I 'll undertake the directing of all the lady-guests thither, and then the meat must follow.

*Cler.* For God's sake, let 's effect it; it will be an excellent comedy of affliction, so many several noises.

*Daup.* But are they not at the other place, already, think you?

*True.* I 'll warrant you for the college-honours: one o'their faces has not the priming colour laid on yet, nor the other her smock sleek'd.[1]

*Cler.* O, but they 'll rise earlier than ordinary to a feast.

*True.* Best go see, and assure ourselves.

*Cler.* Who knows the house?

*True.* I 'll lead you. Were you never there yet?

*Daup.* Not I.

*Cler.* Nor I.

*True.* Where ha' you liv'd then? not know Tom Otter!

*Cler.* No: for God's sake, what is he?

*True.* An excellent animal, equal with your Daw or La-Foole, if not transcendent; and does Latin it as much as your barber. He is his wife's subject; he calls her princess, and at such times as these follows her up and down the house like a page, with his hat off, partly for heat, partly for reverence. At this instant he is marshalling of his bull, bear, and horse.

*Daup.* What be those, in the name of Sphinx?

*True.* Why, sir, he has been a great man at the Bear-garden[2]

[5] Altogether, completely.                    [6] With authority.
[7] The omens (literally, birds) being favorable.          [8] Bring across.
[9] Wedding feast.              [1] Ironed.
[2] Arena on the south bank of the Thames, near the theatres, where bear-baitings were held.

in his time; and from that subtle sport has ta'en the witty denomination[3] of his chief carousing cups. One he calls his bull, another his bear, another his horse. And then he has his lesser glasses, that he calls his deer and his ape; and several degrees of 'em too; and never is well, nor thinks any entertainment perfect, till these be brought out, and set o' the cupboard.

*Cler.* For God's love! — we should miss this, if we should not go.

*True.* Nay, he has a thousand things as good, that will speak[4] him all day. He will rail on his wife, with certain commonplaces,[5] behind her back; and to her face —

*Daup.* No more of him. Let 's go see him, I petition you.

[*Exeunt.*]

## Act III.   Scene I

### Otter, Mrs. Otter, [later] Truewit, Clerimont, Dauphine

[*Ott.*]   Nay, good princess, hear me *pauca verba*.[6]

*Mrs. Ott.* By that light, I 'll ha' you chain'd up, with your bull-dogs and bear-dogs, if you be not civil the sooner. I 'll send you to kennel, i' faith. You were best bait me with your bull, bear, and horse. Never a time that the courtiers or collegiates come to the house, but you make it a Shrove-Tuesday! I would have you get your Whitsuntide velvet cap, and your staff i' your hand, to entertain 'em: yes, in troth, do.

*Ott.* Not so, princess, neither; but under correction, sweet princess, gi' me leave. — These things I am known to the courtiers by. It is reported to them for my humour,[7] and they receive it so, and do expect it. Tom Otter's bull, bear, and horse is known all over England, *in rerum natura*.[8]

*Mrs. Ott.* 'Fore me, I will *na-ture* 'em over to Paris-garden,[9] and *na-ture* you thither too, if you pronounce 'em again. Is a bear a fit beast, or a bull, to mix in society with great ladies? think, i' your discretion, in any good polity?[1]

*Ott.* The horse then, good princess.

*Mrs. Ott.* Well, I am contented for the horse; they love to be well hors'd, I know. I love it myself.

*Ott.* And it is a delicate fine horse this: *Poetarum Pegasus*.[2] Under correction, princess, Jupiter did turn himself into a — *taurus*, or bull, under correction, good princess.

---

[3] Naming.              [4] Reveal.              [5] Clichés.
[6] Few words.           [7] Oddity.              [8] In the nature of things.
[9] The Bear-garden.              [1] Society.
[2] The poets' Pegasus.

*[Enter Truewit, Clerimont, and Dauphine, behind]*

*Mrs. Ott.* By my integrity, I 'll send you over to the Bank-side; I 'll commit you to the master of the Garden, if I hear but a syllable more. Must my house or my roof be polluted with the scent of bears and bulls, when it is perfum'd for great ladies? Is this according to the instrument,[3] when I married you? that I would be princess, and reign in mine own house; and you would be my subject, and obey me? What did you bring me, should make you thus peremptory? Do I allow you your half-crown a day, to spend where you will, among your gamesters, to vex and torment me at such times as these? Who gives you your main-tenance, I pray you? who allows you your horse-meat[4] and man's meat? your three suits of apparel a year? your four pair of stock-ings, one silk, three worsted? your clean linen, your bands and cuffs, when I can get you to wear 'em? — 't is marle[5] you ha' 'em on now. — Who graces you with courtiers or great personages, to speak to you out of their coaches, and come home to your house? Were you ever so much as look'd upon by a lord or a lady, before I married you, but on the Easter or Whitsun-holidays? and then out at the banqueting-house[6] windore, when Ned Whiting or George Stone[7] were at the stake?

*True.* [*Aside.*] For God's sake, let 's go stave her off him.

*Mrs. Ott.* Answer me to that. And did not I take you up from thence, in an old greasy buff-doublet, with points,[8] and green vel-let[9] sleeves, out at the elbows? You forget this.

*True.* [*Aside.*] She 'll worry him, if we help not in time.

*[They come forward.]*

*Mrs. Ott.* O, here are some o' the gallants! Go to, behave yourself distinctly,[1] and with good morality; or, I protest, I 'll take away your exhibition.[2]


## Act III.   Scene II

### Truewit, Mrs. Otter, Cap. Otter, Clerimont, Dauphine, [later] Cutbeard

*[True.]* By your leave, fair mistress Otter, I 'll be bold to enter these gentlemen in your acquaintance.

*Mrs. Ott.* It shall not be obnoxious, or difficil, sir.

[3] Legal agreement.
[5] Marvel.
[7] Names of champion bears.
[9] Velvet.
[2] Allowance.

[4] Horse fodder.
[6] At Whitehall palace.
[8] Laces.
[1] With distinction.

*True.* How does my noble captain? Is the bull, bear, and horse *in rerum natura* still?

*Ott.* Sir, *sic visum superis.*[3]

*Mrs. Ott.* I would you would but intimate[4] 'em, do. Go your ways in, and get toasts and butter made for the woodcocks: that 's a fit province for you.                    [*Drives him off.*]

*Cler.* Alas, what a tyranny is this poor fellow married to!

*True.* O, but the sport will be anon, when we get him loose.

*Daup.* Dares he ever speak?

*True.* No Anabaptist ever rail'd with the like license: but mark her language in the mean time, I beseech you.

*Mrs. Ott.* Gentlemen, you are very aptly come. My cousin, Sir Amorous, will be here briefly.

*True.* In good time, lady. Was not Sir John Daw here, to ask for him, and the company?

*Mrs. Ott.* I cannot assure you, master Truewit. Here was a very melancholy knight in a ruff, that demanded my subject[5] for somebody, a gentleman, I think.

*Cler.* Ay, that was he, lady.

*Mrs. Ott.* But he departed straight, I can resolve[6] you.

*Daup.* What an excellent choice phrase this lady expresses in.

*True.* O, sir, she is the only authentical courtier, that is not naturally bred one, in the city.

*Mrs. Ott.* You have taken that report upon trust, gentlemen.

*True.* No, I assure you, the court governs[7] it so, lady, in your behalf.

*Mrs. Ott.* I am the servant of the court and courtiers, sir.

*True.* They are rather your idolators.

*Mrs. Ott.* Not so, sir.

### [*Enter Cutbeard*]

*Daup.* How now, Cutbeard! any cross?

*Cut.* O no, sir, *omnia bene.*[8] 'T was never better o' the hinges;[9] all 's sure. I have so pleas'd him with a curate, that he 's gone to 't almost with the delight he hopes for soon.

*Daup.* What is he for a vicar?

*Cut.* One that has catch'd a cold, sir, and can scarce be heard six inches off; as if he spoke out of a bulrush that were not pick'd, or his throat were full of pith: a fine quick fellow, and an excellent barber of prayers. I came to tell you, sir, that you might *omnem movere lapidem,*[1] as they say, be ready with your vexation.

---

[3] Thus has it seemed good to those above.        [4] Refer to.
[5] Viz., Otter.        [6] Assure.        [7] Determines.
[8] All's well.        [9] Never swung more easily.
[1] Move every stone.

*Daup.* Gramercy, honest Cutbeard! be thereabouts with thy key, to let us in.

*Cut.* I will not fail you, sir; *ad manum*.[2]          [*Exit.*]

*True.* Well, I 'll go watch my coaches.

*Cler.* Do; and we 'll send Daw to you, if you meet him not.

                         [*Exit Truewit.*]

*Mrs. Ott.* Is master Truewit gone?

*Daup.* Yes, lady, there is some unfortunate business fallen out.

*Mrs. Ott.* So I judged by the physiognomy of the fellow that came in; and I had a dream last night too of the new pageant,[3] and my lady mayoress, which is always very ominous to me. I told it my lady Haughty t' other day, when her honour came hither to see some China stuffs; and she expounded it out of Artemidorus,[4] and I have found it since very true. It has done me many affronts.

*Cler.* Your dream, lady?

*Mrs. Ott.* Yes, sir, anything I do but dream o' the city. It stain'd me a damask tablecloth, cost me eighteen pound, at one time; and burnt me a black satin gown, as I stood by the fire, at my lady Centaure's chamber in the college, another time. A third time, at the lords' masque, it dropp'd all my wire[5] and my ruff with wax candle, that I could not go up to the banquet. A fourth time, as I was taking coach to go to Ware, to meet a friend, it dash'd me a new suit all over (a crimson satin doublet, and black velvet skirts) with a brewer's horse, that I was fain to go in and shift[6] me, and kept my chamber a leash[7] of days for the anguish of it.

*Daup.* These were dire mischances, lady.

*Cler.* I would not dwell in the city, an 't were so fatal to me.

*Mrs. Ott.* Yes, sir; but I do take advice of my doctor to dream of it as little as I can.

*Daup.* You do well, mistress Otter.

[*Enter Sir John Daw, and is taken aside by Clerimont*]

*Mrs. Ott.* Will it please you to enter the house farther, gentlemen?

*Daup.* And your favour, lady: but we stay to speak with a knight, Sir John Daw, who is here come. We shall follow you, lady.

*Mrs. Ott.* At your own time, sir. It is my cousin Sir Amorous his feast —

*Daup.* I know it, lady.

---

[2] At hand.
[3] Procession at the installation of a new Lord Mayor.
[4] Greek writer on dreams.          [5] Support for the ruff.
[6] Change my dress.          [7] Trio

*Mrs. Ott.* And mine together. But it is for his honour, and therefore I take no name of it, more than of the place.

*Daup.*    You are a bounteous kinswoman.

*Mrs. Ott.*    Your servant, sir.                                              [*Exit.*]


## *Act III.   Scene III*

### *Clerimont, Daw, La-Foole, Dauphine, Otter*

[*Cler. coming forward with Daw.*]    Why, do not you know it, Sir John Daw?

*Daw.*    No, I am a rook if I do.

*Cler.*    I 'll tell you, then; she 's married by this time. And, whereas you were put i' the head, that she was gone with Sir Dauphine, I assure you, Sir Dauphine has been the noblest, honestest friend to you, that ever gentleman of your quality could boast of. He has discover'd the whole plot, and made your mistress so acknowledging and indeed so ashamed of her injury to you, that she desires you to forgive her, and but grace her wedding with your presence to-day. — She is to be married to a very good fortune, she says, his uncle, old Morose; and she will'd me in private to tell you, that she shall be able to do you more favours, and with more security now than before.

*Daw.*    Did she say so, i' faith?

*Cler.*    Why, what do you think of me, Sir John? ask Sir Dauphine.

*Daw.*    Nay, I believe you. — Good Sir Dauphine, did she desire me to forgive her?

*Daup.*    I assure you, Sir John, she did.

*Daw.*    Nay, then, I do with all my heart, and I 'll be jovial.

*Cler.*    Yes, for look you, sir, this was the injury to you. La-Foole intended this feast to honour her bridal day, and made you the property[8] to invite the college ladies, and promise to bring her; and then at the time she should have appear'd, as his friend, to have given you the dor. Whereas now, Sir Dauphine has brought her to a feeling of it, with this kind of satisfaction, that you shall bring all the ladies to the place where she is, and be very jovial; and there, she will have a dinner, which shall be in your name: and so disappoint La-Foole, to make you good again, and, as it were, a saver[9] i' the main.

*Daw.*    As I am a knight, I honour her; and forgive her heartily.

[8] Tool.

[9] In gambling, one who escaped loss. The "main" was the thrower's call.

*Cler.* About it then presently. Truewit is gone before to con-
front the coaches, and to acquaint you with so much, if he meet
you. Join with him, and 't is well. —

[*Enter Sir Amorous La-Foole*]

See; here comes your antagonist; but take you no notice, but be
very jovial.

*La-F.* Are the ladies come, Sir John Daw, and your mistress?
[*Exit Daw.*] — Sir Dauphine! you are exceeding welcome, and
honest master Clerimont. Where 's my cousin? did you see no
collegiates, gentlemen?

*Daup.* Collegiates! do you not hear, Sir Amorous, how you
are abus'd?

*La-F.* How, sir!

*Cler.* Will you speak so kindly to Sir John Daw, that has done
you such an affront?

*La-F.* Wherein, gentlemen? Let me be a suitor to you to know,
I beseech you.

*Cler.* Why, sir, his mistress is married to-day to Sir Dauphine's
uncle, your cousin's neighbour, and he has diverted all the ladies,
and all your company thither, to frustrate your provision,[1] and
stick a disgrace upon you. He was here now to have entic'd us
away from you too: but we told him his own, I think.

*La-F.* Has Sir John Daw wrong'd me so inhumanely?

*Daup.* He has done it, Sir Amorous, most maliciously and
treacherously: but, if you 'll be rul'd by us, you shall quit him,[2]
i' faith.

*La-F.* Good gentlemen, I 'll make one, believe it. How, I pray?

*Daup.* Marry, sir, get me your pheasants, and your godwits, and
your best meat, and dish it in silver dishes of your cousin's presently; and say nothing, but clap me a clean towel about you, like
a sewer;[3] and, bare-headed, march afore it with a good confidence,
('t is but over the way, hard by,) and we 'll second you, where
you shall set it o' the board, and bid 'em welcome to 't, which
shall show 't is yours, and disgrace his preparation utterly: and
for your cousin, whereas she should be troubled here at home
with care of making and giving welcome, she shall transfer all that
labour thither, and be a principal guest herself; sit rank'd with the
college-honours, and be honour'd, and have her health drunk as
often, as bare[4] and as loud as the best of 'em.

*La-F.* I 'll go tell her presently. It shall be done, that 's resolv'd.                                                              [*Exit.*]

---

[1] Preparations.                    [2] Pay him back.
[3] Server, waiter.                   [4] Bareheaded.

*Cler.*   I thought he would not hear it out, but 't would take him.

*Daup.*   Well, there be guests and meat now; how shall we do for music?

*Cler.*   The smell of the venison, going through the street, will invite one noise[5] of fiddlers or other.

*Daup.*   I would it would call the trumpeters thither!

*Cler.*   Faith, there is hope: they have intelligence of all feasts. There 's good correspondence[6] betwixt them and the London cooks: 't is twenty to one but we have 'em.

*Daup.*   'T will be a most solemn day for my uncle, and an excellent fit of mirth for us.

*Cler.*   Ay, if we can hold up the emulation betwixt Foole and Daw, and never bring them to expostulate.[7]

*Daup.*   Tut, flatter 'em both, as Truewit says, and you may take their understandings in a purse-net.[8] They 'll believe themselves to be just such men as we make 'em, neither more nor less. They have nothing, not the use of their senses, but by tradition.

*Cler.*   See! Sir Amorous has his towel on already.

*He enters like a sewer.*

Have you persuaded your cousin?

*La-F.*   Yes, 't is very feasible: she 'll do any thing, she says, rather than the La-Fooles shall be disgrac'd.

*Daup.*   She is a noble kinswoman. It will be such a pestling[9] device, Sir Amorous; it will pound all your enemy's practices to powder, and blow him up with his own mine, his own train.

*La.-F.*   Nay, we 'll give fire, I warrant you.

*Cler.*   But you must carry[1] it privately, without any noise, and take no notice by any means —

### [Enter Captain Otter]

*Ott.*   Gentlemen, my princess says you shall have all her silver dishes, *festinate:*[2] and she 's gone to alter her tire a little, and go with you —

*Cler.*   And yourself too, Captain Otter?

*Daup.*   By any means, sir.

*Ott.*   Yes, sir, I do mean it: but I would entreat my cousin Sir Amorous, and you, gentlemen, to be suitors to my princess, that I may carry my bull and my bear, as well as my horse.

*Cler.*   That you shall do, Captain Otter.

*La-F.*   My cousin will never consent, gentlemen.

---

[5] Band.              [6] Communication.              [7] Explain.
[8] Purse with a mouth drawn together by a string.
[9] Like a pestle, i.e., crushing.
[1] Manage.              [2] In haste.

*Daup.*  She must consent, Sir Amorous, to reason.

*La-F.*  Why, she says they are no decorum among ladies.

*Ott.*  But they are *decora*,[3] and that 's better, sir.

*Cler.*  Ay, she must hear argument. Did not Pasiphaë, who was a queen, love a bull?[4] and was not Calisto, the mother of Arcas, turn'd into a bear, and made a star, mistress Ursula,[5] i' the heavens?

*Ott.*  O God! that I could ha' said as much! I will have these stories painted i' the Bear-garden, *ex Ovidii Metamorphosi*.[6]

*Daup.*  Where is your princess, captain? pray, be our leader.

*Ott.*  That I shall, sir.

*Cler.*  Make haste, good Sir Amorous.                    [*Exeunt.*]


## Act III.   Scene IIII

### *Morose, Epicœne, Parson, Cutbeard*

[*Mor.*]  Sir, there 's an angel[7] for yourself, and a brace of angels for your cold. Muse not at this manage of my bounty. It is fit we should thank fortune, double to[8] nature, for any benefit she confers upon us; besides, it is your imperfection, but my solace.

*Par.*  I thank your worship; so is it mine, now.

                    *The Parson speaks as having a cold.*

*Mor.*  What says he, Cutbeard?

*Cut.*  He says, *præsto*,[9] sir, whensoever your worship needs him, he can be ready with the like. He got this cold with sitting up late, and singing catches with cloth-workers.

*Mor.*  No more. I thank him.

*Par.*  God keep your worship, and give you much joy with your fair spouse! — umh, umh.                    *He coughs.*

*Mor.*  O, O! stay, Cutbeard! let him give me five shillings of my money back. As it is bounty to reward benefits, so is it equity to mulct injuries. I will have it. What says he?

*Cler.*  He cannot change it, sir.

*Mor.*  It must be changed.

*Cut.*  [*Aside to Parson.*]  Cough again.

*Mor.*  What says he?

*Cut.*  He will cough out the rest, sir.

*Par.*  Umh, umh, umh.                    *Again.*

*Mor.*  Away, away with him! stop his mouth! away! I forgive it. —                    [*Exit Cut. thrusting out the Par.*]

---

[3] Beautiful.                    [4] The disguise taken by Jupiter.
[5] The constellation of Ursa Minor, the lesser bear.
[6] Out of Ovid's *Metamorphoses*.                    [7] A gold coin.
[8] I.e., twice as much as we do to.                    [9] I am at hand.

*Epi.* Fie, master Morose, that you will use this violence to a man of the church.

*Mor.* How!

*Epi.* It does not become your gravity, or breeding, as you pretend, in court, to have offer'd this outrage on a waterman,[1] or any more boisterous creature, much less on a man of his civil coat.

*Mor.* You can speak then!

*Epi.* Yes, sir.

*Mor.* Speak out, I mean.

*Epi.* Ay, sir. Why, did you think you had married a statue, or a motion[2] only? one of the French puppets, with the eyes turn'd with a wire? or some innocent[3] out of the hospital, that would stand with her hands thus, and a plaise mouth,[4] and look upon you?

*Mor.* O immodesty! a manifest woman! What, Cutbeard!

*Epi.* Nay, never quarrel with Cutbeard, sir; it is too late now. I confess it doth bate[5] somewhat of the modesty I had, when I writ simply maid: but I hope I shall make it a stock still competent to[6] the estate and dignity of your wife.

*Mor.* She can talk!

*Epi.* Yes, indeed, sir.

*[Enter Mute]*

*Mor.* What sirrah! None of my knaves there? Where is this impostor Cutbeard?                                    *[Mute makes signs.]*

*Epi.* Speak to him, fellow, speak to him! I'll have none of this coacted,[7] unnatural dumbness in my house, in a family where I govern.                                                           *[Exit Mute.]*

*Mor.* She is my regent already! I have married a Penthesilea,[8] a Semiramis;[9] sold my liberty to a distaff.

## Act III.   Scene V

### *Truewit, Morose, Epicœne*

*[True.]* Where's master Morose?

*Mor.* Is he come again? Lord have mercy upon me!

*True.* I wish you all joy, mistress Epicœne, with your grave and honourable match.

*Epi.* I return you the thanks, master Truewit, so friendly a wish deserves.

---

[1] Thames boatman.                    [2] Puppet.                      [3] Half wit.
[4] A mouth drawn on one side.          [5] Reduce.
[6] Supply sufficient for.              [7] Enforced.
[8] Queen of the Amazons.         [9] Another warrior queen of antiquity.

*Mor.*  She has acquaintance, too!

*True.*  God save you, sir, and give you all contentment in your
fair choice, here!  Before, I was the bird of night to you, the
owl; but now I am the messenger of peace, a dove, and bring you
the glad wishes of many friends to the celebration of this good hour.

*Mor.*  What hour, sir?

*True.*  Your marriage hour, sir.  I commend your resolution,
that, notwithstanding all the dangers I laid afore you, in the voice
of a night-crow, would yet go on, and be yourself.  It shows you
are a man constant to your own ends, and upright to your purposes, that would not be put off with left-handed[1] cries.

*Mor.*  How should you arrive at the knowledge of so much?

*True.*  Why, did you ever hope, sir, committing the secrecy of
it to a barber, that less than the whole town should know it?  You
might as well ha' told it the conduit, or the bake-house, or the in-
fantry[2] that follow the court, and with more security.  Could your
gravity forget so old and noted a remnant, as, *lippis et tonsoribus
notum?*[3]  Well, sir, forgive it yourself now, the fault, and be com-
municable with your friends.  Here will be three or four fashionable
ladies from the college to visit you presently, and their train of
minions and followers.

*Mor.*  Bar my doors! bar my doors!  Where are all my eaters?
my mouths, now? —

*[Enter Servants]*

Bar up my doors, you varlets!

*Epi.*  He is a varlet that stirs to such an office.  Let 'em stand
open.  I would see him that dares move his eyes toward it.  Shall
I have a barricado made against my friends, to be barr'd of any
pleasure they can bring in to me with honourable visitation?

*[Exeunt Ser.]*

*Mor.*  O Amazonian impudence!

*True.*  Nay, faith, in this, sir, she speaks but reason; and, methinks, is more continent than you.  Would you go to bed so
presently, sir, afore noon?  A man of your head and hair should
owe more to that reverend ceremony, and not mount the marriage-bed like a town bull, or a mountain-goat; but stay the due
season; and ascend it then with religion and fear.  Those delights
are to be steep'd in the humour and silence of the night; and give
the day to other open pleasures, and jollities of feast, of music,
of revels, of discourse.  We 'll have all, sir, that may make your
Hymen[4] high and happy.

---

[1] Ill-omened.          [2] Servants.
[3] Known even to the bleary-eyed barbers.
[4] Wedding celebration.

*Mor.* O my torment, my torment!

*True.* Nay, if you endure the first half hour, sir, so tediously, and with this irksomeness; what comfort or hope can this fair gentlewoman make to herself hereafter, in the consideration of so many years as are to come —

*Mor.* Of my affliction. Good sir, depart, and let her do it alone.

*True.* I have done, sir.

*Mor.* That cursed barber!

*True.* Yes, faith, a cursed wretch indeed, sir.

*Mor.* I have married his cittern,[5] that 's common to all men. Some plague above the plague —

*True.* All Egypt's ten plagues.

*Mor.* Revenge me on him!

*True.* 'T is very well, sir. If you laid on a curse or two more, I 'll assure you he 'll bear 'em. As, that he may get the pox with seeking to cure it, sir; or, that while he is curling another man's hair, his own may drop off; or, for burning some male-bawd's lock, he may have his brain beat out with the curling iron.

*Mor.* No, let the wretch live wretched. May he get the itch, and his shop so lousy, as no man dare come at him, nor he come at no man!

*True.* Ay, and if he would swallow all his balls[6] for pills, let not them purge him.

*Mor.* Let his warming-pan be ever cold.

*True.* A perpetual frost underneath it, sir.

*Mor.* Let him never hope to see fire again.

*True.* But in hell, sir.

*Mor.* His chairs be always empty, his scissors rust, and his combs mould in their cases.

*True.* Very dreadful that! And may he lose the invention, sir, of carving lanterns in paper.

*Mor.* Let there be no bawd carted that year, to employ a basin[7] of his: but let him be glad to eat his sponge for bread.

*True.* And drink lotium[8] to it, and much good do him.

*Mor.* Or, for want of bread —

*True.* Eat ear-wax, sir. I 'll help you. Or, draw his own teeth, and add them to the lute-string.[9]

*Mor.* No, beat the old ones to powder, and make bread of them.

---

[5] These instruments were available in barbers' shops to entertain waiting customers.

[6] Of soap.

[7] Spectators hired barbers' basins to make a din.

[8] Lotion.

[9] Barbers also acted as dentists, and hung up extracted teeth in their shops.

*True.* Yes, make meal o' the mill-stones.

*Mor.* May all the botches and burns that he has cur'd on others break out upon him.

*True.* And he now forget the cure of 'em in himself, sir; or, if he do remember it, let him ha' scrap'd all his linen into lint for 't, and have not a rag left him to set up with.

*Mor.* Let him never set up again, but have the gout in his hands for ever! — Now, no more, sir.

*True.* O, that last was too high set; you might go less with him, i' faith, and be reveng'd enough: as, that he be never able to new-paint his pole —

*Mor.* Good sir, no more, I forgot myself.

*True.* Or, want credit to take up with a comb-maker —

*Mor.* No more, sir.

*True.* Or, having broken his glass in a former despair, fall now into a much greater, of ever getting another —

*Mor.* I beseech you, no more.

*True.* Or, that he never be trusted with trimming of any but chimney-sweepers —

*Mor.* Sir —

*True.* Or, may he cut a collier's throat with his razor, by chance-medley,[1] and yet hang for 't.

*Mor.* I will forgive him, rather than hear any more. I beseech you, sir.


## *Act III.  Scene VI*

### *Daw, Morose, Truewit, Haughty, Centaure, Mavis, Trusty*

[*Daw.*]  This way, madam.

*Mor.* O, the sea breaks in upon me! another flood! an inundation! I shall be o'erwhelmed with noise. It beats already at my shores. I feel an earthquake in myself for 't.

*Daw.* 'Give you joy, mistress.

*Mor.* Has she servants too!

*Daw.* I have brought some ladies here to see and know you. My lady Haughty — (*She kisses them severally as he presents them.*) this is my lady Centaure — mistress Dol Mavis — mistress Trusty, my lady Haughty's woman. Where 's your husband? Let 's see him: can he endure no noise? Let me come to him.

*Mor.* What nomenclator[2] is this!

---

[1] Homicide by misadventure.

[2] Servant to announce names of guests.

*True.*   Sir John Daw, sir, your wife's servant, this.

*Mor.*   A Daw, and her servant! O, 't is decreed, 't is decreed of me, and she have such servants.                        [*Going.*]

*True.*   Nay, sir, you must kiss the ladies; you must not go away, now: they come toward you to seek you out.

*Hau.*   I' faith, master Morose, would you steal a marriage thus, in the midst of so many friends, and not acquaint us? Well, I 'll kiss you, notwithstanding the justice of my quarrel. You shall give me leave, mistress, to use a becoming familiarity with your husband.

*Epi.*   Your ladyship does me an honour in it, to let me know he is so worthy your favour: as you have done both him and me grace to visit so unprepar'd a pair to entertain you.

*Mor.*   Compliment! compliment!

*Epi.*   But I must lay the burden of that upon my servant here.

*Hau.*   It shall not need, mistress Morose; we will all bear, rather than one shall be oppress'd.

*Mor.*   I know it: and you will teach her the faculty, if she be to learn it.                    [*Walks aside while the rest talk apart.*]

*Hau.*   Is this the Silent Woman?

*Cen.*   Nay, she has found her tongue since she was married, master Truewit says.

*Hau.*   O, master Truewit! 'save you. What kind of creature is your bride here? She speaks, methinks!

*True.*   Yes, madam, believe it, she is a gentlewoman of very absolute behaviour, and of a good race.

*Hau.*   And Jack Daw told us she could not speak!

*True.*   So it was carried in plot, madam, to put her upon this old fellow, by Sir Dauphine, his nephew, and one or two more of us: but she is a woman of an excellent assurance, and an extraordinary happy wit and tongue. You shall see her make rare sport with Daw ere night.

*Hau.*   And he brought us to laugh at her!

*True.*   That falls out often, madam, that he that thinks himself the master-wit, is the master-fool. I assure your ladyship, ye cannot laugh at her.

*Hau.*   No, we 'll have her to the college. And she have wit, she shall be one of us, shall she not, Centaure? We 'll make her a collegiate.

*Cen.*   Yes, faith, madam, and Mavis and she will set up a side.[3]

*True.*   Believe it, madam, and mistress Mavis, she will sustain her part.

*Mav.*   I 'll tell you that, when I have talk'd with her, and tried her.

---

[3] Act as partners in a game.

*Hau.*  Use her very civilly, Mavis.

*Mav.*  So I will, madam.                    [*Whispers her.*]

*Mor.*  [*Aside.*]  Blessed minute! that they would whisper thus ever!

*True.*  In the mean time, madam, would but your ladyship help to vex him a little: you know his disease, talk to him about the wedding ceremonies, or call for your gloves,[4] or —

*Hau.*  Let me alone.  Centaure, help me. — Master bridegroom, where are you?

*Mor.*  [*Aside.*]  O, it was too miraculously good to last!

*Hau.*  We see no ensigns[5] of a wedding here; no character of a bride-ale: where be our scarves and our gloves?  I pray you, give 'em us.  Let 's know your bride's colours, and yours at least.

*Cen.*  Alas, madam, he has provided none.

*Mor.*  Had I known your ladyship's painter, I would.

*Hau.*  He has given it you, Centaure, i' faith.  But do you hear, master Morose? a jest will not absolve you in this manner.  You that have suck'd the milk of the court, and from thence have been brought up to the very strong meats and wine of it; been a courtier from the biggen[6] to the night-cap, as we may say, and you to offend in such a high point of ceremony as this, and let your nuptials want all marks of solemnity!  How much plate have you lost to-day, (if you had but regarded your profit,) what gifts, what friends, through your mere rusticity!

*Mor.*  Madam —

*Hau.*  Pardon me, sir, I must insinuate your errors to you; no gloves? no garters? no scarves? no epithalamium? no masque?

*Daw.*  Yes, madam, I 'll make an epithalamium, I promis'd my mistress; I have begun it already: will your ladyship hear it

*Hau.*  Ay, good Jack Daw.

*Mor.*  Will it please your ladyship command a chamber, and be private with your friend?  You shall have your choice of rooms to retire to after: my whole house is yours.  I know it hath been your ladyship's errand into the city at other times, however now you have been unhappily diverted upon me; but I shall be loath to break any honourable custom of your ladyship's.  And therefore, good madam —

*Epi.*  Come, you are a rude bridegroom, to entertain ladies of honour in this fashion.

*Cen.*  He is a rude groom indeed.

*True.*  By that light, you deserve to be grafted,[7] and have your horns reach from one side of the island to the other. — Do not

[4] At weddings the ladies were presented with gloves.
[5] Signs.          [6] Baby's bonnet.          [7] Cuckolded.

mistake me, sir; I but speak this to give the ladies some heart again, not for any malice to you.

*Mor.* Is this your bravo,[8] ladies?

*True.* As God help me, if you utter such another word, I 'll take mistress bride in, and begin to you in a very sad cup; do you see? Go to, know your friends, and such as love you.

## Act III.   Scene VII

### Clerimont,  Morose,  Truewit,  Dauphine,  La-Foole,
### Otter, Mrs. Otter, &c.

[*Cler.*]   By your leave, ladies.  Do you want any music?  I have brought a variety of noises.  Play, sirs, all of you.   *Music of all sorts.*

*Mor.*   O, a plot, a plot, a plot, a plot, upon me! This day I shall be their anvil to work on, they will grate me asunder. 'T is worse than the noise of a saw.

*Cler.*   No, they are hair, rosin, and guts: I can give you the receipt.

*True.*   Peace, boys!

*Cler.*   Play! I say.

*True.*   Peace, rascals! You see who 's your friend now, sir: take courage, put on a martyr's resolution. Mock down all their attemptings with patience. 'T is but a day, and I would suffer heroically. Should an ass exceed me in fortitude? No. You betray your infirmity with your hanging dull ears, and make them insult: bear up bravely and constantly.   *La-Foole passes over sewing[9] the meat.* Look you here, sir, what honour is done you unexpected, by your nephew; a wedding-dinner come, and a knight-sewer before it, for the more reputation: and fine mistress Otter, your neighbour, in the rump or tail of it.

*Mor.*   Is that Gorgon, that Medusa come! hide me, hide me.

*True.*   I warrant you, sir, she will not transform[1] you, entertain her, and conduct your guests in. No? — Mistress bride, will you entreat in the ladies? your bridegroom is so shame-fac'd, here.

*Epi.*   Will it please your ladyship, madam?

*Hau.*   With the benefit of your company, mistress.

*Epi.*   Servant, pray you perform your duties.

*Daw.*   And glad to be commanded, mistress.

*Cen.*   How like you her wit, Mavis?

*Mav.*   Very prettily, absolutely well.

---

[8] Bully.          [9] Serving.
[1] Into stone, as the Gorgon did.

*Mrs. Ott.*  'T is my place.          [*Trying to take precedence.*]

*Mav.*  You shall pardon me, mistress Otter.

*Mrs. Ott.*  Why, I am a collegiate.

*Mav.*  But not in ordinary.

*Mrs. Ott.*  But I am.

*Mav.*  We 'll dispute that within.          [*Exeunt Ladies.*]

*Cler.*  Would this had lasted a little longer.

*True.*  And that they had sent for the heralds.[2]

[*Enter Captain Otter*]

— Captain Otter! what news

*Ott.*  I have brought my bull, bear, and horse, in private, and yonder are the trumpeters without, and the drum, gentlemen.

                              *The drum and trumpets sound.*

*Mor.*  O, O, O!

*Ott.*  And we will have a rouse in each of 'em, anon, for bold Britons, i' faith.          [*They sound again.*]

*Mor.*  O, O, O!                        [*Exit hastily.*]

*All.*  Follow, follow, follow!          [*Exeunt.*]


## Act IIII.  Scene 1

### Truewit, Clerimont, Dauphine

[*True.*]  Was there ever poor bridegroom so tormented? or man, indeed?

*Cler.*  I have not read of the like in the chronicles of the land.

*True.*  Sure, he cannot but go to a place of rest, after all this purgatory.

*Cler.*  He may presume it, I think.

*True.*  The spitting, the coughing, the laughter, the neezing,[3] the farting, dancing, noise of the music, and her masculine and loud commanding, and urging the whole family,[4] makes him think he has married a fury.

*Cler.*  And she carries it up bravely.

*True.*  Ay, she takes any occasion to speak: that 's the height on 't.

*Cler.*  And how soberly Dauphine labours to satisfy him, that it was none of his plot!

[2] Who settled disputes over precedence.
[3] Sneezing.                    [4] Household.

*True.* And has almost brought him to the faith, i' the article. Here he comes. —

[*Enter Sir Dauphine*]

Where is he now? what's become of him, Dauphine?

*Daup.* O, hold me up a little, I shall go away i' the jest else. He has got on his whole nest of night-caps, and lock'd himself up i' the top o' the house, as high as ever he can climb from the noise. I peep'd in at a cranny, and saw him sitting over a cross-beam o' the roof, like him o' the saddler's horse[5] in Fleetstreet, upright: and he will sleep there.

*Cler.* But where are your collegiates?

*Daup.* Withdrawn with the bride in private.

*True.* O, they are instructing her i' the college-grammar. If she have grace with them, she knows all their secrets instantly.

*Cler.* Methinks the lady Haughty looks well to-day, for all my dispraise of her i' the morning. I think, I shall come about to thee again, Truewit.

*True.* Believe it, I told you right. Women ought to repair the losses time and years have made i' their features, with dressings. And an intelligent woman, if she know by herself the least defect, will be most curious[6] to hide it: and it becomes her. If she be short, let her sit much, lest, when she stands, she be thought to sit. If she have an ill foot, let her wear her gown the longer, and her shoe the thinner. If a fat hand, and scald[7] nails, let her carve the less, and act in gloves. If a sour breath, let her never discourse fasting, and always talk at her distance. If she have black and rugged teeth, let her offer the less at laughter, especially if she laugh wide and open.

*Cler.* O, you shall have some women, when they laugh, you would think they bray'd, it is so rude and —

*True.* Ay, and others, that will stalk i' their gait like an estrich,[8] and take huge strides. I cannot endure such a sight. I love measure[9] i' the feet, and number[1] i' the voice: they are gentlenesses, that oft-times draw no less than the face.

*Daup.* How cam'st thou to study these creatures so exactly? I wish thou wouldst make me a proficient.

*True.* Yes, but you must leave[2] to live i' your chamber, then, a month together upon *Amadis de Gaul*,[3] or *Don Quixote*, as you are wont; and come abroad where the matter is frequent, to court, to tiltings, public shows and feasts, to plays, and church sometimes: thither they come to show their new tires too, to see, and to be

---

[5] Presumably a reference to a dummy in a shop window.
[6] Painstaking.          [7] Scabby.          [8] Ostrich.
[9] Graceful gait.          [1] Rhythm.          [2] Cease.
[3] Famous romance of knight errantry.

seen. In these places a man shall find whom to love, whom to play
with, whom to touch once, whom to hold ever. The variety arrests his judgment. A wench to please a man comes not down
dropping from the ceiling, as he lies on his back droning[4] a tobacco-
pipe. He must go where she is.

*Daup.*   Yes, and be never the near.[5]

*True.*   Out, heretic! That diffidence makes thee worthy it should
be so.

*Cler.*   He says true to you, Dauphine.

*Daup.*   Why?

*True.*   A man should not doubt to overcome any woman. Think
he can vanquish 'em and he shall: for though they deny, their desire is to be tempted. Penelope herself cannot hold out long. Os-
tend,[6] you saw, was taken at last. You must perséver, and hold to
your purpose. They would solicit us, but that they are afraid.
Howsoever, they wish in their hearts we should solicit them. Praise
'em, flatter 'em, you shall never want eloquence or trust: even the
chastest delight to feel themselves that way rubb'd. With praises
you must mix kisses too. If they take them, they 'll take more —
though they strive, they would be overcome.

*Cler.*   O, but a man must beware of force.

*True.*   It is to them an acceptable violence, and has oft-times the
place of the greatest courtesy. She that might have been forc'd,
and you let her go free without touching, though she then seem to
thank you, will ever hate you after; and glad i' the face, is assuredly
sad at the heart.

*Cler.*   But all women are not to be taken all ways.

*True.*   'T is true; no more than all birds, or all fishes. If you
appear learned to an ignorant wench, or jocund to a sad, or witty
to a foolish, why she presently begins to mistrust herself. You
must approach them i' their own height, their own line; for the contrary makes many, that fear to commit themselves to noble and
worthy fellows, run into the embraces of a rascal. If she love wit,
give verses, though you borrow 'em of a friend, or buy 'em to have
good. If valour, talk of your sword, and be frequent in the mention
of quarrels, though you be staunch in fighting.[7] If activity, be seen
o' your barbary[8] often, or leaping over stools, for the credit of your
back. If she love good clothes or dressing, have your learned council about you every morning, your French tailor, barber, linener,
&c. Let your powder, your glass, and your comb be your dearest
acquaintance. Take more care for the ornament of your head, than

---

[4] Sucking at.                    [5] Nearer.
[6] Captured in 1604 after a three years' siege.
[7] I.e., really brave, and not boastful.
[8] Barbary horse.

the safety; and wish the commonwealth rather troubled, than a hair about you. That will take her. Then, if she be covetous and craving, do you promise anything, and perform sparingly; so shall you keep her in appetite still. Seem as you would give, but be like a barren field, that yields little; or unlucky dice to foolish and hoping gamesters. Let your gifts be slight and dainty, rather than precious. Let cunning[9] be above cost. Give cherries at time of year, or apricots; and say, they were sent you out o' the country, though you bought 'em in Cheapside. Admire her tires: like her in all fashions; compare her in every habit to some deity; invent excellent dreams to flatter her, and riddles; or, if she be a great one, perform always the second parts to her: like what she likes, praise whom she praises, and fail not to make the household and servants yours, yea the whole family, and salute 'em by their names, ('t is but light cost, if you can purchase 'em so,) and make her physician your pensioner, and her chief woman. Nor will it be out of your gain to make love to her too, so she follow, not usher her lady's pleasure. All blabbing is taken away, when she comes to be a part of the crime.

*Daup.*   On what courtly lap hast thou late slept, to come forth so sudden and absolute a courtling?[1]

*True.*   Good faith, I should rather question you, that are so heark'ning after these mysteries. I begin to suspect your diligence, Dauphine. Speak, art thou in love in earnest?

*Daup.*   Yes, by my troth, am I; 't were ill dissembling before thee.

*True.*   With which of 'em, I pray thee?

*Daup.*   With all the collegiates.

*Cler.*   Out on thee! We 'll keep you at home, believe it, i' the stable, and you be such a stallion.

*True.*   No; I like him well. Men should love wisely, and all women; some one for the face, and let her please the eye; another for the skin, and let her please the touch; a third for the voice, and let her please the ear; and where the objects mix, let the senses so too. Thou would'st think it strange, if I should make 'em all in love with thee afore night!

*Daup.*   I would say, thou hadst the best philtre i' the world, and couldst do more than madam Medea,[2] or doctor Foreman.[3]

*True.*   If I do not, let me play the mountebank for my meat, while I live, and the bawd for my drink.

*Daup.*   So be it, I say.

---

9 Skill.                    1 Courtier.
2 Who was celebrated for her skill in magic.
3 Astrologer and quack, who was still alive when this play was first performed.

## Act IIII.   Scene II

*Otter, Clerimont, Daw, Dauphine, Morose, Truewit,*
*La-Foole, Mrs. Otter*

[*Ott.*]   O lord, gentlemen, how my knights and I have miss'd you here!

*Cler.*   Why, captain, what service, what service?

*Ott.*   To see me bring up my bull, bear, and horse to fight.

*Daw.*   Yes, faith, the captain says we shall be his dogs to bait 'em.

*Daup.*   A good employment.

*True.*   Come on, let 's see a course,[4] then.

*La-F.*   I am afraid my cousin will be offended, if she come.

*Ott.*   Be afraid of nothing. — Gentlemen, I have plac'd the drum and the trumpets, and one to give 'em the sign when you are ready. Here 's my bull for myself, and my bear for Sir John Daw, and my horse for Sir Amorous. Now set your foot to mine, and yours to his, and —

*La-F.*   Pray God my cousin come not.

*Ott.*   St. George, and St. Andrew, fear no cousins. Come, sound, sound! [*Drum and trumpets sound.*] *Et rauco strepuerunt cornua cantu.*[5]                                    [*They drink.*]

*True.*   Well said, captain, i' faith; well fought at the bull.

*Cler.*   Well held at the bear.

*True.*   Low, low! captain.

*Daup.*   O, the horse has kick'd off his dog already.

*La-F.*   I cannot drink it, as I am a knight.

*True.*   Gods so! off with his spurs, somebody.

*La-F.*   It goes again my conscience. My cousin will be angry with it.

*Daw.*   I ha' done mine.

*True.*   You fought high and fair, Sir John.

*Cler.*   At the head.

*Daup.*   Like an excellent bear-dog.

*Cler.*   You take no notice of the business, I hope?

*Daw.*   Not a word, sir; you see we are jovial.

*Ott.*   Sir Amorous, you must not equivocate. It must be pull'd down for all my cousin.

*Cler.*   'Sfoot, if you take not your drink, they 'll think you are discontented with something; you 'll betray all, if you take the least notice.

---

[4] Encounter at bear-baiting.
[5] And the horns blared out with hoarse sound.

*La-F.*  Not I; I 'll both drink and talk then.

*Ott.*  You must pull the horse on his knees, Sir Amorous; fear no cousins. *Jacta est alea.*[6]

*True.*  O, now he 's in his vein, and bold. The least hint given him of his wife now, will make him rail desperately.

*Cler.*  Speak to him of her.

*True.*  Do you, and I 'll fetch her to the hearing of it.     [*Exit.*]

*Daup.*  Captain He-Otter, your She-Otter is coming, your wife.

*Ott.*  Wife! buz? *titivilitium!*[7]  There 's no such thing in nature. I confess, gentlemen, I have a cook, a laundress, a house-drudge, that serves my necessary turns, and goes under that title; but he 's an ass that will be so uxurious to tie his affections to one circle. Come, the name dulls appetite. Here, replenish again; another bout. [*Fills the cups again.*] Wives are nasty, sluttish animals.

*Daup.*  O, captain.

*Ott.*  As ever the earth bare, *tribus verbis.*[8] — Where 's master Truewit?

*Daw.*  He 's slipp'd aside, sir.

*Cler.*  But you must drink and be jovial.

*Daw.*  Yes, give it me.

*La-F.*  And me too.

*Daw.*  Let 's be jovial.

*La-F.*  As jovial as you will.

*Ott.*  Agreed. Now you shall ha' the bear, cousin, and Sir John Daw the horse, and I 'll ha' the bull still. Sound, Tritons o' the Thames! [*Drum and trumpets sound again.*] *Nunc est bibendum, nunc pede libero —*[9]

*Mor.*  Villains, murderers, sons of the earth, and traitors, what do you there?

*Morose speaks from above: the trumpets sounding.*

*Cler.*  O, now the trumpets have wak'd him, we shall have his company.

*Ott.*  A wife is a scurvy clogdogdo,[1] an unlucky thing, a very foresaid bear-whelp, without any good fashion or breeding, *mala bestia.*[2]

*His wife is brought out to hear him.*

*Daup.*  Why did you marry one then, captain?

*Ott.*  A pox! — I married with six thousand pound, I.  I was in love with that. I ha' not kissed my Fury these forty weeks.

[6] The die is cast.                [7] Good-for-nothing.
[8] In three words.
[9] Now it is time to drink, now with free foot —
[1] (Exact meaning uncertain).                [2] Evil beast.

*Cler.*  The more to blame you, captain.

*True.*  Nay, mistress Otter, hear him a little first.

*Ott.*  She has a breath worse than my grandmother's, *profecto*.[3]

*Mrs. Ott.*  A treacherous liar! Kiss me, sweet master Truewit, and prove him a slandering knave.

*True.*  I 'll rather believe you, lady.

*Ott.*  And she has a peruke that 's like a pound of hemp, made up in shoe-threads.

*Mrs. Ott.*  O viper, mandrake!

*Ott.*  O most vile face! and yet she spends me forty pound a year in mercury and hogs-bones.[4] All her teeth were made i' the Black-friars, both her eyebrows i' the Strand, and her hair in Silverstreet. Every part o' the town owns a piece of her.

*Mrs. Ott.* [*Comes forward.*]  I cannot hold.

*Ott.*  She takes herself asunder still when she goes to bed, into some twenty boxes; and about next day noon is put together again, like a great German clock: and so comes forth, and rings a tedious larum to the whole house, and then is quiet again for an hour, but for her quarters — Ha' you done me right, gentlemen?

*Mrs. Ott.*  No, sir, I 'll do you right with my quarters, with my quarters.                    *She falls upon him and beats him.*

*Ott.*  O, hold, good princess.

*True.*  Sound, sound!                    [*Drum and trumpets sound.*]

*Cler.*  A battle, a battle!

*Mrs. Ott.*  You notorious stinkardly bearward, does my breath smell?

*Ott.*  Under correction, dear princess. — Look to my bear and my horse, gentlemen.

*Mrs. Ott.*  Do I want teeth, and eyebrows, thou bull-dog?

*True.*  Sound, sound still.                    [*They sound again.*]

*Ott.*  No, I protest, under correction —

*Mrs. Ott.*  Ay, now you are under correction, you protest: but you did not protest before correction, sir. Thou Judas, to offer to betray thy princess! I 'll make thee an example —     [*Beats him.*]

*Morose descends with a long sword.*

*Mor.*  I will have no such examples in my house, lady Otter.

*Mrs. Ott.*  Ah! —     [*Mrs. Otter, Daw, and La-Foole, run off.*]

*Mor.*  Mistress Mary Ambree,[5] your examples are dangerous. — Rogues, hell-hounds, Stentors! out of my doors, you sons of noise

---

[3] Assuredly.                    [4] Used in compounding cosmetics.

[5] Heroine of a ballad who disguised herself as a soldier and served at the siege of Ghent in 1584.

and tumult, begot on an ill May-day,[6] or when the galley-foist[7] is afloat to Westminster! [*Drives out the musicians.*] A trumpeter could not be conceiv'd but then.

*Daup.*   What ails you, sir?

*Mor.*   They have rent my roof, walls, and all my windores asunder, with their brazen throats.                    [*Exit.*]

*True.*   Best follow him, Dauphine.

*Daup.*   So I will.                    [*Exit.*]

*Cler.*   Where 's Daw and La-Foole?

*Ott.*   They are both run away, sir. Good gentlemen, help to pacify my princess, and speak to the great ladies for me. Now must I go lie with the bears this fortnight, and keep out o' the way, till my peace be made, for this scandal[8] she has taken. Did you not see my bull-head, gentlemen?

*Cler.*   Is 't not on, captain?

*True.*   No; but he may make a new one, by that is on.

*Ott.*   O, here 'tis. And you come over, gentlemen, and ask for Tom Otter, we 'll go down to Ratcliff,[9] and have a course i' faith, for all these disasters. There 's *bona spes*[1] left.

*True.*   Away, captain, get off while you are well.

*Cler.*   I am glad we are rid of him.

*True.*   You had never been, unless we had put his wife upon him. His humour is as tedious at last, as it was ridiculous at first.

[*Exeunt.*]


## Act IIII.   Scene III

*Haughty, Mrs. Otter, Mavis, Daw, La-Foole, Centaure,*
*Epicœne, Truewit, Clerimont*

[*Hau.*]   We wonder'd why you shriek'd so, mistress Otter.

*Mrs. Ott.*   O God, madam, he came down with a huge long naked weapon in both his hands, and look'd so dreadfully! Sure he 's beside himself.

*Mav.*   Why, what made you there, mistress Otter

*Mrs. Ott.*   Alas, mistress Mavis, I was chastising my subject, and thought nothing of him.

*Daw.*   Faith, mistress, you must do so too: learn to chastise. Mistress Otter corrects her husband so, he dares not speak but under correction.

*La-F.*   And with his hat off to her: 't would do you good to see.

---

[6] Day of riots against foreigners in 1517, long remembered.

[7] State barge that took the new Lord Mayor to Westminster, where he took the oath of office.

[8] Offence.                    [9] On the Thames, below London.

[1] Good hope.

*Hau.*  In sadness,[2] 't is good nature and mature counsel; practise it, Morose. I 'll call you Morose still now, as I call Centaure and Mavis; we four will be all one.

*Cen.*  And you 'll come to the college, and live with us?

*Hau.*  Make him give milk and honey.

*Mav.*  Look how you manage him at first, you shall have him ever after.

*Cen.*  Let him allow you your coach, and four horses, your woman, your chamber-maid, your page, your gentleman-usher, your French cook, and four grooms.

*Hau.*  And go with us to Bedlam, to the china-houses, and to the Exchange.

*Cen.*  It will open the gate to your fame.

*Hau.*  Here 's Centaure has immortaliz'd herself, with taming of her wild male.

*Mav.*  Ay, she has done the miracle of the kingdom.

*Epi.*  But, ladies, do you count it lawful to have such plurality of servants, and do 'em all graces?

*Hau.*  Why not? why should women deny their favours to men? are they the poorer or the worse?

*Daw.*  Is the Thames the less for the dyers' water, mistress?

*La-F.*  Or a torch for lighting many torches?

*True.*  Well said, La-Foole; what a new one he has got!

*Cen.*  They are empty losses women fear in this kind.

*Hau.*  Besides, ladies should be mindful of the approach of age, and let no time want his due use. The best of our days pass first.

*Mav.*  We are rivers, that cannot be call'd back, madam: she that excludes her lovers, may live to lie a forsaken beldame, in a frozen bed.

*Cen.*  'T is true, Mavis: and who will wait on us to coach then? or write, or tell us the news then? make anagrams of our names, and invite us to the Cockpit,[3] and kiss our hands all the play-time, and draw their weapons for our honours?

*Hau.*  Not one.

*Daw.*  Nay, my mistress is not altogether unintelligent of these things; here be in presence have tasted of her favours.

*Cler.*  What a neighing hobby-horse is this!

*Epi.*  But not with intent to boast 'em again, servant. — And have you those excellent receipts, madam, to keep yourselves from bearing of children?

*Hau.*  O yes, Morose: how should we maintain our youth and beauty else? Many births of a woman make her old, as many crops make the earth barren.

---

[2] In all seriousness.                    [3] Theatre at Whitehall.

## *Act IIII.   Scene IIII*

*Morose, Dauphine, Truewit, Epicœne, Clerimont, Daw,*
*Haughty, La-Foole, Centaure, Mavis, Mrs. Otter, [later]*
*Trusty*

[*Mor.*]   O my cursed angel, that instructed me to this fate!

*Daup.*   Why, sir?

*Mor.*   That I should be seduc'd by so foolish a devil as a barber
will make?

*Daup.*   I would I had been worthy, sir, to have partaken your
counsel; you should never have trusted it to such a minister.

*Mor.*   Would I could redeem it with the loss of an eye, nephew,
a hand, or any other member.

*Daup.*   Marry, God forbid, sir that you should geld yourself, to
anger your wife.

*Mor.*   So it would rid me of her! — and, that I did superogatory
penance in a belfry, at Westminster-hall, i' the Cockpit, at the fall
of a stag, the Tower-wharf — what place is there else? — London-
bridge, Paris-garden, Billingsgate, when the noises are at their height
and loudest. Nay, I would sit out a play, that were nothing but
fights at sea, drum, trumpet, and target.[4]

*Daup.*   I hope there shall be no such need, sir. Take patience,
good uncle. This is but a day, and 't is well worn too now.

*Mor.*   O, 't will be so for ever, nephew, I foresee it, for ever.
Strife and tumult are the dowry that comes with a wife.

*True.*   I told you so, sir, and you would not believe me.

*Mor.*   Alas, do not rub those wounds, master Truewit, to blood
again: 't was my negligence. Add not affliction to affliction. I have
perceiv'd the effect of it, too late, in madame Otter.

*Epi.*   How do you, sir?

*Mor.*   Did you ever hear a more unnecessary question? as if she
did not see! Why, I do as you see, empress, empress.

*Epi.*   You are not well, sir; you look very ill: something has distemper'd you.

*Mor.*   O horrible, monstrous impertinencies! Would not one of
these have serv'd, do you think, sir? would not one of these have
serv'd?

*True.*   Yes, sir; but these are but notes of female kindness, sir;
certain tokens that she has a voice, sir.

*Mor.*   O, is 't so! Come, and 't be no otherwise —— What say
you?

*Epi.*   How do you feel yourself, sir?

[4] Shield.

*Mor.*   Again that!

*True.*   Nay, look you, sir, you would be friends with your wife upon unconscionable terms; her silence.

*Epi.*   They say you are run mad, sir.

*Mor.*   Not for love, I assure you, of you; do you see?

*Epi.*   O lord, gentlemen! lay hold on him, for God's sake. What shall I do? Who 's his physician, can you tell, that knows the state of his body best, that I might send for him? Good sir, speak; I 'll send for one of my doctors else.

*Mor.*   What, to poison me, that I might die intestate, and leave you possess'd of all!

*Epi.*   Lord, how idly he talks, and how his eyes sparkle! He looks green about the temples! do you see what blue spots he has!

*Cler.*   Ay, it 's melancholy.

*Epi.*   Gentlemen, for Heaven's sake, counsel me. Ladies! — Servant, you have read Pliny and Paracelsus;⁵ ne'er a word now to comfort a poor gentlewoman? Ay me, what fortune had I, to marry a distracted man!

*Daw.*   I 'll tell you, mistress —

*True.*   How rarely she holds it up!                [*Aside to Cler.*]

*Mor.*   What mean you, gentlemen?

*Epi.*   What will you tell me, servant?

*Daw.*   The disease in Greek is called μανια,⁶ in Latin *insania*, *furor, vel ecstasis melancholica,* that is *egressio,* when a man *ex melancholico evadit fanaticus.*⁷

*Mor.*   Shall I have a lecture read upon me alive?

*Daw.*   But he may be but *phreneticus* yet, mistress; and *phrenetis* is only *delirium,* or so.

*Epi.*   Ay, that is for the disease, servant; but what is this to the cure? We are sure enough of the disease.

*Mor.*   Let me go.

*True.*   Why, we 'll entreat her to hold her peace, sir.

*Mor.*   O no, labour not to stop her. She is like a conduit-pipe, that will gush out with more force when she opens again.

*Hau.*   I 'll tell you, Morose, you must talk divinity to him altogether, or moral philosophy.

*La-F.*   Ay, and there 's an excellent book of moral philosophy, madam, of Reynard the Fox, and all the beasts, call'd *Doni's Philosophy.*⁸

⁵ Pliny had written on natural history, Paracelsus on medicine.
⁶ Mania.
⁷ Insanity, madness, or melancholic ecstasy, that is, a losing of his wits, when a man from being melancholy ends up a madman.
⁸ Doni was an Italian who had made a popular collection of fables which had been translated into English by Sir Thomas North.

*Cen.* There is indeed, Sir Amorous La-Foole.

*Mor.* O misery!

*La-F.* I have read it, my lady Centaure, all over, to my cousin here.

*Mrs. Ott.* Ay, and 't is a very good book as any is, of the moderns.

*Daw.* Tut, he must have Seneca read to him, and Plutarch, and the ancients; the moderns are not for this disease.

*Cler.* Why, you discommended them too, to-day, Sir John.

*Daw.* Ay, in some cases: but in these they are best, and Aristotle's *Ethics.*

*Mav.* Say you so, Sir John? I think you are deceiv'd; you took it upon trust.

*Hau.* Where 's Trusty, my woman? I 'll end this difference. I prithee, Otter, call her. Her father and mother were both mad, when they put her to me.

*Mor.* I think so. — Nay, gentlemen, I am tame. This is but an exercise, I know, a marriage ceremony, which I must endure.

*Hau.* And one of 'em, I know not which, was cur'd with the Sick Man's Salve,[9] and the other with Greene's Groat's-worth of Wit.[1]

*True.* A very cheap cure, madam.

### [*Enter Trusty*]

*Hau.* Ay, it 's very feasible.

*Mrs. Ott.* My lady call'd for you, mistress Trusty: you must decide a controversy.

*Hau.* O, Trusty, which was it you said, your father, or your mother, that was cur'd with the Sick Man's Salve?

*Trus.* My mother, Madam, with the Salve.

*True.* Then it was the sick woman's salve?

*Trus.* And my father with the Groat's-worth of Wit. But there was other means us'd: we had a preacher that would preach folk asleep still; and so they were prescrib'd to go to church, by an old woman that was their physician, thrice a week —

*Epi.* To sleep?

*Trus.* Yes, forsooth: and every night they read themselves asleep on those books.

*Epi.* Good faith, it stands with great reason. I would I knew where to procure those books.

*Mor.* Oh!

*La-F.* I can help you with one of 'em, mistress Morose, the Groat's-worth of Wit.

---

[9] A devotional tract by Thomas Becon, published in 1562.
[1] First published in 1592.

*Epi.*   But I should disfurnish you, Sir Amorous: can you spare it?

*La-F.*   O yes, for a week, or so; I 'll read it myself to him.

*Epi.*   No, I must do that, sir; that must be my office.

*Mor.*   Oh, oh!

*Epi.*   Sure he would do well enough, if he could sleep.

*Mor.*   No, I should do well enough, if you could sleep. Have I no friend that will make her drunk, or give her a little laudanum, or opium?

*True.*   Why, sir, she talks ten times worse in her sleep.

*Mor.*   How!

*Cler.*   Do you not know that, sir? never ceases all night.

*True.*   And snores like a porcpisce.[2]

*Mor.*   O redeem me, fate; redeem me, fate! For how many causes may a man be divorc'd, nephew?

*Daup.*   I know not, truly, sir.

*True.*   Some divine must resolve you in that, sir, or canon-lawyer.

*Mor.*   I will not rest, I will not think of any other hope or comfort, till I know.        [*Exit with Dauphine.*]

*Cler.*   Alas, poor man!

*True.*   You 'll make him mad indeed, ladies, if you pursue this.

*Hau.*   No, we 'll let him breathe now, a quarter of an hour or so.

*Cler.*   By my faith, a large truce!

*Hau.*   Is that his keeper, that is gone with him?

*Daw.*   It is his nephew, madam.

*La-F.*   Sir Dauphine Eugenie.

*Cen.*   He looks like a very pitiful knight —

*Daw.*   As can be. This marriage has put him out of all.

*La-F.*   He has not a penny in his purse, madam.

*Daw.*   He is ready to cry all this day.

*La-F.*   A very shark;[3] he set me i' the nick[4] t' other night at primero.[5]

*True.*   How these swabbers[6] talk!

*Cler.*   Ay, Otter's wine has swell'd their humours above a spring-tide.

*Hau.*   Good Morose, let 's go in again. I like your couches exceeding well; we 'll go lie and talk there.

       [*Exeunt Hau., Cen., Mav., Trus., La-Foole, and Daw.*]

*Epi.* [*Following them.*]   I wait on you, madam.

*True.* [*Stopping her.*]   'Slight, I will have 'em as silent as signs, and their posts too, ere I ha' done. Do you hear, lady-bride? I

---

[2] Porpoise.        [3] Card sharper.
[4] Took me down.       [5] A card game.
[6] Low fellows.

pray thee now, as thou art a noble wench, continue this discourse of Dauphine within; but praise him exceedingly: magnify him with all the height of affection thou canst; — I have some purpose in 't: and but beat off these two rooks, Jack Daw and his fellow, with any discontentment hither, and I 'll honour thee for ever.

*Epi.* I was about it here. It angered me to the soul, to hear 'em begin to talk so malapert.[7]

*True.* Pray thee perform it, and thou winn'st me an idolater to thee everlasting.

*Epi.* Will you go in and hear me do it?

*True.* No, I 'll stay here. Drive 'em out of your company, 'tis all I ask; which cannot be any way better done, than by extolling Dauphine, whom they have so slighted.

*Epi.* I warrant you; you shall expect one of 'em presently.

[*Exit.*]

*Cler.* What a cast of kastrils[8] are these, to hawk after ladies, thus!

*True.* Ay, and strike at such an eagle as Dauphine.

*Cler.* He will be mad when we tell him. Here he comes.

## Act IIII.   Scene V
### Clerimont, Truewit, Dauphine,
### [*later*] Daw, La-Foole

[*Cler to Daup.*]    O sir, you are welcome.

*True.* Where 's thine uncle?

*Daup.* Run out o' doors in his night-caps, to talk with a casuist[9] about his divorce. It works admirably.

*True.* Thou wouldst ha' said so, and thou hadst been here! The ladies have laugh'd at thee most comically, since thou went'st, Dauphine.

*Cler.* And ask'd, if thou wert thine uncle's keeper.

*True.* And the brace of baboons answer'd, "Yes"; and said thou wert a pitiful poor fellow, and didst live upon posts[1] and hadst nothing but three suits of apparel, and some few benevolences that the lords ga' thee to fool to 'em, and swagger.

*Daup.* Let me not live, I 'll beat 'em: I 'll bind 'em both to grand-madam's bed-posts, and have 'em baited[2] with monkeys.

---

[7] Impudently.                        [8] Pair of base hawks.
[9] Theologian who decided cases of conscience.
[1] Run errands like a lackey.                        [2] Attacked.

*True*. Thou shalt not need, they shall be beaten to thy hand, Dauphine. I have an execution[3] to serve upon 'em, I warrant thee, shall serve; trust my plot.

*Daup*. Ay, you have many plots! so you had one to make all the wenches in love with me.

*True*. Why, if I do not yet afore night, as near as 't is, and that they do not every one invite thee, and be ready to scratch for thee, take the mortgage of my wit.

*Cler*. 'Fore God, I 'll be his witness thou shalt have it, Dauphine: thou [*to True*.] shalt be his fool for ever, if thou dost not.

*True*. Agreed. Perhaps 't will be the better estate. Do you observe this gallery, or rather lobby, indeed? Here are a couple of studies, at each end one: here will I act such a tragi-comedy between the Guelphs and the Ghibellines,[4] Daw and La-Foole — which of 'em comes out first, will I seize on; — you two shall be the chorus behind the arras, and whip out between the acts and speak. — If I do not make 'em keep the peace for this remnant of the day, if not of the year, I have fail'd once. —— I hear Daw coming: hide, [*they withdraw*] and do not laugh, for God's sake.

### [*Enter Daw*]

*Daw*. Which is the way into the garden, trow?

*True*. O, Jack Daw! I am glad I have met with you. In good faith, I must have this matter go no furder between you: I must ha' it taken up.

*Daw*. What matter, sir? between whom?

*True*. Come, you disguise it: Sir Amorous and you. If you love me, Jack, you shall make use of your philosophy now, for this once, and deliver me your sword. This is not the wedding the Centaurs[5] were at, though there be a she one here. [*Takes his sword*.] The bride has entreated me I will see no blood shed at her bridal: you saw her whisper me erewhile.

*Daw*. As I hope to finish Tacitus,[6] I intend no murder.

*True*. Do you not wait for Sir Amorous?

*Daw*. Not I, by my knighthood.

*True*. And your scholarship too?

*Daw*. And my scholarship too.

*True*. Go to, then I return you your sword, and ask you mercy; but put it not up, for you will be assaulted. I understood that you had apprehended it, and walk'd here to brave him; and that you had held your life contemptible, in regard of your honour.

---

[3] Writ.                    [4] Rival parties in mediaeval Italy.
[5] The fatal quarrel between the Centaurs and the Lapithae broke out at a wedding.
[6] The Roman historian.

*Daw.* No, no; no such thing, I assure you. He and I parted now, as good friends as could be.

*True.* Trust not you to that vizor.[7] I saw him since dinner with another face. I have known many men in my time vex'd with losses, with deaths, and with abuses; but so offended a wight as Sir Amorous did I never see or read of. For taking away his guests, sir, to-day, that 's the cause; and he declares it behind your back with such threatenings and contempts. He said to Dauphine, you were the arrant'st ass —

*Daw.* Ay, he may say his pleasure.

*True.* And swears you are so protested[8] a coward, that he knows you will never do him any manly or single right; and therefore he will take his course.

*Daw.* I 'll give him any satisfaction, sir — but fighting.

*True.* Ay, sir: but who knows what satisfaction he 'll take? Blood he thirsts for, and blood he will have; and whereabouts on you he will have it, who knows but himself?

*Daw.* I pray you, master Truewit, be you a mediator.

*True.* Well, sir, conceal yourself then in this study till I return. (*He puts him up.*) Nay, you must be content to be lock'd in; for, for mine own reputation, I would not have you seen to receive a public disgrace, while I have the matter in managing. Gods so, here he comes; keep your breath close, that he do not hear you sigh. — In good faith, Sir Amorous, he is not this way; I pray you be merciful, do not murder him! he is a Christian, as good as you: you are arm'd as if you sought a revenge on all his race. Good Dauphine, get him away from this place. I never knew a man's choler so high, but he would speak to his friends, he would hear reason. — Jack Daw, Jack Daw! asleep?

*Daw.* [*Within.*]   Is he gone, master Truewit?

*True.* Ay; did you hear him?

*Daw.* O God! yes.

*True.* What a quick ear fear has!

*Daw.* [*Comes out of the closet.*] But is he so arm'd, as you say?

*True.* Arm'd! did you ever see a fellow set out to take possession?[9]

*Daw.* Ay, sir.

*True.* That may give you some light to conceive of him; but 't is nothing to the principal.[1] Some false brother i' the house has furnish'd him strangely;[2] or, if it were out o' the house, it was Tom Otter.

---

[7] Mask.          [8] Declared.

[9] Of property to which the title was in dispute.          [1] Real thing.

[2] Fitted him up extravagantly.

*Daw.* Indeed he 's a captain, and his wife is his kinswoman.

*True.* He has got some body's old two-hand sword, to mow you off at the knees; and that sword hath spawn'd such a dagger! — But then he is so hung with pikes, halberds, petronels, calivers[3] and muskets, that he looks like a justice of peace's hall; a man of two thousand a year is not cess'd[4] at so many weapons as he has on. There was never fencer challeng'd at so many several foils. You would think he meant to murder all St. Pulchre's[5] parish. If he could but victual himself for half a-year in his breeches,[6] he is sufficiently arm'd to over-run a country.

*Daw.* Good lord! what means he, sir? I pray you, master Truewit, be you a mediator.

*True.* Well, I 'll try if he will be appeas'd with a leg or an arm; if not, you must die once.

*Daw.* I would be loath to lose my right arm, for writing madrigals.

*True.* Why, if he will be satisfied with a thumb or a little finger, all 's one to me. You must think, I 'll do my best.

*Daw.* Good sir, do.

> *He puts him up again and then comes forth.*

*Cler.* What hast thou done?

*True.* He will let me do nothing, man; he does all afore me; he offers his left arm.

*Cler.* His left wing for a Jack Daw.

*Daup.* Take it by all means.

*True.* How! maim a man for ever, for a jest? What a conscience hast thou!

*Daup.* 'T is no loss to him; he has no employment for his arms, but to eat spoon-meat. Beside, as good maim his body as his reputation.

*True.* He is a scholar and a wit, and yet he does not think so. But he loses no reputation with us; for we all resolv'd him an ass before. To your places again.

*Cler.* I pray thee, let me be in at the other a little.

*True.* Look, you 'll spoil all; these be ever your tricks.

*Cler.* No, but I could hit of some things that thou wilt miss, and thou wilt say are good ones.

*True.* I warrant you. I pray forbear, I 'll leave it off, else.

*Daup.* Come away, Clerimont.

> [*Daup, and Cler. withdraw as before. Enter La-Foole.*]

*True.* Sir Amorous!

---

[3] Petronels and calivers were different kinds of firearms.
[4] Assessed.
[5] The church of St. Sepulchre, on the west side of the City of London.
[6] Which were worn large and padded.

*La-F.*  Master Truewit.

*True.*  Whither were you going?

*La-F.*  Down into the court to make water.

*True.*  By no means, sir; you shall rather tempt your breeches.

*La-F.*  Why, sir?

*True.*  Enter here, if you love your life.

[*Opening the door of the other study.*]

*La-F.*  Why? why?

*True.*  Question till your throat be cut, do: dally till the enraged soul find you.

*La-F.*  Who 's that?

*True.*  Daw it is: will you in?

*La-F.*  Ay, ay, I 'll in: what 's the matter?

*True.*  Nay, if he had been cool enough to tell us that, there had been some hope to atone you; but he seems so implacably enrag'd!

*La-F.*  'Slight, let him rage! I 'll hide myself.

*True.*  Do, good sir. But what have you done to him within, that should provoke him thus? You have broke some jest upon him afore the ladies.

*La-F.*  Not I, never in my life, broke jest upon any man. The bride was praising Sir Dauphine, and he went away in snuff,[7] and I followed him; unless he took offence at me in his drink erewhile, that I would not pledge all the horse full.

*True.*  By my faith, and that may be; you remember well: but he walks the round up and down, through every room o' the house, with a towel in his hand, crying "Where 's La-Foole? Who saw La-Foole?" And when Dauphine and I demanded the cause, we can force no answer from him, but — "O revenge, how sweet art thou! I will strangle him in this towel" — which leads us to conjecture that the main cause of his fury is, for bringing your meat to-day, with a towel about you, to his discredit.

*La-F.*  Like enough. Why, and he be angry for that, I 'll stay here till his anger be blown over.

*True.*  A good becoming resolution, sir; if you can put it on o' the sudden.

*La-F.*  Yes, I can put it on: or, I 'll away into the country presently.

*True.*  How will you get out o' the house, sir? He knows you are i' the house, and he 'll watch you this se'ennight, but he 'll have you: he 'll outwait a sergeant[8] for you.

*La-F.*  Why, then I 'll stay here.

*True.*  You must think how to victual yourself in time then.

---

[7] Resentment.

[8] Sheriff's officer.

*La-F.* Why, sweet master Truewit, will you entreat my cousin Otter to send me a cold venison pasty, a bottle or two of wine, and a chamber-pot?

*True.* A stool were better, sir, of Sir Ajax[9] his invention.

*La-F.* Ay, that will be better, indeed; and a pallet to lie on.

*True.* O, I would not advise you to sleep by any means.

*La-F.* Would you not, sir? Why, then I will not.

*True.* Yet there 's another fear —

*La-F.* Is there, sir! What is 't?

*True.* No, he cannot break open this door with his foot, sure.

*La-F.* I 'll set my back against it, sir. I have a good back.

*True.* But then if he should batter.

*La-F.* Batter! if he dare, I 'll have an action of batt'ry against him.

*True.* Cast[1] you the worst. He has sent for powder already, and what he will do with it, no man knows: perhaps blow up the corner o' the house where he suspects you are. Here he comes; in quickly. I protest, Sir John Daw *He feigns as if one were* he is not this way: what will *present, to fright the other, who* *is run in to hide himself.* you do? Before God, you shall hang no petard[2] here. I 'll die rather. Will you not take my word? I never knew one but would be satisfied. — Sir Amorous, [*speaks through the key-hole,*] there 's no standing out: he has made a petard of an old brass pot, to force your door. Think upon some satisfaction, or terms to offer him.

*La-F.* [*Within.*] Sir, I 'll give him any satisfaction. I dare give any terms.

*True.* You 'll leave it to me then?

*La-F.* Ay, sir: I 'll stand to any condi- *He calls forth* tions. *Clerimont and Dauphine.*

*True.* How now, what think you, sirs? Were 't not a difficult thing to determine which of these two fear'd most?

*Cler.* Yes, but this fears the bravest:[3] the other a whiniling[4] dastard, Jack Daw! But La-Foole, a brave heroic coward! and is afraid in a great look and a stout accent; I like him rarely.

*True.* Had it not been pity these two should ha' been conceal'd?

*Cler.* Shall I make a motion?

*True.* Briefly: for I must strike while 't is hot.

*Cler.* Shall I go fetch the ladies to the catastrophe?

*True.* Umph! ay, by my troth.

---

[9] A reference to Sir John Harrington's book with the punning title, *The Metamorphosis of Ajax.*

[1] Be ready for.                    [2] Bomb.

[3] Best.                    [4] Whining.

*Daup.*   By no mortal means. Let them continue in the state of ignorance, and err still; think 'em wits and fine fellows, as they have done. 'T were sin to reform them.

*True.*   Well, I will have 'em fetch'd, now I think on 't, for a private purpose of mine: do, Clerimont, fetch 'em, and discourse to 'em all that 's past, and bring 'em into the gallery here.

*Daup.*   This is thy extreme vanity, now: thou think'st thou wert undone, if every jest thou mak'st were not publish'd.

*True.*   Thou shalt see how unjust thou art presently. Clerimont, say it was Dauphine's plot. [*Exit Clerimont.*] Trust me not, if the whole drift be not for thy good. There 's a carpet[5] i' the next room, put it on, with this scarf over thy face, and a cushion o' thy head, and be ready when I call Amorous. Away! [*Exit Daup.*] John Daw!          [*Goes to Daw's closet and brings him out.*]

*Daw.*   What good news, sir?

*True.*   Faith, I have followed and argued with him hard for you. I told him you were a knight, and a scholar, and that you knew fortitude did consist *magis patiendo quam faciendo, magis ferendo quam feriendo.*[6]

*Daw.*   It doth so indeed, sir.

*True.*   And that you would suffer, I told him: so at first he demanded by my troth, in my conceit, too much.

*Daw.*   What was it, sir?

*True.*   Your upper lip, and six o' your foreteeth.

*Daw.*   'T was unreasonable.

*True.*   Nay, I told him plainly, you could not spare 'em all. So after long argument *pro et con.* as you know, I brought him down to your two butter-teeth,[7] and them he would have.

*Daw.*   O, did you so? Why, he shall have 'em.

*True.*   But he shall not, sir, by your leave. The conclusion is this, sir: because you shall be very good friends hereafter, and this never to be remembered or upbraided; besides, that he may not boast he has done any such thing to you in his own person; he is to come here in disguise, give you five kicks in private, sir, take your sword from you, and lock you up in that study during pleasure: which will be but a little while, we 'll get it releas'd presently.

*Daw.*   Five kicks! he shall have six, sir, to be friends.

*True.*   Believe me, you shall not over-shoot yourself, to send him that word by me.

*Daw.*   Deliver it, sir; he shall have it with all my heart, to be friends.

---

[5] Table cover.
[6] More in enduring than in doing, more in bearing than in striking.
[7] Front teeth.

*True.* Friends! Nay, and he should not be so, and heartily too, upon these terms, he shall have me to enemy while I live. Come, sir, bear it bravely.

*Daw.* O God, sir, 't is nothing.

*True.* True: what 's six kicks to a man that reads Seneca?

*Daw.* I have had a hundred, sir.

*True.* Sir Amorous! —

No speaking one to another, or rehearsing old matters.

### Dauphine comes forth and kicks him

*Daw.* One, two, three, four, five. I protest, Sir Amorous, you shall have six.

*True.* Nay, I told you, you should not talk. Come give him six, and he will needs. [*Dauphine kicks him again.*] — Your sword. [*Takes his sword.*] Now return to your safe custody; you shall presently meet afore the ladies, and be the dearest friends one to another. [*Puts Daw into the study.*] — Give me the scarf now, thou shalt beat the other bare-fac'd. Stand by. [*Dauphine retires, and Truewit releases La-Foole.*] — Sir Amorous!

*La-F.* What 's here! A sword?

*True.* I cannot help it, without I should take the quarrel upon myself. Here he has sent you his sword —

*La-F.* I 'll receive none on 't.

*True.* And he wills you to fasten it against a wall, and break your head in some few several places against the hilts.

*La-F.* I will not: tell him roundly. I cannot endure to shed my own blood.

*True.* Will you not?

*La-F.* No. I 'll beat it against a fair flat wall, if that will satisfy him: if not, he shall beat it himself, for Amorous.

*True.* Why, this is strange starting off, when a man undertakes for you! I offer'd him another condition; will you stand to that?

*La-F.* Ay, what is 't?

*True.* That you will be beaten in private.

*La-F.* Yes, I am content, at the blunt.[8]

[*Enter, above, Haughty, Centaure, Mavis, Mistress Otter, Epicœne, and Trusty*]

*True.* Then you must submit yourself to be hoodwink'd[9] in this scarf, and be led to him, where he will take your sword from you, and make you bear a blow over the mouth, gules,[1] and tweaks by the nose *sans nombre.*

[8] With a weapon whose point is capped, like a fencer's.
[9] Blindfolded.      [1] So as to draw blood.

*La-F.*  I am content. But why must I be blinded?

*True.*  That 's for your good, sir; because, if he should grow
insolent upon this, and publish it hereafter to your disgrace, (which
I hope he will not do,) you might swear safely, and protest, he
never beat you, to your knowledge.

*La-F.*  O, I conceive.

*True.*  I do not doubt but you 'll be perfect good friends upon
't, and not dare to utter an ill thought one of another in future.

*La-F.*  Not I, as God help me, of him.

*True.*  Nor he of you, sir. If he should, — [*binds his eyes.*] —
Come, sir [*leads him forward.*] — *All hid,*[2] Sir John!

#### *Dauphine enters to tweak him*

*La-F.*  O, Sir John, Sir John! Oh, o-o-o-o-o-Oh —

*True.*  Good Sir John, leave tweaking, you 'll blow his nose
off. — 'T is Sir John's pleasure, you should retire into the study.
[*Puts him up again.*] — Why, now you are friends. All bitterness
between you, I hope, is buried; you shall come forth by and by,
Damon and Pythias upon 't, and embrace with all the rankness of
friendship that can be. — I trust, we shall have 'em tamer i' their
language hereafter. Dauphine, I worship thee. — God's will, the
ladies have surpris'd us!

## Act IIII.  Scene VI

*Haughty, Centaure, Mavis, Mrs. Otter, Epicœne, Trusty*
(*having discover'd part of the past scene above*);
*Dauphine, Truewit, &c.*

[*Hau.*]  Centaure, how our judgments were impos'd on by these
adulterate knights!

*Cen.*  Nay, madam, Mavis was more deceiv'd than we; 'twas
her commendation utter'd[3] 'em in the college.

*Mav.*  I commended but their wits, madam, and their braveries.[4]
I never look'd toward their valours.

*Hau.*  Sir Dauphine is valiant, and a wit too, it seems.

*Mav.*  And a bravery[5] too.

*Hau.*  Was this his project?

*Mrs. Ott.*  So master Clerimont intimates, madam.

*Hau.*  Good Morose, when you come to the college, will you
bring him with you?  He seems a very perfect gentleman.

2 Cry in hide and seek.               3 Introduced.
4 Finery.             5 Gallant.

*Epi.*  He is so, madam, believe it.

*Cen.*  But when will you come, Morose?

*Epi.*  Three or four days hence, madam, when I have got me a coach and horses.

*Hau.*  No, to-morrow, good Morose; Centaure shall send you her coach.

*Mav.*  Yes faith, do, and bring Sir Dauphine with you.

*Hau.*  She has promis'd that, Mavis.

*Mav.*  He is a very worthy gentleman in his exteriors, madam.

*Hau.*  Ay, he shows he is judicial in his clothes.

*Cen.*  And yet not so superlatively neat as some, madam, that have their faces set in a brake.[6]

*Hau.*  Ay, and have every hair in form.

*Mav.*  That wear purer linen than ourselves, and profess more neatness than the French hermaphrodite![7]

*Epi.*  Ay, ladies, they, what they tell one of us, have told a thousand; and are the only thieves of our fame, that think to take us with that perfume, or with that lace, and laugh at us unconscionably when they have done.

*Hau.*  But Sir Dauphine's carelessness becomes him.

*Cen.*  I could love a man for such a nose.

*Mav.*  Or such a leg.

*Cen.*  He has an exceeding good eye, madam.

*Mav.*  And a very good lock.

*Cen.*  Good Morose, bring him to my chamber first.

*Mrs. Ott.*  Please your honours to meet at my house, madam.

*True.*  See how they eye thee, man! they are taken, I warrant thee.                                      [*Haughty comes forward.*]

*Hau.*  You have unbrac'd[8] our brace of knights here, master Truewit.

*True.*  Not I, madam; it was Sir Dauphine's ingine:[9] who, if he have disfurnish'd your ladyship of any guard or service by it, is able to make the place good again in himself.

*Hau.*  There 's no suspicion of that, sir.

*Cen.*  God so, Mavis, Haughty is kissing.

*Mav.*  Let us go too, and take part.        [*They come forward.*]

*Hau.*  But I am glad of the fortune (beside the discovery of two such empty caskets) to gain the knowledge of so rich a mine of virtue as Sir Dauphine.

*Cen.*  We would be all glad to style him of our friendship, and see him at the college.

---

[6] So that they cannot move it.

[7] A sideshow. See *The Knight of the Burning Pestle*, p. 174.

[8] Bared, shown up.        [9] Device, scheme.

*Mav.*   He cannot mix with a sweeter society, I 'll prophesy; and I hope he himself will think so.

*Daup.*   I should be rude to imagine otherwise, lady.

*True.*   Did not I tell thee, Dauphine! Why, all their actions are governed by crude opinion, without reason or cause; they know not why they do anything; but, as they are inform'd, believe, judge, praise, condemn, love, hate, and in emulation one of another, do all these things alike. Only they have a natural inclination sways 'em generally to the worst, when they are left to themselves. But pursue it, now thou hast 'em.

*Hau.*   Shall we go in again, Morose?

*Epi.*   Yes, madam.

*Cen.*   We 'll entreat Sir Dauphine's company.

*True.*   Stay, good madam, the interview of the two friends, Pylades and Orestes: I 'll fetch 'em out to you straight.

*Hau.*   Will you, master Truewit?

*Daup.*   Ay, but, noble ladies, do not confess in your countenance, or outward bearing to 'em, any discovery of their follies, that we may see how they will bear up again, with what assurance and erection.[1]

*Hau.*   We will not, Sir Dauphine.

*Cen. Mav.*   Upon our honours, Sir Dauphine.

*True.*   [*Goes to the first closet.*]   Sir Amorous, Sir Amorous! The ladies are here.

*La-F.* [*Within.*]   Are they?

*True.*   Yes; but slip out by and by, as their backs are turn'd, and meet Sir John here, as by chance, when I call you. [*Goes to the other.*] — Jack Daw.

*Daw.* [*Within.*]   What say you, sir?

*True.*   Whip out behind me suddenly, and no anger i' your looks to your adversary. Now, now!

[*La-Foole and Daw slip out of their respective closets, and salute each other.*]

*La-F.*   Noble Sir John Daw, where have you been?

*Daw.*   To seek you, Sir Amorous.

*La-F.*   Me! I honour you.

*Daw.*   I prevent you, sir.

*Cler.*   They have forgot their rapiers.

*True.*   O, they meet in peace, man.

*Daup.*   Where 's your sword, Sir John?

*Cler.*   And yours, Sir Amorous?

*Daw.*   Mine! my boy had it forth to mend the handle, e'en now.

*La.-F.*   And my gold handle was broke too, and my boy had it forth.

---

[1] Impudence.

*Daup.*   Indeed, sir! — How their excuses meet!

*Cler.*   What a consent there is i' the handles!

*True.*   Nay, there is so i' the points too, I warrant you.

*Mrs. Ott.*   O me! madam, he comes again, the madman! Away!

[*Ladies, Daw, and La-Foole, run off.*]


## Act IIII.   Scene VII

### *Morose, Truewit, Clerimont, Dauphine*

[*Mor.*]   What make these naked weapons     *He had found the two*
here, gentlemen?                                        *swords drawn within.*

*True.*   O sir! here hath like to been murder since you went; a
couple of knights fallen out about the bride's favours! We were
fain to take away their weapons; your house had been begg'd[2] by
this time else.

*Mor.*   For what?

*Cler.*   For manslaughter, sir, as being accessary.

*Mor.*   And for her favours?

*True.*   Ay, sir, heretofore, not present. — Clerimont, carry 'em
their swords now. They have done all the hurt they will do.

[*Exit Cler. with the two swords.*]

*Daup.*   Ha' you spoke with a lawyer, sir?

*Mor.*   O no! there is such a noise i' the court, that they have
frighted me home with more violence than I went! such speaking
and counter-speaking, with their several voices of citations, appel-
lations, allegations, certificates, attachments, intergatories,[3] refer-
ences, convictions, and afflictions indeed, among the doctors and
proctors,[4] that the noise here is silence to 't, a kind of calm midnight!

*True.*   Why, sir, if you would be resolv'd indeed, I can bring
you hither a very sufficient lawyer, and a learned divine, that shall
inquire into every least scruple for you.

*Mor.*   Can you, master Truewit?

*True.*   Yes, and are very sober, grave persons, that will dispatch
it in a chamber, with a whisper or two.

*Mor.*   Good sir, shall I hope this benefit from you, and trust
myself into your hands?

*True.*   Alas, sir! your nephew and I have been asham'd and oft-
times mad, since you went, to think how you are abus'd. Go in,

---

[2] Begged for by some courtier in anticipation of the confiscation of
Morose's property as that of a criminal.

[3] I.e., interrogatories.

[4] Attorneys in the ecclesiastical courts.

good sir, and lock yourself up till we call you; we 'll tell you more anon, sir.

*Mor.* Do your pleasure with me, gentlemen; I believe in you, and that deserves no delusion.                                    [*Exit.*]

*True.* You shall find none, sir; — but heap'd, heap'd plenty of vexation.

*Daup.* What wilt thou do now, Wit?

*True.* Recover me hither[5] Otter and the barber, if you can, by any means, presently.

*Daup.* Why? to what purpose?

*True.* O, I 'll make the deepest divine, and gravest lawyer, out o' them two for him —

*Daup.* Thou canst not, man; these are waking dreams.

*True.* Do not fear me. Clap but a civil gown[6] with a welt[7] o' the one, and a canonical cloak with sleeves o' the other, and give 'em a few terms i' their mouths, if there come not forth as able a doctor and complete a parson, for this turn, as may be wish'd, trust not my election: and I hope, without wronging the dignity of either profession, since they are but persons put on, and for mirth's sake, to torment him. The barber smatters Latin, I remember.

*Daup.* Yes, and Otter too.

*True.* Well then, if I make 'em not wrangle out this case to his no comfort, let me be thought a Jack Daw or La-Foole or anything worse. Go you to your ladies, but first send for them.    [*Exeunt.*]

## Act V.  Scene I
### La-Foole, Clerimont, Daw, [later] Mavis

[*La-F.*]    Where had you our swords, master Clerimont?

*Cler.*  Why, Dauphine took 'em from the madman.

*La-F.*  And he took 'em from our boys, I warrant you.

*Cler.*  Very like, sir.

*La-F.*  Thank you, good master Clerimont. Sir John Daw and I are both beholden to you.

*Cler.*  Would I knew how to make you so, gentlemen!

*Daw.*  Sir Amorous and I are your servants, sir.

#### [Enter Mavis]

*Mav.*  Gentlemen, have any of you a pen and ink? I would fain write out a riddle in Italian, for Sir Dauphine to translate.

---

[5] Bring back here to me.                  [6] Gown of a civil lawyer.
[7] Border.

*Cler.*   Not I, in troth, lady; I am no scrivener.[8]

*Daw.*   I can furnish you, I think, lady. [*Exeunt Daw and Mavis.*]

*Cler.*   He has it in the haft of a knife, I believe.

*La-F.*   No, he has his box of instruments.

*Cler.*   Like a surgeon!

*La-F.*   For the mathematics: his squire,[9] his compasses, his brass pens, and black-lead, to draw maps of every place and person where he comes.

*Cler.*   How, maps of persons!

*La.-F.*   Yes, sir, of Nomentack[1] when he was here, and of the Prince of Moldavia,[2] and of his mistress, mistress Epicœne.

### [*Enter Daw*]

*Cler.*   Away! he has not found out her latitude, I hope.

*La-F.*   You are a pleasant gentleman, sir.

*Cler.*   Faith, now we are in private, let's wanton it a little, and talk waggishly. — Sir John, I am telling Sir Amorous here, that you two govern the ladies where'er you come; you carry the feminine gender afore you.

*Daw.*   They shall rather carry us afore them, if they will, sir.

*Cler.*   Nay, I believe that they do, withal — but that you are the prime men in their affections, and direct all their actions —

*Daw.*   Not I; Sir Amorous is.

*La-F.*   I protest, Sir John is.

*Daw.*   As I hope to rise i' the state, Sir Amorous, you ha' the person.

*La-F.*   Sir John, you ha' the person, and the discourse too.

*Daw.*   Not I, sir. I have no discourse — and then you have activity beside.

*La-F.*   I protest, Sir John, you come as high from Tripoly as I do, every whit:[3] and lift as many join'd stools, and leap over 'em, if you would use it.

*Cler.*   Well, agree on 't together, knights; for between you, you divide the kingdom or comonwealth of ladies' affections: I see it, and can perceive a little how they observe you, and fear you, indeed. You could tell strange stories, my masters, if you would, I know.

*Daw.*   Faith, we have seen somewhat, sir.

*La-F.*   That we have — velvet petticoats, and wrought smocks, or so.

[8] Professional scribe.                     [9] Square.
[1] Indian chief from Virginia, brought to England in 1605.
[2] Who sought the hand of the King's cousin, Lady Arabella Stuart.
[3] You are as active as I am, every bit.

*Daw.*  Ay, and —

*Cler.*  Nay, out with it, Sir John; do not envy your friend the pleasure of hearing, when you have had the delight of tasting.

*Daw.*  Why — a —— Do you speak, Sir Amorous.

*La-F.*  No, do you, Sir John Daw.

*Daw.*  I' faith, you shall.

*La-F.*  I' faith, you shall.

*Daw.*  Why, we have been —

*La-F.*  In the great bed at Ware[4] together in our time.  On, Sir John.

*Daw.*  Nay, do you, Sir Amorous.

*Cler.*  And these ladies with you, knights?

*La-F.*  No, excuse us, sir.

*Daw.*  We must not wound reputation.

*La-F.*  No matter — they were these, or others.  Our bath cost us fifteen pound when we came home.

*Cler.*  Do you hear, Sir John?  You shall tell me but one thing truly, as you love me.

*Daw.*  If I can, I will, sir.

*Cler.*  You lay in the same house with the bride here?

*Daw.*  Yes, and convers'd with her hourly, sir.

*Cler.*  And what humour is she of?  Is she coming and open, free?

*Daw.*  O, exceeding open, sir.  I was her servant, and Sir Amorous was to be.

*Cler.*  Come, you have both had favours from her: I know, and have heard so much.

*Daw.*  O no, sir.

*La-F.*  You shall excuse us, sir; we must not wound reputation.

*Cler.*  Tut, she is married now, and you cannot hurt her with any report; and therefore speak plainly: how many times, i' faith? which of you led first? ha!

*La-F.*  Sir John had her maidenhead, indeed.

*Daw.*  O, it pleases him to say so, sir; but Sir Amorous knows what 's what, as well.

*Cer.*  Dost thou, i' faith, Amorous?

*La-F.*  In a manner, sir.

*Cler.*  Why, I commend you, lads.  Little knows Don Bridegroom of this; nor shall he, for me.

*Daw.*  Hang him, mad ox!

*Cler.*  Speak softly; here comes his nephew, with the lady Haughty: he 'll get the ladies from you, sirs, if you look not to him in time.

---

[4] A famous bed eleven feet square, now in the Victoria and Albert Museum, supposed to be capable of accommodating twelve people.

*La-F.*  Why, if he do, we 'll fetch 'em home again, I warrant you.                    [*Exit with Daw. Cler. walks aside.*]


## Act V.  Scene II

### Haughty, Dauphine, Centaure, Mavis, Clerimont

[*Hau.*]  I assure you, Sir Dauphine, it is the price and estimation of your virtue only, that hath embark'd me to this adventure; and I could not but make out to tell you so: nor can I repent me of the act, since it is always an argument of some virtue in our selves, that we love and affect it so in others.

*Daup.*  Your ladyship sets too high a price on my weakness.

*Hau.*  Sir, I can distinguish gems from pebbles —

*Daup.*  [*Aside.*]  Are you so skilful in stones?

*Hau.*  And howsoever I may suffer in such a judgment as yours, by admitting equality of rank or society with Centaure or Mavis —

*Daup.*  You do not, madam; I perceive they are your mere foils.

*Hau.*  Then are you a friend to truth, sir; it makes me love you the more. It is not the outward, but the inward man that I affect. They are not apprehensive of an eminent perfection, but love flat and dully.

*Cen.*  [*Within.*]  Where are you, my lady Haughty?

*Hau.*  I come presently, Centaure. — My chamber, sir, my page shall show you; and Trusty, my woman, shall be ever awake for you: you need not fear to communicate any thing with her, for she is a Fidelia.[5]  I pray you, wear this jewel for my sake, Sir Dauphine —


[*Enter Centaure*]

Where 's Mavis, Centaure?

*Cen.*  Within, madam, a-writing. I 'll follow you presently. [*Exit Hau.*] I 'll but speak a word with Sir Dauphine.

*Daup.*  With me, madam?

*Cen.*  Good Sir Dauphine, do not trust Haughty, nor make any credit to her[6] whatever you do besides. Sir Dauphine, I give you this caution, she is a perfect courtier, and loves nobody but for her uses; and for her uses she loves all. Besides, her physicians give her out to be none o' the clearest; whether she pay 'em or no, heaven knows; and she 's above fifty too, and pargets![7] See her in a forenoon. Here comes Mavis, a worse face than she! you would not like this by candlelight.

---

[5] A faithful one.          [6] Do not give any credit to her.
[7] Plasters herself (with make-up).

[*Enter Mavis*]

If you 'll come to my chamber one o' these mornings early, or late
in an evening, I 'll tell you more. Where 's Haughty, Mavis?

*Mav.*   Within, Centaure.

*Cen.*   What ha' you there?

*Mav.*   An Italian riddle for Sir Dauphine, — you shall not see it,
i' faith, Centaure. — [*Exit Cen.*] Good Sir Dauphine, solve it for
me: I 'll call for it anon.                                    [*Exit.*]

*Cler.* [*Coming forward.*]   How now, Dauphine! how dost thou
quit thyself of these females?

*Daup.*   'Slight, they haunt me like fairies, and give me jewels
here; I cannot be rid of 'em.

*Cler.*   O, you must not tell though.

*Daup.*   Mass, I forgot that: I was never so assaulted. One loves
for virtue, and bribes me with this: [*shows the jewel.*] — another
loves me with caution, and so would possess me; a third brings me a
riddle here: and all are jealous, and rail each at other.

*Cler.*   A riddle! pray le' me see 't.          *He reads the paper.*

Sir Dauphine, I chose this way of intimation for privacy. The ladies
here, I know, have both hope and purpose to make a collegiate and
servant of you. If I might be so honour'd, as to appear at any end of so
noble a work, I would enter into a fame[8] of taking physic to-morrow,
and continue it four or five days, or longer, for your visitation.

                                                               MAVIS

By my faith, subtle one! Call you this a riddle? what 's their
plain-dealing, trow?

*Daup.*   We lack Truewit to tell us that.

*Cler.*   We lack him for somewhat else too: his knights reforma-
dos[9] are wound up as high and insolent as ever they were.

*Daup.*   You jest.

*Cler.*   No drunkards, either with wine or vanity, ever confess'd
such stories of themselves. I would not give a fly's leg in balance
against all the women's reputations here, if they could be but
thought to speak truth: and for the bride, they have made their
affidavit against her directly —

*Daup.*   What, that they have lien with her?

*Cler.*   Yes; and tell times and circumstances, with the cause why,
and the place where. I had almost brought 'em to affirm that they
had done it to-day.

*Daup.*   Not both of 'em?

*Cler.*   Yes, faith; with a sooth[1] or two more I had effected it.
They would ha' set it down under their hands.

---

8 Rumor.              9 Discharged, set loose.              1 Cajolery.

*Daup.* Why, they will be our sport, I see, still, whether we will or no.

## Act V. Scene III

### Truewit, Morose, Otter, Cutbeard, Clerimont, Dauphine

[*True.*] O, are you here? Come, Dauphine; go call your uncle presently: I have fitted my divine and my canonist, dyed their beards and all. The knaves do not know themselves, they are so exalted and alter'd. Perferment changes any man. Thou shalt keep one door and I another, and then Clerimont in the midst, that he may have no means of escape from their cavilling, when they grow hot once. And then the women, as I have given the bride her instructions, to break in upon him i' the l'envoy.[2] O, will be full and twanging![3] Away! fetch him.                           [*Exit Dauphine.*]

[*Enter Otter disguised as a divine, and Cutbeard as a canon lawyer*]

Come, master doctor, and master parson, look to your parts now, and discharge 'em bravely; you are well set forth, perform it as well. If you chance to be out, do not confess it with standing still, or humming, or gaping one at another; but go on, and talk aloud and eagerly; use vehement action, and only remember your terms, and you are safe. Let the matter go where it will: you have many will do so. But at first be very solemn and grave, like your garments, though you loose your selves after, and skip out like a brace of jugglers on a table. Here he comes: set your faces, and look superciliously, while I present you.

[*Enter Dauphine with Morose*]

*Mor.* Are these the two learned men?

*True.* Yes, sir; please you salute 'em.

*Mor.* Salute 'em! I had rather do any thing, than wear out time so unfruitfully, sir. I wonder how these common forms, as "God save you," and "You are welcome," are come to be a habit in our lives: or, "I am glad to see you!" when I cannot see what the profit can be of these words, so long as it is no whit better with him whose affairs are sad and grievous, that he hears this salutation.

*True.* 'T is true, sir; we 'll go to the matter then. — Gentlemen, master doctor, and master parson, I have acquainted you

---

[2] End.                   [3] Fine.

sufficiently with the business for which you are come hither; and you are not now to inform yourselves in the state of the question, I know. This is the gentleman who expects your resolution, and therefore, when you please, begin.

*Ott.* Please you, master doctor.

*Cut.* Please you, good master parson.

*Ott.* I would hear the canon-law speak first.

*Cut.* It must give place to positive divinity, sir.

*Mor.* Nay, good gentlemen, do not throw me into circumstances. Let your comforts arrive quickly at me, those that are. Be swift in affording me my peace, if so I shall hope any. I love not your disputations, or your court-tumults. And that it be not strange to you, I will tell you. My father, in my education, was wont to advise me, that I should always collect and contain my mind, not suffering it to flow loosely; that I should look to what things were necessary to the carriage of my life, and what not; embracing the one and eschewing the other: in short, that I should endear myself to rest, and avoid turmoil; which now is grown to be another nature to me. So that I come not to your public pleadings, or your places of noise; not that I neglect those things that make for the dignity of the commonwealth; but for the mere avoidance of clamours and impertinencies of orators, that know not how to be silent. And for the cause of noise, am I now a suitor to you. You do not know in what a misery I have been exercis'd this day, what a torrent of evil! my very house turns round with the tumult! I dwell in a windmill: the perpetual motion is here, and not at Eltham.[4]

*True.* Well, good master doctor, will you break the ice? master parson will wade after.

*Cut.* Sir, though unworthy, and the weaker, I will presume.

*Ott.* 'T is no presumption, *domine* doctor.

*Mor.* Yet again!

*Cut.* Your question is, For how many causes a man may have *divortium legitimum*, a lawful divorce? First, you must understand the nature of the word, divorce, *a divertendo*[5] —

*Mor.* No excursions upon words, good doctor; to the question briefly.

*Cut.* I answer then, the canon law affords divorce but in few cases; and the principal is in the common case, the adulterous case. But there are *duodecim impedimenta*, twelve impediments, as we call 'em, all which do not *dirimere contractum*, but *irritum reddere*

---

[4] Where a Dutchman, Cornelis Drebbel, lived, who claimed to have invented a machine with perpetual motion.

[5] From "diverting" or separating.

*matrimonium*, as we say in the canon law, *not take away the bond, but cause a nullity therein.*

*Mor.* I understood you before: good sir, avoid your impertinency of translation.

*Ott.* He cannot open[6] this too much, sir, by your favour.

*Mor.* Yet more!

*True.* O, you must give the learned men leave, sir. — To your impediments, master doctor.

*Cut.* The first is *impedimentum erroris*.

*Ott.* Of which there are several species.

*Cut.* Ay, as *error personæ*.

*Ott.* If you contract yourself to one person, thinking her another.

*Cut.* Then, *error fortunæ*.

*Ott.* If she be a beggar, and you thought her rich.

*Cut.* Then, *error qualitatis*.

*Ott.* If she proves stubborn or headstrong, that you thought obedient.

*Mor.* How! is that, sir, a lawful impediment? One at once, I pray you, gentlemen.

*Ott.* Ay, *ante copulam*, but not *post copulam*, sir.

*Cut.* Master parson says right. *Nec post nuptiarum benedictionem.*[7] It doth indeed but *irritata reddere sponsalia*, annul the contract;[8] after marriage it is no obstancy.[9]

*True.* Alas, sir, what a hope are we fall'n from by this time!

*Cut.* The next is *conditio*: if you thought her free born, and she proves a bond-woman, there is impediment of estate and condition.

*Ott.* Ay, but, master doctor, those servitudes are *sublatæ*[1] now, among us Christians.

*Cut.* By your favour, master parson —

*Ott.* You shall give me leave, master doctor.

*Mor.* Nay, gentlemen, quarrel not in that question; it concerns not my case: pass to the third.

*Cut.* Well then, the third is *votum*: if either party have made a vow of chastity. But that practice, as master parson said of the other, is taken away among us, thanks be to discipline.[2] The fourth is *cognatio*; if the persons be of kin within the degrees.

*Ott.* Ay: do you know what the degrees are, sir?

*Mor.* No, nor I care not, sir; they offer me no comfort in the question, I am sure.

---

[6] Make clear.
[8] I.e., the betrothal.
[1] Abolished.

[7] And not after the benediction of the marriage.
[9] Obstacle.
[2] Teaching (of the church).

*Cut.* But there is a branch of this impediment may, which is *cognatio spiritualis:* if you were her godfather, sir, then the marriage is incestuous.

*Ott.* That comment is absurd and superstitious, master doctor: I cannot endure it. Are we not all brothers and sisters, and as much akin in that, as godfathers and goddaughters?

*Mor.* O me! to end the controversy, I never was a godfather, I never was a godfather in my life, sir. Pass to the next.

*Cut.* The fift is *crimen adulterii;* the known case. The sixt, *cultus disparitas*, difference of religion: Have you ever examin'd her, what religion she is of?

*Mor.* No, I would rather she were of none, than be put to the trouble of it.

*Ott.* You may have it done for you, sir.

*Mor.* By no means, good sir; on to the rest! Shall you ever come to an end, think you?

*True.* Yes, he has done half, sir — On to the rest. — Be patient, and expect, sir.

*Cut.* The seventh is, *vis:* if it were upon compulsion or force.

*Mor.* O no, it was too voluntary, mine; too voluntary.

*Cut.* The eight is, *ordo;* if ever she have taken holy orders.

*Ott.* That's superstitious, too.

*Mor.* No matter, master parson. Would she would go into a nunnery yet.

*Cut.* The ninth is, *ligamen;* if you were bound, sir, to any other before.

*Mor.* I thrust myself too soon into these fetters.

*Cut.* The tenth is *publica honestas;*[3] which is *inchoata quædam affinitas.*[4]

*Ott.* Ay, or *affinitas orta ex sponsalibus;*[5] and is but *leve impedimentum.*[6]

*Mor.* I feel no air of comfort blowing to me, in all this.

*Cut.* The eleventh is, *affinitas ex fornicatione.*[7]

*Ott.* Which is less *vera affinitas,*[8] than the other, master doctor.

*Cut.* True, *quæ oritur ex legitimo matrimonio.*[9]

*Ott.* You say right, venerable doctor: and, *nascitur ex eo, quod per conjugium duæ personæ efficiuntur una caro*[1] —

*Mor.* Hey-day, now they begin!

---

[3] Public reputation.
[4] Some incomplete relationship by marriage.
[5] Relationship arising out of betrothal.   [6] Slight impediment.
[7] Relationship from fornication.   [8] True relationship.
[9] Which arises out of lawful matrimony.
[1] It begins in this, that through marriage two persons are made one flesh.

*Cut.* I conceive you, master parson: *ita per fornicationem æque est verus pater, qui sic generat*[2] —

*Ott.* *Et vere filius qui sic generatur*[3] —

*Mor.* What 's all this to me?

*Cler.* Now it grows warm.

*Cut.* The twelfth and last is, *si forte coire nequibis.*[4]

*Ott.* Aye, that is *impedimentum gravissimum:*[5] it doth utterly annul, and annihilate, that. If you have *manifestam frigiditatem,*[6] you are well, sir.

*True.* Why, there is comfort come at length, sir. Confess yourself but a man unable, and she will sue to be divorc'd first.

*Ott.* Ay, or if there be *morbus perpetuus, et insanabilis;*[7] as *paralysis, elephantiasis,* or so —

*Daup.* O, but *frigiditas* is the fairer way, gentlemen.

*Ott.* You say troth, sir, and as it is in the canon, master doctor —

*Cut.* I conceive you, sir.

*Cler.* Before he speaks!

*Ott.* That a boy, or child, under years, is not fit for marriage, because he cannot *reddere debitum.*[8] So your *omnipotentes* —

*True.* Your *impotentes*, you whoreson lobster! [*Aside to Ott.*]

*Ott.* Your *impotentes*, I should say, are *minime apti ad contrahenda matrimonium.*[9]

*True.* *Matrimonium!* we shall have most unmatrimonial Latin with you: *matrimonia*, and be hang'd!

*Daup.* You put 'em out, man.

*Cut.* But then there will arise a doubt, master parson, in our case, *post matrimonium:*[1] that *frigiditate præditus*[2] — do you conceive me, sir?

*Ott.* Very well, sir.

*Cut.* Who cannot *uti uxore pro uxore*, may *habere eam pro sorore.*[3]

*Ott.* Absurd, absurd, absurd, and merely apostatical!

*Cut.* You shall pardon me, master parson, I can prove it.

*Ott.* You can prove a will, master doctor; you can prove nothing else. Does not the verse of your own canon say,

> *Hæc socianda vetant connubia, facta retractant?*[4]

[2] Thus he is equally a true father who thus begets —
[3] And truly a son who is thus begotten.
[4] If perchance you shall be incapable of coition.
[5] A very serious impediment.    [6] Manifest frigidity.
[7] A perpetual and incurable disease.    [8] Pay his debt.
[9] Least fitted to contract marriage.    [1] After the marriage.
[2] A man afflicted with frigidity.
[3] Use a wife as a wife may her for a sister.
[4] These things forbid marriages to be joined, and when made revoke them.

*Cut.*  I grant you; but how do they *retractare*, master parson?

*Mor.*  O, this was it I feared.

*Ott.*  *In æternum,*[5] sir.

*Cut.*  That 's false in divinity, by your favour.

*Ott.*  'T is false in humanity to say so. Is he not *prorsus inutilis ad thorum?*[6] Can he *præstare fidem datam?*[7] I would fain know.

*Cut.*  Yes; how if he do *convalere*[8]?

*Ott.*  He cannot *convalere*, it is impossible.

*True.*  Nay, good sir, attend the learned men; they 'll think you neglect 'em else.

*Cut.*  Or, if he do *simulare* himself *frigidum, odio uxoris,*[9] or so?

*Ott.*  I say, he is *adulter manifestus*[1] then.

*Daup.*  They dispute it very learnedly, i' faith.

*Ott.*  And *prostitutor uxoris;*[2] and this is positive.

*Mor.*  Good sir, let me escape.

*True.*  You will not do me that wrong, sir?

*Ott.*  And, therefore, if he be *manifeste frigidus*, sir —

*Cut.*  Ay, if he be *manifeste frigidus*, I grant you —

*Ott.*  Why, that was my conclusion.

*Cut.*  And mine too.

*True.*  Nay, hear the conclusion, sir.

*Ott.*  Then, *frigiditatis causa* —

*Cut.*  Yes, *causa frigiditatis* —

*Mor.*  O, mine ears!

*Ott.*  She may have *libellum divortii*[3] against you.

*Cut.*  Ay, *divortii libellum* she will sure have.

*Mor.*  Good echoes, forbear.

*Ott.*  If you confess it. —

*Cut.*  Which I would do, sir —

*Mor.*  I will do anything.

*Ott.*  And clear myself *in foro conscientiæ*[4] —

*Cut.*  Because you want indeed —

*Mor.*  Yet more!

*Ott.*  *Exercendi potestate.*[5]

---

[5] For ever.
[6] Altogether useless in the marriage bed.
[7] Perform the promise given.
[8] Recover.
[9] Pretend himself to be frigid out of hatred for his wife.
[1] Manifest adulterer.
[2] Prostituter of his wife.
[3] Libel of divorce.
[4] At the bar of conscience.
[5] The power of achieving.

## Act V.  Scene IIII

*Epicœne, Morose, Haughty, Centaure, Mavis, Mrs.
Otter, Daw, Truewit, Dauphine, Clerimont, La-Foole,
Otter, Cutbeard*

[*Epi.*]  I will not endure it any longer. Ladies, I beseech you,
help me. This is such a wrong as never was offer'd to poor bride
before: upon her marriage-day to have her husband conspire against
her, and a couple of mercenary companions to be brought in for
form's sake, to persuade a separation! If you had blood or virtue in
you, gentlemen, you would not suffer such earwigs about a husband, or scorpions to creep between man and wife.

*Mor.*  O the variety and changes of my torment!

*Hau.*  Let 'em be cudgell'd out of doors by our grooms.

*Cen.*  I 'll lend you my footman.

*Mav.*  We 'll have our men blanket[6] 'em i' the hall.

*Mrs. Ott.*  As there was one at our house, madam, for peeping
in at the door.

*Daw.*  Content, i' faith.

*True.*  Stay, ladies and gentlemen; you 'll hear before you proceed?

*Mav.*  I 'd ha 'the bridegroom blanketed too.

*Cen.*  Begin with him first.

*Hau.*  Yes, by my troth.

*Mor.*  O mankind[7] generation!

*Daup.*  Ladies, for my sake forbear.

*Hau.*  Yes, for Sir Dauphine's sake.

*Cen.*  He is as fine a gentleman of his inches, madam, as any is
about the town, and wears as good colours when he list.

*True.*  Be brief, sir, and confess your infirmity; she 'll be a-fire to
quit of you, if she but hear that nam'd once; you shall not entreat
her to stay. She 'll fly you like one that had the marks upon him.

*Mor.*  Ladies, I must crave all your pardons —

*True.*  Silence, ladies.

*Mor.*  For a wrong I have done to your whole sex in marrying
this fair and virtuous gentlewoman —

*Cler.*  Hear him, good ladies.

*Mor.*  Being guilty of an infirmity, which, before I conferr'd
with these learned men, I thought I might have conceal'd —

*True.*  But now being better inform'd in his conscience by them,
he is to declare it, and give satisfaction, by asking your public forgiveness.

---

[6] Toss in a blanket.          [7] Crazed.

*Mor.*  I am no man, ladies.

*All.*  How!

*Mor.*  Utterly unabled in nature, by reason of frigidity, to perform the duties, or any the least office of a husband.

*Mav.*  Now out upon him, prodigious[8] creature!

*Cen.*  Bridegroom uncarnate[9]!

*Hau.*  And would you offer it to a young gentlewoman?

*Mrs. Ott.*  A lady of her longings?

*Epi.*  Tut, a device, a device, this! It smells rankly, ladies. A mere comment of his own.

*True.*  Why, if you suspect that, ladies, you may have him search'd —

*Daw.*  As the custom is, by a jury of physicians.

*La-F.*  Yes, faith, 't will be brave.

*Mor.*  O me, must I undergo that?

*Mrs. Ott.*  No, let women search him, madam; we can do it ourselves.

*Mor.*  Out on me! worse.

*Epi.*  No, ladies, you shall not need, I 'll take him with all his faults.

*Mor.*  Worst of all!

*Cler.*  Why then, 't is no divorce, doctor, if she consent not?

*Cut.*  No, if the man be *frigidus*, it is *de parte uxoris*, that we grant *libellum divortii*, in the law.

*Ott.*  Ay, it is the same in theology.

*Mor.*  Worse, worse than worst!

*True.*  Nay, sir, be not utterly disheartn'd; we have yet a small relic of hope left, as near as our comfort is blown out. Clerimont, produce your brace of knights. What was that, master parson, you told me *in errore qualitatis*, e'en now? —Dauphine, whisper the bride, that she carry it as if she were guilty, and asham'd.    [*Aside.*]

*Ott.*  Marry, sir, *in errore qualitatis*, (which master doctor did forbear to urge), if she be found *corrupta*, that is, vitiated or broken up, that wes *pro virgine desponsa*, espous'd for a maid —

*Mor.*  What then, sir?

*Ott.*  It doth *dirimere contractum*, and *irritum reddere*[1] too.

*True.*  If this be true, we are happy again, sir, once more. Here are an honourable brace of knights, that shall affirm so much.

*Daw.*  Pardon us, good master Clerimont.

*La-F.*  You shall excuse us, master Clerimont.

*Cler.*  Nay, you must make it good now, knights, there is no

---

[8] Unnatural.                    [9] Without flesh and blood.

[1] Cancel the contract and render it null and void.

remedy; I 'll eat no words for you, nor no men: you know you spoke it to me.

*Daw.*   Is this gentleman-like, sir?

*True.*   Jack Daw, he 's worse than Sir Amorous; fiercer a great deal. [*Aside to Daw.*] Sir Amorous, beware, there be ten Daws in this Clerimont.                          [*Aside to La-Foole.*]

*La-F.*   I 'll confess it, sir.

*Daw.*   Will you, Sir Amorous, will you wound reputation?

*La-F.*   I am resolv'd.

*True.*   So should you be too, Jack Daw: what should keep you off? She is but a woman, and in disgrace: he 'll be glad on 't.

*Daw.*   Will he? I thought he would ha' been angry.

*Cler.*   You will dispatch, knights; it must be done, i' faith.

*True.*   Why, an it must, it shall, sir, they say: they 'll ne'er go back. — Do not tempt his patience.           [*Aside to them.*]

*Daw.*   It is true indeed, sir.

*La-F.*   Yes, I assure you, sir.

*Mor.*   What is true, gentlemen? what do you assure me?

*Daw.*   That we have known your bride, sir —

*La-F.*   In good fashion. She was our mistress, or so —

*Cler.*   Nay, you must be plain, knights, as you were to me.

*Ott.*   Ay, the question is, if you have *carnaliter*, or no?

*La-F.*   *Carnaliter!* what else, sir?

*Ott.*   It is enough; a plain nullity.

*Epi.*   I am undone, I am undone!

*Mor.*   O let me worship and adore you, gentlemen!

*Epi.*   I am undone.                              [*Weeps.*]

*Mor.*   Yes, to my hand, I thank these knights. Master parson, let me thank you otherwise.             [*Gives him money.*]

*Cen.*   And ha' they confess'd?

*Mav.*   Now out upon 'em, informers!

*True.*   You see what creatures you may bestow your favours on, madams.

*Hau.*   I would except against 'em as beaten knights, wench, and not good witnesses in law.

*Mrs. Ott.*   Poor gentlewoman, how she takes it!

*Hau.*   Be comforted, Morose, I love you the better for 't.

*Cen.*   So do I, I protest.

*Cut.*   But, gentlemen, you have not known her since *matrimonium?*

*Daw.*   Not to-day, master doctor.

*La-F.*   No, sir, not to-day.

*Cut.*   Why, then I say, for any act before, the *matrimonium* is good and perfect; unless the worshipful bridegroom did precisely, before witness, demand, if she were *virgo ante nuptias.*

*Epi.* No, that he did not, I assure you, master doctor.

*Cut.* If he cannot prove that, it is *ratum conjugium,*[2] nothwithstanding the premises; and they do no way *impedire.* And this is my sentence, this I pronounce.

*Ott.* I am of master doctor's resolution too, sir; if you made not that demand *ante nuptias.*

*Mor.* O my heart! wilt thou break? wilt thou break? this is worst of all worst worsts that hell could have devis'd! Marry a whore, and so much noise!

*Daup.* Come, I see now plain confederacy in this doctor and this parson, to abuse a gentleman. You study his affliction. I pray be gone, companions. — And, gentlemen, I begin to suspect you for having parts with 'em. — Sir, will it please you hear me?

*Mor.* O do not talk to me; take not from me the pleasure of of dying in silence, nephew.

*Daup.* Sir, I must speak to you. I have been long your poor despis'd kinsman, and many a hard thought has strengthen'd you against me: but now it shall appear if either I love you or your peace, and prefer them to all the world beside. I will not be long or grievous to you, sir. If I free you of this unhappy match abolutely, and instantly, after all this trouble, and almost in your despair, now —

*Mor.* It cannot be.

*Daup.* Sir, that you be never troubled with a murmur of it more, what shall I hope for, or deserve of you?

*Mor.* O, what thou wilt, nephew! thou shalt deserve me, and have me.

*Daup.* Shall I have your favour perfect to me, and love hereafter?

*Mor.* That, and anything beside. Make thine own conditions. My whole estate is thine; manage it, I will become thy ward.

*Daup.* Nay, sir, I will not be so unreasonable.

*Epi.* Will Sir Dauphine be mine enemy too?

*Daup.* You know I have been long a suitor to you, uncle, that out of your estate, which is fifteen hundred a-year, you would allow me but five hundred during life, and assure the rest upon me after; to which I have often, by myself and friends, tendered you a writing to sign, which you would never consent or incline to. If you please but to effect it now —

*Mor.* Thou shalt have it, nephew: I will do it, and more.

*Daup.* If I quit you not presently, and for ever, of this cumber,[3]

2 Valid marriage.          3 Encumbrance.

you shall have power instantly, afore all these, to revoke your act, and I will become whose slave you will give me to, for ever.

*Mor.* Where is the writing? I will seal to it, or to a blank, and write thine own conditions.

*Epi.* O me, most unfortunate, wretched gentlewoman!

*Hau.* Will Sir Dauphine do this?

*Epi.* Good sir, have some compassion on me.

*Mor.* O, my nephew knows you, belike; away, crocodile!

*Cen.* He does it not, sure, without good ground.

*Daup.* Here, sir.      [*Gives him the parchments.*]

*Mor.* Come, nephew, give me the pen; I will subscribe to any-thing, and seal to what thou wilt, for my deliverance. Thou are my restorer. Here, I deliver it thee as my deed. If there be a word in it lacking, or writ with false orthography, I protest before heaven I will not take the advantage.      [*Returns the writings.*]

*Daup.* Then here is your release, sir. —      *He takes off* You have married a boy, a gentleman's son,      *Epicœne's peruke.* that I have brought up this half year at my great charges, and for this composition, which I have now made with you. — What say you, master doctor? This is *justum impedimentum*, I hope, *error personæ?*

*Ott.* Yes, sir *in primo gradu.*

*Cut.* *In primo gradu.*

*Daup.* I thank you, good doctor Cutbeard, and parson Otter. — You are beholden to 'em, sir, that      *He pulls off their* have taken this pains for you;      *beards and disguises.* and my friend, master Truewit, who enabled 'em for the business. Now you may go in and rest; be as private as you will, sir. [*Exit Morose.*] I 'll not trouble you, till you trouble me with your funeral, which I care not how soon it come. — Cutbeard, I 'll make your lease good. "Thank me not, but with your leg, Cutbeard." And Tom Otter, your princess shall be reconcil'd to you. — How now, gentlemen, do you look at me?

*Cler.* A boy!

*Daup.* Yes, mistress Epicœne.

*True.* Well, Dauphine, you have lurch'd[4] your friends of the better half of the garland,[5] by concealing this part of the plot: but much good do it thee, thou deserv'st it, lad. And, Clerimont, for thy unexpected bringing in these two to confession, wear my part of it freely. Nay, Sir Daw and Sir La-Foole, you see the gentle-woman that has done you the favours! we are all thankful to you, and so should the woman-kind here, specially for lying on her, though not with her! you meant so, I am sure. But that we have

---

[4] Cheated.      [5] Glory, credit.

stuck it upon you today, in your own imagin'd persons, and so lately, this Amazon, the champion of the sex, should beat you now thriftily, for the common slanders which ladies receive from such cuckoos as you are. You are they that, when no merit or fortune can make you hope to enjoy their bodies, will yet lie with their reputations, and make their fame suffer. Away, you common moths of these, and all ladies' honours. Go, travel to make legs and faces, and come home with some new matter to be laugh'd at; you deserve to live in an air as corrupted as that wherewith you feed rumour. [*Exeunt Daw and La-Foole.*] — Madams, you are mute, upon this new metamorphosis! But here stands she that has vindicated your fames. Take heed of such *insectæ* hereafter. And let it not trouble you, that you have discover'd any mysteries to this young gentleman. He is almost of years, and will make a good visitant within this twelvemonth. In the mean time, we 'll all undertake for his secrecy, that can speak so well of his silence. [*Coming forward.*] — Spectators, if you like this comedy, rise cheerfully, and now Morose is gone in, clap your hands. It may be, that noise will cure him, at least please him.                [*Exeunt.*]

**THE END**

# THE
# TRAGEDY
## *of The Dutchesse of Malfy.*

*As it was Presented priuatly, at the Black-Friers; and publiquely at the Globe, By the* Kings Maiesties Seruants.

*The Perfect and exact Copy, with diuerse things Printed, that the length of the Play would* not beare in the Presentment.

## Written by *John Webster*

HORA. —— *Si quid* ——
—— *Candidus Imperti si non bis utere mecum.*[1]

## LONDON:
Printed by Nicholas Okes, for Iohn Waterson, and are to be sold at the signe of the Crowne, in Paules Church-yard. 1 6 2 3 .

---

[1] If aught [better than these you know] kindly tell me; if not, make use of these with me.

# The Duchess of Malfi

≥ *JOHN WEBSTER*
was born free of the Merchant Taylor's Company of London,
since his father was already a member, but the date of his birth
is uncertain and may be placed in any year between 1570 and
1580. He is first heard of as a dramatist in 1602 when he received
several payments from Henslowe for work he was doing for the
company. He collaborated for a while with Dekker, and in 1612
published his first important play, *The White Devil*. Very little
is known of the facts of Webster's life. He wrote *The Devil's
Law Case*, a comedy, about 1620 and subsequently collaborated
with Massinger and Ford. He died some time after 1627, and in
1634 was referred to as dead.

*The Duchess of Malfi* was printed in 1623, and was evidently
seen through the press by Webster himself, since the title page
informs us that the cuts in the text made by the producer have
been restored. The play was acted at both their theatres by Shakespeare's company, the King's Men, and the list of *dramatis personae* shows the names of the actors who played the various parts.
There are two distinct casts here; the first belongs to performances
before William Ostler's death on 21 December 1614, and the
second to performances after Richard Burbage's death on 13
March 1619. The earlier cast is almost certainly that of the original performances.

The Duchess and her two brothers were actual people, the children of Ferdinand I, King of Naples. Giovanna, the daughter,
was married at the age of twelve to the heir of the Duke of Amalfi
and was left a widow at twenty; she carried on the government of
the duchy on behalf of her infant son. The story of her persecution by her brothers for secretly marrying Antonio Bologna and
her subsequent death is told by Matteo Bandello in his *Novelle*
(I, 26). Bandello narrates the tale as told by Antonio himself to a
certain Delio, who last saw Antonio just before his assassination.
Delio was a name used elsewhere by Bandello as a disguise for
himself, so it is very probable that he rendered the tale much as he
had heard it from Antonio. Webster, however, probably found
the story in the English version of William Painter in his *Palace of*

*Pleasure*, 1567; he did not hesitate to use it freely and make alterations for the purpose of the play.

Books. The standard edition of Webster is *The Complete Works*, edited by F. L. Lucas, 4 volumes, London, 1927. Rupert Brooke's *John Webster and the Elizabethan Drama*, London and New York, 1916, is a stimulating work that is still worth reading; a more recent study is C. Leech, *John Webster, a critical study*, London, 1951.

## The Actors' Names

BOSOLA, *J. Lowin*
FERDINAND [Duke of Calabria], *1 R. Burbidge. 2 J. Taylor*
CARDINAL [his Brother], *1 H. Cundaile. 2 R. Robinson*
ANTONIO [BOLOGNA, Steward to the Duchess],
  *1 W. Ostler. 2 R. Benfeild*
DELIO, *J. Underwood*
FOROBOSCO, *N. Towley*
MALATESTE
MARQUESSE OF PESCARA, *J. Rice*
SILVIO, *T. Pollard*
[CASTRUCHIO, an Old Lord, Husband of Julia]
[RODERIGO and GRISOLAN, Gentlemen attending the Duke]
The Several Madmen, *N. Towley, J. Underwood, &c.*

THE DUCHESS, *R. Sharpe*
The Cardinal's Mistress [JULIA], *J. Tomson*

The Doctor, ⎫
CARIOLA, ⎬ *R. Pallant*
Court Officers, ⎭

[Old Lady]
  Three Young Children; Two Pilgrims; [Executioners, and Other
  Attendants]

(SCENE: The Duchess's palace, Amalfi; Cardinal's palace, Rome;
  Loretto and neighboring country; Milan.)

301

## Actus Primus.  Scena Prima

*Antonio and Delio, [later] Bosola, Cardinal*

*Delio.*   You are welcome to your country, dear Antonio;
You have been long in France, and you return
A very formal Frenchman in your habit.[2]
How do you like the French court?
    *Ant.*                                    I admire it.
In seeking to reduce both state and people
To a fix'd order, their judicious king
Begins at home; quits[3] first his royal palace
Of flatt'ring sycophants, of dissolute
And infamous persons, — which he sweetly terms
His Master's masterpiece, the work of heaven;
Considering duly that a prince's court
Is like a common fountain, whence should flow
Pure silver drops in general, but if 't chance
Some curs'd example poison 't near the head,
Death and diseases through the whole land spread.
And what is 't makes this blessed government
But a most provident council, who dare freely
Inform him the corruption of the times?
Though some o' th' court hold it presumption
To instruct princes what they ought to do,
It is a noble duty to inform them
What they ought to foresee. — Here comes Bosola,
The only court-gall; yet I observe his railing
Is not for simple love of piety:
Indeed, he rails at those things which he wants;
Would be as lecherous, covetous, or proud,
Bloody, or envious, as any man,
If he had means to be so. — Here 's the cardinal.

*[Enter Cardinal and Bosola]*

    *Bos.*   I do haunt you still.
    *Card.*   So.
    *Bos.*   I have done you better service than to be slighted thus.
Miserable age, where only the reward of doing well is the doing
of it!
    *Card.*   You enforce your merit too much.

---

  [2] Clothing.          [3] Rids.

*Bos.*   I fell into the galleys[4] in your service; where, for two years together, I wore two towels instead of a shirt, with a knot on the shoulder, after the fashion of a Roman mantle. Slighted thus! I will thrive some way. Blackbirds fatten best in hard weather; why not I in these dog-days?

*Card.*   Would you could become honest!

*Bos.*   With all your divinity do but direct me the way to it. I have known many travel far for it, and yet return as arrant knaves as they went forth, because they carried themselves always along with them. [*Exit Cardinal.*] Are you gone? Some fellows, they say, are possessed with the devil, but this great fellow were able to possess the greatest devil, and make him worse.

*Ant.*   He hath denied thee some suit?

*Bos.*   He and his brother are like plum-trees that grow crooked over standing-pools;[5] they are rich and o'erladen with fruit, but none but crows, pies,[6] and caterpillars feed on them. Could I be one of their flattering pandars, I would hang on their ears like a horseleech, till I were full, and then drop off. I pray, leave me. Who would rely upon these miserable dependences, in expectation to be advanc'd tomorrow? What creature ever fed worse than hoping Tantalus? Nor ever died any man more fearfully than he that hop'd for a pardon. There are rewards for hawks and dogs when they have done us service; but for a soldier that hazards his limbs in a battle, nothing but a kind of geometry is his last supportation.[7]

*Delio.*   Geometry?

*Bos.*   Ay, to hang in a fair pair of slings, take his latter swing in the world upon an honourable pair of crutches, from hospital to hospital. Fare ye well, sir: and yet do not you scorn us; for places in the court are but like beds in the hospital, where this man's head lies at that man's foot, and so lower and lower.          [*Exit.*]

*Del.*   I knew this fellow seven years in the galleys
For a notorious murther; and 't was thought
The cardinal suborn'd it: he was releas'd
By the French general, Gaston de Foix,
When he recover'd Naples.

*Ant.*                              'T is great pity
He should be thus neglected: I have heard
He 's very valiant. This foul melancholy
Will poison all his goodness; for, I 'll tell you,
If too immoderate sleep be truly said
To be an inward rust unto the soul,

---

[4] Which were rowed by condemned criminals.
[5] Stagnant pools.          [6] Magpies.          [7] Support.

It then doth follow want of action
Breeds all black malcontents; and their close rearing,
Like moths in cloth, do hurt for want of wearing.

## SCENA II

*Antonio, Delio. [Enter to them] Silvio, Castruchio, Julia,*
*Roderigo, and Grisolan*

*Delio.*   The presence 'gins to fill; you promis'd me
To make me the partaker of the natures
Of some of your great courtiers.
*Ant.*                                The lord cardinal's
And other strangers' that are now in court?
I shall. — Here comes the great Calabrian duke.

*[Enter Ferdinand and Attendants]*

*Ferd.*   Who took the ring[8] oft'nest?
*Sil.*   Antonio Bologna, my lord.
*Ferd.*   Our sister duchess' great master of her household?  Give
him the jewel. — When shall we leave this sportive action, and fall
to action indeed?
*Cast.*   Methinks, my lord, you should not desire to go to war in
person.
*Ferd.*   Now for some gravity. — Why, my lord?
*Cast.*   It is fitting a soldier arise to be a prince, but not necessary
a prince descend to be a captain.
*Ferd.*   No?
*Cast.*   No, my lord; he were far better do it by a deputy.
*Ferd.*   Why should he not as well sleep or eat by a deputy?  This
might take idle, offensive, and base office from him, whereas the
other deprives him of honour.
*Cast.*   Believe my experience: that realm is never long in quiet
where the ruler is a soldier.
*Ferd.*   Thou told'st me thy wife could not endure fighting.
*Cast.*   True, my lord.
*Ferd.*   And of a jest she broke[9] of a captain she met full of
wounds: I have forgot it.
*Cast.*   She told him, my lord, he was a pitiful fellow, to lie, like
the children of Ismael, all in tents.[1]
*Ferd.*   Why, there 's a wit were able to undo all the chirurgeons[2]

---

[8] In the sport of riding at the ring.          [9] Made.
[1] Surgical dressings.                    [2] Surgeons.

o' the city; for although gallants should quarrel, and had drawn their weapons, and were ready to go to it, yet her persuasions would make them put up.

*Cast.* That she would, my lord. — How do you like my Spanish jennet?[3]

*Rod.* He is all fire.

*Ferd.* I am of Pliny's opinion: I think he was begot by the wind; he runs as if he were ballass'd[4] with quicksilver.

*Sir.* True, my lord, he reels from the tilt often.

*Rod., Gris.* Ha, ha, ha!

*Ferd.* Why do you laugh? Methinks you that are courtiers should be my touch-wood, take fire when I give fire; that is, laugh when I laugh, were the subject never so witty.

*Cast.* True, my lord: I myself have heard a very good jest, and have scorn'd to seem to have so silly a wit as to understand it.

*Ferd.* But I can laugh at your fool, my lord.

*Cast.* He cannot speak, you know, but he makes faces; my lady cannot abide him.

*Ferd.* No?

*Cast.* Nor endure to be in merry company; for she says too much laughing, and too much company, fills her too full of the wrinkle.

*Ferd.* I would, then, have a mathematical instrument made for her face, that she might not laugh out of compass.[5] — I shall shortly visit you at Milan, Lord Silvio.

*Sil.* Your grace shall arrive most welcome.

*Ferd.* You are a good horseman, Antonio: you have excellent riders in France. What do you think of good horsemanship?

*Ant.* Nobly, my lord: as out of the Grecian horse[6] issued many famous princes, so out of brave horsemanship arise the first sparks of growing resolution, that raise the mind to noble action.

*Ferd.* You have bespoke it worthily.

*Sil.* Your brother, the lord cardinal, and sister duchess.

[*Enter Cardinal, with Duchess, and Cariola*]

*Card.* Are the galleys come about?

*Gris.* They are, my lord.

*Ferd.* Here 's the Lord Silvio is come to take his leave.

*Delio.* Now, sir, your promise: what 's that cardinal?
I mean his temper. They say he 's a brave fellow,
Will play his five thousand crowns at tennis, dance,
Court ladies, and one that hath fought single combats.

[3] A breed of horse.     [4] Ballasted.
[5] Measure.     [6] At Troy.

*Ant.* Some such flashes superficially hang on him for form; but observe his inward character: he is a melancholy churchman. The spring in his face is nothing but the engend'ring of toads; where he is jealous of any man, he lays worse plots for them than ever was impos'd on Hercules, for he strews in his way flatterers, pandars, intelligencers,[7] atheists, and a thousand such political monsters. He should have been Pope; but instead of coming to it by the primitive decency of the church, he did bestow bribes so largely and so impudently as if he would have carried it away without heaven's knowledge. Some good he hath done ——

*Delio.* You have given too much of him. What 's his brother?

*Ant.* The duke there? A most perverse and turbulent nature.
What appears in him mirth is merely outside;
If he laugh heartily, it is to laugh
All honesty out of fashion.

*Delio.*                    Twins?

*Ant.*                              In quality.
He speaks with others' tongues, and hears men's suits
With others' ears; will seem to sleep o' th' bench
Only to entrap offenders in their answers;
Dooms men to death by information;
Rewards by hearsay.

*Delio.*            Then the law to him
Is like a foul, black cobweb to a spider, —
He makes it his dwelling and a prison
To entangle those shall feed him.

*Ant.*                              Most true:
He never pays debts unless they be shrewd[8] turns,
And those he will confess that he doth owe.
Last, for his brother there, the cardinal,
They that do flatter him most say oracles
Hang at his lips; and verily I believe them,
For the devil speaks in them.
But for their sister, the right noble duchess,
You never fix'd your eye on three fair medals
Cast in one figure, of so different temper.
For her discourse, it is so full of rapture,
You only will begin then to be sorry
When she doth end her speech, and wish, in wonder,
She held it less vain-glory to talk much,
Than your penance to hear her. Whilst she speaks,
She throws upon a man so sweet a look
That it were able raise one to a galliard[9]

7 Spies.                 8 Bad.                 9 Lively dance.

That lay in a dead palsy, and to dote
On that sweet countenance; but in that look
There speaketh so divine a continence
As cuts off all lascivious and vain hope.
Her days are practis'd in such noble virtue,
That sure her nights, nay, more, her very sleeps,
Are more in heaven than other ladies' shrifts.[1]
Let all sweet ladies break their flatt'ring glasses,
And dress themselves in her.

   *Delio.*                 Fie, Antonio,
You play the wire-drawer with[2] her commendations.

   *Ant.*    I 'll case the picture up:[3] only thus much;
All her particular worth grows to this sum, —
She stains[4] the time past, lights the time to come.

   *Cari.*    You must attend my lady in the gallery,
Some half an hour hence.

   *Ant.*    I shall.          [*Exeunt Antonio and Delio.*]

   *Ferd.*    Sister, I have a suit to you.

   *Duch.*              To me, sir?

   *Ferd.*    A gentleman here, Daniel de Bosola,
One that was in the galleys ——

   *Duch.*             Yes, I know him.

   *Ferd.*    A worthy fellow he 's: pray, let me entreat for
The provisorship[5] of your horse.

   *Duch.*           Your knowledge of him
Commends him and prefers him.

   *Ferd.*            Call him hither. [*Exit Attendants.*]
We are now upon parting. Good Lord Silvio,
Do us commend to all our noble friends
At the leaguer.[6]

   *Sil.*        Sir, I shall.

   *Duch.*        You are for Milan?

   *Sil.*    I am.

   *Duch.*    Bring the caroches.[7] — We 'll bring you down
To the haven.

        [*Exeunt Duchess, Silvio, Castruchio, Roderigo, Grisolan,*
                          *Cariola, Julia, and Attendants.*]

   *Card.*    Be sure you entertain that Bosola
For your intelligence.[8] I would not be seen in 't;
And therefore many times I have slighted him,
When he did court our furtherance,[9] as this morning.

---

[1] Confessions.          [2] Prolong.        [3] Put it away.
[4] Deprives of lustre.      [5] Office of purveyor.      [6] Camp.
[7] Carriages.      [8] Obtaining of secret information.      [9] Aid.

*Ferd.*   Antonio, the great master of her household,
Had been far fitter.

*Card.*               You are deceiv'd in him.
His nature is too honest for such business. —
He comes: I 'll leave you.                              [*Exit.*]

[*Re-enter Bosola*]

*Bos.*                I was lur'd to you.

*Ferd.*   My brother here, the cardinal, could never
Abide you.

*Bos.*      Never since he was in my debt.

*Ferd.*   May be some oblique character[1] in your face
Made him suspect you.

*Bos.*                Doth he study physiognomy?
There 's no more credit to be given to th' face
Than to a sick man's urine, which some call
The physician's whore, because she cozens him.
He did suspect me wrongfully.

*Ferd.*                For that
You must give great men leave to take their times.
Distrust doth cause us seldom be deceiv'd.
You see, the oft shaking of the cedar-tree
Fastens it more at root.

*Bos.*                Yet take heed;
For to suspect a friend unworthily
Instructs him the next[2] way to suspect you,
And prompts him to deceive you.

*Ferd.*                There 's gold.

*Bos.*                                So:
What follows? — [*Aside.*] Never rain'd such showers as these
Without thunderbolts i' th' tail of them. — Whose throat must I
cut?

*Ferd.*   Your inclination to shed blood rides post[3]
Before my occasion to use you. I give you that
To live i' th' court here, and observe the duchess;
To note all the particulars of her haviour,
What suitors do solicit her for marriage,
And whom she best affects. She 's a young widow:
I would not have her marry again.

*Bos.*                No, sir?

*Ferd.*   Do not you ask the reason; but be satisfied.
I say I would not.

---

[1] Sign of evil.          [2] Nearest.          [3] Hurries ahead.

*Bos.* It seems you would create me
One of your familiars.[4]

*Ferd.* Familiar! What 's that?

*Bos.* Why, a very quaint[5] invisible devil in flesh, —
An intelligencer.

*Ferd.* Such a kind of thriving thing
I would wish thee; and ere long thou mayst arrive
At a higher place by 't.

*Bos.* Take your devils,
Which hell calls angels![6] These curs'd gifts would make
You a corrupter, me an impudent traitor;
And should I take these, they 'd take me to hell.

*Ferd.* Sir, I 'll take nothing from you that I have given.
There is a place that I procur'd for you
This morning, the provisorship o' th' horse.
Have you heard on 't?

*Bos.* No.

*Ferd.* 'T is yours: is 't not worth thanks?

*Bos.* I would have you curse yourself now, that your bounty
(Which makes men truly noble) e'er should make me
A villain. O, that to avoid ingratitude
For the good deed you have done me, I must do
All the ill man can invent! Thus the devil
Candies all sins o'er: and what heaven terms vild,[7]
That names he complimental.[8]

*Ferd.* Be yourself;
Keep your old garb of melancholy; 't will express
You envy those that stand above your reach,
Yet strive not to come near 'em. This will gain
Access to private lodgings, where yourself
May, like a politic dormouse ——

*Bos.* As I have seen some
Feed in a lord's dish, half asleep, not seeming
To listen to any talk; and yet these rogues
Have cut his throat in a dream. What 's my place?
The provisorship o' th' horse? Say, then, my corruption
Grew out of horse-dung: I am your creature.

*Ferd.* Away! [*Exit.*]

*Bos.* Let good men, for good deeds, covet good fame,
Since place and riches oft are bribes of shame.
Sometimes the devil doth preach. *Exit Bosola.*

---

[4] Evil spirits.  [5] Cunning.
[6] Gold coins.  [7] Vile.
[8] A polite accomplishment.

[SCENE III]

[*Enter Ferdinand, Duchess, Cardinal, and Cariola*]

*Card.*   We are to part from you; and your own discretion
Must now be your director.
*Ferd.*                           You are a widow:
You know already what man is; and therefore
Let not youth, high promotion, eloquence ——
*Card.*   No,
Nor anything without the addition, honour,
Sway your high blood.
*Ferd.*                         Marry! They are most luxurious[9]
Will wed twice.
*Card.*         O, fie!
*Ferd.*                       Their livers are more spotted
Than Laban's sheep.
*Duch.*                 Diamonds are of most value,
They say, that have pass'd through most jewellers' hands.
*Ferd.*   Whores by that rule are precious.
*Duch.*                                       Will you hear me?
I 'll never marry.
*Card.*           So most widows say;
But commonly that motion lasts no longer
Than the turning of an hour-glass: the funeral sermon
And it end both together.
*Ferd.*                     Now hear me:
You live in a rank pasture, here, i' th' court;
There is a kind of honey-dew that 's deadly;
'T will poison your fame; look to 't. Be not cunning;
For they whose faces do belie their hearts
Are witches ere they arrive at twenty years,
Ay, and give the devil suck.
*Duch.*   This is terrible good counsel.
*Ferd.*   Hypocrisy is woven of a fine small thread,
Subtler than Vulcan's engine:[1] yet, believe 't,
Your darkest actions, nay, your privat'st thoughts,
Will come to light.
*Card.*             You may flatter yourself,
And take your own choice; privately be married
Under the eaves of night ——
*Ferd.*                         Think 't the best voyage

---

[9] Lustful.
[1] The fine net with which he captured Mars.

That e'er you made; like the irregular crab,
Which, though 't goes backward, thinks that it goes right
Because it goes its own way: but observe,
Such weddings may more properly be said
To be executed than celebrated.
    *Card.*                  The marriage night
Is the entrance into some prison.
    *Ferd.*                And those joys,
Those lustful pleasures, are like heavy sleeps
Which do fore-run man's mischief.
    *Card.*            Fare you well.
Wisdom begins at the end: remember it.         [*Exit.*]
    *Duch.*   I think this speech between you both was studied,
It came so roundly off.
    *Ferd.*          You are my sister;
This was my father's poniard, do you see?
I 'd be loath to see 't look rusty, 'cause 't was his.
I would have you to give o'er these chargeable revels:
A visor and a mask are whispering-rooms
That were never built for goodness. Fare ye well —
And women like that part which, like the lamprey,[2]
Hath never a bone in 't.
    *Duch.*         Fie, sir!
    *Ferd.*            Nay,
I mean the tongue: variety of courtship.
What cannot a neat knave with a smooth tale
Make a woman believe? Farewell, lusty widow.    [*Exit.*]
    *Duch.*   Shall this move me? If all my royal kindred
Lay in my way unto this marriage,
I 'd make them my low footsteps.[3] And even now,
Even in this hate, as men in some great battles,
By apprehending danger, have achiev'd
Almost impossible actions (I have heard soldiers say so),
So I through frights and threat'nings will assay
This dangerous venture. Let old wives report
I wink'd[4] and chose a husband. — Cariola,
To thy known secrecy I have given up
More than my life, — my fame.
    *Cari.*          Both shall be safe;
For I 'll conceal this secret from the world
As warily as those that trade in poison

---

[2] Fish like an eel.
[3] Steps of a staircase, or rungs of a ladder.
[4] Closed my eyes.

Keep poison from their children.

 *Duch.*        Thy protestation

Is ingenious[5] and hearty; I believe it.

Is Antonio come?

 *Cari.*   He attends you.

 *Duch.*       Good dear soul,

Leave me; but place thyself behind the arras,

Where thou may'st overhear us. Wish me good speed;

For I am going into a wilderness,

Where I shall find nor path nor friendly clue

To be my guide.   [*Cariola goes behind the arras.*]

[*Enter Antonio*]

      I sent for you: sit down;

Take pen and ink, and write. Are you ready?

 *Ant.*          Yes.

 *Duch.* What did I say?

 *Ant.*  That I should write somewhat.

 *Duch.*        O, I remember.

After these triumphs[6] and this large expense

It 's fit, like thrifty husbands, we inquire

What 's laid up for to-morrow.

 *Ant.*  So please your beauteous excellence.

 *Duch.*       Beauteous!

Indeed, I thank you. I look young for your sake;

You have ta'en my cares upon you.

 *Ant.*       I 'll fetch your grace

The particulars of your revenue and expense.

 *Duch.* O, you are

An upright treasurer, but you mistook;

For when I said I meant to make inquiry

What 's laid up for to-morrow, I did mean

What 's laid up yonder for me.

 *Ant.*      Where?

 *Duch.*       In heaven.

I am making my will (as 't is fit princes should,

In perfect memory), and, I pray, sir, tell me,

Were not one better make it smiling, thus,

Than in deep groans and terrible ghastly looks,

As if the gifts we parted with procur'd[7]

That violent distraction?[8]

 *Ant.*    O, much better.

 *Duch.* If I had a husband now, this care were quit:[9]

<hr/>

[5] Ingenuous.     [6] Festivities.     [7] Brought on.

[8] Confusion.     [9] Removed.

But I intend to make you overseer.[1]
What good deed shall we first remember? Say.

   *Ant.*    Begin with that first good deed began i' th' world.
After man's creation, the sacrament of marriage.
I 'd have you first provide for a good husband:
Give him all.

   *Duch.*        All!

   *Ant.*            Yes, your excellent self.

   *Duch.*    In a winding-sheet?

   *Ant.*                In a couple.

   *Duch.*    Saint Winfrid, that were a strange will!

   *Ant.*    'T were stranger if there were no will in you
To marry again.

   *Duch.*            What do you think of marriage?

   *Ant.*    I take 't, as those that deny purgatory:
It locally contains or heaven or hell;
There 's no third place in 't.

   *Duch.*                How do you affect it?

   *Ant.*    My banishment, feeding my melancholy,
Would often reason thus: —

   *Duch.*            Pray, let 's hear it.

   *Ant.*    Say a man never marry, nor have children,
What takes that from him? Only the bare name
Of being a father, or the weak delight
To see the little wanton ride-a-cock-horse
Upon a painted stick, or hear him chatter
Like a taught starling.

   *Duch.*            Fie, fie, what 's all this?
One of your eyes is blood-shot; use my ring to 't.
They say 't is very sovereign. 'T was my wedding-ring,
And I did vow never to part with it
But to my second husband.

   *Ant.*    You have parted with it now.

   *Duch.*    Yes, to help your eye-sight.

   *Ant.*    You have made me stark blind.

   *Duch.*                How?

   *Ant.*    There is a saucy and ambitious devil
Is dancing in this circle.

   *Duch.*            Remove him.

   *Ant.*                How?

   *Duch.*    There needs small conjuration, when your finger
May do it: thus. Is it fit?

                 *[She puts the ring upon his finger;]*
                    *he kneels.*

---

[1] Person appointed to oversee and assist the executors of a will.

*Ant.*                     What said you?

*Duch.*                                             Sir,

This goodly roof of yours is too low built;
I cannot stand upright in 't nor discourse,
Without I raise it higher. Raise yourself;
Or, if you please my hand to help you: so!          [*Raises him.*]

*Ant.* Ambition, madam, is a great man's madness.
That is not kept in chains and close-pent rooms,
But in fair lightsome lodgings, and is girt
With the wild noise of prattling visitants,
Which makes it lunatic beyond all cure.
Conceive not I am so stupid but I aim
Whereto your favours tend: but he 's a fool
That, being a-cold, would thrust his hands i' th' fire
To warm them.

*Duch.*          So, now the ground 's broke,
You may discover what a wealthy mine
I make you lord of.

*Ant.*                     O my unworthiness!

*Duch.*   You were ill to sell yourself:
This dark'ning of your worth is not like that
Which tradesmen use i' th' city; their false lights
Are to rid bad wares off: and I must tell you,
If you will know where breathes a complete man
(I speak it without flattery), turn your eyes,
And progress through yourself.

*Ant.*   Were there nor heaven nor hell,
I should be honest: I have long serv'd virtue,
And never ta'en wages of her.

*Duch.*                     Now she pays it.
The misery of us that are born great!
We are forc'd to woo, because none dare woo us;
And as a tyrant doubles with his words
And fearfully equivocates, so we
Are forc'd to express our violent passions
In riddles and in dreams, and leave the path
Of simple virtue, which was never made
To seem the thing it is not. Go, go brag
You have left me heartless; mine is in your bosom:
I hope 't will multiply love there. You do tremble:
Make not your heart so dead a piece of flesh,
To fear more than to love me. Sir, be confident:
What is 't distracts you? This is flesh and blood, sir;
'T is not the figure cut in alabaster

Kneels at my husband's tomb. Awake, awake, man!
I do here put off all vain ceremony,
And only do appear to you a young widow
That claims you for her husband, and, like a widow,
I use but half a blush in 't.

   *Ant.*             Truth speak for me:
I will remain the constant sanctuary
Of your good name.

   *Duch.*           I thank you, gentle love:
And 'cause you shall not come to me in debt,
(Being now my steward) here upon your lips
I sign your *Quietus est.* This you should have begg'd now.
I have seen children oft eat sweetmeats thus,
As fearful to devour them too soon.

   *Ant.*   But for your brothers?

   *Duch.*              Do not think of them:
All discord without[2] this circumference
Is only to be pitied, and not fear'd:
Yet, should they know it, time will easily
Scatter the tempest.

   *Ant.*        These words should be mine,
And all the parts you have spoke, if some part of it
Would not have savour'd flattery.

   *Duch.*                Kneel.

                [*Cariola comes from behind the arras.*]

   *Ant.*                         Ha!

   *Duch.*   Be not amaz'd: this woman 's of my counsel.
I have heard lawyers say, a contract in a chamber
*Per verba* [*de*] *presenti*[3] is absolute marriage.

               [*She and Antonio kneel.*]
Bless, heaven, this sacred Gordian,[4] which let violence
Never untwine.

   *Ant.*   And may our sweet affections, like the spheres,
Be still in motion!

   *Duch.*         Quick'ning, and make
The like soft music!

   *Ant.*   That we may imitate the loving palms,
Best emblem of a peaceful marriage,
That never bore fruit, divided!

   *Duch.*   What can the church force more?

---

  [2] Outside.
  [3] By words referring to the present time (in contrast to those referring to the future).
  [4] Gordian knot.

*Ant.*    That fortune may not know an accident,
Either of joy or sorrow, to divide
Our fixed wishes!
    *Duch.*        How can the church build faster?
We now are man and wife, and 't is the church
That must but echo this. — Maid, stand apart:
I now am blind.
    *Ant.*        What 's your conceit in this?
    *Duch.*    I would have you lead your fortune by the hand
Unto your marriage-bed:
(You speak in me this, for we now are one).
We 'll only lie and talk together, and plot
T' appease my humorous[5] kindred; and if you please,
Like the old tale in *Alexander and Lodowick*,[6]
Lay a naked sword between us, keep us chaste.
O, let me shroud my blushes in your bosom,
Since 't is the treasury of all my secrets!
                      *[Exeunt Duchess and Antonio.]*
    *Cari.*    Whether the spirit of greatness or of woman
Reign most in her, I know not; but it shows
A fearful madness. I owe her much of pity.        *Exit.*

## *Actus II.  Scena I*

### *[Enter] Bosola and Castruchio*

*Bos.*    You say you would fain be taken for an eminent courtier?
*Cast.*    'T is the very main[7] of my ambition.
*Bos.*    Let me see: you have a reasonable good face for 't already,
and your night-cap[8] expresses[9] your ears sufficient largely. I would
have you learn to twirl the strings of your band[1] with a good grace,
and in a set speech, at th' end of every sentence, to hum three or
four times, or blow your nose till it smart again, to recover your
memory. When you come to be a president in criminal causes, if
you smile upon a prisoner, hang him; but if you frown upon him
and threaten him, let him be sure to scape the gallows.
*Cast.*    I would be a very merry president.
·*Bos.*    Do not sup o' nights; 't will beget you an admirable wit.
*Cast.*    Rather it would make me have a good stomach to quarrel;

---

[5] Capricious.
[6] Two faithful friends, subjects of a popular ballad.
[7] Height.         [8] Coif, worn by senior lawyers.
[9] Reveals.       [1] Collar.

for they say, your roaring boys[2] eat meat seldom, and that makes them so valiant. But how shall I know whether the people take me for an eminent fellow?

*Bos.* I will teach a trick to know it: give out you lie a-dying, and if you hear the common people curse you, be sure you are taken for one of the prime night-caps.

[*Enter an Old Lady*]

You come from painting now.

*Old Lady.* From what?

*Bos.* Why, from your scurvy face-physic. To behold thee not painted inclines somewhat near a miracle. These in thy face here were deep ruts and foul sloughs the last progress.[3] There was a lady in France that, having had the small-pox, flayed the skin off her face to make it more level; and whereas before she looked like a nutmeg-grater, after she resembled an abortive hedgehog.

*Old Lady.* Do you call this painting?

*Bos.* No, no, but I call it careening[4] of an old morphew'd[5] lady, to make her disembogue[6] again: there 's rough-cast phrase to your plastic.[7]

*Old Lady.* It seems you are well acquainted with my closet.

*Bos.* One would suspect it for a shop of witchcraft, to find it the fat of serpents, spawn of snakes, Jews' spittle, and their young children's ordure: and all these for the face. I would sooner eat a dead pigeon taken from the soles of the feet of one sick of the plague, than kiss one of you fasting. Here are two of you, whose sin of your youth is the very patrimony of the physcian; makes him renew his foot-cloth[8] with the spring, and change his high-pric'd courtesan with the fall of the leaf. I do wonder you do not loathe yourselves. Observe my meditation now:

What thing is in this outward form of man
To be belov'd? We account it ominous,
If nature do produce a colt, or lamb,
A fawn, or goat, in any limb resembling
A man, and fly from 't as a prodigy.
Man stands amaz'd to see his deformity
In any other creature but himself.
But in our own flesh though we bear diseases
Which have their true names only ta'en from beasts, —

[2] Bullies and roisterers.
[3] State journey of the sovereign through the provinces.
[4] Turning a ship on its side to scrape the hull.
[5] Covered with scurf.          [6] Put to sea again.
[7] Modeling.          [8] Trappings of a horse.

As the most ulcerous wolf[9] and swinish measle, —
Though we are eaten up of lice and worms,
And though continually we bear about us
A rotten and dead body, we delight
To hide it in rich tissue: all our fear,
Nay, all our terror, is, lest our physician
Should put us in the ground to be made sweet. —
Your wife 's gone to Rome: you two couple, and get you to the
wells at Lucca to recover your aches. I have other work on foot.

### [*Exeunt Castruchio and Old Lady*]

I observe our duchess
Is sick a-days, she pukes, her stomach seethes,
The fins[1] of her eye-lids look most teeming[2] blue,
She wanes i' the cheek, and waxes fat i' th' flank,
And, contrary to our Italian fashion,
Wears a loose-bodied gown: there 's somewhat in 't.
I have a trick may chance discover it,
A pretty one: I have bought some apricocks,
The first our spring yields.

### [*Enter Antonio and Delio, talking together apart*]

*Delio.*   And so long since married? You amaze me.

*Ant.*   Let me seal your lips for ever: For, did I think that any-
thing but th' air
Could carry these words from you, I should wish
You had no breath at all. — Now, sir, in your contemplation?
You are studying to become a great wise fellow.

*Bos.*   O, sir, the opinion of wisdom is a foul tetter[3] that runs
all over a man's body: if simplicity direct us to have no evil, it
directs us to a happy being; for the subtlest folly proceeds from the
subtlest wisdom. Let me be simply honest.

*Ant.*   I do understand your inside.

*Bos.*                              Do you so?

*Ant.*   Because you would not seem to appear to th' world
Puff'd up with your preferment, you continue
This out-of-fashion melancholy: leave it, leave it.

*Bos.*   Give me leave to be honest in any phrase, in any compliment whatsoever. Shall I confess myself to you? I look no higher
than I can reach: they are the gods that must ride on winged
horses. A lawyer's mule of a slow pace will both suit my disposition

---

[9] A form of ulcer known as "lupus."         [1] Rims.
[2] Like those in pregnancy.         [3] Skin disease.

and business; for, mark me, when a mans' mind rides faster than his
horse can gallop, they quickly both tire.

*Ant.*   You would look up to heaven, but I think
The devil, that rules i' th' air, stands in your light.

*Bos.*   O, sir, you are lord of the ascendant,[4] chief man with the
duchess: a duke was your cousin-german remov'd. Say you were
lineally descended from King Pepin,[5] or he himself, what of this?
Search the heads of the greatest rivers in the world, you shall find
them but bubbles of water. Some would think the souls of princes
were brought forth by some more weighty cause than those of
meaner persons: they are deceiv'd, there 's the same hand to them;
the like passions sway them; the same reason that makes a vicar go
to law for a tithe-pig, and undo his neighbours, makes them spoil
a whole province, and batter down goodly cities with the cannon.

*[Enter Duchess and Ladies]*

*Duch.*   Your arm, Antonio: do I not grow fat? I am exceeding
short-winded. — Bosola,
I would have you, sir, provide for me a litter;
Such a one as the Duchess of Florence rode in.

*Bos.*   The duchess us'd one when she was great with child.

*Duch.*   I think she did. — Come hither, mend my ruff:
Here, when? thou art such a tedious lady; and
Thy breath smells of lemon-peels: would thou hadst done!
Shall I sound[6] under thy fingers? I am
So troubled with the mother[7]!

*Bos. [Aside.]*          I fear, too much.

*Duch.*   I have heard you say that the French courtiers
Wear their hats on 'fore the king.

*Ant.*   I have seen it.

*Duch.*          In the presence?

*Ant.*          Yes.

*Duch.*   Why should not we bring up that fashion?
'T is ceremony more than duty that consists
In the removing of a piece of felt.
Be you the example to the rest o' th' court;
Put on your hat first.

*Ant.*          You must pardon me:
I have seen, in colder countries than in France,

---

[4] Planet whose sign is entering the first house into which the heavens
were divided.
[5] King of France 752–768, and father of Charlemagne.
[6] Swoon.
[7] Hysteria.

Nobles stand bare to th' prince; and the distinction
Methought show'd reverently.

 *Bos.* I have a present for your grace.

 *Duch.*        For me, sir?

 *Bos.* Apricocks, madam.

 *Duch.*      O, sir, where are they?
I have heard of none to-year.[8]

 *Bos.* [*Aside.*]    Good; her colour rises.

 *Duch.* Indeed, I thank you: they are wondrous fair ones.
What an unskilful fellow is our gardener!
We shall have none this month.

 *Bos.* Will not your grace pare them?

 *Duch.* No: they taste of musk, methinks; indeed they do.

 *Bos.* I know not: yet I wish your grace had par'd 'em.

 *Duch.* Why?

 *Bos.* I forgot to tell you, the knave gardener,
(Only to raise his profit by them the sooner)
Did ripen them in horse-dung.

 *Duch.*      O, you jest. —
You shall judge: pray, taste one.

 *Ant.*      Indeed, madam,
I do not love the fruit.

 *Duch.*    Sir, you are loath
To rob us of our dainties. 'T is a delicate fruit;
They say they are restorative.

 *Bos.*     'T is a pretty art,
This grafting.

 *Duch.* 'T is so; a bettering of nature.

 *Bos.* To make a pippin grow upon a crab,[9]
A damson on a black-thorn. — [*Aside.*] How greedily she eats
  them!
A whirlwind strike off these bawd-farthingales![1]
For, but for that and the loose-bodied gown,
I should have discover'd apparently[2]
The young springal[3] cutting a caper in her belly.

 *Duch.* I thank you, Bosola: they were right good ones,
If they do not make me sick.

 *Ant.*     How now, madam!

 *Duch.* This green fruit and my stomach are not friends:
How they swell me!

 *Bos.* [*Aside.*] Nay, you are too much swell'd already.

---

[8] This year.      [9] Crab apple.
[1] Farthingales were hooped skirts.    [2] Clearly.
[3] Stripling.

*Duch.*   O, I am in an extreme cold sweat!

*Bos.*                              I am very sorry. [*Exit.*]

*Duch.*   Lights to my chamber! — O good Antonio,
I fear I am undone!

*Delio.*              Lights there, lights! *Exit Duchess* [*with Ladies*].

*Ant.*   O my most trusty Delio, we are lost!
I fear she 's fall'n in labour; and there 's left
No time for her remove.

*Delio.*                  Have you prepar'd
Those ladies to attend her; and procur'd
That politic[4] safe conveyance for the midwife
Your duchess plotted?

*Ant.*          I have.

*Delio.*   Make use, then, of this forc'd occasion.
Give out that Bosola hath poison'd her
With these apricocks; that will give some colour
For keeping her close.

*Ant.*              Fie, fie, the physicians
Will then flock to her.

*Delio.*   For that you may pretend
She 'll use some prepar'd antidote of her own,
Lest the physicians should re-poison her.

*Ant.*   I am lost in amazement: I know not what to think on 't.

                                              *Exeunt.*


### Scena II

*Bosola* [*and a little later*] *Old Lady*

*Bos.*   So, so, there 's no question but her tetchiness[5] and most
vulturous eating of the apricocks are apparent signs of breeding. —
Now?

*Old Lady.*   I am in haste, sir.

*Bos.*   There was a young waiting-woman had a monstrous desire
to see the glass-house[6] ——

*Old Lady.*   Nay, pray, let me go.

*Bos.*   And it was only to know what strange instrument it was
should swell up a glass to the fashion of a woman's belly.

*Old Lady.*   I will hear no more of the glass-house. You are still
abusing women!

*Bos.*   Who? I? No; only (by the way now and then) mention

---

[4] Crafty, secret.              [5] Irritability.
[6] Glass factory, one of the sights of Jacobean London.

your frailties. The orange-tree bears ripe and green fruit and blossoms all together; and some of you give entertainment for pure love, but more for more precious reward. The lusty spring smells well; but drooping autumn tastes well. If we have the same golden showers that rained in the time of Jupiter the thunderer, you have the same Danaës still, to hold up their laps to receive them. Didst thou never study the mathematics?

*Old Lady.* What 's that, sir?

*Bos.* Why, to know the trick how to make a many lines meet in one centre. Go, go, give your foster-daughters good counsel: tell them, that the devil takes delight to hang at a woman's girdle, like a false rusty watch, that she cannot discern how the time passes.                              [*Exit Old Lady.*]

### [*Enter Antonio, Roderigo, and Grisolan*]

*Ant.*   Shut up the court-gates.

*Rod.*                              Why, sir? What 's the danger?

*Ant.*   Shut up the posterns presently, and call
All the officers o' th' court.

*Gris.*                    I shall instantly.              [*Exit.*]

*Ant.*   Who keeps the key o' th' park-gate?

*Rod.*                              Forobosco.

*Ant.*   Let him bring 't presently.

### [*Re-enter Grisolan with Servants*]

*1 Serv.*   O, gentlemen o' th' court, the foulest treason!

*Bos.* [*Aside.*]   If that these apricocks should be poison'd now,
Without my knowledge!

*1 Serv.*   There was taken even now a Switzer in the duchess'
bed-chamber ——

*2 Serv.*   A Switzer!

*1 Serv.*   With a pistol in his great codpiece.

*Bos.*   Ha, ha, ha!

*1 Serv.*   The codpiece was the case for 't.

*2 Serv.*   There was a cunning traitor. Who would have search'd
his codpiece?

*1 Serv.*   True; if he had kept out of the ladies' chambers. And
all the moulds of his buttons were leaden bullets.

*2 Serv.*   O wicked cannibal! A fire-lock in 's codpiece!

*1 Serv.*   'T was a French plot, upon my life.

*2 Serv.*   To see what the devil can do!

*Ant.*   All the officers here?

*Servants.*   We are.

*Ant.*   Gentlemen,

We have lost much plate, you know; and but this evening
Jewels, to the value of four thousand ducats,
Are missing in the duchess' cabinet.
Are the gates shut?

    *Serv.*          Yes.

    *Ant.*                 'T is the duchess' pleasure
Each officer be lock'd into his chamber
Till the sun-rising; and to send the keys
Of all their chests and of their outward doors
Into her bed-chamber. She is very sick.

    *Rod.*    At her pleasure.

    *Ant.*    She entreats you take 't not ill: the innocent
Shall be the more approv'd by it.

    *Bos.*    Gentleman o' th' wood-yard, where 's your Switzer now?

    1 *Serv.*    By this hand, 't was credibly reported by one o' th'
black guard.                 [*Exeunt all except Antonio and Delio.*]

    *Delio.*    How fares it with the duchess?

    *Ant.*                    She 's expos'd
Unto the worst of torture, pain and fear.

    *Delio.*    Speak to her all happy comfort.

    *Ant.*    How I do play the fool with mine own danger!
You are this night, dear friend, to post to Rome:
My life lies in your service.

    *Delio.*                Do not doubt me.

    *Ant.*    O, 't is far from me: and yet fear presents me
Somewhat that looks like danger.

    *Delio.*                Believe it,
'T is but the shadow of your fear, no more.
How superstitious we mind our evils!
The throwing down salt, or crossing of a hare,
Bleeding at nose, the stumbling of a horse,
Or singing of a cricket, are of power
To daunt whole man in us. Sir, fare you well:
I wish you all the joys of a bless'd father;
And (for my faith) lay this unto your breast:
Old friends, like old swords, still are trusted best.        [*Exit.*]

                [*Enter Cariola*]

    *Cari.*    Sir, you are the happy father of a son:
Your wife commends him to you.

    *Ant.*                  Blessed comfort! —
For heaven' sake, tend her well: I 'll presently
Go set a figure[7] for 's nativity.             *Exeunt.*

    [7] Cast a horoscope.

SCENA III

*Bosola [with a dark lantern, and later] Antonio*

*Bos.*   Sure I did hear a woman shriek: list, ha!
And the sound came, if I receiv'd it right,
From the duchess' lodgings. There 's some stratagem
In the confining all our courtiers
To their several wards:[8] I must have part of it;
My intelligence will freeze else. List, again!
It may be 't was the melancholy bird,
Best friend of silence and of solitariness,
The owl, that scream'd so. — Ha! Antonio!

[*Enter Antonio with a candle, his sword drawn*]

*Ant.*   I heard  some  noise. — who 's there?  What art thou?
    Speak.
*Bos.*   Antonio? put not your face nor body
To such a forc'd expression of fear:
I am Bosola, your friend.
    *Ant.*        Bosola? —
[*Aside.*] This mole does undermine me. —Heard you not
A noise even now?
    *Bos.*        From whence?
    *Ant.*               From the duchess' lodging.
*Bos.*   Not I: did you?
    *Ant.*        I did, or else I dream'd.
*Bos.*   Let 's walk toward it.
    *Ant.*          No: it may be 't was
But the rising of the wind.
    *Bos.*        Very likely.
Methinks 't is very cold, and yet you sweat:
You look wildly.
    *Ant.*      I have been setting a figure
For the duchess' jewels.
    *Bos.*      Ah, and how falls your question?
Do you find it radical[9]?
    *Ant.*      What 's that to you?
'T is rather to be question'd what design,
When all men are commanded to their lodgings,
Makes you a night-walker.
    *Bos.*      In sooth, I 'll tell you:
Now all the court 's asleep, I thought the devil

---

8 Quarters.
9 Capable of being resolved by astrology.

Had least to do here. I came to say my prayers;
And if it do offend you I do so,
You are a fine courtier.

　　*Ant.* [*Aside.*]　This fellow will undo me! —
You gave the duchess apricocks today:
Pray heaven they were not poison'd!

　　*Bos.*　Poison'd! a Spanish fig[1]
For the imputation!

　　*Ant.*　　　　　　　Traitors are ever confident
Till they are discover'd. There were jewels stol'n too:
In my conceit,[2] none are to be suspected
More than yourself.

　　*Bos.*　　　　　You are a false steward.

　　*Ant.*　Saucy slave, I 'll pull thee up by the roots.

　　*Bos.*　May be the ruin will crush you to pieces.

　　*Ant.*　You are an impudent snake indeed, sir:
Are you scarce warm, and do you show your sting?
You libel well, sir?

　　*Bos.*　　　　　No, sir: copy it out,
And I will set my hand to 't.

　　*Ant.* [*Aside.*]　　　　My nose bleeds.
One that were superstitious would count
This ominous, when it merely comes by chance.
Two letters,[3] that are wrought here for my name,
Are drown'd in blood!
Mere accident. — For you, sir, I 'll take order.
I' th' morn you shall be safe. — [*Aside.*] 'T is that must colour
Her lying-in. — Sir, this door you pass not:
I do not hold it fit that you come near
The duchess' lodgings, till you have quit yourself.[4] —
[*Aside.*]　The great are like the base; nay, they are the same,
When they seek shameful ways to avoid shame.　　　*Exit.*

　　*Bos.*　Antonio hereabout did drop a paper: —
Some of your help, false friend.[5] O, here it is.
What 's here? a child's nativity calculated!　　　[*Reads.*]
'*The duchess was deliver'd of a son 'tween the hours twelve and
one in the night, Anno Dom.* 1504.' — that 's this year — '*decimo
nono Decembris*,'[6] — that 's this night — '*taken according to the
meridian of Malfi*,' — that 's our duchess: happy discovery! — '*The
lord of the first house being combust*[7] *in the ascendant signifies*

---

[1] (A term of contempt).　　　　　　　[2] Thought, idea.
[3] (Embroidered on his handkerchief).　　　　　[4] Proved your innocence.
[5] His dark lantern.　　　　　　[6] Nineteenth of December.
[7] In a position close to the sun, where his influence could not be exerted.

*short life; and Mars being in a human sign,*[8] *joined to the tail of the Dragon, in the eight house, doth threaten a violent death. Cætera non scrutantur.'*[9]

Why now 't is most apparent; this precise fellow
Is the duchess' bawd: — I have it to my wish!
This is a parcel of intelligency[1]
Our courtiers were cas'd up for.  It needs must follow
That I must be committed on pretence
Of poisoning her; which I 'll endure, and laugh at.
If one could find the father now! but that
Time will discover.  Old Castruchio
I' th' morning posts to Rome: by him I 'll send
A letter that shall make her brothers' galls
O'erflow their livers.  This was a thrifty way!
Though Lust do mask in ne'er so strange disguise,
She 's oft found witty, but is never wise.          [*Exit.*]


SCENA IIII

*Cardinal and Julia, [later] Servant, and Delio*

   *Card.*    Sit: thou art my best of wishes.  Prithee, tell me
What trick didst thou invent to come to Rome
Without thy husband?
   *Julia.*                    Why, my lord, I told him
I came to visit an old anchorite
Here for devotion.
   *Card.*                    Thou art a witty false one, —
I mean, to him.
   *Julia.*          You have prevail'd with me
Beyond my strongest thoughts; I would not now
Find you inconstant.
   *Card.*                    Do not put thyself
To such a voluntary torture, which proceeds
Out of your own guilt.
   *Julia.*                    How, my lord!
   *Card.*                              You fear
My constancy, because you have approv'd
Those giddy and wild turnings in yourself.
   *Julia.*    Did you e'er find them?

---

[8] One of the four signs of the zodiac named for persons.
[9] The rest are not investigated.
[1] Piece of news.

*Card.*                              Sooth, generally for women,
A man might strive to make glass malleable,
Ere he should make them fixed.
   *Julia.*                              So, my lord.
   *Card.*   We had need go borrow that fantastic glass[2]
Invented by Galileo, the Florentine,
To view another spacious world i' the moon,
And look to find a constant woman there.
   *Julia.*   This is very well, my lord.
   *Card.*                              Why do you weep?
Are tears your justification? The self-same tears
Will fall into your husband's bosom, lady,
With a loud protestation that you love him
Above the world. Come, I 'll love you wisely,
That 's jealously; since I am very certain
You cannot make me cuckold.
   *Julia.*                              I 'll go home
To my husband.
   *Card.*          You may thank me, lady.
I have taken you off your melancholy perch,
Bore you upon my fist, and show'd you game,
And let you fly at it. — I pray thee, kiss me. —
When thou wast with thy husband, thou wast watch'd
Like a tame elephant: — still you are to thank me: —
Thou hadst only kisses from him and high feeding:
But what delight was that? 'T was just like one
That hath a little fing'ring on the lute,
Yet cannot tune it: — still you are to thank me.
   *Julia.*   You told me of a piteous wound i' th' heart,
And a sick liver, when you woo'd me first,
And spake like one in physic.
   *Card.*                              Who 's that? —


[*Enter Servant*]

Rest firm! for my affection to thee,
Lightning moves slow to 't.
   *Serv.*                              Madam, a gentleman
That 's comes post from Malfi, desires to see you.
   *Card.*   Let him enter: I 'll withdraw.                    *Exit.*
   *Serv.*                              He says
Your husband, old Castruchio, is come to Rome,
Most pitifully tir'd with riding post.                    [*Exit.*]

   [2] I.e., the telescope.

*[Enter Delio]*

*Julia.* [*Aside.*]    Signior Delio! 't is one of my old suitors.

*Delio.*    I was bold to come and see you.

*Julia.*                              Sir, you are welcome.

*Delio.*    Do you lie here?

*Julia.*                              Sure, your own experience
Will satisfy you no: our Roman prelates
Do not keep lodging for ladies.

*Delio.*                              Very well:
I have brought you no commendations from your husband,
For I know none by him.

*Julia.*                              I hear he 's come to Rome.

*Delio.*    I never knew man and beast, of a horse and a knight,
So weary of each other.  If he had had a good back,
He would have undertook to have borne his horse,
His breech was so pitifully sore.

*Julia.*                              Your laughter
Is my pity.

*Delio.*    Lady, I know not whether
You want money, but I have brought some.

*Julia.*    From my husband?

*Delio.*                              No, from mine own allowance.

*Julia.*    I must hear the condition, ere I be bound to take it.

*Delio.*    Look on 't, 't is gold; hath it not a fine colour?

*Julia.*    I have a bird more beautiful.

*Delio.*                              Try the sound on 't.

*Julia.*    A lute-string far exceeds it.
It hath no smell, like cassia[3] or civet;
Nor is it physical,[4] though some fond doctors
Persuade us seethe 't in cullises.[5]  I 'll tell you,
This is a creature bred by ——

*[Re-enter Servant]*

*Serv.*                              Your husband 's come,
Hath deliver'd a letter to the Duke of Calabria
That, to my thinking, hath put him out of his wits.    [*Exit.*]

*Julia.*    Sir, you hear:
Pray, let me know your business and your suit
As briefly as can be.

*Delio.*    With good speed: I would wish you
(At such time as you are non-resident
With your husband) my mistress.

---

[3] Cinnamon.                    [4] Remedial.                    [5] Strengthening broths.

*Julia.*   Sir, I 'll go ask my husband if I shall,
And straight return your answer.                                    *Exit.*
  *Delio.*                                                    Very fine!
Is this her wit, or honesty, that speaks thus?
I heard one say the duke was highly mov'd
With a letter sent from Malfi.  I do fear
Antonio is betray'd.  How fearfully
Shows his ambition now!  Unfortunate fortune!
They pass through whirl-pools, and deep woes do shun,
Who the event[6] weigh ere the action 's done.            *Exit.*


### Scena V

*Cardinal and Ferdinand with a letter*

*Ferd.*   I have this night digg'd up a mandrake.[7]
*Card.*           Say you?
*Ferd.*   And I am grown mad with 't.
*Card.*                              What 's the prodigy?
*Ferd.*   Read there, — a sister damn'd: she 's loose i' th' hilts;
Grown a notorious strumpet.
*Card.*                        Speak lower.
*Ferd.*                                      Lower!
Rogues do not whisper 't now, but seek to publish 't
(As servants do the bounty of their lords)
Aloud; and with a covetous searching eye,
To mark who note them.  O, confusion seize her!
She hath had most cunning bawds to serve her turn,
And more secure conveyances for lust
Than towns of garrison for service.
  *Card.*                              Is 't possible?
Can this be certain?
  *Ferd.*               Rhubarb!  O, for rhubarb
To purge this choler!  Here 's the cursed day
To prompt my memory; and here 't shall stick
Till of her bleeding heart I make a sponge
To wipe it out.
  *Card.*         Why do you make yourself
So wild a tempest?
  *Ferd.*            Would I could be one,

[6] Outcome.
[7] The mandrake was supposed to shriek on being pulled up, and whoever heard the shriek lost his reason.

That I might toss her palace 'bout her ears,
Root up her goodly forests, blast her meads,
And lay her general territory as waste
As she hath done her honours.

   *Card.*                     Shall our blood,
The royal blood of Arragon and Castile,
Be thus attainted?

   *Ferd.*           Apply desperate physic:
We must not now use balsamum,[8] but fire,
The smarting cupping-glass,[9] for that 's the mean
To purge infected blood, such blood as hers.
There is a kind of pity in mine eye, —
I 'll give it to my handkercher; and now 't is here.
I 'll bequeath this to her bastard.

   *Card.*                   What to do?

   *Ferd.*   Why, to make soft lint for his mother's wounds,
When I have hew'd her to pieces.

   *Card.*                Curs'd creature!
Unequal nature, to place women's hearts
So far upon the left side!

   *Ferd.*            Foolish men,
That e'er will trust their honour in a bark
Made of so slight weak bulrush as is woman,
Apt every minute to sink it!

   *Card.*   Thus ignorance, when it hath purchas'd[1] honour,
It cannot wield[2] it.

   *Ferd.*         Methinks I see her laughing, —
Excellent hyena! Talk to me somewhat, quickly,
Or my imagination will carry me
To see her in the shameful act of sin.

   *Card.*   With whom?

   *Ferd.*   Happily with some strong-thigh'd bargeman,
Or one o' th' wood-yard that can quoit the sledge[3]
Or toss the bar, or else some lovely squire
That carries coals up to her privy lodgings.

   *Card.*   You fly beyond your reason.

   *Ferd.*                Go to, mistress!
'T is not your whore's milk that shall quench my wild-fire,
But your whore's blood.

   *Card.*   How idly shows this rage, which carries you,
As men convey'd by witches through the air,
On violent whirlwinds! This intemperate noise
Fitly resembles deaf men's shrill discourse,

---

8 Balm.            9 Used in drawing blood from the patient.
1 Obtained.         2 Use skilfully.        3 Throw the hammer.

Who talk aloud, thinking all other men
To have their imperfection.

*Ferd.*                     Have not you
My palsy?

*Card.*   Yes, yet I can be angry
Without this rupture.[4]  There is not in nature
A thing that makes man so deform'd, so beastly,
As doth intemperate anger.  Chide yourself.
You have divers men who never yet express'd
Their strong desire of rest but by unrest,
By vexing of themselves.  Come, put yourself
In tune.

*Ferd.*   So I will only study to seem
The thing I am not.  I could kill her now,
In you, or in myself; for I do think
It is some sin in us heaven doth revenge
By her.

*Card.*   Are you stark mad?

*Ferd.*                        I would have their bodies
Burnt in a coal-pit with the ventage[5] stopp'd,
That their curs'd smoke might not ascend to heaven;
Or dip the sheets they lie in in pitch or sulphur,
Wrap them in 't, and then light them like a match;
Or else to boil their bastard to a cullis,
And give 't his lecherous father to renew
The sin of his back.

*Card.*           I 'll leave you.

*Ferd.*                        Nay, I have done.
I am confident, had I been damn'd in hell,
And should have heard of this, it would have put me
Into a cold sweat.  In, in; I 'll go sleep.
Till I know who leaps my sister, I 'll not stir:
That known, I 'll find scorpions to string my whips,
And fix her in a general eclipse.                    *Exeunt.*


## Actus III.  Scena I

### *Antonio and Delio, [later,] Duchess, Ferdinand, Bosola*

*Ant.*   Our noble friend, my most beloved Delio!
O, you have been a stranger long at court.
Came you along with the Lord Ferdinand?

*Delio.*   I did, sir: and how fares your noble duchess?

*Ant.*   Right fortunately well: she 's an excellent

---

[4] Outbreak.            [5] Vent hole.

Feeder of pedigrees; since you last saw her,
She hath had two children more, a son and daughter.

*Delio.* Methinks 't was yesterday. Let me but wink,
And not behold your face, which to mine eye
Is somewhat leaner, verily I should dream
It were within this half hour.

*Ant.* You have not been in law, friend Delio,
Nor in prison, nor a suitor at the court,
Nor begg'd the reversion of some great man's place,
Nor troubled with an old wife, which doth make
Your time so insensibly hasten.

*Delio.* Pray, sir, tell me,
Hath not this news arriv'd yet to the ear
Of the lord cardinal?

*Ant.* I fear it hath:
The Lord Ferdinand, that 's newly come to court,
Doth bear himself right dangerously.

*Delio.* Pray, why?

*Ant.* He is so quiet that he seems to sleep
The tempest out, as dormice do in winter.
Those houses that are haunted are most still,
Till the devil be up.

*Delio.* What say the common people?

*Ant.* The common rabble do directly say
She is a strumpet.

*Delio.* And your graver heads
Which would be politic,[6] what censure[7] they?

*Ant.* They do observe I grow to infinite purchase,[8]
The left-hand way; and all suppose the duchess
Would amend it, if she could; for, say they,
Great princes, though they grudge their officers
Should have such large and unconfined means
To get wealth under them, will not complain,
Lest thereby they should make them odious
Unto the people. For other obligation,
Of love or marriage between her and me,
They never dream of.

*Delio.* The Lord Ferdinand
Is going to bed.

[*Enter Duchess, Ferdinand, and Attendants*]

*Ferd.* I 'll instantly to bed,

---

[6] Statesmanlike.   [7] Think.
[8] Riches.

For I am weary. — I am to bespeak
A husband for you.

   *Duch.*           For me, sir! Pray, who is 't?

   *Ferd.*   The great Count Malateste.

   *Duch.*           Fie upon him!
A count! He's a mere stick of sugar-candy;
You may look quite thorough him. When I choose
A husband, I will marry for your honour.

   *Ferd.*   You shall do well in 't. — How is 't, worthy Antonio?

   *Duch.*   But, sir, I am to have private conference with you
About a scandalous report is spread
Touching mine honour.

   *Ferd.*           Let me be ever deaf to 't:
One of Pasquil's[9] paper-bullets, court-calumny,
A pestilent air, which princes' palaces
Are seldom purg'd of. Yet, say that it were true,
I pour it in your bosom, my fix'd love
Would strongly excuse, extenuate, nay, deny
Faults, were they apparent in you. Go, be safe
In your own innocency.

   *Duch.* [*Aside*].     O bless'd comfort!
This deadly air is purg'd.

               *Exeunt* [*Duchess, Antonio, Delio, and Attendants*].

   *Ferd.*           Her guilt treads on
Hot-burning coulters.[1]


                  [*Enter Bosola*]

                  Now, Bosola,
How thrives our intelligence?

   *Bos.*           Sir, uncertainly:
'T is rumour'd she hath had three bastards, but
By whom we may go read i' th' stars.

   *Ferd.*           Why, some
Hold opinion all things are written there.

   *Bos.*   Yes, if we could find spectacles to read them.
I do suspect there hath been some sorcery
Us'd on the duchess.

   *Ferd.*         Sorcery! to what purpose?

   *Bos.*   To make her dote on some desertless fellow
She shames to acknowledge.

   *Ferd.*         Can your faith give way

   [9] Statue in Rome on which lampoons were fixed.
   [1] The cutting part of the plow.

To think there 's power in potions or in charms,
To make us love whether we will or no?
   *Bos.*   Most certainly.
   *Ferd.*   Away! these are mere gulleries, horrid things,
Invented by some cheating mountebanks
To abuse us.  Do you think that herbs or charms
Can force the will?  Some trials have been made
In this foolish practice, but the ingredients
Were lenitive[2] poisons, such as are of force
To make the patient mad; and straight the witch
Swears by equivocation[3] they are in love.
The witchcraft lies in her rank blood.  This night
I will force confession from her.  You told me
You had got, within these two days, a false key
Into her bed-chamber.
   *Bos.*          I have.
   *Ferd.*          As I would wish.
   *Bos.*   What do you intend to do?
   *Ferd.*          Can you guess?
   *Bos.*          No.
   *Ferd.*          Do not ask, then:
He that can compass me, and know my drifts,[4]
May say he hath put a girdle 'bout the world,
And sounded all her quick-sands.
   *Bos.*          I do not
Think so.
   *Ferd.*   What do you think, then, pray?
   *Bos.*          That you
Are your own chronicle too much, and grossly
Flatter yourself.
   *Ferd.*   Give me thy hand; I thank thee:
I never gave pension but to flatterers,
Till I entertained thee.  Farewell.
That friend a great man's ruin strongly checks,
Who rails into his belief all his defects.       *Exeunt.*

### SCENA II

*Duchess, Antonio, Cariola, [and later]*
*Ferdinand, Bosola, Officers*

   *Duch.*   Bring me the casket hither, and the glass. —
You get no lodging here to-night, my lord.

    2 Slow.         3 A quibble.        4 Intentions.

*Ant.*   Indeed, I must persuade one.

*Duch.*                              Very good:
I hope in time 't will grow into a custom,
That noblemen shall come with cap and knee
To purchase a night's lodging of their wives.

*Ant.*   I must lie here.

*Duch.*   Must! You are a lord of mis-rule.[5]

*Ant.*   Indeed, my rule is only in the night.

*Duch.*   To what use will you put me?

*Ant.*                              We 'll sleep together.

*Duch.*   Alas, what pleasure can two lovers find in sleep?

*Cari.*   My lord, I lie with her often, and I know
She 'll much disquiet you.

*Ant.*                      See, you are complain'd of.

*Cari.*   For she 's the sprawling'st bedfellow.

*Ant.*   I shall like her the better for that.

*Cari.*   Sir, shall I ask you a question?

*Ant.*   I pray thee, Cariola.

*Cari.*   Wherefore still[6] when you lie with my lady
Do you rise so early?

*Ant.*                  Labouring men
Count the clock oft'nest, Cariola,
Are glad when their task 's ended.

*Duch.*   I 'll stop your mouth. [*Kisses him.*]

*Ant.*   Nay, that 's but one; Venus had two soft doves
To draw her chariot: I must have another. —

                                        [*She kisses him again.*]
When wilt thou marry, Cariola?

*Cari.*                          Never, my lord.

*Ant.*   O, fie upon this single life! forgo it.
We read how Daphne, for her peevish slight,
Became a fruitless bay-tree; Syrinx turn'd
To the pale empty reed; Anaxarete
Was frozen into marble: whereas those
Which married, or prov'd kind unto their friends,
Were by a gracious influence trans-shap'd
Into the olive, pomegranate, mulberry,
Became flowers, precious stones, or eminent stars.

*Cari.*   This is a vain poety: but I pray you, tell me,
If there were propos'd me wisdom, riches, and beauty,
In three several young men, which should I choose?

*Ant.*   'T is a hard question. This was Paris' case,

[5] Who ruled over the revels during the Christmas season.
[6] Always.

And he was blind in 't, and there was great cause;
For how was 't possible he could judge right,
Having three amorous goddesses in view,
And they stark naked? 'T was a motion
Were able to benight the apprehension
Of the severest counsellor of Europe.
Now I look on both your faces so well form'd,
It puts me in mind of a question I would ask.
 *Cari.* What is 't?
 *Ant.* I do wonder why hard-favour'd[7] ladies,
For the most part, keep worse-favour'd waiting-women
To attend them, and cannot endure fair ones.
 *Duch.* O, that 's soon answer'd.
Did you ever in your life know an ill painter
Desire to have his dwelling next door to the shop
Of an excellent picture-maker? 'T would disgrace
His face-making, and undo him. I prithee,
When were we so merry? My hair tangles.
 *Ant.* Pray thee, Cariola, let 's steal forth the room,
And let her talk to herself. I have divers times
Serv'd her the like, when she hath chaf'd extremely.
I love to see her angry. Softly, Cariola.
       *Exeunt* [*Antonio and Cariola*].
 *Duch.* Doth not the colour of my hair 'gin to change?
When I wax gray, I shall have all the court
Powder their hair with arras, to be like me.
You have cause to love me; I ent'red you into my heart

    [*Enter Ferdinand unseen*]

Before you would vouchsafe to call for the keys.
We shall one day have my brothers take you napping.
Methinks his presence, being now in court,
Should make you keep your own bed; but you 'll say
Love mix'd with fear is sweetest. I 'll assure you,
You shall get no more children till my brothers
Consent to be your gossips.[8] Have you lost your tongue?
'T is welcome:
For know, whether I am doom'd to live or die,
I can do both like a prince.
 *Ferd.*     Die, then, quickly.
       *Ferdinand gives her a poniard.*
Virtue, where art thou hid? What hideous thing
Is it that doth eclipse thee?

  [7] Homely.      [8] Godfathers to your children.

*Duch.*                    Pray, sir, hear me.

*Ferd.*    Or is it true thou art but a bare name,
And no esssential thing?

*Duch.*                    Sir ——

*Ferd.*                         Do not speak.

*Duch.*    No, sir:
I will plant my soul in mine ears, to hear you.

*Ferd.*    O most imperfect light of human reason,
That mak'st us so unhappy to foresee
What we can least prevent!  Pursue thy wishes,
And glory in them: there 's in shame no comfort
But to be past all bounds and sense of shame.

*Duch.*    I pray, sir, hear me: I am married.

*Ferd.*                         So!

*Duch.*    Happily, not to your liking: but for that,
Alas, your shears do come untimely now
To clip the bird's wings that 's already flown!
Will you see my husband?

*Ferd.*                    Yes, if I could change
Eyes with a basilisk.[9]

*Duch.*              Sure, you came hither
By his confederacy.

*Ferd.*                The howling of a wolf
Is music to thee, screech-owl: prithee, peace. —
Whate'er thou art that hast enjoy'd my sister,
For I am sure thou hear'st me, for thine own sake
Let me not know thee.  I came hither prepar'd
To work thy discovery; yet am now persuaded
It would beget such violent effects
As would damn us both.  I would not for ten millions
I had beheld thee: therefore use all means
I never may have knowledge of thy name.
Enjoy thy lust still, and a wretched life,
On that condition. — And for thee, vild woman,
If thou do wish thy lecher may grow old
In thy embracements, I would have thee build
Such a room for him as our anchorites
To holier use inhabit.  Let not the sun
Shine on him till he 's dead; let dogs and monkeys
Only converse with him, and such dumb things
To whom nature denies use to sound his name;
Do not keep a paraquito,[1] lest she learn it.

[9] Fabulous monster, the very sight of which was fatal.
[1] Parrot.

If thou do love him, cut out thine own tongue,
Lest it bewray him.
    *Duch.*          Why might not I marry?
I have not gone about in this to create
Any new world or custom.
    *Ferd.*          Thou art undone;
And thou hast ta'en that massy sheet of lead
That hid thy husband's bones, and folded it
About my heart.
    *Duch.*    Mine bleeds for 't.
    *Ferd.*          Thine! thy heart!
What should I name 't, unless a hollow bullet
Fill'd with unquenchable wild-fire?
    *Duch.*          You are in this
Too strict; and were you not my princely brother,
I would say, too wilful: my reputation
Is safe.
    *Ferd.*   Dost thou know what reputation is?
I 'll tell thee, — to small purpose, since th' instruction
Comes now too late.
Upon a time Reputation, Love, and Death
Would travel o'er the world; and it was concluded
That they should part, and take three several ways.
Death told them, they should find him in great battles,
Or cities plagu'd with plagues; Love gives them counsel
To inquire for him 'mongst unambitious shepherds,
Where dowries were not talk'd of, and sometimes
'Mongst quiet kindred that had nothing left
By their dead parents. 'Stay,' quoth Reputation,
'Do not forsake me; for it is my nature,
If once I part from any man I meet,
I am never found again.' And so for you:
You have shook hands with Reputation,
And made him invisible. So, fare you well:
I will never see you more.
    *Duch.*          Why should only I,
Of all the other princes of the world,
Be cas'd up, like a holy relic? I have youth
And a little beauty.
    *Ferd.*          So you have some virgins
That are witches. I will never see thee more.        *Exit.*

       *Enter Antonio with a pistol* [*and Cariola*]

    *Duch.*   You saw this apparition?
    *Ant.*              Yes: we are

Betray'd. How came he hither?  I should turn
This to thee, for that.
   *Cari.*                Pray, sir, do; and when
That you have cleft my heart, you shall read there
Mine innocence.
   *Duch.*        That gallery gave him entrance.
   *Ant.*  I would this terrible thing would come again,
That, standing on my guard, I might relate
My warrantable love. —          *She shows the poniard.*
                Ha! what means this?
   *Duch.*  He left this with me.
   *Ant.*               And it seems did wish
You would use it on yourself?
   *Duch.*            His action seem'd
To intend so much.
   *Ant.*         This hath a handle to 't,
As well as a point: turn it towards him, and
So fasten the keen edge in his rank gall.     [*Knocking within.*]
How now! who knocks?  More earthquakes?
   *Duch.*                I stand
As if a mine beneath my feet were ready
To be blown up.
   *Cari.*        'T is Bosola.
   *Duch.*          Away!
O misery! methinks unjust actions
Should wear these masks and curtains, and not we.
You must instantly part hence: I have fashion'd it already.
                            *Exit Antonio.*


               [*Enter Bosola*]

   *Bos.*  The duke your brother is ta'en up in a whirlwind;
Hath took horse, and 's rid post to Rome.
   *Duch.*                So late?
   *Bos.*  He told me, as he mounted into th' saddle,
You were undone.
   *Duch.*        Indeed, I am very near it.
   *Bos.*  What 's the matter?
   *Duch.*  Antonio, the master of our household,
Hath dealt so falsely with me in 's accounts.
My brother stood engag'd with me for money
Ta'en up of certain Neapolitan Jews,
And Antonio lets the bonds be forfeit.
   *Bos.*  Strange! — [*Aside.*]  This is cunning.
   *Duch.*               And hereupon

My brother's bills at Naples are protested
Against. — Call up our officers.

 *Bos.*     I shall.       *Exit.*

### [Re-enter Antonio]

 *Duch.* The place that you must fly to is Ancona:
Hire a house there. I 'll send after you
My treasure and my jewels. Our weak safety
Runs upon enginous[2] wheels: short syllables
Must stand for periods.[3] I must now accuse you
Of such a feigned crime as Tasso calls
*Magnanima menzogna,* a noble lie.
'Cause it must shield our honours. — Hark! they are coming.

### [Re-enter Bosola and Officers]

 *Ant.* Will your grace hear me?
 *Duch.* I have got well by you; you have yielded me
A million of loss: I am like to inherit
The people's curses for your stewardship.
You had the trick in audit-time to be sick,
Till I had sign'd your quietus;[4] and that cur'd you
Without help of a doctor. — Gentlemen,
I would have this man be an example to you all;
So shall you hold my favour; I pray, let him;
For h'as done that, alas, you would not think of,
And (because I intend to be rid of him)
I mean not to publish. — Use your fortune elsewhere.
 *Ant.* I am strongly arm'd to brook[5] my overthrow,
As commonly men bear with a hard year.
I will not blame the cause on 't; but do think
The necessity of my malevolent star
Procures this, not her humour. O, the inconstant
And rotten ground of service! You may see,
'T is e'en like him, that in a winter night,
Takes a long slumber o'er a dying fire,
As loath to part from 't; yet parts thence as cold
As when he first sat down.
 *Duch.*     We do confiscate,
Towards the satisfying of your accounts,
All that you have.
 *Ant.* I am all yours; and 't is very fit
All mine should be so.
 *Duch.*    So, sir, you have your pass.

----

 [2] Ingenious.     [3] Long and complex sentences.
 [4] Acquittance.     [5] Endure.

*Ant.* You may see, gentlemen, what 't is to serve
A prince with body and soul.                          *Exit.*

*Bos.* Here 's an example for extortion: what moisture is drawn
out of the sea, when foul weather comes, pours down, and runs into
the sea again.

*Duch.* I would know what are your opinions
Of this Antonio.

*2 Off.* He could not abide to see a pig's head gaping: I thought
your grace would find him a Jew.

*3 Off.* I would you had been his officer, for your own sake.

*4 Off.* You would have had more money.

*1 Off.* He stopp'd his ears with black wool, and to those came
to him for money said he was thick of hearing.

*2 Off.* Some said he was an hermaphrodite, for he could not
abide a woman.

*4 Off.* How scurvy proud he would look when the treasury was
full! Well, let him go.

*1 Off.* Yes, and the chippings[6] of the buttery fly after him, to
scour his gold chain.[7]

*Duch.* Leave us. ——                          *Exeunt [Officers].*
What do you think of these?

*Bos.* That these are rogues that in 's prosperity,
But to have waited on his fortune, could have wish'd
His dirty stirrup riveted through their noses,
And follow'd after 's mule, like a bear in a ring;
Would have prostituted their daughters to his lust;
Made their first-born intelligencers; thought none happy
But such as were born under his blest planet.
And wore his livery: and do these lice drop off now?
Well, never look to have the like again:
He hath left a sort[8] of flatt'ring rogues behnd him;
Their doom must follow. Princes pay flatterers
In their own money: flatterers dissemble their vices,
And they dissemble their lies; that 's justice.
Alas, poor gentleman!

*Duch.* Poor! he hath amply fill'd his coffers.

*Bos.* Sure, he was too honest. Pluto, the god of riches,
When he 's sent by Jupiter to any man,
He goes limping, to signify that wealth
That comes on God's name comes slowly; but when he 's sent
On the devil's errand, he rides post and comes in by scuttles.
Let me show you what a most unvalu'd jewel
You have in a wanton humour thrown away,
To bless the man shall find him. He was an excellent

---

[6] Bread crumbs.          [7] The sign of his stewardship.          [8] Set.

Courtier and most faithful; a soldier that thought it
As beastly to know his own value too little
As devilish to acknowledge it too much.
Both his virtue and form deserv'd a far better fortune:
His discourse rather delighted to judge itself than show itself:
His breast was fill'd with all perfection,
And yet it seem'd a private whisp'ring-room,
It made so little noise of 't.
 *Duch.* But he was basely descended.
 *Bos.* Will you make yourself a mercenary herald,
Rather to examine men's pedigrees than virtues?
You shall want him:
For know, an honest statesman to a prince
Is like a cedar planted by a spring;
The spring bathes the tree's root, the grateful tree
Rewards it with his shadow: you have not done so.
I would sooner swim to the Bermooths[9] on
Two politicians' rotten bladders, tied
Together with an intelligencer's heart-string,
Than depend on so changeable a prince's favour.
Fare thee well, Antonio! Since the malice of the world
Would needs down with thee, it cannot be said yet
That any ill happen'd unto thee, considering thy fall
Was accompanied with virtue.
 *Duch.* O, you render me excellent music!
 **Bos.**        Say you?
 *Duch.* This good one that you speak of is my husband.
 *Bos.* Do I not dream? Can this ambitious age
Have so much goodness in 't as to prefer
A man merely for worth, without these shadows
Of wealth and painted honours? Possible?
 *Duch.* I have had three children by him.
 *Bos.*        Fortunate lady!
For you have made your private nuptial bed
The humble and fair seminary of peace,
No question but: many an unbenefic'd scholar
Shall pray for you for this deed, and rejoice
That some preferment in the world can yet
Arise from merit. The virgins of your land
That have no dowries shall hope your example
Will raise them to rich husbands. Should you want
Soldiers, 't would make the very Turks and Moors
Turn Christians, and serve you for this act.

 [9] Bermuda.

Last, the neglected poets of your time,
In honour of this trophy[1] of a man,
Rais'd by that curious engine, your white hand,
Shall thank you in your grave for 't, and make that
More reverend than all the cabinets[2]
Of living princes. For Antonio,
His fame shall likewise flow from many a pen,
When heralds shall want coats to sell to men.
   *Duch.*   As I taste comfort in this friendly speech,
So would I find concealment.
   *Bos.*   O, the secret of my prince,
Which I will wear on th' inside of my heart!
   *Duch.*   You shall take charge of all my coin and jewels,
And follow him; for he retires himself
To Ancona.
   *Bos.*        So.
   *Duch.*            Whither, within few days,
I mean to follow thee.
   *Bos.*                Let me think:
I would wish your grace to feign a pilgrimage
To our Lady of Loretto, scarce seven leagues
From fair Ancona; so may you depart
Your country with more honour, and your flight
Will seem a princely progress, retaining
Your usual train about you.
   *Duch.*                Sir, your direction
Shall lead me by the hand.
   *Cari.*                In my opinion,
She were better progress to the baths at Lucca,
Or go visit the Spa
In Germany; for, if you will believe me,
I do not like this jesting with religion,
This feigned pilgrimage.
   *Duch.*   Thou art a superstitious fool!
Prepare us instantly for our departure.
Past sorrows, let us moderately lament them,
For those to come, seek wisely to prevent them.
              *Exit* [*Duchess with Cariola*].
   *Bos.*   A politician is the devil's quilted anvil;
He fashions all sins on him, and the blows
Are never heard: he may work in a lady's chamber
(As here for proof). What rests but I reveal

---

[1] Monument of virtue.
[2] Collections of rarities.

All to my lord?  O, this base quality[3]
Of intelligencer!  Why, every quality i' th' world
Prefers[4] but gain or commendation:
Now, for this act I am certain to be rais'd,
And men that paint weeds to the life are prais'd.          *Exit.*


SCENA III

*Cardinal, Ferdinand, Malateste, Pescara, Silvia, Delio,*
*[and later] Bosola*

*Card.*  We must turn soldier, then?
*Mal.*                              The emperor,
Hearing your worth that way (ere you attain'd
This reverend garment), joins you in commission
With the right fortunate soldier, the Marquis of Pescara,
And the famous Lannoy.
*Card.*                    He that had the honour
Of taking the French king prisoner?
*Mal.*                      The same.
Here 's a plot drawn for a new fortification
At Naples.
*Ferd.*  This great Count Malateste, I perceive,
Hath got employment?
*Delio.*             No employment, my lord,
A marginal note in the muster-book that he is
A voluntary[5] lord.
*Ferd.*        He 's no soldier?
*Delio.*  He has worn gun-powder in 's hollow tooth for the
    tooth-ache.
*Sil.*  He comes to the leaguer with a full intent
To eat fresh beef and garlic, means to stay
Till the scent be gone, and straight return to court.
*Delio.*  He hath read all the late service
As the City Chronicle relates it;
And keeps two pewterers[6] going, only to express
Battles in model.
*Sil.*          Then he 'll fight by the book.[7]
*Delio.*  By the same almanac, I think,
To choose good days and shun the critical.
That 's his mistress' scarf.

3 Profession.                    4 Provides.
5 Volunteer.                     6 To make lead soldiers.
7 According to the rules.

*Sil.*                    Yes, he protests
He would do much for that taffeta.

*Delio.*   I think he would run away from a battle,
To save it from taking prisoner.

*Sil.*                              He is horribly afraid
Gun-powder will spoil the perfume on 't.

*Delio.*   I saw a Dutchman break his pate once
For calling him a pot-gun;[8] he made his head
Have a bore in 't like a musket.

*Sil.*   I would he had made a touch-hole to 't.
He is indeed a guarded sumpter-cloth,[9]
Only for the remove of the court.

### [*Enter Bosola*]

*Pes.*   Bosola arriv'd!  What should be the business?
Some falling-out amongst the cardinals.
These factions amongst great men, they are like
Foxes: when their heads are divided,
They carry fire in their tails, and all the country
About them goes to wrack for 't.

*Sil.*                              What 's that Bosola?

*Delio.*   I knew him in Padua, — a fantastical scholar, like such
who study to know how many knots was in Hercules' club, of
what colour Achilles' beard was, or whether Hector were not
troubled with the tooth-ache. He hath studied himself half blear-
ey'd to know the true symmetry of Cæsar's nose by a shoeing-horn;
and this he did to gain the name of a speculative man.

*Pes.*   Mark Prince Ferdinand:
A very salamander lives in 's eye,
To mock the eager violence of fire.

*Sil.*   That cardinal hath made more bad faces with his oppression than ever Michael Angelo made good ones. He lifts up 's nose,
like a foul porpoise before a storm.

*Pes.*   The Lord Ferdinand laughs.

*Delio.*                              Like a deadly cannon
That lightens ere it smokes.

*Pes.*   These are your true pangs of death,
The pangs of life, that struggle with great statesmen.

*Delio.*   In such a deformed silence witches whisper their charms.

*Card.*   Doth she make religion her riding-hood
To keep her from the sun and tempest?

*Ferd.*   That, that damns her. Methinks her fault and beauty,
Blended together, show like leprosy,

---

[8] Pop-gun, i.e., a braggart.          [9] Ornamented saddle blanket.

The whiter the fouler. I make it a question
Whether her beggarly brats were ever christ'n'd.

   *Card.*   I will instantly solicit the state of Ancona
To have them banish'd.

   *Ferd.*             You are for Loretto?
I shall not be at your ceremony, fare you well. —
Write to the Duke of Malfi, my young nephew,
She had by her first husband, and acquaint him
With 's mother's honesty.

   *Bos.*             I will.

   *Ferd.*                 Antonio!
A slave that only smell'd of ink and counters,
And nev'r in 's life look'd like a gentleman,
But in the audit-time. — Go, go presently,[1]
Draw me out an hundreth and fifty of our horse,
And meet me at the fort-bridge.[2]         *Exeunt.*

## Scena IIII

### *Two Pilgrims to the Shrine of our Lady of Loretto*

   *1 Pil.*   I have not seen a goodlier shrine than this;
Yet I have visited many.

   *2 Pil.*             The cardinal of Arragon
Is this day to resign his cardinal's hat;
His sister duchess likewise is arriv'd
To pay her vow of pilgrimage. I expect
A noble ceremony.

   *1 Pil.*         No question. — They come.

> *Here the ceremony of the Cardinal's instalment in the habit of a soldier: perform'd in delivering up his cross, hat, robes and ring at the shrine, and investing him with sword, helmet, shield, and spurs. Then Antonio, the Duchess and their children, having presented themselves at the shrine, are (by a form of banishment in dumb show expressed towards them by the Cardinal and the state of Ancona) banished. During all which ceremony, this ditty is sung, to very solemn music, by divers churchmen; and then exeunt [all except the two Pilgrims].*

---

[1] Immediately.        [2] Drawbridge.

Arms and honours deck thy story,
To thy fame's eternal glory!
Adverse fortune ever fly thee;
No disastrous fate come nigh thee!
I alone will sing thy praises,
Whom to honour virtue raises,
And thy study, that divine is,
Bent to martial discipline is.
Lay aside all those robes lie by thee;
Crown thy arts with arms, they 'll beautify thee.

*The Author*
*disclaims*
*this ditty*
*to be his*


O worthy of worthiest name, adorn'd in this manner,
Lead bravely thy forces on under war's warlike banner!
O, mayst thou prove fortunate in all martial courses!
Guide thou still by skill in arts and forces!
Victory attend thee nigh, whilst fame sings loud thy powers;
Triumphant conquest crown thy head, and blessings pour down
    showers!


   1 *Pil.*   Here 's a strange turn of state! who would have thought
So great a lady would have match'd herself
Unto so mean a person?  Yet the Cardinal
Bears himself much too cruel.
   2 *Pil.*              They are banish'd.
   1 *Pil.*   But I would ask what power hath this state
Of Ancona to determine of a free prince?
   2 *Pil.*   They are a free state, sir, and her brother show'd
How that the Pope, fore-hearing of her looseness,
Hath seiz'd into th' protection of the church
The dukedom which she held as dowager.
   1 *Pil.*   But by what justice?
   2 *Pil.*              Sure, I think by none,
Only her brother's instigation.
   1 *Pil.*   What was it with such violence he took
Off from her finger?
   2 *Pil.*          'T was her wedding-ring;
Which he vow'd shortly he would sacrifice
To his revenge.
   1 *Pil.*       Alas, Antonio!
If that a man be thrust into a well,
No matter who sets hand to 't, his own weight
Will bring him sooner to th' bottom.  Come, let 's hence.
Fortune makes this conclusion general:
All things do help th' unhappy man to fall.
                           *Exeunt.*

## SCENA V

*Antonio, Duchess, Children, Cariola, Servants, [and later] Bosola, Soldiers, with Vizards*[3]

*Duch.*    Banish'd Ancona!
*Ant.*                        Yes, you see what power
Lightens in great men's breath.
*Duch.*                        Is all our train
Shrunk to this poor remainder?
*Ant.*                        These poor men,
Which have got little in your service, vow
To take your fortune: but your wiser buntings,[4]
Now they are fledg'd, are gone.
*Duch.*                        They have done wisely.
This puts me in mind of death: physicians thus,
With their hands full of money, use to give o'er
Their patients.
*Ant.*        Right the fashion of the world:
From decay'd fortunes every flatterer shrinks;
Men cease to build where the foundation sinks.
*Duch.*    I had a very strange dream to-night.[5]
*Ant.*                        What was 't?
*Duch.*    Methought I wore my coronet of state,
And on a sudden all the diamonds
Were chang'd to pearls.
*Ant.*                My interpretation
Is, you'll weep shortly; for to me the pearls
Do signify your tears.
*Duch.*            The birds, that live i' th' field
On the wild benefit of nature, live
Happier than we: for they may choose their mates.
And carol their sweet pleasures to the spring.

*[Enter Bosola with a letter]*

*Bos.*    You are happily o'erta'en.
*Duch.*                        From my brother?
*Bos.*    Yes, from the Lord Ferdinand, your brother,
All love and safety.
*Duch.*            Thou dost blanch mischief,
Would'st make it white. See, see, like to calm weather
At sea before a tempest, false hearts speak fair
To those they intend most mischief.    *[Reads.] A Letter.*

---

[3] Masks.            [4] Small migratory birds.            [5] Last night.

"Send Antonio to me; I want his head in a business."
A political equivocation!
He doth not want your counsel, but your head;
That is, he cannot sleep till you be dead.
And here 's another pitfall that 's strew'd o'er
With roses; mark, 't is a cunning one:     [*Reads.*]
"I stand engaged for your husband for several debts at Naples: let
not that trouble him; I had rather have his heart than his
     money." —
And I believe so too.

    *Bos.*          What do you believe?
    *Duch.*   That he so much distrusts my husband's love,
He will by no means believe his heart is with him
Until he see it. The devil is not cunning enough
To circumvent us in riddles.
    *Bos.*   Will you reject that noble and free league
Of amity and love which I present you?
    *Duch.*   Their league is like that of some politic kings,
Only to make themselves of strength and power
To be our after-ruin: tell them so.
    *Bos.*   And what from you?
    *Ant.*          Thus tell him: I will not come.
    *Bos.*   And what of this?
    *Ant.*          My brothers have dispers'd
Bloodhounds abroad; which till I hear are muzzl'd,
No truce, though hatch'd with ne'er such politic skill,
Is safe, that hangs upon upon our enemies' will.
I 'll not come at them.
    *Bos.*         This proclaims your breeding.
Every small thing draws a base mind to fear
As the adamant[6] draws iron. Fare you well, sir;
You shall shortly hear from 's.          *Exit.*
    *Duch.*         I suspect some ambush;
Therefore by all my love I do conjure you
To take your eldest son, and fly towards Milan,
Let us not venture all this poor remainder
In one unlucky bottom.
    *Ant.*         You counsel safely.
Best of my life, farewell. Since we must part,
Heaven hath a hand in 't; but no otherwise
Than as some curious artist takes in sunder
A clock or watch, when it is out of frame,
To bring 't in better order.

    [6] Lodestone.

*Duch.*     I know not which is best,
To see you dead, or part with you.  Farewell, boy:
Thou art happy that thou hast not understanding
To know thy misery; for all our wit
And reading brings us to a truer sense
Of sorrow. — In the eternal church, sir,
I do hope we shall not part thus.
     *Ant.*                         O, be of comfort!
Make patience a noble fortitude,
And think not how unkindly we are us'd:
Man, like to cassia, is prov'd best, being bruis'd.
     *Duch.*     Must I, like to a slave-born Russian,
Account it praise to suffer tyranny?
And yet, O heaven, thy heavy hand is in 't!
I have seen my little boy oft scourge his top,
And compar'd myself to 't: naught made me e'er
Go right but heaven's scourge-stick.
     *Ant.*                         Do not weep:
Heaven fashion'd us of nothing; and we strive
To bring ourselves to nothing. — Farewell, Cariola,
And thy sweet armful. — If I do never see thee more,
Be a good mother to your little ones,
And save them from the tiger: fare you well.
     *Duch.*     Let me look upon you once more, for that speech
Came from a dying father.  Your kiss is colder
Than that I have seen an holy anchorite
Give to a dead man's skull.
     *Ant.*     My heart is turn'd to a heavy lump of lead,
With which I sound[7] my danger: fare you well.
                              *Exit* [*with his son.*]
     *Duch.*     My laurel is all withered.
     *Cari.*     Look, madam, what a troop of armed men
Make toward us!

          *Enter Bosola* [*vizarded,*] *with a Guard*

     *Duch.*               O, they are very welcome:
When Fortune's wheel is over-charg'd with princes,
The weight makes it move swift: I would have my ruin
Be sudden. — I am your adventure,[8] am I not?
     *Bos.*     You are: you must see your husband no more.
     *Duch.*     What devil art thou that counterfeits heaven's thunder?
     *Bos.*     Is that terrible?  I would have you tell me whether

[7] I.e., take soundings of.
[8] The object of your search.

Is that note worse that frights the silly birds
Out of the corn, or that which doth allure them
To the nets?  You have heark'ned to the last too much.
  *Duch.*   O misery! like to a rusty o'ercharg'd cannon,
Shall I never fly in pieces?  Come, to what prison?
  *Bos.*   To none.
  *Duch.*             Whither, then?
  *Bos.*                       To your palace.
  *Duch.*                               I have heard
That Charon's boat serves to convey all o'er
The dismal lake, but brings none back again.
  *Bos.*   Your brothers mean you safety and pity.
  *Duch.*                             Pity!
With such a pity men preserve alive
Pheasants and quails, when they are not fat enough
To be eaten.
  *Bos.*        These are your children?
  *Duch.*                       Yes.
  *Bos.*                         Can they prattle?
  *Duch.*   No:
But I intend, since they were born accurs'd,
Curses shall be their first language.
  *Bos.*                       Fie, madam!
Forget this base, low fellow.
  *Duch.*                   Were I a man,
I 'd beat that counterfeit face[9] into thy other.
  *Bos.*   One of no birth.
  *Duch.*             Say that he was born mean,
Man is most happy when 's own actions
Be arguments and examples of his virtue.
  *Bos.*   A barren, beggarly virtue.
  *Duch.*   I prithee, who is greatest?  Can you tell?
Sad tales befit my woe: I 'll tell you one.
A salmon, as she swam unto the sea,
Met with a dog-fish, who encounters her
With this rough language: 'Why art thou so bold
To mix thyself with our high state of floods,
Being no eminent courtier, but one
That for the calmest and fresh time o' th' year
Dost live in shallow rivers, rank'st thyself
With silly smelts and shrimps?  And darest thou
Pass by our dog-ship without reverence?'
'O,' quoth the salmon, 'sister, be at peace:

  [9] I.e., his mask.

Thank Jupiter we both have pass'd the net!
Our value never can be truly known,
Till in the fisher's basket we be shown:
I' th' market then my price may be the higher,
Even when I am nearest to the cook and fire.'
So to great men the moral may be stretched;
Men oft are valu'd high, when th' are most wretched. —
But come, whither you please. I am arm'd 'gainst misery;
Bent to all sways of the oppressor's will.
There's no deep valley but near some great hill.          *Exeunt.*

## *Actus IIII. Scena I*

### *Ferdinand, Bosola, [and later,] Duchess, Cariola, Servants*

*Ferd.*   How doth our sister duchess bear herself
In her imprisonment?
    *Bos.*                 Nobly: I 'll describe her.
She 's sad as one long us'd to 't, and she seems
Rather to welcome the end of misery
Than shun it; a behaviour so noble
As gives a majesty to adversity.
You may discern the shape of loveliness
More perfect in her tears than in her smiles:
She will muse four hours together; and her silence,
Methinks, expresseth more than if she spake.
    *Ferd.*   Her melancholy seems to be fortified
With a strange disdain.
    *Bos.*                 'T is so; and this restraint,
(Like English mastiffs that grow fierce with tying)
Makes her too passionately apprehend
Those pleasures she 's kept from.
    *Ferd.*                 Curse upon her!
I will no longer study in the book
Of another's heart. Inform her what I told you.          *Exit.*

### [*Enter Duchess and Attendants*]

    *Bos.*   All comfort to your grace!
    *Duch.*                 I will have none.
Pray thee, why dost thou wrap thy poison'd pills
In gold and sugar?
    *Bos.*   Your elder brother, the Lord Ferdinand,
Is come to visit you, and sends you word,

'Cause once he rashly made a solemn vow
Never to see you more, he comes i' th' night;
And prays you gently neither torch nor taper
Shine in your chamber. He will kiss your hand,
And reconcile himself; but for his vow
He dares not see you.

 *Duch.*    At his pleasure. —
Take hence the lights. — He 's come.

         *[Exeunt Attendants with lights.]*

      *[Enter Ferdinand]*

 *Ferd.*    Where are you?
 *Duch.*      Here, sir.
 *Ferd.* This darkness suits you well.
 *Duch.*      I would ask you pardon.
 *Ferd.* You have it;
For I account it the honourabl'st revenge,
Where I may kill, to pardon. — Where are your cubs?
 *Duch.* Whom?
 *Ferd.*    Call them your children;
For though our national law distinguish bastards
From true legitimate issue, compassionate nature
Makes them all equal.
 *Duch.*    Do you visit me for this?
You violate a sacrament o' th' church
Shall make you howl in hell for 't.
 *Ferd.*      It had been well,
Could you have liv'd thus always; for, indeed,
You were too much i' th' light. — But no more;
I come to seal my peace with you. Here 's a hand

       *Gives her a dead man's hand.*
To which you have vow'd much love; the ring upon 't
You gave.
 *Duch.*  I affectionately kiss it.
 *Ferd.* Pray, do, and bury the print of it in your heart.
I will leave this ring with you for a love-token;
And the hand as sure as the ring: and do not doubt
But you shall have the heart too. When you need a friend,
Send it to him that ow'd[1] it; you shall see
Whether he can aid you.
 *Duch.*    You are very cold:
I fear you are not well after your travel. —
Ha! lights! —— O, horrible!

 [1] Owned.

*Ferd.*   Let her have lights enough.                              *Exit.*

*Duch.*   What witchcraft doth he practise, that he hath left
A dead man's hand here?

> *Here is discover'd, behind a traverse,[2]*
> *the artificial figures of Antonio and*
> *his children, appearing as if they*
> *were dead.*

*Bos.*   Look you, here 's the piece from which 't was ta'en.
He doth present you this sad spectacle,
That, now you know directly they are dead,
Hereafter you may wisely cease to grieve
For that which cannot be recovered.

*Duch.*   There is not between heaven and earth one wish
I stay for after this.  It wastes me more
Than were 't my picture, fashion'd out of wax,
Stuck with a magical needle, and then buried
In some foul dung-hill; and yond 's an excellent property[3]
For a tyrant, which I would account mercy.

*Bos.*                              What 's that?

*Duch.*   If they would bind me to that liveless trunk,
And let me freeze to death.

*Bos.*                  Come, you must live.

*Duch.*   That 's the greatest torture souls feel in hell:
In hell that they must live, and cannot die.
Portia,[4] I 'll new-kindle thy coals again,
And revive the rare and almost dead example
Of a loving wife.

*Bos.*          O, fie! despair?  Remember
You are a Christian.

*Duch.*          The church enjoins fasting:
I 'll starve myself to death.

*Bos.*                  Leave this vain sorrow.
Things being at the worst begin to mend: the bee
When he hath shot his sting into your hand,
May then play with your eye-lid.

*Duch.*                  Good comfortable fellow,
Persuade a wretch that 's broke upon the wheel
To have all hs bones new set; entreat him live
To be executed again.  Who must despatch me?
I account this world a tedious theatre,
For I do play a part in 't 'gainst my will.

*Bos.*   Come, be of comfort: I will save your life.

---

[2] Curtain.          [3] Appropriate act.
[4] Wife of Brutus; cf. Shakespeare's *Julius Caesar*, IV.iii.152–56.

*Duch.*   Indeed, I have not leisure to tend so small a business.
*Bos.*   Now, by my life, I pity you.
*Duch.*                          Thou art a fool, then,
To waste thy pity on a thing so wretched
As cannot pity itself. I am full of daggers.
Puff, let me blow these vipers from me.

[*Enter Servant*]

What are you?
*Serv.*          One that wishes you long life.
*Duch.*   I would thou wert hang'd for the horrible curse
Thou hast given me: I shall shortly grow one
Of the miracles of pity. I 'll go pray! —          [*Exit Serv.*]
No, I 'll go curse.
*Bos.*          O, fie!
*Duch.*                  I could curse the stars —
*Bos.*                                  O, fearful!
*Duch.*   And those three smiling seasons of the year
Into a Russian winter; nay, the world
To its first chaos.
*Bos.*          Look you, the stars shine still.
*Duch.*   O, but you must
Remember, my curse hath a great way to go. —
Plagues, that make lanes through largest families,
Consume them! —
*Bos.*          Fie, lady!
*Duch.*                  Let them, like tyrants,
Never be remember'd but for the ill they have done;
Let all the zealous prayers of mortified
Churchmen forget them! —
*Bos.*                  O, uncharitable!
*Duch.*   Let heaven a little while cease crowning martyrs,
To punish them! —
Go, howl them this, and say, I long to bleed:
It is some mercy when men kill with speed.          *Exit.*

[*Re-enter Ferdinand*]

*Ferd.*   Excellent, as I would wish; she 's plagu'd in art.
These presentations are but fram'd in wax
By the curious master in that quality,
Vincentio Lauriola, and she takes them
For true substantial bodies.
*Bos.*                  Why do you do this?
*Ferd.*   To bring her to despair.

*Bos.*                         Faith, end here,
And go no farther in your cruelty.
Send her a penitential garment to put on
Next to her delicate skin, and furnish her
With beads and prayer-books.
    *Ferd.*                 Damn her! that body of hers,
While that my blood ran pure in 't, was more worth
Than that which thou wouldst comfort, call'd a soul.
I will send her masques of common courtesans,
Have her meat serv'd up by bawds and ruffians,
And, 'cause she 'll needs be mad, I am resolv'd
To remove forth the common hospital
All the mad-folk, and place them near her lodging;
There let them practise together, sing and dance,
And act their gambols to the full o' th' moon:
If she can sleep the better for it, let her.
Your work is almost ended.
    *Bos.*                     Must I see her again?
    *Ferd.*  Yes.
    *Bos.*        Never.
    *Ferd.*              You must.
    *Bos.*                     Never in mine own shape;
That 's forfeited by my intelligence[5]
And this last cruel lie: when you send me next,
The business shall be comfort.
    *Ferd.*                 Very likely!
Thy pity is nothing of kin to thee.  Antonio
Lurks about Milan: thou shalt shortly thither,
To feed a fire as great as my revenge,
Which never will slack till it hath spent his fuel:
Intemperate agues make physicians cruel.              *Exeunt.*


SCENA II

*Duchess, Cariola, [and later] Servant, Madmen, Bosola,*
*Executioners, Ferdinand*

*Duch.*   What hideous noise was that?
    *Cari.*                         'T is the wild consort[6]
Of madmen, lady, which your tyrant brother
Hath plac'd about your lodging.  This tyranny,
I think, was never practis'd till this hour.
    *Duch.*   Indeed, I thank him.  Nothing but noise and folly

---

[5] My having acted as an intelligencer, or spy.          [6] Band.

Can keep me in my right wits; whereas reason
And silence make me stark mad.  Sit down;
Discourse to me some dismal tragedy.

 *Cari.* O, 't will increase your melancholy!

 *Duch.*        Thou art deceiv'd:
To hear of greater grief would lessen mine.
This is a prison?

 *Cari.*    Yes, but you shall live
To shake this durance off.

 *Duch.*     Thou art a fool:
The robin-red-breast and the nightingale
Never live long in cages.

 *Cari.*     Pray, dry your eyes.
What think you of, madam?

 *Duch.*     Of nothing;
When I muse thus, I sleep.

 *Cari.* Like a madman, with your eyes open?

 *Duch.* Dost thou think we shall know one another
In th' other world?

 *Cari.*     Yes, out of question.

 *Duch.* O, that it were possible we might
But hold some two days' conference with the dead!
From them I should learn somewhat, I am sure,
I never shall know here.  I 'll tell thee a miracle:
I am not mad yet, to my cause of sorrow:
The' heaven o'er my head seems made of molten brass,
The earth of flaming sulphur, yet I am not mad.
I am acquainted with sad misery
As the tann'd galley-slave is with his oar;
Necessity makes me suffer constantly,
And custom makes it easy.  Who do I look like now?

 *Cari.* Like to your picture in the gallery,
A deal of life in show, but none in practice;
Or rather like some reverend monument
Whose ruins are even pitied.

 *Duch.*     Very proper;
And Fortune seems only to have her eye-sight
To behold my tragedy. — How now!
What noise is that?

[*Enter Servant*]

 *Serv.*     I am come to tell you,
Your brother hath intended you some sport.
A great physician, when the Pope was sick

Of a deep melancholy, presented him
With several sorts of madmen, which wild object
(Being full of change and sport) forc'd him to laugh,
And so th' imposthume[7] broke: the self-same cure
The duke intends on you.

    *Duch.*             Let them come in.

    *Serv.*   There 's a mad lawyer; and a secular priest;
A doctor that hath forfeited his wits
By jealousy; an astrologian
That in his works said such a day o' th' month
Should be the day of doom, and, falling of 't,
Ran mad; an English tailor, craz'd i' th' brain
With the study of new fashion; a gentleman-usher
Quite beside himself with care to keep in mind
The number of his lady's salutations,
Or 'How do you,' she employ'd him in each morning;
A farmer, too, an excellent knave in grain,
Mad 'cause he was hinder'd transportation:[8]
And let one broker that 's mad loose to these,
You 'd think the devil were among them.

    *Duch.*   Sit, Cariola. — Let them loose when you please,
For I am chain'd to endure all your tyranny.

*[Enter Madmen]*

*Here by a Madman this song is sung to a dismal kind of*
*music.*

O, let us howl some heavy note,
    Some deadly dogged howl,
Sounding as from the threat'ning throat
    Of beasts and fatal fowl!
As ravens, screech-owls, bulls, and bears,
    We' ll bell,[9] and bawl our parts,
Till irksome noise have cloy'd your ears
    And corrosiv'd[1] your hearts.
At last, when as our choir wants breath,
    Our bodies being blest,
We 'll sing, like swans, to welcome death,
    And die in love and rest.

    1 *Madman.*  Doom's-day not come yet! I 'll draw it nearer by a
perspective, or make a glass that shall set all the world on fire upon
an instant. I cannot sleep; my pillow is stuff'd with a litter of por-
cupines.

    [7] Ulcer.             [8] Prevented from exporting his grain.
    [9] Bellow.          [1] Corroded.

2 *Madman.*   Hell is a mere glass-house, where the devils are continually blowing up women's souls on hollow irons, and the fire
never goes out.

3 *Madman.*   I will lie with every woman in my parish the tenth
night. I will tithe them over like hay-cocks.

4 *Madman.*   Shall my 'pothecary out-go me, because I am a
cuckold? I have found out his roguery: he makes alum of his
wife's urine, and sells it to Puritans that have sore throats with
over-straining.

1 *Madman.*   I have skill in heraldry.

2 *Madman.*   Hast?

1 *Madman.*   You do give for your crest a woodcock's head with
the brains pick'd out on 't; you are a very ancient gentleman.

3 *Madman.*   Greek is turn'd Turk: we are only to be sav'd by
the Helvetian translation.[2]

1 *Madman.*   Come on, sir, I will lay the law to you.

2 *Madman.*   O, rather lay a corrosive: the law will eat to the
bone.

3 *Madman.*   He that drinks but to satisfy nature is damn'd.

4 *Madman.*   If I had my glass here, I would show a sight should
make all the women here call me mad doctor.

1 *Madman.*   What 's he? A rope-maker?

2 *Madman.*   No, no, no; a snuffling knave that while he shows
the tombs, will have his hand in a wench's placket.

3 *Madman.*   Woe to the caroche that brought home my wife
from the masque at three o'clock in the morning! It had a large
feather-bed in it.

4 *Madman.*   I have pared the devil's nails forty times, roasted
them in raven's eggs, and cur'd agues with them.

3 *Madman.*   Get me three hundred milchbats, to make possets[3]
to procure sleep.

4 *Madman.*   All the college may throw their caps at me: I have
made a soap-boiler costive;[4] it was my masterpiece.

> *Here the dance, consisting of Eight Madmen, with mu-
> sic answerable thereunto; after which, Bosola (like an
> old man) enters.*

Duch.   Is he mad too?

Serv.                    Pray, question him. I 'll leave you.

                         [*Exeunt Servant and Madmen.*]

Bos.   I am come to make thy tomb.

Duch.                    Ha! my tomb!

[2] The Geneva Bible of 1560, favored by the Puritans.
[3] Warm soothing drink made of milk and other ingredients.
[4] Constipated.

Thou speak'st as if I lay upon my death-bed,
Gasping for breath. Dost thou perceive me sick?

*Bos.* Yes, and the more dangerously, since thy sickness is insensible.

*Duch.* Thou art not mad, sure: dost know me?

*Bos.* Yes.

*Duch.* Who am I?

*Bos.* Thou art a box of worm-seed, at best but a salvatory of green mummy.[5] What 's this flesh? A little crudded[6] milk, fantastical puff-paste. Our bodies are weaker than those paper-prisons boys use to keep flies in; more contemptible, since ours is to preserve earth-worms. Didst thou ever see a lark in a cage? Such is the soul in the body: this world is like her little turf of grass, and the heaven o'er our heads, like her looking-glass, only gives us a miserable knowledge of the small compass of our prison.

*Duch.* Am not I thy duchess?

*Bos.* Thou are some great woman, sure, for riot begins to sit on thy forehead (clad in gray hairs) twenty years sooner than on a merry milk-maid's. Thou sleep'st worse than if a mouse should be forc'd to take up her lodging in a cat's ear: a little infant that breeds its teeth, should it lie with thee, would cry out, as if thou wert the more unquiet bedfellow.

*Duch.* I am Duchess of Malfi still.

*Bos.* That makes thy sleeps so broken:
Glories, like glow-worms, afar off shine bright,
But, look'd to near, have neither heat nor light.

*Duch.* Thou art very plain.

*Bos.* My trade is to flatter the dead, not the living; I am a tomb-maker.

*Duch.* And thou com'st to make my tomb?

*Bos.* Yes.

*Duch.* Let me be a little merry: — of what stuff wilt thou make it?

*Bos.* Nay, resolve me first of what fashion?

*Duch.* Why, do we grow fantastical[7] in our deathbed?
Do we affect fashion in the grave?

*Bos.* Most ambitiously. Princes' images on their tombs do not lie, as they were wont, seeming to pray up to heaven; but with their hands under their cheeks, as if they died of the tooth-ache. They are not carved with their eyes fix'd upon the stars; but, as their minds were wholly bent upon the world, the selfsame way they seem to turn their faces.

---

[5] Ointment box of fresh mummy, a drug supposed to be extracted from embalmed bodies.

[6] Curdled.                    [7] Whimsical.

*Duch.* Let me know fully therefore the effect
Of this thy dismal preparation,
This talk fit for a charnel.
    *Bos.*                   Now I shall: —

    *[Enter Executioners, with] A coffin, cords, and a bell*

Here is a present from your princely brothers;
And may it arrive welcome, for it brings
Last benefit, last sorrow.
    *Duch.*                Let me see it:
I have so much obedience in my blood,
I wish it in their veins to do them good.
    *Bos.* This is your last presence-chamber.
    *Cari.* O my sweet lady!
    *Duch.*            Peace; it affrights not me.
    *Bos.* I am the common bellman
That usually is sent to condemn'd persons
The night before they suffer.
    *Duch.*           Even now thou said'st
Thou wast a tomb-maker.
    *Bos.*          'T was to bring you
By degrees to mortification. Listen.

*Hark, now everything is still,*
*The screech-owl and the whistler shrill*
*Call upon our dame aloud,*
*And bid her quickly don her shroud!*
*Much you had of land and rent;*
*Your length in clay 's now competent:*
*A long war disturb'd your mind;*
*Here your perfect peace is sign'd.*
*Of what is 't fools make such vain keeping?*
*Sin their conception, their birth weeping,*
*Their life a general mist of error,*
*Their death a hideous storm of terror.*
*Strew your hair with powders sweet,*
*Don clean linen, bathe your feet,*
*And (the foul field more to check)*
*A crucifix let bless your neck.*
*'T is now full tide 'tween night and day;*
*End your groan, and come away.*

    *Cari.* Hence, villains, tyrants, murderers! Alas!
What will you do with my lady? — Call for help!
    *Duch.* To whom? To our next neighbours? They are **mad-**
    **folks.**

*Bos.*  Remove that noise.

*Duch.*                    Farewell, Cariola.
In my last will I have not much to give:
A many hungry guests have fed upon me;
Thine will be a poor reversion.

    *Cari.*                    I will die with her.

    *Duch.*  I pray thee, look thou giv'st my little boy
Some syrup for his cold, and let the girl
Say her prayers ere she sleep.

                *[Cariola is forced out by the Executioners.]*
What death?

    *Bos.*  Strangling: here are your executioners.

    *Duch.*  I forgive them:
The apoplexy, catarrh, or cough o' th' lungs,
Would do as much as they do.

    *Bos.*  Doth not death fright you?

    *Duch.*                    Who would be afraid on 't,
Knowing to meet such excellent company
In th' other world?

    *Bos.*  Yet, methinks,
The manner of your death should much afflict you:
This cord should terrify you.

    *Duch.*                    Not a whit:
What would it pleasure me to have my throat cut
With diamonds? or to be smothered
With cassia? or to be shot to death with pearls?
I know death hath ten thousand several doors
For men to take their exits; and 't is found
They go on such strange geometrical hinges,
You may open them both ways: any way, for heaven-sake,
So I were out of your whispering.  Tell my brothers
That I perceive death, now I am well awake,
Best gift is they can give or I can take.
I would fain put off my last woman's-fault:
I 'd not be tedious to you.

    *Execut.*                    We are ready.

    *Duch.*  Dispose my breath how please you; but my body
Bestow upon my women, will you?

    *Execut.*                    Yes.

    *Duch.*  Pull, and pull strongly, for your able strength
Must pull down heaven upon me: —
Yet stay; heaven-gates are not so highly arch'd
As princes' palaces; they that enter there
Must go upon their knees [*kneels*]. — Come violent death,

Serve for mandragora[8] to make me sleep! —
Go tell my brothers, when I am laid out,
They then may feed in quiet.                    *They strangle her.*
    *Bos.* Where 's the waiting-woman?
Fetch her: some other strangle the children.

#### [*Enter Cariola*]

Look you, there sleeps your mistress.
    *Cari.*                    O, you are damn'd
Perpetually for this! My turn is next; —
Is 't not so order'd?
    *Bos.*          Yes, and I am glad
You are so well prepared for 't.
    *Cari.*                  You are deceiv'd, sir,
I am not prepar'd for 't, I will not die;
I will first come to my answer, and know
How I have offended.
    *Bos.*          Come, despatch her. —
You kept her counsel; now you shall keep ours.
    *Cari.* I will not die, I must not; I am contracted
To a young gentleman.
    *Execut.*          Here 's your wedding-ring.
    *Cari.* Let me but speak with the duke, I 'll discover
Treason to his person.
    *Bos.*          Delays: — throttle her.
    *Execut.* She bites and scratches.
    *Cari.*                    If you kill me now,
I am damn'd; I have not been at confession
This two years.
    *Bos.* [*To Executioners.*]   When!
    *Cari.*                  I am quick with child.
    *Bos.*                          Why, then,
Your credit 's saved.          [*Executioners strangle Cariola.*]
            Bear her into th' next room;
Let this lie still.          [*Exeunt Executioners with body of Cariola.*

#### Enter Ferdinand]

    *Ferd.* Is she dead?
    *Bos.*          She is what
You 'd have her. But here begin your pity:
            *Shows the Children strangled.*
Alas, how have these offended?

  [8] Plant of the nightshade family.

*Ferd.*                    The death
Of young wolves is never to be pitied.
    *Bos.*   Fix your eye here.
    *Ferd.*                 Constantly.
    *Bos.*                            Do you not weep?
Other sins only speak; murther shrieks out.
The element of water moistens the earth,
But blood flies upwards and bedews the heavens.
    *Ferd.*   Cover her face; mine eyes dazzle: she died young.
    *Bos.*   I think not so; her infelicity
Seem'd to have years too many.
    *Ferd.*   She and I were twins;
And should I die this instant, I had liv'd
Her time to a minute.
    *Bos.*                It seems she was born first:
You have bloodily approv'd the ancient truth,
That kindred commonly do worse agree
Than remote strangers.
    *Ferd.*                Let me see her face
Again. Why didst not thou pity her? What
An excellent honest man mightst thou have been,
If thou hadst borne her to some sanctuary!
Or, bold in a good cause, oppos'd thyself,
With thy advanced sword above thy head,
Between her innocence and my revenge!
I bade thee, when I was distracted of my wits,
Go kill my dearest friend, and thou hast done 't.
For let me but examine well the cause:
What was the meanness of her match to me?
Only I must confess I had a hope,
Had she continu'd widow, to have gain'd
An infinite mass of treasure by her death:
And that was the main cause, — her marriage,
That drew a stream of gall quite through my heart.
For thee (as we observe in tragedies
That a good actor many times is curs'd
For playing a villain's part) I hate thee for 't.
And, for my sake, say, thou hast done much ill well.
    *Bos.*   Let me quicken your memory, for I perceive
You are falling into ingratitude: I challenge
The reward due to my service.
    *Ferd.*                    I'll tell thee
What I'll give thee.
    *Bos.*          Do.

*Ferd.*                    I 'll give thee a pardon
For this murther.
   *Bos.*          Ha!
   *Ferd.*                Yes, and 't is
The largest bounty I can study to do thee.
By what authority didst thou execute
This bloody sentence?
   *Bos.*                By yours.
   *Ferd.*   Mine!  Was I her judge?
Did any ceremonial form of law
Doom her to not-being?  Did a complete jury
Deliver her conviction up i' th' court?
Where shalt thou find this judgment register'd,
Unless in hell?  See, like a bloody fool,
Thou 'st forfeited thy life, and thou shalt die for 't.
   *Bos.*   The office of justice is perverted quite
When one thief hangs another.  Who shall dare
To reveal this?
   *Ferd.*        O, I 'll tell thee;
The wolf shall find her grave, and scrape it up,
Not to devour the corpse, but to discover
The horrid murther.
   *Bos.*                You, not I, shall quake for 't.
   *Ferd.*   Leave me.
   *Bos.*                I will first receive my pension.
   *Ferd.*   You are a villain.
   *Bos.*                When your ingratitude
Is judge, I am so.
   *Ferd.*        O horror,
That not the fear of him which binds the devils
Can prescribe man obedience! —
Never look upon me more.
   *Bos.*                Why, fare thee well.
Your brother and yourself are worthy men!
You have a pair of hearts are hollow graves,
Rotten, and rotting others; and your vengeance,
Like two chain'd bullets, still goes arm in arm.
You may be brothers; for treason, like the plague,
Doth take much in a blood.[9]  I stand like one
That long hath ta'en a sweet and golden dream:
I am angry with myself, now, that I wake.
   *Ferd.*   Get thee into some unknown part o' th' world,
That I may never see thee.

   [9] Goes in families.

   *Bos.*             Let me know
Wherefore I should be thus neglected.  Sir,
I serv'd your tyranny, and rather strove
To satisfy yourself than all the world:
And though I loath'd the evil, yet I lov'd
You that did counsel it; and rather sought
To appear a true servant than an honest man.
   *Ferd.*   I 'll go hunt the badger by owl-light:
'T is a deed for darkness.                   *Exit.*
   *Bos.*   He 's much distracted.  Off, my painted honour!
While with vain hopes our faculties we tire,
We seem to sweat in ice and freeze in fire.
What would I do, were this to do again?
I would not change my peace of conscience
For all the wealth of Europe. — She stirs; here 's life: —
Return, fair soul, from darkness, and lead mine
Out of this sensible hell! — she 's warm, she breathes: —
Upon thy pale lips I will melt my heart,
To store them with fresh colour. — Who 's there?
Some cordial drink! — Alas! I dare not call:
So pity would destroy pity. — Her eye opes,
And heaven in it seems to ope, that late was shut
To take me up to mercy.
   *Duch.*   Antonio!
   *Bos.*            Yes, madam, he is living;
The dead bodies you saw were but feign'd statues.
He 's reconciled to your brothers; the Pope hath wrought
The atonement.
   *Duch.*       Mercy!             *She dies.*
   *Bos.*   O, she 's gone again! there the cords of life broke.
O sacred innocence, that sweetly sleeps
On turtles'[1] feathers, whilst a guilty conscience
Is a black register wherein is writ
All our good deeds and bad, a perspective[2]
That shows us hell!  That we cannot be suffer'd
To do good when we have a mind to it!
This is manly sorrow!
These tears, I am very certain, never grew
In my mother's milk.  My estate is sunk
Below the degree of fear: where were
These penitent fountains while she was living?
O, they were frozen up!  Here is a sight
As direful to my soul as is the sword

---

[1] Turtledoves'.             [2] Peep show.

Unto a wretch hath slain his father.
Come, I 'll bear thee hence,
And execute thy last will; that 's deliver
Thy body to the reverend dispose
Of some good women: that the cruel tyrant
Shall not deny me. Then I 'll post to Milan,
Where somewhat I will speedily enact
Worth my dejection.[3]                    *Exit [with the body].*


### Actus V.  Scena 1

*Antonio, Delio [and later] Pescara, Julia*

*Ant.*  What think you of my hope of reconcilement
To the Arragonian brethren?
 *Delio.*      I misdoubt it;
For though they have sent their letters of safe-conduct
For your repair to Milan, they appear
But nets to entrap you. The Marquis of Pescara,
Under whom you hold certain land in cheat,[4]
Much 'gainst his noble nature hath been mov'd
To seize those lands; and some of his dependants
Are at this instant making it their suit
To be invested in your revenues.
I cannot think they mean well to your life
That do deprive you of your means of life,
Your living.
 *Ant.*  You are still an heretic
To any safety I can shape myself.
 *Delio.*  Here comes the marquis: I will make myself
Petitioner for some part of your land,
To know whether it is flying.
 *Ant.*       I pray, do. *[Withdraws.]*

### [Enter Pescara]

*Delio.*  Sir, I have a suit to you.
 *Pes.*     To me?
 *Delio.*       An easy one:
There is the Citadel of Saint Bennet,
With some demesnes, of late in the possession
Of Antonio Bologna, — please you bestow them on me.
 *Pes.*  You are my friend; but this is such a suit,
Nor fit for me to give, nor you to take.

---

³ Suitable to my distress.     ⁴ Subject to forfeiture.

*Delio.*    No, sir?
*Pes.*    I will give you ample reason for 't
Soon in private.  Here 's the cardinal's mistress.

[*Enter Julia*]

*Julia.*    My lord, I am grown your poor petitioner,
And should be an ill beggar, had I not
A great man's letter here (the cardinal's)
To court you in my favour.                    [*Gives a letter.*]
*Pes.*                    He entreats for you
The Citadel of Saint Bennet, that belong'd
To the banish'd Bologna.
*Julia.*                    Yes.
*Pes.*    I could not have thought of a friend I could rather
Pleasure with it: 't is yours.
*Julia.*                    Sir, I thank you;
And he shall know how doubly I am engag'd,
Both in your gift, and speediness of giving,
Which makes your grant the greater.                    *Exit.*
*Ant. [Aside.]*                    How they fortify
Themselves with my ruin!
*Delio.*                    Sir, I am
Little bound to you.
*Pes.*                    Why?
*Delio.*    Because you denied this suit to me, and gave 't
To such a creature.
*Pes.*                    Do you know what it was?
It was Antonio's land: not forfeited
By course of law, but ravish'd from his throat
By the cardinal's entreaty.  It were not fit
I should bestow so main a piece of wrong
Upon my friend: 't is a gratification
Only due to a strumpet, for it is injustice.
Shall I sprinkle the pure blood of innocents
To make those followers I call my friends
Look ruddier upon me?  I am glad
This land, ta'en from the owner by such wrong,
Returns again unto so foul an use
As salary for his lust.  Learn, good Delio,
To ask noble things of me, and you shall find
I 'll be a noble giver.
*Delio.*                    You instruct me well.
*Ant. [Aside.]*    Why, here 's a man now would fright impudence
From sauciest beggars.

*Pes.*                    Prince Ferdinand's come to Milan,
Sick, as they give out, of an apoplexy;
But some say 't is a frenzy. I am going
To visit him.                                        *Exit.*

*Ant.*          'T is a noble old fellow.

*Delio.*   What course do you mean to take, Antonio?

*Ant.*   This night I mean to venture all my fortune,
Which is no more than a poor ling'ring life,
To the cardinal's worst of malice. I have got
Private access to his chamber; and intend
To visit him about the mid of night,
As once his brother did our noble duchess.
It may be that the sudden apprehension
Of danger, — for I 'll go in mine own shape, —
When he shall see it fraight[5] with love and duty,
May draw the poison out of him, and work
A friendly reconcilement. If it fail,
Yet it shall rid me of this infamous calling;
For better fall once than be ever falling.

*Delio.*   I 'll second you in all danger; and, howe'er,
My life keeps rank with yours.

*Ant.*   You are still my lov'd and best friend.          *Exeunt.*


SCENA II

*Pescara, a Doctor, [later] Ferdinand, Cardinal, Mala-
teste, Bosola, Julia*

*Pes.*   Now, doctor, may I visit your patient?

*Doc.*   If 't please your lordship; but he 's instantly
To take the air here in the gallery
By my direction.

*Pes.*          Pray thee, what 's his disease?

*Doc.*   A very pestilent disease, my lord,
They call lycanthropia.

*Pes.*          What 's that?
I need a dictionary to 't.

*Doc.*          I 'll tell you.
In those that are possess'd with 't there o'erflows
Such melancholy humour they imagine
Themselves to be transformed into wolves;
Steal forth to church-yards in the dead of night,

5 Fraught.

And dig dead bodies up: as two nights since
One met the duke 'bout midnight in a lane
Behind Saint Mark's church, with the leg of a man
Upon his shoulder; and he howl'd fearfully;
Said he was a wolf, only the difference
Was, a wolf's skin was hairy on the outside,
His on the inside; bade them take their swords,
Rip up his flesh; and try. Straight I was sent for,
And, having minister'd to him, found his grace
Very well recovered.

    *Pes.*  I am glad on 't.

    *Doc.*              Yet not without some fear
Of a relapse. If he grow to his fit again,
I 'll go a nearer way to work with him
Than ever Paracelsus[6] dream'd of; if
They 'll give me leave, I 'll buffet his madness out of him.
Stand aside; he comes.

        [*Enter Ferdinand, Cardinal, Malateste, and Bosola*]

    *Ferd.*  Leave me.

    *Mal.*  Why doth your lordship love this solitariness?

    *Ferd.*  Eagles commonly fly alone: they are crows, daws, and starlings that flock together. Look, what 's that follows me?

    *Mal.*  Nothing, my lord.

    *Ferd.*  Yes.

    *Mal.*  'T is your shadow.

    *Ferd.*  Stay it; let it not haunt me.

    *Mal.*  Impossible, if you moved, and the sun shine.

    *Ferd.*  I will throttle it.   [*Throws himself down on his shadow.*]

    *Mal.*  O, my lord, you are angry with nothing.

    *Ferd.*  You are a fool: how is 't possible I should catch my shadow, unless I fall upon 't? When I go to hell, I mean to carry a bribe; for, look you, good gifts evermore make way for the worst persons.

    *Pes.*  Rise, good my lord.

    *Ferd.*  I am studying the art of patience.

    *Pes.*  'T is a noble virtue.

    *Ferd.*  To drive six snails before me from this town to Moscow; neither use goad nor whip to them, but let them take their own time; — the patient'st man i' the world match me for an experiment! And I 'll crawl after like a sheepbiter.[7]

    *Card.*  Force him up.            [*They raise him.*]

    [6] A reformer of medical theory.
    [7] A dog that worries sheep.

*Ferd.*  Use me well, you were best.  What I have done, I have done: I 'll confess nothing.

*Doc.*  Now let me come to him. — Are you mad, my lord? Are you out of your princely wits?

*Ferd.*                          What 's he?

*Pes.*                          Your doctor.

*Ferd.*  Let me have his beard saw'd off, and his eye-brows fil'd more civil.[8]

*Doc.*  I must do mad tricks with him, for that 's the only way on 't. — I have brought your grace a salamander's skin to keep you from sunburning.

*Ferd.*  I have cruel sore eyes.

*Doc.*  The white of a cockatrix's[9] egg is present remedy.

*Ferd.*  Let it be a new-laid one, you were best.  Hide me from him: physicians are like kings, — They brook no contradiction.

*Doc.*  Now he begins to fear me: now let me alone with him.

          [*Puts off his four cloaks, one after another.*]

*Card.*  How now! put off your gown?

*Doc.*  Let me have some forty urinals filled with rose-water: he and I 'll go pelt one another with them. — Now he begins to fear me. — Can you fetch a frisk,[1] sir? — Let him go, let him go, upon my peril.  I find by his eye he stands in awe of me: I 'll make him as tame as a dormouse.

*Ferd.*  Can you fetch your frisks, sir! — I will stamp him into a cullis, flay off his skin to cover one of the anatomies[2] this rogue hath set i' th' cold yonder in Barber-Chirurgeons's-hall. — Hence, hence! you are all of you like beasts for sacrifice. [*Throws the Doctor down and beats him.*]  There 's nothing left of you but tongue and belly, flattery and lechery.                    [*Exit.*]

*Pes.*  Doctor, he did not fear you thoroughly.

*Doc.*  True; I was somewhat too forward.

*Bos.*  Mercy upon me, what a fatal judgment Hath fall'n upon this Ferdinand!

*Pes.*                          Knows your grace What accident hath brought unto the prince This strange distraction?

*Card.* [*Aside.*]  I must feign somewhat. — Thus they say it grew. You have heard it rumour'd, for these many years, None of our family dies but there is seen The shape of an old woman, which is given By tradition to us to have been murther'd By her nephews for her riches.  Such a figure

---

[8] Becomingly.
[1] Cut a caper.

[9] Fabulous monster, identified with the basilisk.
[2] Skeletons.

One night, as the prince sat up late at 's book,
Appear'd to him; when crying out for help,
The gentleman of 's chamber found his grace
All on a cold sweat, alter'd much in face
And language: since which apparition,
He hath grown worse and worse, and I much fear
He cannot live.

    *Bos.*        Sir, I would speak with you.

    *Pes.*  We 'll leave your grace,
Wishing to the sick prince, our noble lord,
All health and mind and body.

    *Card.*          You are most welcome.

                    [*Exeunt Pescara, Malateste, and Doctor*]

Are you come? so. — [*Aside.*] This fellow must not know
By any means I had intelligence
In our duchess' death; for, though I counsell'd it,
The full of all th' engagement[3] seem'd to grow
From Ferdinand. — Now, sir, how fares our sister?
I do not think but sorrow makes her look
Like to an oft-dy'd garment: she shall now
Taste comfort from me. Why do you look so wildly?
O, the fortune of your master here, the prince,
Dejects you; but be you of happy comfort:
If you 'll do one thing for me I 'll entreat,
Though he had a cold tomb-stone o'er his bones,
I 'd make you what you would be.

    *Bos.*             Anything!
Give it me in a breath, and let me fly to 't.
They that think long small expedition[4] win,
For musing much o' th' end cannot begin.

                [*Enter Julia*]

    *Julia.*  Sir, will you come in to supper?

    *Card.*              I am busy; leave me.

    *Julia.* [*Aside.*]  What an excellent shape hath that fellow!  *Exit.*

    *Card.*  'T is thus. Antonio lurks here in Milan:
Inquire him out, and kill him. While he lives,
Our sister cannot marry; and I have thought
Of an excellent match for her. Do this, and style me
Thy advancement.

    *Bos.*  But by what means shall I find him out?

    *Card.*  There is a gentleman call'd Delio
Here in the camp, that hath been long approv'd

---

[3] The whole of Bosola's employment.         [4] Haste.

His loyal friend. Set eye upon that fellow;
Follow him to mass; may be Antonio,
Although he do account religion
But a school-name, for fashion of the world
May accompany him; or else go inquire out
Delio's confessor, and see if you can bribe
Him to reveal it. There are a thousand ways
A man might find to trace him: as to know
What fellows haunt the Jews for taking up
Great sums of money, for sure he 's in want;
Or else to go to th' picture-makers, and learn
Who bought her picture lately: some of these
Happily may take.

    _Bos._          Well, I 'll not freeze i' th' business:
I would see that wretched thing, Antonio,
Above all sights i' th' world.

    _Card._          Do, and be happy.          _Exit._

    _Bos._  This fellow doth breed basilisks in 's eyes,
He 's nothing else but murder; yet he seems
Not to have notice of the duchess' death.
'T is his cunning: I must follow his example;
There cannot be a surer way to trace
Than that of an old fox.

            _[Re-enter Julia, with a pistol]_

    _Julia._  So, sir, you are well met.

    _Bos._          How now!

    _Julia._  Nay, the doors are fast enough:
Now, sir, I will make you confess your treachery.

    _Bos._  Treachery!

    _Julia._          Yes, confess to me
Which of my women 't was you hir'd out to put
Love-powder into my drink?

    _Bos._  Love-powder!

    _Julia._          Yes, when I was at Malfi.
Why should I fall in love with such a face else?
I have already suffer'd for thee so much pain,
The only remedy to do me good
Is to kill my longing.

    _Bos._          Sure, your pistol holds
Nothing but perfumes or kissing-comfits.
Excellent lady!
You have a pretty way on 't to discover
Your longing. Come, come, I 'll disarm you,

And arm you thus: yet this is wondrous strange.

   *Julia.*  Compare thy form and my eyes together,
You 'll find my love no such great miracle.
Now you 'll say
I am wanton. This nice modesty in ladies
Is but a troublesome familiar
That haunts them.

   *Bos.*  Know you me: I am a blunt soldier.

   *Julia.*                       The better:
Sure, there wants fire where there are no lively sparks
Of roughness.

   *Bos.*        And I want compliment.

   *Julia.*                     Why, ignorance
In courtship cannot make you do amiss,
If you have a heart to do well.

   *Bos.*              You are very fair.

   *Julia.*  Nay, if you lay beauty to my charge,
I must plead unguilty.

   *Bos.*             Your bright eyes
Carry a quiver of darts in them, sharper
Than sun-beams.

   *Julia.*       You will mar me with commendation,
Put yourself to the charge of courting me,
Whereas now I woo you.

   *Bos.* [*Aside.*]  I have it, I will work upon this creature. —
Let us grow most amorously familiar.
If the great cardinal now should see me thus,
Would he not count me a villain?

   *Julia.*  No; he might count me a wanton,
Not lay a scruple of offence on you;
For if I see and steal a diamond,
The fault is not i' th' stone, but in me the thief
That purloins it. I am sudden with you.
We that are great women of pleasure use to cut off
These uncertain wishes and unquiet longings,
And in an instant join the sweet delight
And the pretty excuse together. Had you been i' th' street,
Under my chamber-window, even there
I should have courted you.

   *Bos.*  O, you are an excellent lady!

   *Julia.*  Bid me do somewhat for you presently
To express I love you.

   *Bos.*            I will; and if you love me,
Fail not to effect it.

The cardinal is grown wondrous melancholy:
Demand the cause, let him not put you off
With feign'd excuse; discover the main ground on 't.
 *Julia.* Why would you know this?
 *Bos.*       I have depended on him,
And I hear that he is fall'n in some disgrace
With the emperor: if he be, like the mice
That forsake falling houses, I would shift
To other dependance.
 *Julia.*     You shall not need
Follow the wars: I 'll be your maintenance.
 *Bos.* And I your loyal servant: but I cannot
Leave my calling.
 *Julia.*    Not leave an ungrateful
General for the love of a sweet lady!
You are like some cannot sleep in feather-beds,
But must have blocks for their pillows.
 *Bos.*      Will you do this?
 *Julia.* Cunningly.
 *Bos.* To-morrow I 'll expect th' intelligence.
 *Julia.* To-morrow! Get you into my cabinet;[5]
You shall have it with you. Do not delay me,
No more than I do you: I am like one
That is condemn'd; I have my pardon promis'd,
But I would see it seal'd. Go, get you in:
You shall see me wind my tongue about his heart
Like a skein of silk.      *[Exit Bosola.]*


     *[Re-enter Cardinal]*

 *Card.*     Where are you?

     *[Enter Servants]*

*Servants.*        Here.
 *Card.* Let none, upon your lives, have conference
With the Prince Ferdinand, unless I know it. —
*[Aside.]* In this distraction he may reveal
The murther.       *[Exeunt Servants.]*
    Yond 's my lingering consumption:
I am weary of her, and by any means
Would be quit of.
 *Julia.*   How now, my lord! what ails you?
 *Card.* Nothing.

 [5] Closet.

*Julia.*                    O, you are much alter'd:
Come, I must be your secretary,[6] and remove
This lead from off your bosom: what 's the matter?
    *Card.*   I may not tell you.
    *Julia.*   Are you so far in love with sorrow
You cannot part with part of it? Or think you
I cannot love your grace when you are sad
As well as merry? Or do you suspect
I, that have been a secret to your heart
These many winters, cannot be the same
Unto your tongue?
    *Card.*          Satisfy thy longing. —
The only way to make thee keep my counsel
Is, not to tell thee.
    *Julia.*          Tell your echo this,
Or flatterers, that like echoes still report
What they hear, though most imperfect, and not me;
For if that you be true unto yourself,
I 'll know.
    *Card.*   Will you rack me?
    *Julia.*                    No, judgment shall
Draw it from you: it is an equal fault,
To tell one's secrets unto all or none.
    *Card.*   The first argues folly.
    *Julia.*   But the last tyranny.
    *Card.*   Very well: why, imagine I have committed
Some secret deed which I desire the world
May never hear of.
    *Julia.*          Therefore may not I know it?
You have conceal'd for me as great a sin
As adultery. Sir, never was occasion
For perfect trial of my constancy
Till now; sir, I beseech you ——
    *Card.*                    You 'll repent it.
    *Julia.*   Never.
    *Card.*   It hurries thee to ruin: I 'll not tell thee.
Be well advis'd, and think what danger 't is
To receive a prince's secrets. They that do,
Had need have their breasts hoop'd with adamant
To contain them. I pray thee, yet be satisfied;
Examine thine own frailty; 't is more easy
To tie knots than unloose them. 'T is a secret
That, like a ling'ring poison, many chance lie
Spread in thy veins, and kill thee seven year hence.

---

[6] Repository of secrets.

*Julia.*   Now you dally with me.
*Card.*                    No more; thou shalt know it.
By my appointment, the great Duchess of Malfi
And two of her young children, four nights since,
Were strangled.
*Julia.*   O heaven! sir, what have you done!
*Card.*   How now?  How settles this?  Think you your bosom
Will be a grave dark and obscure enough
For such a secret?
*Julia.*                You have undone yourself, sir.
*Card.*   Why?
*Julia.*            It lies not in me to conceal it.
*Card.*                         No?
Come, I will swear you 't upon this book.
*Julia.*   Most religiously.
*Card.*                  Kiss it.          [*She kisses the book.*]
Now you shall never utter it; thy curiosity
Hath undone thee: thou 'rt poison'd with that book.
Because I knew thou couldst not keep my counsel,
I have bound thee to 't by death.

### [Re-enter Bosola]

*Bos.*   For pity sake, hold!
*Card*                Ha, Bosola!
*Julia.*                       I forgive you
This equal piece of justice you have done,
For I betray'd your counsel to that fellow.
He overheard it: that was the cause I said
It lay not in me to conceal it.
*Bos.*   O foolish woman,
Couldst not thou have poison'd him?
*Julia.*                ’T is weakness
Too much to think what should have been done.  I go,
I know not whither.                    [*Dies.*]
*Card.*            Wherefore com'st thou hither?
*Bos.*   That I might find a great man like yourself,
Not out of his wits, as the Lord Ferdinand,
To remember my service.
*Card.*   I 'll have thee hew'd in pieces.
*Bos.*   Make not yourself such a promise of that life
Which is not yours to dispose of.
*Card.*                  Who plac'd thee here?
*Bos.*   Her lust, as she intended.
*Card.*                    Very well:
Now you know me for your fellow-murderer.

*Bos.*    And wherefore should you lay fair marble colours
Upon your rotten purposes to me?
Unless you imitate some that do plot great treasons,
And when they have done, go hide themselves i' th' graves
Of those were actors in 't?
    *Card.*                    No more; there is
A fortune attends thee.
    *Bos.*    Shall I go sue to Fortune any longer?
'T is the fool's pilgrimage.
    *Card.*    I have honours in store for thee.
    *Bos.*    There are a many ways that conduct to seeming
Honour, and some of them very dirty ones.
    *Card.*    Throw to the devil
Thy melancholy.  The fire burns well;
What need we keep a-stirring of 't, and make
A greater smother?  Thou wilt kill Antonio?
    *Bos.*  Yes.
    *Card.*        Take up that body.
    *Bos.*                        I think I shall
Shortly grow the common bier for church-yards.
    *Card.*    I will allow thee some dozen of attendants
To aid thee in the murther.
    *Bos.*    O, by no means.  Physicians that apply horse-leeches to any
rank swelling use to cut off their tails, that the blood may run
through them the faster: let me have no train when I go to shed
blood, less it make me have a greater when I ride to the gallows.
    *Card.*    Come to me after midnight, to help to remove
That body to her own lodging.  I 'll give out
She died o' th' plague; 't will breed the less inquiry
After her death.
    *Bos.*    Where 's Castruchio her husband?
    *Card.*    He 's rode to Naples, to take possession
Of Antonio's citadel.
    *Bos.*    Believe me, you have done a very happy turn.
    *Card.*    Fail not to come.  There is the master-key
Of our lodgings; and by that you may conceive
What trust I plant in you.                              *Exit.*
    *Bos.*                    You shall find me ready.
O poor Antonio, though nothing be so needful
To thy estate as pity, yet I find
Nothing so dangerous!  I must look to my footing.
In such slippery ice-pavements men had need
To be frost-nail'd[7] well: they may break their necks else.

    [7] Hob-nailed.

The precedent 's here afore me. How this man
Bears up in blood![8] seems fearless! Why, 't is well:
Security some men call the suburbs of hell,
Only a dead wall between. Well, good Antonio,
I 'll seek thou out; and all my care shall be
To put thee into safety from the reach
Of these most cruel biters that have got
Some of thy blood already. It may be,
I 'll join with thee in a most just revenge.
The weakest arm is strong enough that strikes
With the sword of justice. Still methinks the duchess
Haunts me: there, there! — 'T is nothing but my melancholy.
O Penitence, let me truly taste thy cup,
That throws men down only to raise them up!       *Exit.*

## Scena III

*Antonio, Delio, Echo (from the Duchess' Grave)*

*Delio.*    Yond 's the cardinal's window. This fortification
Grew from the ruins of an ancient abbey;
And to yond side o' th' river lies a wall,
Piece of a cloister, which in my opinion
Gives the best echo that you have heard,
So hollow and so dismal, and withal
So plain in the distinction of our words,
That many have suppos'd it is a spirit
That answers.
    *Ant.*        I do love these ancient ruins.
We never tread upon them but we set
Our foot upon some reverend history;
And, questionless, here in this open court,
Which now lies naked to the injuries
Of stormy weather, some men lie interr'd
Lov'd the church so well, and gave so largely to 't,
They thought it should have canopied their bones
Till dooms-day. But all things have their end;
Churches and cities, which have diseases like to men,
Must have like death that we have.
    *Echo.*              *Like death that we have.*
    *Delio.*   Now the echo hath caught you.
    *Ant.*   It groan'd, methought, and gave
A very deadly accent.

[8] Keeps his courage.

*Echo.*              *Deadly accent.*

*Delio.*   I told you 't was a pretty one.  You may make it
A huntsman, or a falconer, a musician,
Or a thing of sorrow.

 *Echo.*              *A thing of sorrow.*

 *Ant.*   Ay, sure, that suits it best.

 *Echo.*                   *That suits it best.*

 *Ant.*   'T is very like my wife's voice.

 *Echo.*                        *Ay, wife's voice.*

 *Delio.*   Come, let 's us walk farther from 't.
I would not have you go to th' cardinal's tonight:
Do not.

 *Echo.   Do not.*

 *Delio.*   Wisdom doth not more moderate wasting sorrow
Than time.  Take time for 't; be mindful of thy safety.

 *Echo.   Be mindful of thy safety.*

 *Ant.*   Necessity compels me.
Make scrutiny throughout the passages
Of your own life, you 'll find it impossible
To fly your fate.

 *Echo.*              *O, fly your fate!*

 *Delio.*   Hark! the dead stones seem to have pity on you,
And give you good counsel.

 *Ant.*   Echo, I will not talk with thee,
For thou art a dead thing.

 *Echo.*                   *Thou art a dead thing.*

 *Ant.*   My duchess is asleep now,
And her little ones, I hope sweetly.  O heaven,
Shall I never see her more?

 *Echo.*                   *Never see her more.*

 *Ant.*   I mark'd not one repetition of the echo
But that; and on the sudden a clear light
Presented me a face folded in sorrow.

 *Delio.*   Your fancy merely.

 *Ant.*                        Come, I 'll be out of this ague.
For to live thus is not indeed to live:
It is a mockery and abuse of life.
I will not henceforth save myself by halves;
Lose all, or nothing.

 *Delio.*              Your own virtue save you!
I 'll fetch your eldest son, and second you.
It may be that the sight of his own blood,
Spread in so sweet a figure, may beget
The more compassion.  However, fare you well.

Though in our miseries Fortune have a part,
Yet in our noble suff'rings she hath none.
Contempt of pain, that we may call our own.        *Exeunt.*


SCENA IIII

*Cardinal, Pescara, Malateste, Roderigo, Grisolan,* [*later*]
*Bosola, Ferdinand, Antonio, Servant*

*Card.*    You shall not watch to-night by the sick prince;
His grace is very well recover'd.
*Mal.*    Good my lord, suffer us.
*Card.*                          O, by no means;
The noise, and change of object in his eye,
Doth more distract him. I pray, all to bed;
And though you hear him in his violent fit,
Do not rise, I entreat you.
*Pes.*    So, sir; we shall not.
*Card.*                          Nay, I must have you promise
Upon your honours, for I was enjoin'd to 't
By himself; and he seem'd to urge it sensibly.
*Pes.*    Let our honours bind this trifle!
*Card.*    Nor any of your followers.
*Mal.*    Neither.
*Card.*    It may be, to make trial of your promise,
When he 's asleep, myself will rise and feign
Some of his mad tricks, and cry out for help,
And feign myself in danger.
*Mal.*    If your throat were cutting,
I 'd not come at you, now I have protested against it.
*Card.*    Why, I thank you.
*Gris.*                          'T was a foul storm to-night.
*Rod.*    The Lord Ferdinand's chamber shook like an osier.
*Mal.*    'T was nothing but pure kindness in the devil
To rock his own child.        *Exeunt* [*all except the Cardinal*].
*Card.*    The reason why I would not suffer these
About my brother, is, because at midnight
I may with better privacy convey
Julia's body to her own lodging. O, my conscience!
I would pray now; but the devil takes away my heart
For having any confidence in prayer.
About this hour I appointed Bosola
To fetch the body. When he hath serv'd my turn,
He dies.        *Exit.*

*[Enter Bosola]*

*Bos.*   Ha! 't was the cardinal's voice; I heard him name Bosola and my death. Listen; I hear one's footing.

*[Enter Ferdinand]*

*Ferd.*   Strangling is a very quiet death.

*Bos.* [*Aside.*]   Nay, then, I see I must stand upon my guard.

*Ferd.*   What say to that? Whisper softly: do you agree to 't? So; it must be done i' th' dark: the cardinal would not for a thousand pounds the doctor should see it.                          *Exit.*

*Bos.*   My death is plotted; here 's the consequence of murther. We value not desert nor Christian breath, When we know black deeds must be cur'd with death.

*[Enter Antonio and Servant]*

*Serv.*   Here stay, sir, and be confident, I pray; I 'll fetch you a dark lantern.                          *Exit.*

*Ant.*   Could I take him at his prayers. There were hope of pardon.

*Bos.*   Fall right, my sword! —                     [*Stabs him.*] I 'll not give thee so much leisure as to pray,

*Ant.*   O, I am gone! Thou hast ended a long suit In a minute.

*Bos.*        What art thou?

*Ant.*                          A most wretched thing, That only have thy benefit in death, To appear myself.

*[Re-enter Servant with a lantern]*

*Serv.*   Where are you, sir?

*Ant.*   Very near my home. — Bosola!

*Serv.*   O, misfortune!

*Bos.*   Smother thy pity, thou art dead else. — Antonio! The man I would have sav'd 'bove mine own life! We are merely the stars' tennis-balls, struck and bandied Which way please them. — O good Antonio, I 'll whisper one thing in thy dying ear Shall make thy heart break quickly! Thy fair duchess And two sweet children ——

*Ant.*                          Their very names Kindle a little life in me.

*Bos.*                  Are murder'd.

*Ant.*   Some men have wish'd to die At the hearing of sad tidings; I am glad

That I shall do 't in sadness.[9] I would not now
Wish my wounds balm'd nor heal'd, for I have no use
To put my life to.  In all our quest of greatness,
Like wanton boys whose pastimes is their care,
We follow after bubbles blown in th' air.
Pleasure of life, what is 't?  Only the good hours
Of an ague, merely a preparative to rest,
To endure vexation.  I do not ask
The process of my death; only commend me
To Delio.
    *Bos.*   Break, heart!
    *Ant.*   And let my son fly the courts of princes.       [*Dies.*]
    *Bos.*   Thou seem'st to have lov'd Antonio.
    *Serv.*   I brought him hither,
To have reconcil'd him to the cerdinal.
    *Bos.*   I do not ask thee that.
Take him up, if thou tender thine own life,
And bear him where the lady Julia
Was wont to lodge. — O, my fate moves swift!
I have this cardinal in the forge already;
Now I 'll bring him to th' hammer.  O direful misprision![1]
I will not imitate things glorious,
No more than base: I 'll be mine own example. —
On, on, and look thou represent, for silence,
The thing thou bear'st.               *Exeunt.*

### Scena V

*Cardinal, with a book. [Later,] Bosola, Pescara, Mala-
teste, Roderigo, Ferdinand, Delio, Servant with Antonio's body*

    *Card.*   I am puzzl'd in a question about hell;
He says, in hell there 's one material fire,
And yet it shall not burn all men alike.
Lay him by.  How tedious is a guilty conscience!
When I look into the fish-ponds in my garden,
Methinks I see a thing arm'd with a rake,
That seems to strike at me.

    [*Enter Bosola and Servant bearing Antonio's body*]

                              Now, art thou come?
Thou look'st ghastly;

[9] Reality.               [1] Mistake.

There sits in thy face some great determination,
Mix'd with some fear.

    *Bos.*               Thus it lightens into action:
I am come to kill thee.

    *Card.*            Ha! — Help! our guard!

    *Bos.*   Thou art deceiv'd: they are out of thy howling.

    *Card.*   Hold; and I will faithfully divide
Revenues with thee.

    *Bos.*            Thy prayers and proffers
Are both unseasonable.

    *Card.*           Raise the watch!
We are betray'd!

    *Bos.*        I have confin'd your flight:
I 'll suffer your retreat to Julia's chamber,
But no further.

    *Card.*       Help! we are betray'd!

*[Enter, above, Pescara, Malateste, Roderigo, and Griso-*
*lan]*

    *Mal.*   Listen.

    *Card.*   My dukedom for rescue!

    *Rod.*   Fie upon his counterfeiting!

    *Mal.*   Why, 't is not the cardinal.

    *Rod.*   Yes, yes, 't is he:
But I 'll see him hang'd ere I 'll go down to him.

    *Card.*   Here 's a plot upon me; I am assaulted; I am lost,
Unless some rescue!

    *Gris.*         He doth this pretty well;
But it will not serve to laugh me out of mine honour.

    *Card.*   The sword 's at my throat!

    *Rod.*            You would not bawl so loud then.

    *Mal.*   Come, come, let 's go to bed: he told us thus much afore-
hand.

    *Pes.*   He wish'd you should not come at him; but, believe 't,
The accent of the voice sounds not in jest.
I 'll down to him, howsoever, and with engines
Force ope the doors.                  *[Exit above.]*

    *Rod.*          Let 's follow him aloof,
And note how the cardinal will laugh at him.

*[Exeunt, above, Malateste, Roderigo, and Grisolan]*

    *Bos.*   There 's for you first,
'Cause you shall not unbarricade the door
To let in rescue.                *He kills the Servant.*

*Card.*           What cause hast thou to pursue my life?
*Bos.*                                             Look there.
*Card.*   Antonio!
*Bos.*            Slain by my hand unwittingly.
Pray, and be sudden. When thou kill'd'st thy sister,
Thou took'st from Justice her most equal balance,
And left her naught but her sword.
    *Card.*               O, mercy!
    *Bos.*   Now it seems thy greatness was only outward;
For thou fall'st faster of thyself than calamity
Can drive thee. I 'll not waste longer time; there!    [*Stabs him.*]
    *Card.*   Thou hast hurt me.
    *Bos.*          Again!
    *Card.*              Shall I die like a leveret,[2]
Without any resistance? — Help, help, help!
I am slain!

[*Enter Ferdinand*]

    *Ferd.*   Th' alarum! Give me a fresh horse!
Rally the vaunt-guard,[3] or the day is lost!
Yield, yield! I give you the honour of arms,[4]
Shake my sword over you; will you yield?
    *Card.*   Help me; I am your brother!
    *Ferd.*            The devil!
My brother fight upon the adverse party!
                  *He wounds the Cardinal, and (in the*
                   *scuffle) gives Bosola his death-wound.*
There flies your ransom.
    *Card.*   O justice!
I suffer now for what hath former been:
Sorrow is held the eldest child of sin.
    *Ferd.*   Now you 're brave fellows. Cæsar's fortune was harder
than Pompey's: Cæsar died in the arms of prosperity, Pompey at
the feet of disgrace. You both died in the field. The pain 's noth-
ing; pain many times is taken away with the apprehension of
greater, as the tooth-ache with the sight of a barber that comes to
pull it out. There 's philosophy for you.
    *Bos.*   Now my revenge is perfect. — Sink, thou main cause
                              *He kills Ferdinand.*
Of my undoing! — The last part of my life
Hath done me best service.
    *Ferd.*   Give me some wet hay; I am broken-winded.
I do account this world but a dog-kennel:

---

[2] Young hare.                 [3] Vanguard.
[4] Honorable terms of surrender.

I will vault credit[5] and affect high pleasures
Beyond death.
    *Bos.*           He seems to come to himself,
Now he 's so near the bottom.
    *Ferd.*   My sister, O my sister! there 's the cause on 't.
Whether we fall by ambition, blood, or lust,
Like diamonds, we are cut with our own dust.        *[Dies.]*
    *Card.*   Thou hast thy payment too.
    *Bos.*    Yes, I hold my weary soul in my teeth;
'T is ready to part from me. I do glory
That thou, which stood'st like a huge pyramid
Begun upon a large and ample base,
Shalt end in a little point, a kind of nothing.

> *[Enter, below, Pescara, Malateste, Roderigo, and Griso-*
> *lan]*

    *Pes.*   How now, my lord!
    *Mal.*             O sad disaster!
    *Rod.*                  How comes this?
    *Bos.*   Revenge for the Duchess of Malfi murdered
By th' Arragonian brethren; for Antonio
Slain by this hand; for lustful Julia
Poison'd by this man; and lastly for myself,
That was an actor in the main of all
Much 'gainst mine own good nature, yet i' th' end
Neglected.
    *Pes.*   How now, my lord!
    *Card.*             Look to my brother:
He gave us these large wounds, as we were struggling
Here i' th' rushes. And now, I pray, let me
Be laid by and never thought of.        *[Dies.]*
    *Pes.*   How fatally, it seems, he did withstand
His own rescue!
    *Mal.*         Thou wretched thing of blood,
How came Antonio by his death?
    *Bos.*   In a mist; I know not how.
Such a mistake as I have often seen
In a play. O, I am gone!
We are only like dead walls or vaulted graves,
That, ruin'd, yields no echo. Fare you well!
It may be pain, but no harm, to me to die
In so good a quarrel. O, this gloomy world!
In what a shadow, or deep pit of darkness,

    [5] Exceed probability.

Doth womanish and fearful mankind live!
Let worthy minds ne'er stagger in distrust
To suffer death or shame for what is just:
Mine is another voyage.                              [*Dies.*]
   *Pes.*   The noble Delio, as I came to th' palace,
Told me of Antonio's being here, and show'd me
A pretty gentleman, his son and heir.

        [*Enter Delio, and Antonio's Son*]

   *Mal.*   O sir, you come too late!
   *Delio.*               I heard so, and
Was arm'd for 't, ere I came. Let us make noble use
Of this great ruin; and join all our force
To establish this young hopeful gentleman
In 's mother's right. These wretched eminent things
Leave no more fame behind 'em, than should one
Fall in a frost, and leave his print in snow:
As soon as the sun shines, it ever melts,
Both form and matter. I have ever thought
Nature doth nothing so great for great men
As when she 's pleas'd to make them lords of truth:
Integrity of life is fame's best friend,
Which nobly, beyond death, shall crown the end.          *Exeunt.*

                FINIS

# THE BROKEN HEART.

## A Tragedy.

*ACTED*
By the King's Majesties Seruants
at the priuate House in the
BLACK-FRIERS.

*Fide Honor.*[1]

LONDON:
Printed by I. B. for Hugh Beeston, and are to
be sold at his Shop, neere the Castle in
Corne-hill. 1 6 3 3 .

---

[1]Honor through faith; an anagram on the author's name (Iohn Forde).

# The Broken Heart

### ❧ JOHN FORD

was the younger son of an old Devonshire family, and was born in 1586. He was admitted to the Middle Temple in 1602 and was a law student for several years. Some verses have survived from his pen that were written between 1606 and 1610, but he does not seem to have turned to the drama until the 1620's. His earliest surviving play is *The Witch of Edmonton*, written about 1621 in collaboration with Thomas Dekker. Besides *The Broken Heart*, his best-known plays are *'Tis Pity She's a Whore* (written about 1626) and *Perkin Warbeck* (printed in 1634). Ford is last heard of in London in 1639; he either died in that year or retired to his native Devonshire to spend the rest of his life there.

*The Broken Heart* was entered in the Stationers' Register on 28 March 1633 and printed in the same year. There was no author's name on the title page, but the dedicatory epistle is signed "Iohn Ford" and the motto on the title page "Fide Honor" is an anagram of the author's name. The play had been performed by what was still the leading company of actors in London, the "King's Majesties Seruants," at their "priuate House in the Black-friers." There is no decisive evidence for the date of the play, but all authorities agree in believing that it must have been written not very long before it was published. We may therefore assign it to a date "c. 1630."

Much of the plot of *The Broken Heart* was probably of Ford's own invention. The Sparta of the action is not, of course, the Sparta of ancient Greek history, but that of Sir Philip Sidney's famous romance, the *Arcadia*. In the Prologue Ford declares:

> What may be thought a fiction, when time's youth
> Wanted some riper years, was known a truth,

so it is likely that parts of the plot are based on actual fact. It has been pointed out that the situation involving Penthea, Orgilus, and Bassanes parallels in many respects the relations of Penelope Devereux (Sidney's Stella, whom he addressed in *Astrophel and Stella*), her husband Lord Rich (to whom she was married against her will), and Sidney himself. Ford's earliest surviving verses were

391

dedicated to Lady Rich, so he apparently knew her, and must almost certainly have had her story in mind in writing this play.

Books. There is no adequate modern edition of Ford's plays; the best available is William Gifford's edition of the *Works*, as revised by Alexander Dyce and A. H. Bullen, London, 2 vols., 1895. Useful critical studies are R. Davril, *Le drame de John Ford*, Paris, 1954; C. Leech, *John Ford and the Drama of his Time*, London, 1957; H. J. Oliver, *The Problem of John Ford*, Melbourne, 1955; M. J. Sargeaunt, *John Ford*, Oxford, 1935.

## The Speakers' Names, Fitted to Their Qualities

AMYCLAS, *Common to the Kings of Laconia*
ITHOCLES, *Honour of loveliness*, a Favourite
ORGILUS, *Angry*, son to Crotolon
BASSANES, *Vexation*, a jealous Nobleman
ARMOSTES, *an Appeaser*, a Councillor of State
CROTOLON, *Noise*, another Councillor
PROPHILUS, *Dear*, Friend to Ithocles
NEARCHUS, *Young Prince*, Prince of Argos
TECNICUS, *Artist*, a Philosopher
LEMOPHIL,[2] *Glutton,*
GRONEAS, *Tavern-haunter,* } two Courtiers
AMELUS, *Trusty*, Friend to Nearchus
PHULAS, *Watchful*, Servant to Bassanes
CALANTHA, *Flower of beauty*, the King's Daughter
PENTHEA, *Complaint*, Sister to Ithocles [and Wife to Bassanes]
EUPHRANEA, *Joy*, a Maid of honour [Daughter to Crotolon]
CHRISTALLA, *Christal,*
PHILEMA, *A Kiss,* } Maids of honour
GRAUSIS, *Old Beldam*, Overseer of Penthea

### PERSONS INCLUDED

THRASUS, *Fierceness*, Father of Ithocles
APLOTES, *Simplicity*, Orgilus so disguised

The Scene, SPARTA

2 Frequently "Hemophil" in the original edition.

## The Prologue

Our scene is Sparta. He whose best of art.
Hath drawn this piece calls it *The Broken Heart*.
The title lends no expectation here
Of apish laughter, or of some lame jeer
At place or persons; no pretended clause[3]
Of jests fit for a brothel courts applause
From vulgar admiration: such low songs,
Tun'd to unchaste ears, suit not modest tongues.
The Virgin Sisters[4] then deserv'd fresh bays,
When Innocence and Sweetness crown'd their lays;
Then vices gasp'd for breath, whose whole commerce
Was whipp'd to exile by unblushing verse.
This law we keep in our presentment now,
Not to take freedom more than we allow.
What may be here thought a fiction, when time's youth
Wanted some riper years, was known a truth:
In which, if words have cloth'd the subject right,
You may partake a pity with delight.

[3] Section.
[4] The Muses.

## Actus Primus.  Scæna prima

### Enter Crotolon and Orgilus

*Crot.*   Dally not further; I will know the reason
That speeds thee to this journey.

*Org.*                              Reason! good sir,
I can yield many.

*Crot.*               Give me one, a good one;
Such I expect, and ere we part must have.
Athens! Pray, why to Athens? You intend not
To kick against the world, turn Cynic, Stoic?
Or read the logic lecture? or become
An Areopagite,[5] and judge in causes
Touching the commonwealth? for, as I take it,
The budding of your chin cannot prognosticate
So grave an honour.

*Org.*               All this I acknowledge.

*Crot.*   You do! Then, son, if books and love of knowledge
Inflame you to this travel, here in Sparta
You may as freely study.

*Org.*                    'T is not that, sir.

*Crot.*   Not that, sir! As a father, I command thee
To acquaint me with the truth.

*Org.*                         Thus I obey ye.
After so many quarrels as dissension,
Fury, and rage had broach'd in blood, and sometimes
With death to such confederates as sided
With now-dead Thrasus and yourself, my lord;
Our present king, Amyclas, reconcil'd
Your eager swords and seal'd a gentle peace.
Friends you profess'd yourselves; which to confirm,
A resolution for a lasting league
Betwixt your families was entertain'd,
By joining in a Hymenean bond
Me and the fair Penthea, only daughter
To Thrasus.

*Crot.*   What of this?

*Org.*                  Much, much, dear sir.
A freedom of converse, an interchange

---

[5] I.e., a lawyer.

395

Of holy and chaste love, so fix'd our souls
In a firm growth of holy union, that no time
Can eat into the pledge. We had enjoy'd
The sweets our vows expected, had not cruelty
Prevented all those triumphs[6] we prepar'd for
By Thrasus his untimely death.

   *Crot.*              Most certain.

   *Org.*   From this time sprouted up that poisonous **stalk**
Of aconite, whose ripen'd fruit hath ravish'd
All health, all comfort of a happy life;
For Ithocles, her brother, proud of youth,
And prouder in his power, nourish'd closely
The memory of former discontents,
To glory in revenge. By cunning partly,
Partly by threats, 'a woos at once and forces
His virtuous sister to admit a marriage
With Bassanes, a nobleman, in honour
And riches, I confess, beyond my fortunes.

   *Crot.*   All this is no sound reason to importu**ne**
My leave for thy departure.

   *Org.*            Now it follows.
Beauteous Penthea, wedded to this torture
By an insulting brother, being secretly
Compell'd to yield her virgin freedom up
To him who never can usurp her heart,
Before contracted mine, is now so yok'd
To a most barbarous thraldom, misery,
Affliction, that he savours not humanity,
Whose sorrow melts not into more than pity
In hearing but her name.

   *Crot.*          As how, pray?

   *Org.*                 Bassanes,
The man that calls her wife, considers truly
What heaven of perfections he is lord of
By thinking fair Penthea his. This thought
Begets a kind of monster-love, which love
Is nurse unto a fear so strong and servile
As brands all dotage with a jealousy:
All eyes who gaze upon that shrine of beauty,
He doth resolve, do homage to the miracle;
Some one, he is assur'd, may now or then,
If opportunity but sort,[7] prevail.
So much, out of a self-unworthiness,

---

   **6** Festivities.                **7** Chance to come about.

His fears transport him; not that he finds cause
In her obedience, but his own distrust.

   *Crot.*   You spin out your discouse.

   *Org.*                       My griefs are violent:
For knowing how the maid was heretofore
Courted by me, his jealousies grow wild
That I should steal again into her favours,
And undermine her virtues; which the gods
Know I nor dare nor dream of. Hence, from hence
I undertake a voluntary exile;
First, by my absence to take off the cares
Of jealous Bassanes; but chiefly, sir,
To free Penthea from a hell on earth;
Lastly, to lose the memory of something
Her presence makes to live in me afresh.

   *Crot.*   Enough, my Orgilus, enough. To Athens!
I give a full consent. — Alas, good lady! —
We shall hear from thee often?

   *Org.*                    Often.

   *Crot.*                      See,
Thy sister comes to give a farewell.

*Enter Euphranea*

   *Euph.*                      Brother!

   *Org.*   Euphranea, thus upon thy cheeks I print
A brother's kiss; more careful of thine honour,
Thy health, and thy well-doing, than my life.
Before we part, in presence of our father,
I must prefer a suit t' ye.

   *Euph.*                You may style it,
My brother, a command.

   *Org.*               That you will promise
To pass never to any man, however
Worthy, your faith, till, with our father's leave,
I give a free consent.

   *Crot.*          An easy motion!
I 'll promise for her, Orgilus.

   *Org.*             Your pardon;
Euphranea's oath must yield me satisfaction.

   *Euph.*   By Vesta's sacred fires I swear.

   *Crot.*                 And I,
By great Apollo's beams, join in the vow,
Not without thy allowance to bestow her
On any living.

*Org.*        Dear Euphranea,
Mistake me not: far, far 't is from my thought,
As far from any wish of mine, to hinder
Preferment to an honourable bed
Or fitting fortune. Thou art young and handsome;
And 't were injustice, — more, a tyranny, —
Not to advance thy merit. Trust me, sister,
It shall be my first care to see thee match'd
As may become thy choice and our contents.
I have your oath.
    *Euph.*   You have. But mean you, brother,
To leave us, as you say?
    *Crot.*                Ay, ay, Euphranea.
He has just grounds direct him. I will prove
A father and a brother to thee.
    *Euph.*                Heaven
Does look into the secrets of all hearts.
Gods, you have mercy with ye, else —
    *Crot.*                Doubt nothing;
Thy brother will return in safety to us.
    *Org.*   Souls sunk in sorrows never are without 'em;
They change fresh airs, but bear their griefs about 'em.

*Exeunt omnes.*

## Scene 2

*Flourish. Enter Amyclas the King, Armostes,
Prophilus, and Attendants*

*Amy.*   The Spartan gods are gracious; our humility
Shall bend before their altars, and perfume
Their temples with abundant sacrifice.
See, lords, Amyclas, your old king, is ent'ring
Into his youth again! I shall shake off
This silver badge of age, and change this snow
For hairs as gay as are Apollo's locks.
Our heart leaps in new vigour.
    *Arm.*                May old time
Run back to double your long life, great sir!
    *Amy.*   It will, it must, Armostes. Thy bold nephew,
Death-braving Ithocles, brings to our gates
Triumphs and peace upon his conquering sword.
Laconia is a monarchy at length;

Hath in this latter war trod under foot
Messene's pride; Messene bows her neck
To Lacedæmon's royalty. O, 't was
A glorious victory, and doth deserve
More than a chronicle — a temple, lords,
A temple to the name of Ithocles. —
Where didst thou leave him, Prophilis?
   *Pro.*                                   At Pephon,
Most gracious sovereign. Twenty of the noblest
Of the Messenians there attend your pleasure,
For such conditions as you shall propose
In settling peace, and liberty of life.
   *Amy.*   When comes your friend, the general?
   *Pro.*                                   He promis'd
To follow with all speed convenient.

     *Enter Crotolon, Calantha, Christalla, Philema*
       *[with a garland] and Euphranea*

   *Amy.*   Our daughter! — Dear Calantha, the happy news,
The conquest of Messene, hath already
Enrich'd thy knowledge.
   *Cal.*                    With the circumstance
And manner of the fight, related faithfully
By Prophilus himself. — But, pray, sir, tell me,
How doth the youthful general demean
His actions in these fortunes?
   *Pro.*                       Excellent princess,
Your own fair eyes may soon report a truth
Unto your judgment, with what moderation,
Calmness of nature, measure,[8] bounds, and limits
Of thankfulness and joy, 'a doth digest
Such amplitude of his success as would
In others, moulded of a spirit less clear,
Advance 'em to comparison with heaven.
But Ithocles —
   *Cal.*         Your friend —
   *Pro.*                       He is so, madam,
In which the period[9] of my fate consists:
He, in this firmament of honour, stands
Like a star fix'd, not mov'd with any thunder
Of popular applause or sudden lightning
Of self-opinion. He hath serv'd his country,
And thinks 't was but his duty.

  [8] Restraint.                [9] Whole scope.

*Crot.*                              You describe
A miracle of man.

*Amy.*              Such, Crotolon,
On forfeit of a king's word, thou wilt find him. —              *Flourish.*
Hark, warning of his coming!  All attend him.

*Enter Ithocles, Lemophil, and Groneas; the
rest of the Lords ushering him in*

Return into these arms, thy home, thy sanctuary,
Delight of Sparta, treasure of my bosom,
Mine own, own Ithocles!

*Ith.*                        Your humblest subject.

*Arm.*   Proud of the blood I claim an interest in,
As brother to thy mother, I embrace thee,
Right noble nephew.

*Ith.*                        Sir, your love 's too partial.

*Crot.*   Our country speaks by me, who by thy valour,
Wisdom, and service, shares in this great action;
Returning thee, in part[1] of thy due merits,
A general welcome.

*Ith.*                    You exceed in bounty.

*Cal.*   Christalla, Philema, the chaplet. [*Takes the chaplet from
                        them.*] — Ithocles,
Upon the wings of Fame the singular
And chosen fortune of an high attempt
Is borne so past the view of common sight,
That I myself with mine own hands have wrought,
To crown thy temples, this provincial[2] garland:
Accept, wear, and enjoy it as our gift
Deserv'd, not purchas'd.

*Ith.*                    Y' are a royal maid.

*Amy.*   She is in all our daughter.

*Ith.*                        Let me blush,
Acknowledging how poorly I have serv'd,
What nothings I have done, compar'd with th' honours
Heap'd on the issue[3] of a willing mind.
In that lay mine ability, that only:
For who is he so sluggish from his birth,
So little worthy of a name or country,
That owes not out of gratitude for life
A debt of service, in what kind soever

---

[1] In return for only a part of.
[2] I.e., worn by a conqueror of a province.              [3] Achievement.

Safety or counsel of the commonwealth
Requires, for payment?
    *Cal.*               'A speaks truth.
    *Ith.*                          Whom heaven
Is pleas'd to style victorious, there to such
Applause runs madding, like the drunken priests
In Bacchus' sacrifices, without reason
Voicing the leader-on a demi-god;
Whenas, indeed, each common soldier's blood
Drops down as current coin in that hard purchase
As his whose much more delicate condition
Hath suck'd the milk of ease.  Judgment commands,
But resolution executes.  I use not,
Before this royal presence, these fit slights
As in contempt of such as can direct;
My speech hath other end: not to attribute
All praise to one man's fortune, which is strengthen'd
By many hands.  For instance, here is Prophilus,
A gentleman — I cannot flatter truth —
Of much desert; and, though in other rank,
Both Lemophil and Groneas were not missing
To wish their country's peace; for, in a word,
All there did strive their best, and 't was our duty.
    *Amy.*   Courtiers turn soldiers! — We vouchsafe our hand.
                      [*Lemophil and Groneas kiss his hand.*]
Observe your great example.
    *Lem.*            With all diligence.
    *Gron.*  Obsequiously and hourly.
    *Amy.*              Some repose
After these toils are needful.  We must think on
Conditions for the conquer'd; they expect 'em.
On! — Come, my Ithocles.
    *Euph.*          Sir, with your favour,
I need not a supporter.
    *Pro.*          Fate instructs me.
        *Exeunt.  Manent Lemophil, Groneas, Christalla, et Philema.*
              *Lemophil stays Christalla, Groneas Philema.*
    *Chris.*  With me?
    *Phil.*         Indeed, I dare not stay.
    *Lem.*              Sweet lady,
Soldiers are blunt, — your lip.
    *Chris.*         Fie, this is rudeness:
You went not hence such creatures.

*Gro.*                                    Spirit of valour
Is of a mounting nature.
    *Phil.*                    It appears so. —
Pray, in earnest, how many men apiece
Have you two been the death of?
    *Gro.*                        'Faith, not many;
We were compos'd of mercy.
    *Lem.*                        For our daring,
You have heard the general's approbation
Before the king.
    *Chris.*    You "wish'd your country's peace":
That show'd your charity.  Where are your spoils,
Such as the soldier fights for?
    *Phil.*                    They are coming.
    *Chris.*    By the next carrier, are they not?
    *Gro.*                        Sweet Philema,
When I was in the thickest of mine enemies,
Slashing off one man's head, another's nose,
Another's arms and legs, —
    *Phil.*                And all together.
    *Gro.*    Then would I with a sigh remember thee,
And cry "Dear Philema, 't is for thy sake
I do these deeds of wonder!" — Dost not love me
With all thy heart now?
    *Phil.*            Now as heretofore.
I have not put my love to use;[4] the principal
Will hardly yield an interest.
    *Gro.*                By Mars,
I 'll marry thee!
    *Phil.*        By Vulcan, y' are forsworn,
Except my mind do alter strangely.
    *Gro.*                    One word.
    *Chris.*    You lie beyond all modesty: — forbear me.
    *Lem.*    I 'll make thee mistress of a city; 't is
Mine own by conquest.
    *Chris.*            By petition; sue for 't
*In forma pauperis.*[5] — City! kennel. — Gallants,
Off with your feathers, put on aprons, gallants;
Learn to reel, thrum,[6] or trim a lady's dog,
And be good quiet souls of peace, hobgoblins!
    *Lem.*    Christalla!

[4] On loan.
[5] As a poor man, without any means.
[6] Weave.

*Chris.*          Practise to drill hogs, in hope
To share in the acorns. — Soldiers! corncutters,
But not so valiant: they ofttimes draw blood,
Which you durst never do. When you have practis'd
More wit or more civility, we 'll rank ye
I' th' list of men: till then, brave things-at-arms,
Dare not to speak to us. — most potent Groneas! —
    *Phil.*    And Lemophil the hardy! — at your services.
                              *Exeunt Christalla et Philema.*
    *Gro.*    They scorn us as they did before we went.
    *Lem.*    Hang 'em! let us scorn them, and be reveng'd.
    *Gro.*    Shall we?
    *Lem.*    We will: and when we slight them thus,
Instead of following them, they 'll follow us.
It is a woman's nature.
    *Gro.*              'T is a scurvy one.          *Exeunt omnes*


### Scene 3

*Enter Tecnicus, a philosopher, and Orgilus
disguised like a Scholar of his*

*Tec.*    Tempt not the stars; young man, thou canst not play
With the severity of fate: this change
Of habit and disguise in outward view
Hides not the secrets of thy soul within thee
From their quick-piercing eyes, which dive at all times
Down to thy thoughts. In thy aspect I note
A consequence of danger.[7]
    *Org.*              Give me leave,
Grave Tecnicus, without foredooming destiny,
Under thy roof to ease my silent griefs
By applying to my hidden wounds the balm
Of thy oraculous lectures. If my fortune
Run such a crooked by-way as to wrest
My steps to ruin, yet thy learned precepts
Shall call me back and set my footings straight.
I will not court the world.
    *Tec.*              Ah, Orgilus,
Neglects in young men of delights and life
Run often to extremities; they care not
For harms to others who contemn their own.

---

[7] Dangerous outcome.

*Org.*  But I, most learned artist, am not so much
At odds with nature that I grutch[8] the thrift
Of any true deserver; nor doth malice
Of present hopes so check them with despair
As that I yield to thought of more affliction
Than what is incident to frailty: wherefore
Impute not this retired course of living
Some little time to any other cause
Than what I justly render, — the information
Of an unsettled mind; as the effect
Must clearly witness.

*Tec.*            Spirit of truth inspire thee!
On these conditions I conceal thy change,
And willingly admit thee for an auditor. —
I 'll to my study.

*Org.*         I to contemplations
In these delightful walks.            [*Exit Tecnicus.*]
                     Thus metamorphos'd
I may without suspicion hearken after
Penthea's usage and Euphranea's faith.
Love, thou art full of mystery! The deities
Themselves are not secure in searching out
The secrets of those flames, which, hidden, waste
A breast made tributary to the laws
Of beauty. Physic yet hath never found
A remedy to cure a lover's wound. —
Ha! who are those that cross yon private walk
Into the shadowing grove in amorous foldings?

*Prophilus passeth over, supporting Euphranea,
and whispering*

My sister! O, my sister! 't is Euphranea
With Prophilus: supported too! I would
It were an apparition! Prophilus
Is Ithocles his friend. It strangely puzzles me.
Again! help me, my book; this scholar's habit
Must stand my privilege:[9] my mind is busy,
Mine eyes and ears are open.            *Walks by, reading.*

*Enter again Prophilus and Euphranea*

*Pro.*            Do not waste
The span of this stol'n time, lent by the gods
For precious use, in niceness.[1] Bright Euphranea,

8 Grudge.            9 Be my excuse.            1 Coyness.

Should I repeat old vows, or study new,
For purchase[2] of belief to my desires, —
   *Org.* [*Aside.*]   Desires!
   *Pro.*                      My service, my integrity, —
   *Org.* [*Aside.*]   That's better.
   *Pro.*                      I should but repeat a lesson
Oft conn'd without a prompter but thine eyes.
My love is honourable.
   *Org.* [*Aside.*]          So was mine
To my Penthea, chastely honourable.
   *Pro.*   Nor wants there more addition to my wish
Of happiness than having thee a wife;
Already sure of Ithocles, a friend
Firm and unalterable.
   *Org.* [*Aside.*]          But a brother
More cruel than the grave.
   *Euph.*                      What can you look for,
In answer to your noble protestations,
From an unskilful maid, but language suited
To a divided mind?
   *Org.* [*Aside.*]   Hold out, Euphranea!
   *Euph.*   Know, Prophilus, I never undervalu'd,
From the first time you mention'd worthy love,
Your merit, means, or person. It had been
A fault of judgment in me, and a dulness
In my affections, not to weigh and thank
My better stars that offer'd me the grace
Of so much blissfulness. For, to speak truth,
The law of my desires kept equal pace
With yours; nor have I left that resolution:
But, only in a word, whatever choice
Lives nearest in my heart must first procure
Consent both from my father and my brother,
Ere he can own me his.
   *Org.* [*Aside.*]          She is forsworn else.
   *Pro.*   Leave me that task.
   *Euph.*                      My brother, ere he parted
To Athens, had my oath.
   *Org.* [*Aside.*]          Yes, yes, 'a had, sure.
   *Pro.*   I doubt not, with the means the court supplies,
But to prevail at pleasure.
   *Org.* [*Aside.*]          Very likely!
   *Pro.*   Meantime, best, dearest, I may build my hopes

[2] In order to obtain.

On the foundation of thy constant suff'rance
In any opposition.

    *Euph.*               Death shall sooner
Divorce life and the joys I have in living
Than my chaste vows from truth.

    *Pro.*                   On thy fair hand
I seal the like.

    *Org.* [*Aside.*]   There is no faith in woman.
Passion, O, be contain'd!  My very heartstrings
Are on the tenters.[3]

    *Euph.*             Sir, we are overheard.
Cupid protect us!  'T was a stirring, sir,
Of some one near.

    *Pro.*           Your fears are needless, lady.
None have access into these private pleasures[4]
Except some near in court, or bosom-student
From Tecnicus his oratory, granted
By special favour lately from the king
Unto the grave philosopher.

    *Euph.*              Methinks
I hear one talking to himself, — I see him.

    *Pro.*  'T is a poor scholar, as I told you, lady.

    *Org.* [*Aside.*]  I am discover'd. — [*Half aloud to himself, as if*
                                *studying.*] Say it: is it possible,
With a smooth tongue, a leering countenance,
Flattery, or force of reason — I come t' ye, sir —
To turn or to appease the raging sea?
Answer to that. — Your art! what art to catch
And hold fast in a net the sun's small atoms?
No, no; they 'll out, they 'll out: ye may as easily
Outrun a cloud driven by a northern blast
As fiddle-faddle so!  Peace, or speak sense.

    *Euph.*  Call you this thing a scholar?  'Las, he 's lunatic.

    *Pro.*  Observe him, sweet; 't is but his recreation.

    *Org.*  But will you hear a little?  You are so tetchy,[5]
You keep no rule in argument.  Philosophy
Works not upon impossibilities,
But natural conclusions. — Mew! — absurd!
The metaphysics are but speculations
Of the celestial bodies, or such accidents
As not mix'd perfectly, in the air engend'red,
Appear to us unnatural; that's all.
Prove it.  Yet, with a reverence to your gravity,

---

  **3** Tenter-hooks.             **4** Pleasure grounds.          **5** Peevish.

I 'll balk illiterate sauciness, submitting
My sole opinion to the touch of writers.
   *Pro.*   Now let us fall in with him.     [*They come forward.*]
   *Org.*                       Ha, ha, ha!
These apish boys, when they but taste the grammates[6]
And principles of theory, imagine
They can oppose their teachers. Confidence
Leads many into errors.
   *Pro.*                By your leave, sir.
   *Euph.*   Are you a scholar, friend?
   *Org.*                I am, gay creature,
With pardon of your deities, a mushroom
On whom the dew of heaven drops now and then.
The sun shines on me too, I thank his beams!
Sometime I feel their warmth, and eat and sleep.
   *Pro.*   Does Tecnicus read to thee?
   *Org.*                Yes, forsooth,
He is my master surely; yonder door
Opens upon his study.
   *Pro.*           Happy creatures.
Such people toil not, sweet, in heats of state,
Nor sink in thaws of greatness; their affections
Keep order with the limits of their modesty;
Their love is love of virtue. — what 's thy name?
   *Org.*   Aplotes, sumptuous master, a poor wretch.
   *Euph.*   Dost thou want anything?
   *Org.*              Books, Venus, books.
   *Pro.*   Lady, a new conceit[7] comes in my thought,
And most available for both our comforts.
   *Euph.*   My lord, —
   *Pro.*          Whiles I endeavour to deserve
Your father's blessing to our loves, this scholar
May daily at some certain hours attend
What notice I can write of my success,
Here in this grove, and give it to your hands;
The like from you to me: so can we never,
Barr'd of our mutual speech, want sure intelligence,
And thus our hearts may talk when our tongues cannot.
   *Euph.*   Occasion is most favourable; use it.
   *Pro.*   Aplotes, wilt thou wait us twice a day,
At nine i' th' morning and at four at night,
Here in this bower, to convey such letters
As each shall send to other? Do it willingly,

---

[6] Rudiments.                  [7] Idea.

Safely, and secretly, and I will furnish
Thy study, or what else thou canst desire.

　　*Org.*　Jove, make me thankful, thankful, I beseech thee,
Propitious Jove! I will prove sure and trusty:
You will not fail me books?

　　*Pro.*　　　　　　　Nor aught besides
Thy heart can wish. This lady's name 's Euphranea,
Mine Prophilus.

　　*Org.*　　　I have a pretty memory;
It must prove my best friend. I will not miss
One minute of the hours appointed.

　　*Pro.*　　　　　　　Write
The books thou wouldst have bought thee in a note,
Or take thyself some money.

　　*Org.*　　　　　No, no money.
Money to scholars is a spirit invisible,
We dare not finger it: or books, or nothing.

　　*Pro.*　Books of what sort thou wilt: do not forget
Our names.

　　*Org.*　　I warrant ye, I warrant ye.

　　*Pro.*　Smile, Hymen, on the growth of our desires;
We 'll feed thy torches with eternal fires! *Exeunt. Manet Orgilus.*

　　*Org.*　Put out thy torches, Hymen, or their light
Shall meet a darkness of eternal night!
Inspire me, Mercury, with swift deceits.
Ingenious Fate has leapt into mine arms,
Beyond the compass of my brain. Mortality
Creeps on the dung of earth, and cannot reach
The riddles which are purpos'd by the gods.
Great arts best write themselves in their own stories;
They die too basely who outlive their glories.　　　　　*Exit.*


## Actus Secundus: Scæna prima

### Enter Bassanes and Phulas

　　*Bass.*　I 'll have that window next the street damm'd up.
It gives too full a prospect to temptation,
And courts a gazer's glances. There 's a lust
Committed by the eye, that sweats and travails,
Plots, wakes, contrives, till the deformed bear-whelp,
Adultery, be lick'd into the act,
The very act. That light shall be damm'd up;
D' ye hear, sir?

*Phu.*　　　　I do hear, my lord; a mason
Shall be provided suddenly.[8]
　*Bass.*　　　　　　Some rogue.
Some rogue of your confederacy, — factor[9]
For slaves and strumpets! — to convey close packets
From this spruce springal[1] and the t' other youngster,
That gaudy earwig, or my lord your patron,
Whose pensioner you are. — I 'll tear thy throat out,
Son of a cat, ill-looking hound's-head, rip up
Thy ulcerous maw, if I but scent a paper,
A scroll, but half as big as what can cover
A wart upon thy nose, a spot, a pimple,
Directed to my lady. It may prove
A mystical[2] preparative to lewdness.
　*Phu.* Care shall be had: I will turn every thread
About me to an eye.[3] — [*Aside.*] Here 's a sweet life!
　*Bass.* The city housewives, cunning in the traffic
Of chamber merchandise, set all at price
By wholesale; yet they wipe their mouths and simper,
Cull,[4] kiss, and cry "sweetheart," and stroke the head
Which they have branch'd;[5] and all is well again!
Dull clods of dirt, who dare not feel the rubs
Stuck on their foreheads.
　*Phu.*　　　　　　'T is a villainous world;
One cannot hold his own in 't.
　*Bass.*　　　　　　Dames at court,
Who flaunt in riots, run another bias.[6]
Their pleasure heaves the patient ass that suffers
Up on the stilts of office, titles, incomes;
Promotion justifies the shame, and sues for 't.
Poor honour, thou art stabb'd, and bleed'st to death
By such unlawful hire! The country mistress
Is yet more wary, and in blushes hides
Whatever trespass draws her troth to guilt.
But all are false. On this truth I am bold:
No woman but can fall, and doth, or would. —
Now for the newest news about the city;
What blab the voices, sirrah?
　*Phu.*　　　　　　O, my lord,
The rarest, quaintest, strangest, tickling news
That ever —

[8] At once.　　　　　[9] Agent.　　　　　[1] Youth.
[2] Secret.　　　　　[3] Eye of the needle.　　　　　[4] Hug.
[5] Horned, cuckolded.　　　　　[6] Direction.

*Bass.*    Hey-day! up and ride me, rascal!
What is 't?
   *Phu.*    Forsooth, they say the king has mew'd[7]
All his gray beard, instead of which is budded
Another of a pure carnation[8] colour,
Speckled with green and russet.
   *Bass.*              Ignorant block!
   *Phu.*    Yes, truly; and 't is talk'd about the streets
That, since Lord Ithocles came home, the lions
Never left roaring, at which noise the bears
Have danc'd their very hearts out.
   *Bass.*              Dance out thine too.
   *Phu.*    Besides, Lord Orgilus is fled to Athens
Upon a fiery dragon, and 't is thought
'A never can return.
   *Bass.*    Grant it, Apollo!
   *Phu.*    Moreover, please your lordship, 't is reported
For certain, that whoever is found jealous,
Without apparent proof that 's wife is wanton,
Shall be divorc'd: but this is but she-news;
I had it from a midwife. I have more yet.
   *Bass.*    Antic,[9] no more! Idiots and stupid fools
Grate[1] my calamities. Why, to be fair
Should yield presumption of a faulty soul! —
Look to the doors.
   *Phu.[Aside.]*    The horn of plenty crest him!      *Exit Phulas.*
   *Bass.*    Swarms of confusion huddle in my thoughts
In rare distemper. — Beauty! O, it is
An unmatch'd blessing or a horrid curse.

          *Enter Penthea and Grausis, an old Lady*

        She comes, she comes! so shoots the morning forth,
Spangled with pearls of transparent dew. —
The way to poverty is to be rich,
As I in her am wealthy; but for her,
In all contents[2] a bankrupt. —
                  Lov'd Penthea!
How fares my heart's best joy?
   *Grau.*              In sooth, not well.
She is so over-sad.
   *Bass.*         Leave chattering, magpie. —
Thy brother is returned, sweet, safe, and honour'd

---

   [7] Moulted.          [8] Flesh-colored.         [9] Buffoon.
   [1] Irritate.            [2] Happinesses.

With a triumphant victory: thou shalt visit him.
We will to court, where, if it be thy pleasure,
Thou shalt appear in such a ravishing lustre
Of jewels above value, that the dames
Who brave it there, in rage to be outshin'd,
Shall hide them in their closets, and unseen
Fret in their tears; whiles every wond'ring eye
Shall crave none other brightness but thy presence.
Choose thine own recreations; be a queen
Of what delights thou fanciest best, what company,
What place, what times. Do anything, do all things
Youth can command, so thou wilt chase these clouds
From the pure firmament of thy fair looks.
   *Grau.*   Now 't is well said, my lord. — What, lady! laugh,
Be merry; time is precious.
   *Bass.* [*Aside.*]          Furies whip thee!
   *Pen.*   Alas, my lord, this language to your hand-maid
Sounds as would music to the deaf. I need
No braveries nor cost of art to draw
The whiteness of my name into offense.
Let such, if any such there are, who covet
A curiosity of admiration,[3]
By laying out their plenty to full view,
Appear in gaudy outsides; my attires
Shall suit the inward fashion of my mind;
From which, if your opinion, nobly plac'd,
Change not the livery your words bestow,[4]
My fortunes with my hopes are at the highest.
   *Bass.*   This house, methinks, stands somewhat too much inward,[5]
It is too melancholy; we 'll remove
Nearer the court: or what thinks my Penthea
Of the delightful island we command?
Rule me as thou canst wish.
   *Pen.*          I am no mistress.
Whither you please, I must attend; all ways
Are alike pleasant to me.
   *Grau.*        Island? prison!
A prison is as gaysome: we 'll no islands;
Marry, out upon 'em! Whom shall we see there?
Sea-gulls, and porpoises, and water-rats,
And crabs, and mews,[6] and dog-fish? goodly gear

---

[3] Who are concerned to take pains to secure admiration.
[4] The attitude of mind indicated by your words.
[5] Secret.      [6] Sea gulls.

For a young lady's dealing, — or an old one's!
On no terms islands; I 'll be stew'd first.
   *Bass.* [*Aside to Grausis.*]   Grausis,
You are a juggling bawd. — This sadness, sweetest,
Becomes not youthful blood. — [*Aside to Grausis.*] I 'll have you
    pounded. —
For my sake put on a more cheerful mirth;
Thou 't mar thy cheeks, and make me old in griefs. —
[*Aside to Grausis.*] Damnable bitch-fox!
   *Grau.*               I am thick of hearing,
Still,[7] when the wind blows southerly. — What think ye,
If your fresh lady breed young bones, my lord?
Would not a chopping[8] boy d' ye good at heart?
But, as you said —
   *Bass.* [*Aside to Grausis.*]   I 'll spit thee on a stake,
Or chop thee into collops[9]!
   *Grau.*            Pray, speak louder.
Sure, sure the wind blows south still.
   *Pen.*               Thou prat'st madly.
   *Bass.*   'T is very hot; I sweat extremely.

*Enter Phulas*

                               Now?

   *Phu.*   A herd of lords, sir.
   *Bass.*            Ha!
   *Phu.*            A flock of ladies.
   *Bass.*   Where?
   *Phu.*        Shoals of horses.
   *Bass.*             Peasant, how?
   *Phu.*                   Caroches
In drifts; th' one enter, th' other stand without, sir:

*Enter Prophilus, Lemophil, Groneas,*
*Christalla, and Philema*

And now I vanish.                     *Exit Phulas.*
   *Pro.*       Noble Bassanes!
   *Bass.*   Most welcome, Prophilus! Ladies, gentlemen,
To all my heart is open; you all honour me, —
[*Aside.*] A tympany[1] swells in my head already, —
Honour me bountifully. — [*Aside.*] How they flutter,
Wagtails and jays together!

    [7] Always.              [8] Vigorous.          [9] Slices of meat.
    [1] Swelling (as of growing horns).

*Pro.*　　　　　　　　From your brother,
By virtue of your love to him, I require
Your instant presence, fairest.

*Pen.*　　　　　　　　He is well, sir?

*Pro.*　The gods preserve him ever! Yet, dear beauty,
I find some alteration in him lately,
Since his return to Sparta. — My good lord,
I pray, use no delay.

*Bass.*　　　　　　　We had not needed
An invitation, if his sister's health
Had not fallen into question. — Haste, Penthea,
Slack not a minute. — Lead the way, good Prophilus;
I 'll follow step by step.

*Pro.*　　　　　　　Your arm, fair madam.

　　　　　　　　　　　*Exeunt omnes sed*[2] *Bassanes & Grausis.*

*Bass.*　One word with your old bawdship: th' hadst been better
Rail'd[3] at the sins thou worshipp'st than have thwarted
My will. I 'll use thee cursedly.

*Grau.*　　　　　　　You dote,
You are beside yourself. A politician[4]
In jealousy? No, y' are too gross, too vulgar.
Pish, teach not me my trade; I know my cue.
My crossing you sinks me into her trust,
By which I shall know all: my trade 's a sure one.

*Bass.*　Forgive me, Grausis, 't was consideration
I relish'd not;[5] but have a care now.

*Grau.*　　　　　　　Fear not,
I am no new-come to 't.

*Bass.*　　　　　　Thy life 's upon it,
And so is mine. My agonies are infinite.　　　*Exeunt omnes.*

## Scene 2

### Enter *Ithocles, alone*

*Ith.*　Ambition! 't is of vipers' breed:[6] it gnaws
A passage through the womb that gave it motion.
Ambition, like a seeled[7] dove, mounts upward,

---

[2] Except (bad Latin!).　　　　[3] Would have done better to have railed.
[4] Crafty schemer.　　　[5] Did not appreciate.
[6] Breeding; (their young were supposed to gnaw their way out of the females).
[7] Blinded by having the eyelids stitched together.

Higher and higher still, to perch on clouds,
But tumbles headlong down with heavier ruin.
So squibs and crackers fly into the air,
Then, only breaking with a noise, they vanish
In stench and smoke.  Morality, appli'd
To timely practice,[8] keeps the soul in tune,
At whose sweet music all our actions dance.
But this is form[9] of books and school-tradition;
It physics not the sickness of a mind
Broken with griefs: strong fevers are not eas'd
With counsel, but with best receipts[1] and means.
Means, speedy means and certain; that's the cure.

*Enter Armostes and Crotolon*

*Arm.*    You stick, Lord Crotolon, upon a point
Too nice and too unnecessary; Prophilus
Is every way desertful.  I am confident,
Your wisdom is too ripe to need instruction
From your son's tutelage.
*Crot.*                      Yet not so ripe,
My Lord Armostes, that it dares to dote
Upon the painted meat[2] of smooth persuasion,
Which tempts me to a breach of faith.
*Ith.*                                    Not yet
Resolv'd, my lord?  Why, if your son's consent
Be so available, we 'll write to Athens
For his repair to Sparta.  The king's hand
Will join with our desires; he has been mov'd to 't.
*Arm.*    Yes, and the king himself impórtun'd Crotolon
For a dispatch.
*Crot.*          Kings may command; their wills
Are laws not to be question'd.
*Ith.*                              By this marriage
You knit an union so devout, so hearty,
Between your loves to me and mine to yours,
As if mine own blood had an interest in it;
For Prophilus is mine, and I am his.
*Crot.*    My lord, my lord! —
*Ith.*    What, good sir?  Speak your thought.
*Crot.*    Had this sincerity been real once,
My Orgilus had not been now unwiv'd,
Nor your lost sister buried in a bride-bed.

---

8 Put into practice early.        9 Method.
1 Prescriptions.              2 Imaginary sustenance.

Your uncle here, Armostes, knows this truth;
For had your father Thrasus liv'd, — but peace
Dwell in his grave! I have done.
    *Arm.*                    Y' are bold and bitter.
    *Ith.* [*Aside.*]  'A presses home the injury; it smarts. —
No reprehensions, uncle; I deserve 'em.
Yet, gentle sir, consider what the heat
Of an unsteady youth, a giddy brain,
Green indiscretion, flattery of greatness,
Rawness of judgment, wilfulness in folly,
Thoughts vagrant as the wind and as uncertain,
Might lead a boy in years to: — 't was a fault,
A capital fault; for then I could not dive
Into the secrets of commanding love;
Since when, experience, by the extremes (in others),
Hath forc'd me to collect. And, trust me, Crotolon,
I will redeem those wrongs with any service
Your satisfaction can require for current.[3]
    *Arm.* Thy acknowledgment is satisfaction. — [*To Crot.*] What
would you more?
    *Crot.*            I 'm conquer'd. If Euphranea
Herself admit the motion, let it be so;
I doubt not my son's liking.
    *Ith.*             Use my fortunes,
Life, power, sword, and heart, — all are your own.

        *Enter Bassanes, Prophilus, Calantha, Penthea,*
         *Euphranea, Christalla, Philema, and Grausis*

    *Arm.* The princess, with your sister!
    *Cal.*                I present 'ee
A stranger here in court, my lord; for did not
Desire of seeing you draw her abroad,
We had not been made happy in her company.
    *Ith.* You are a gracious princess. — Sister, wedlock
Holds too severe a passion in your nature,
Which can engross all duty to your husband,
Without attendance on so dear a mistress. —
[*To Bassanes.*] 'T is not my brother's pleasure I presume,
T' immure her in a chamber.
    *Bass.*              'T is her will;
She governs her own hours. Noble Ithocles,
We thank the gods for your success and welfare.
Our lady has of late been indispos'd,

  [3] As being real and valuable.

Else we had waited on you with the first.

*Ith.*   How does Penthea now?

*Pen.*                       You best know, brother,
From whom my health and comforts are deriv'd.

*Bass.* [*Aside.*]   I like the answer well; 't is sad[4] and modest.
There may be tricks yet, tricks. — Have an eye, Grausis!

*Cal.*   Now, Crotolon, the suit we join'd in must not
Fall by too long demur.

*Crot.*                       'T is granted, princess,
For my part.

*Arm.*      With condition, that his son
Favour the contract.

*Cal.*                 Such delay is easy. —
The joys of marriage make thee, Prophilus,
A proud deserver of Euphranea's love,
And her of thy desert!

*Pro.*                 Most sweetly gracious!

*Bass.*   The joys of marriage are the heaven on earth,
Life's paradise, great princess, the soul's quiet,
Sinews of concord, earthly immortality,
Eternity of pleasures; — no restoratives
Like to a constant woman! — [*Aside.*] But where is she?
'T would puzzle all the gods but to create
Such a new monster. — I can speak by proof,
For I rest in Elysium; 't is my happiness.

*Crot.*   Euphranea, how are you resolv'd, speak freely,
In your affections to this gentleman?

*Euph.*   Nor more nor less than as his love assures me;
Which (if your liking with my brother's warrants)
I cannot but approve in all points worthy.

*Crot.*   So, so! — [*To Prophilus.*]   I know your answer.

*Ith.*                                 'T had been pity
To sunder hearts so equally consented.

### Enter Lemophil

*Lem.*   The king, Lord Ithocles, commands your presence; —
And, fairest princess, yours.

*Cal.*                 We will attend him.

### Enter Groneas

*Gro.*   Where are the lords?  All must unto the king
Without delay: the Prince of Argos —

*Cal.*                             Well, sir?

---

[4] Serious.

*Gro.*   Is coming to the court, sweet lady.

*Cal.*                                   How!

The Prince of Argos?

*Gro.*                     'T was my fortune, madam,

T' enjoy the honour of these happy tidings.

*Ith.*   Penthea! —

*Pen.*             Brother?

*Ith.*                         Let me an hour hence

Meet you alone within the palace-grove;

I have some secret with you. — Prithee, friend,

Conduct her thither, and have special care

The walks be clear'd of any to disturb us.

*Pro.*   I shall.

*Bass.* [*Aside.*]   How 's that?

*Ith.*                         Alone, pray be alone. —

I am your creature, princess. — On, my lords!

*Exeunt.* [*Manet*] *Bassanes.*

*Bass.*   Alone! alone! What means that word "alone"?

Why might not I be there? — hum! — he 's her brother.

Brothers and sisters are but flesh and blood,

And this same whoreson court ease is temptation

To a rebellion in the veins. — Besides,

His fine friend Prophilus must be her guardian:

Why may not he dispatch a business nimbly

Before the other come? — or — pand'ring, pand'ring

For one another, — be 't to sister, mother,

Wife, cousin, anything, — 'mongst youths of mettle

Is in request. It is so — stubborn fate!

But if I be a cuckold, and can know it,

I will be fell,[5] and fell.

### Enter Groneas

*Gro.*                         My lord, y' are call'd for.

*Bass.*   Most heartily I thank ye. Where 's my wife, pray?

*Gro.*   Retir'd amongst the ladies.

*Bass.*                         Still I thank ye.

There 's an old waiter[6] with her; saw you her too?

*Gro.*   She sits i' th' presence-lobby fast asleep, sir.

*Bass.*   Asleep! asleep, sir!

*Gro.*                         Is your lordship troubled?

You will not to the king?

*Bass.*                   Your humblest vassal.

*Gro.*   Your servant, my good lord.

*Bass.*                         I wait[7] your footsteps. *Exeunt.*

[5] Fierce.            [6] Attendant.            [7] Attend upon.

## Scene 3

*Prophilus, Penthea*

*Pro.*   In this walk, lady, will your brother find you:
And, with your favour, give me leave a little
To work a preparation. In his fashion[8]
I have observ'd of late some kind of slackness
To such alacrity as nature once
And custom took delight in. Sadness grows
Upon his recreations, which he hoards
In such a willing silence, that to question
The grounds will argue little skill in friendship,
And less good manners.

*Pen.*                    Sir, I 'm not inquisitive
Of secrecies without an invitation.

*Pro.*   With pardon, lady, not a syllable
Of mine implies so rude a sense; the drift —

*Enter Orgilus [disguised as before]*

[*To Org.*]   Do thy best
To make this lady merry for an hour.                          *Exit.*

*Org.*   Your will shall be a law, sir.

*Pen.*                    Prithee, leave me.
I have some private thoughts I would account with:
Use thou thine own.

*Org.*                    Speak on, fair nymph; our souls
Can dance as well to music of the spheres
As any's who have feasted with the gods.

*Pen.*   Your school-terms are too troublesome.

*Org.*                                What Heaven
Refines mortality from dross of earth
But such as uncompounded beauty hallows
With glorified perfection?

*Pen.*                    Set thy wits
In a less wild proportion.

*Org.*                    Time can never
On the white table of unguilty faith
Write counterfeit dishonour; turn those eyes,
The arrows of pure love, upon that fire,
Which once rose to a flame, perfum'd with vows
As sweetly scented as the incense smoking
On Vesta's altars with the holiest odours,

8 Behavior.

Shed virgin tears, like sprinkled dews, to feed 'em
And to increase their fervour.

    *Pen.*                      Be not frantic.

    *Org.*    All pleasures are but mere imagination,
Feeding the hungry appetite with steam
And sight of banquet, whilst the body pines,
Not relishing the real taste of food:
Such is the leanness of a heart divided
From intercourse of troth-contracted loves.
No horror should deface that precious figure
Seal'd with the lively stamp of equal souls.

    *Pen.*    Away! some fury hath bewitch'd thy tongue.
The breath of ignorance, that flies from thence,
Ripens a knowledge in me of afflictions
Above all suff'rance. — Thing of talk, begone!
Begone, without reply!

    *Org.*            Be just, Penthea,
In thy commands: when thou send'st forth a doom
Of banishment, know first on whom it lights.
Thus I take off the shroud, in which my cares
Are folded up from view of common eyes.

                              *[Removes his Scholar's gown.]*
What is thy sentence next?

    *Pen.*                  Rash man! thou layest
A blemish on mine honour, with the hazard
Of thy too-desperate life. Yet I profess,
By all the laws of ceremonious wedlock,
I have not given admittance to one thought
Of female change since cruelty enforc'd
Divorce betwixt my body and my heart.
Why would you fall from goodness thus?

    *Org.*                     O, rather
Examine me, how I could live to say
I have been much, much wrong'd. 'T is for thy sake
I put on this imposture. Dear Penthea,
If thy soft bosom be not turn'd to marble,
Thou 't pity our calamities; my interest
Confirms me, thou art mine still.

    *Pen.*                    Lend your hand.
With both of mine I clasp it thus, thus kiss it,
Thus kneel before ye.

    *Org.*           You instruct my duty.

    *Pen.*    We may stand up. — Have you aught else to urge
Of new demand? As for the old, forget it;

'T is buried in an everlasting silence,
And shall be, shall be ever.  What more would ye?

   *Org.*   I would possess my wife; the equity
Of very reason bids me.

    *Pen.*          Is that all?

   *Org.*   Why, 't is the all of me, myself.

    *Pen.*                   Remove
Your steps some distance from me: — at this space
A few words I dare change; but first put on
Your borrow'd shape.

    *Org.*         You are obey'd; 't is done.

                        [*He resumes his disguise.*]

    *Pen.*   How, Orgilus, by promise I was thine
The heavens do witness: they can witness too
A rape done on my truth.  How I do love thee
Yet, Orgilus, and yet, must best appear
In tendering thy freedom; for I find
The constant preservation of thy merit,
By thy not daring to attempt my fame
With injury of any loose conceit,
Which might give deeper wounds to discontents.
Continue this fair race: then, though I cannot
Add to thy comfort, yet I shall more often
Remember from what fortune I am fallen,
And pity mine own ruin. — Live, live happy, —
Happy in thy next choice, that thou mayst people
This barren age with virtues in thy issue!
And O, when thou art married, think on me
With mercy, not contempt!  I hope thy wife,
Hearing my story, will not scorn my fall. —
Now let us part.

    *Org.*       Part! yet advise thee better:
Penthea is the wife to Orgilus,
And ever shall be.

    *Pen.*        Never shall nor will.

   *Org.*   How!

    *Pen.*        Hear me; in a word I 'll tell thee why
The virgin-dowry which my birth bestow'd
Is ravish'd by another; my true love
Abhors to think that Orgilus deserv'd
No better favours than a second bed.

    *Org.*   I must not take this reason.

    *Pen.*                 To confirm it,
Should I outlive my bondage, let me meet
Another worse than this and less desir'd,

If, of all the men alive, thou shouldst but touch
My lip or hand again!
   *Org.*               Penthea, now
I tell 'ee, you grow wanton[9] in my sufferance.[1]
Come, sweet, th' art mine.
   *Pen.*            Uncivil sir, forbear!
Or I can turn affection into vengeance;
Your reputation, if you value any,
Lies bleeding at my feet. Unworthy man,
If ever henceforth thou appear in language,
Message, or letter, to betray my frailty,
I 'll call thy former protestations lust,
And curse my stars for forfeit of my judgment.
Go thou, fit only for disguise and walks,
To hide thy shame: this once I spare thy life.
I laugh at mine own confidence; my sorrows
By thee are made inferior to my fortunes.
If ever thou didst harbour worthy love,
Dare not to answer. My good genius guide me,
That I may never see thee more! — Go from me!
   *Org.*  I 'll tear my veil of politic frenzy off,
And stand up like a man resolv'd to do:
Action, not words, shall show me. — O Penthea!    *Exit Orgilus.*
   *Pen.*  'A sigh'd my name, sure, as he parted from me:
I fear I was too rough. Alas, poor gentleman!
'A look'd not like the ruins of his youth,
But like the ruins of those ruins. Honour,
How much we fight with weakness to preserve thee!

                                          [*Walks aside.*]

*Enter Bassanes and Grausis*

   *Bass.*  Fie on thee! damn thee, rotten maggot, damn thee!
Sleep? sleep at court? and now? Aches, convulsions,
Imposthumes, rheums, gouts, palsies, clog thy bones
A dozen years more yet!
   *Grau.*           Now y' are in humours.
   *Bass.*  She 's by herself, there 's hope of that; she 's sad too;
She 's in strong contemplation; yes, and fix'd:
The signs are wholesome.
   *Grau.*           Very wholesome, truly,
   *Bass.*  Hold your chops,[2] nightmare! — Lady, come; your brother
Is carried to his closet;[3] you must thither.
   *Pen.*  Not well, my lord?

   [9] Frivolous.             [1] Forbearance.
   [2] Jaws.              [3] Private room.

*Bass.*                    A sudden fit; 't will off!
Some surfeit or disorder. — How dost, dearest?
    *Pen.*   Your news is none o' the best.

*Enter Prophilus*

    *Pro.*                         The chief of men,
The excellentest Ithocles, desires
Your presence, madam.
    *Bass.*            We are hasting to him.
    *Pen.*   In vain we labour in this course of life
To piece our journey out at length, or crave
Respite of breath: our home is in the grave.
    *Bass.*   Perfect philosophy!
    *Pen.*                    Then let us care
To live so, that our reckonings may fall even[4]
When w' are to make account.
    *Pro.*                    He cannot fear
Who builds on noble grounds: sickness or pain
Is the deserver's exercise;[5] and such
Your virtuous brother to the world is known.
Speak comfort to him, lady; be all gentle:
Stars fall but in the grossness of our sight;
A good man dying, th' earth doth lose a light.        *Exeunt omnes.*

*Actus Tertius: Scæna prima*
*Enter Tecnicus, and Orgilus in his own shape*

    *Tec.*   Be well advis'd; let not a resolution
Of giddy rashness choke the breath of reason.
    *Org.*   It shall not, most sage master.
    *Tec.*                    I am jealous;[6]
For if the borrow'd shape so late put on
Inferr'd a consequence,[7] we must conclude
Some violent design of sudden nature
Hath shook that shadow off, to fly upon
A new-hatch'd execution. Orgilus,
Take heed thou hast not, under our integrity,
Shrouded unlawful plots; our mortal eyes
Pierce not the secrets of your heart, the gods
Are only privy to them.

---

[4] Our books may balance.                [5] A test of the deserving man.
[6] Suspicious.            [7] Intention.

*Org.*                      Learned Tecnicus,
Such doubts are causeless; and, to clear the truth
From misconceit,[8] the present state commands me.
The Prince of Argos comes himself in person
In quest of great Calantha for his bride,
Our kingdom's heir; besides, mine only sister,
Euphranea, is dispos'd to Prophilus;
Lastly, the king is sending letters for me
To Athens, for my quick repair to court:
Please to accept these reasons.
    *Tec.*                   Just ones, Orgilus,
Not to be contradicted: yet beware
Of an unsure foundation.  No fair colours
Can fortify a building faintly jointed.[9]
I have observ'd a growth in thy aspect
Of dangerous extent,[1] sudden, and — look to 't —
I might add, certain —
    *Org.*              My aspéct!  Could art
Run through mine inmost thoughts, it should not sift
An inclination there more than what suited
With justice of mine honour.
    *Tec.*                  I believe it.
But know then, Orgilus, what honour is.
Honour consists not in a bare opinion
By doing any act that feeds content,
Brave in appearance, 'cause we think it brave.
Such honour comes by accident, not nature,
Proceeding from the vices of our passion,
Which makes our reason drunk.  But real honour
Is the reward of virtue, and acquir'd
By justice, or by valour which for basis
Hath justice to uphold it.  He then fails
In honour, who for lucre or revenge
Commits thefts, murthers, treasons, and adulteries,
With suchlike, by intrenching on just laws,
Whose sovereignty is best preserv'd by justice.
Thus, as you see how honour must be grounded
On knowledge, not opinion, — for opinion
Relies on probability and accident,
But knowledge on necessity and truth, —
I leave thee to the fit consideration
Of what becomes the grace of real honour,
Wishing success to all thy virtuous meanings.

---

[8] Misconception.          [9] Weakly constructed.          [1] Vehemence.

*Org.*   The gods increase thy wisdom, reverend oracle,
And in thy precepts make me ever thrifty!
   *Tec.*   I thank thy wish.                            *Exit Orgilus.*
                    Much mystery of fate
Lies hid in that man's fortunes. Curiosity[2]
May lead his actions into rare attempts: —
But let the gods be moderators still;
No human power can prevent their will.

*Enter Armostes [with a casket]*

From whence come ye?
   *Arm.*                From King Amyclas, — pardon
My interruption of your studies. — Here,
In this seal'd box, he sends a treasure dear
To him as his crown. 'A prays your gravity,
You would examine, ponder, sift, and bolt
The pith and circumstance of every tittle
The scroll within contains.
   *Tec.*                What is 't, Armostes?
   *Arm.*   It is the health of Sparta, the king's life,
Sinews and safety of the commonwealth;
The sum of what the oracle deliver'd
When last he visited the prophetic temple
At Delphos: what his reasons are, for which,
After so long a silence, he requires
Your counsel now, grave man, his majesty
Will soon himself acquaint you with.
   *Tec. [Takes the casket.]*            Apollo
Inspire my intellect! — The Prince of Argos
Is entertain'd?
   *Arm.*       He is; and has demanded
Our princess for his wife; which I conceive
One special cause the king importunes you
For resolution of the oracle.
   *Tec.*   My duty to the king, good peace to Sparta,
And fair day to Armostes!
   *Arm.*                Like to Tecnicus!         *Exeunt.*

[SCENE II]

*Soft Music. A Song*

*Can you paint a thought? or number*
*Every fancy in a slumber?*

2 Subtle skill.

> *Can you count soft minutes roving*
> *From a dial's point by moving?*
> *Can you grasp a sigh? or, lastly,*
> *Rob a virgin's honour chastely?*
> > *No, O, no! yet you may*
> *Sooner do both that and this,*
> *This and that, and never miss,*
> > *Than by any praise display*
> *Beauty's beauty; such a glory,*
> *As beyond all fate, all story,*
> > > *All arms, all arts,*
> > > *All loves, all hearts,*
> *Greater than those or they,*
> *Do, shall, and must obey.*

*During which time enters Prophilus, Bassanes, Penthea, Grausis,*
*passing over the stage. Bassanes and Grausis enter again softly,*
*stealing to several stands,[3] and listen.*

*Bass.* All silent, calm, secure. — Grausis, no creaking?
No noise? Dost hear nothing?
   *Grau.*                 Not a mouse,
Or whisper of the wind.
   *Bass.*               The floor is matted;
The bedposts sure are steel or marble. — Soldiers
Should not affect, methinks, strains so effeminate:
Sounds of such delicacy are but fawnings
Upon the sloth of luxury,[4] they heighten
Cinders of covert lust up to a flame.
   *Grau.* What do you mean, my lord? — speak low; that gabbling
Of yours will but undo us.
   *Bass.*             Chamber-combats
Are felt, not heard.
   *Pro. [Within.]*   'A wakes.
   *Bass.*             What 's that?
   *Ith. [Within.]*             Who 's there?
Sister? — All quit the room else.
   *Bass.*             'T is consented!

### Enter Prophilus

   *Pro.* Lord Bassanes, your brother would be private.
We must forbear; his sleep hath newly left him.
Please ye, withdraw.

---

[3] Different positions.
[4] Lust.

*Bass.*               By any means; 't is fit.
*Pro.*   Pray, gentlewoman, walk too.
*Grau.*                         Yes, I will, sir. *Exeunt omnes.*

### *Ithocles discovered in a chair, and Penthea*

*Ith.*   Sit nearer, sister, to me; nearer yet.
We had one father, in one womb took life,
Were brought up twins together, yet have liv'd
At distance, like two strangers. I could wish
That the first pillow whereon I was cradled
Had prov'd to me a grave.
*Pen.*                 You had been happy:
Then had you never known that sin of life,
Which blots all following glories with a vengeance
For forfeiting[5] the last will of the dead,
From whom you had your being.
*Ith.*                 Sad Penthea,
Thou canst not be too cruel; my rash spleen
Hath with a violent hand pluck'd from thy bosom
A love-bless'd heart, to grind it into dust;
For which mine 's now a-breaking.
*Pen.*                 Not yet, Heaven,
I do beseech thee! First let some wild fires
Scorch, not consume it! may the heat be cherish'd
With desires infinite, but hopes impossible!
*Ith.*   Wrong'd soul, thy prayers are heard.
*Pen.*                         Here, lo, I breathe,
A miserable creature, led to ruin
By an unnatural brother!
*Ith.*                 I consume
In languishing affections for that trespass;
Yet cannot die.
*Pen.*         The handmaid to the wages
Of country toil drinks the untroubled streams
With leaping kids and with the bleating lambs,
And so allays her thirst secure;[6] whiles I
Quench my hot sighs with fleetings[7] of my tears.
*Ith.*   The labourer doth eat his coarsest bread,
Earn'd with his sweat, and lies him down to sleep;
While every bit I touch turns in digestion
To gall as bitter as Penthea's curse.
Put me to any penance for my tyranny,
And I will call thee merciful.

[5] Violating.          [6] Free from care.          [7] Flowings.

*Pen.*           Pray kill me,
Rid me from living with a jealous husband;
Then we will join in friendship, be again
Brother and sister. — Kill me, pray; nay, will ye?
   *Ith.*    How does thy lord esteem thee?
   *Pen.*               Such an one
As only you have made me: a faith-breaker,
A spotted whore. — Forgive me, I am one
In act, not in desires, the gods must witness.
   *Ith.*    Thou dost belie thy friend.
   *Pen.*           I do not, Ithocles;
For she that 's wife to Orgilus, and lives
In known adultery with Bassanes,
Is at the best a whore. Wilt kill me now?
The ashes of our parents will assume
Some dreadful figure, and appear to charge
Thy bloody guilt, that hast betray'd their name
To infamy in this reproachful match.
   *Ith.*    After my victories abroad, at home
I meet despair; ingratitude of nature
Hath made my actions monstrous. Thou shalt stand
A deity, my sister, and be worshipp'd
For thy resolved martyrdom: wrong'd maids
And married wives shall to thy hallow'd shrine
Offer their orisons, and sacrifice
Pure turtles,[8] crown'd with myrtle; if thy pity
Unto a yielding brother's pressure lend
One finger but to ease it.
   *Pen.*          O, no more!
   *Ith.*    Death waits to waft me to the Stygian banks,
And free me from this chaos of my bondage;
And till thou wilt forgive, I must endure.
   *Pen.*    Who is the saint you serve?
   *Ith.*           Friendship, or nearness
Of birth to any but my sister, durst not
Have mov'd that question. 'T is a secret, sister,
I dare not murmur to myself.
   *Pen.*        Let me,
By your new protestations, I conjure 'ee,
Partake her name.
   *Ith.*    Her name? — 't is — 't is — I dare not.
   *Pen.*    All your respects[9] are forg'd.

[8] Turtledoves.
[9] Attentions.

*Ith.*                              They are not. — Peace!
Calantha is — the princess — the king's daughter —
Sole heir of Sparta. — Me most miserable!
Do I now love thee? For my injuries
Revenge thyself with bravery,[1] and gossip
My treasons to the king's ears, do. Calantha
Knows it not yet, nor Prophilus, my nearest.

   *Pen.*   Suppose you were contracted to her, would it not
Split even your very soul to see her father
Snatch her out of your arms against her will,
And force her on the Prince of Argos?

   *Ith.*                              Trouble not
The fountains of mine eyes with thine own story;
I sweat in blood for 't.

   *Pen.*             We are reconcil'd.
Alas, sir, being children, but two branches
Of one stock, 't is not fit we should divide.
Have comfort, you may find it.

   *Ith.*                       Yes, in thee;
Only in thee, Penthea mine.

   *Pen.*                    If sorrows
Have not too much dull'd my infected brain,
I 'll cheer invention for an active strain.[2]

   *Ith.*   Mad man! why have I wrong'd a maid so excellent!

*Enter Bassanes with poniard, Prophilus, Groneas, Lemo-
phil, and Grausis*

   *Bass.*   I can forbear no longer; more, I will not.
Keep off your hands, or fall upon my point. —
Patience is tir'd; for, like a slow-pac'd ass,
Ye ride my easy nature, and proclaim
My sloth to vengeance a reproach and property.

   *Ith.*   The meaning of this rudeness?

   *Pro.*                    He 's distracted.

   *Pen.*   O, my griev'd lord! —

   *Grau.*   Sweet lady, come not near him;
He holds his perilous weapon in his hand
To prick 'a cares not whom nor where, — see, see, see!

   *Bass.*   My birth is noble. Though the popular blast
Of vanity, as giddy as thy youth,
Hath rear'd thy name up to bestride a cloud,
Or progress in the chariot of the sun,
I am no clod of trade, to lackey pride,[3]

---

[1] Defiance.                    [2] Into activity.
[3] To be a servant to the proud.

Nor, like your slave of expectation,[4] wait
The bawdy hinges of your doors, or whistle
For mystical[5] conveyance to your bed-sports.

   *Gro.*   Fine humours! they become him.

   *Lem.*                    How 'a stares,
Struts, puffs, and sweats!  Most admirable lunacy!

   *Ith.*   But that I may conceive the spirit of wine
Has took possession of your soberer custom,
I 'd say you were unmannerly.

   *Pen.*              Dear brother! —

   *Bass.*   Unmannerly! — mew, kitling![6] — smooth Formality
Is usher to the rankness of the blood,
But Impudence bears up the train.  Indeed, sir,
Your fiery mettle, or your springal[7] blaze
Of huge renown, is no sufficient royalty
To print upon my forehead the scorn, "cuckold."

   *Ith.*   His jealousy has robb'd him of his wits;
'A talks 'a knows not what.

   *Bass.*             Yes, and 'a knows
To whom 't talks; to one that franks his lust
In swine-security of bestial incest.

   *Ith.*   Ha, devil!

   *Bass.*   I will haloo 't; though I blush more
To name the filthiness than thou to act it.

   *Ith.*   Monster!                  [*Draws his sword.*]

   *Pro.*         Sir, by our friendship —

   *Pen.*                 By our bloods —
Will you quite both undo us, brother?

   *Grau.*               Out on him!
These are his megrims,[8] firks,[9] and melancholies.

   *Lem.*   Well said, old touch-hole.

   *Gro.*            Kick him out at doors.

   *Pen.*   With favour, let me speak. — My lord, what slackness
In my obedience hath deserv'd this rage?
Except humility and silent duty
Have drawn on your unquiet, my simplicity
Ne'er studied your vexation.

   *Bass.*            Light of beauty,
Deal not ungently with a desperate wound!
No breach of reason dares make war with her
Whose looks are sovereignty, whose breath is balm.
O, that I could preserve thee in fruition
As in devotion!

---

  [4] Hopeful lackey.       [5] Secret.       [6] Kitten.
  [7] Youthful.          [8] Whims.       [9] Friskings.

*Pen.*          Sir, may every evil
Lock'd in Pandora's box shower, in your presence,
On my unhappy head, if, since you made me
A partner in your bed, I have been faulty
In one unseemly thought against your honour!
    *Ith.*   Purge not his griefs, Penthea.
    *Bass.*                          Yes, say on,
Excellent creature! — [*To Ithocles.*] Good, be not a hindrance
To peace and praise of virtue. — O, my senses
Are charm'd with sounds celestial! — On, dear, on.
I never gave you one ill word; say, did I?
Indeed I did not.
    *Pen.*             Nor, by Juno's forehead,
Was I e'er guilty of a wanton error.
    *Bass.*   A goddess! let me kneel.
    *Grau.*                       Alas, kind animal!
    *Ith.*   No; but for penance.
    *Bass.*                    Noble sir, what is it?
With gladness I embrace it; yet, pray let not
My rashness teach you to be too unmerciful.
    *Ith.*   When you shall show good proof that manly wisdom,
Not oversway'd by passion or opinion,
Knows how to lead your judgment, then this lady,
Your wife, my sister, shall return in safety
Home, to be guided by you; but, till first
I can out of clear evidence approve it,
She shall be my care.
    *Bass.*             Rip my bosom up,
I 'll stand the execution with a constancy;
This torture is unsufferable.
    *Ith.*                  Well, sir,
I dare not trust her to your fury.
    *Bass.*                       But
Penthea says not so.
    *Pen.*             She needs no tongue
To plead excuse who never purpos'd wrong.
    *Lem.* [*To Grausis.*]   Virgin of reverence and antiquity,
Stay you behind.
    *Gro.*          The court wants not your diligence.
                              *Exeunt omnes sed Bass. & Grau.*
    *Grau.*   What will you do, my lord? My lady 's gone;
I am denied to follow.
    *Bass.*             I may see her,
Or speak to her once more?

    *Grau.*               And feel her too, man.
Be of good cheer, she 's your own flesh and bone.
    *Bass.*   Diseases desperate must find cures alike.
She swore she has been true.
    *Grau.*            True, on my modesty.
    *Bass.*  Let him want truth who credits not her vows?
Much wrong I did her, but her brother infinite;
Rumour will voice me the contempt of manhood,
Should I run on thus.  Some way I must try
To outdo art, and tie up jealousy.           *Exeunt omnes.*


[SCENE III]

*Flourish.  Enter Amyclas, Nearchus, leading Calantha,*
*Armostes,  Crotolon,  Euphranea,  Christalla,  Philema,*
*and Amelus*

    *Amy.*   Cousin of Argos, what the heavens have pleas'd,
In their unchanging counsels, to conclude
For both our kingdoms' weal, we must submit to:
Nor can we be unthankful to their bounties,
Who, when we were even creeping to our grave,
Sent us a daughter, in whose birth our hope
Continues of succession.  As you are
In title next, being grandchild to our aunt,
So we in heart desire you may sit nearest
Calantha's love; since we have ever vow'd
Not to enforce affection by our will,
But by her own choice to confirm it gladly.
    *Near.*   You speak the nature of a right just father.
I come not hither roughly to demand
My cousin's thraldom, but to free mine own.
Report of great Calanthas' beauty, virtue,
Sweetness, and singular perfections, courted
All ears to credit what I find was publish'd
By constant truth; from which, if any service
Of my desert can purchase fair construction,[1]
This lady must command it.
    *Cal.*          Princely sir,
So well you know how to profess observance,[2]
That you instruct your hearers to become

    [1] Can win a good opinion.
    [2] Dutiful service.

Practitioners in duty; of which number
I 'll study to be chief.

   *Near.*              Chief, glorious virgin,
In my devotions, as in all men's wonder.

   *Amy.*   Excellent cousin, we deny no liberty;
Use thine own opportunities. — Armostes,
We must consult with the philosophers;
The business is of weight.

   *Arm.*            Sir, at your pleasure.

   *Amy.*   You told me, Crotolon, your son 's return'd
From Athens: wherefore comes 'a not to court
As we commanded?

   *Crot.*          He shall soon attend
Your royal will, great sir.

   *Amy.*              The marriage
Between young Prophilus and Euphranea
Tastes of too much delay.

   *Crot.*          My lord, —

   *Amy*              Some pleasures
At celebration of it would give life
To th' entertainment of the prince our kinsman.
Our court wears gravity more than we relish.

   *Arm.*   Yet the heavens smile on all your high attempts,
Without a cloud.

   *Crot.*       So may the gods protect us.

   *Cal.*   A prince a subject?

   *Near.*          Yes, to beauty's sceptre:
As all hearts kneel, so mine.

   *Cal.*          You are too courtly.

*To them Ithocles, Orgilus, Prophilus*

   *Ith.*   Your safe return to Sparta is most welcome:
I joy to meet you here, and, as occasion
Shall grant us privacy, will yield you reasons
Why I should covet to deserve the title
Of your respected friend; for, without compliment,
Believe it, Orgilus, 't is my ambition.

   *Org.*   Your lordship may command me, your poor servant.

   *Ith.* [*Aside.*]   So amorously close! — so soon! — so soon! —
      my heart!

   *Pro.*   What sudden change is next?

   *Ith.*               Life to the king!
To whom I here present this noble gentleman,

New come from Athens.  Royal sir, vouchsafe
Your gracious hand in favour of his merit.
                              [*The King gives Orgilus his hand to kiss.*]
  *Crot.* [*Aside.*]    My son preferr'd by Ithocles!
  *Amy.*                                        Our bounties
Shall open to thee, Orgilus; for instance, —
Hark in thine ear, — if, out of those inventions
Which flow in Athens, thou hast there engross'd
Some rarity of wit, to grace the nuptials
Of thy fair sister, and renown our court
In th' eyes of this young prince, we shall be debtor
To thy conceit: think on 't.
  *Org.*                    Your highness honours me.
  *Near.*   My tongue and heart are twins.
  *Cal.*                                        A noble birth;
Becoming such a father. — Worthy Orgilus,
You are a guest most wish'd for.
  *Org.*                    May my duty
Still rise in your opinion, sacred princess!
  *Ith.*   Euphranea's brother, sir; a gentleman
Well worthy of your knowledge.
  *Near.*                      We embrace him,
Proud of so dear acquaintance.
  *Amy.*                      All prepare
For revels and disport; the joys of Hymen,
Like Phœbus in his lustre, put to flight
All mists of dulness, crown the hours with gladness:
No sounds but music, no discourse but mirth!
  *Cal.*   Thine arm, I prithee, Ithocles. — Nay, good
My lord, keep on your way; I am provided.
  *Near.*   I dare not disobey.
  *Ith.*                    Most heavenly lady!            *Exeunt.*


[SCENE IV]

*Enter Crotolon, Orgilus*

  *Crot.*   The king hath spoke his mind.
  *Org.*                            His will he hath;
But were it lawful to hold plea against
The power of greatness, not the reason, haply
Such undershrubs as subjects sometimes might

Borrow of nature justice, to inform[3]
That license sovereignty holds without check
Over a meek obedience.
   *Crot.*              How resolve you
Touching your sister's marriage? Prophilus
Is a deserving and a hopeful youth.
   *Org.*   I envy not his merit, but applaud it;
Could wish him thrift[4] in all his best desires,
And with a willingness inleague our blood
With his, for purchase of full growth in friendship.
He never touch'd on any wrong that malic'd
The honour of our house, nor stirr'd our peace:
Yet, with your favour, let me not forget
Under whose wing he gathers warmth and comfort,
Whose creature he is bound, made, and must live so.
   *Crot.*   Son, son, I find in thee a harsh condition;
No courtesy can win it; 't is too rancorous.
   *Org.*   Good sir, be not severe in your construction.
I am no stranger to such easy calms
As sit in tender bosoms: lordly Ithocles
Hath grac'd my entertainment in abundance,
Too humbly hath descended from that height
Of arrogance and spleen which wrought the rape
On griev'd Penthea's purity; his scorn
Of my untoward fortunes is reclaim'd
Unto a courtship, almost to a fawning: —
I 'll kiss his foot, since you will have it so.
   *Crot.*   Since I will have it so! Friend, I will have it so,
Without our ruin by your politic plots,
Or wolf-of-hatred snarling in your breast.
You have a spirit, sir, have ye? A familiar
That posts i' th' air for your intelligence?
Some such hobgoblin hurried you from Athens,
For yet you come unsent for.
   *Org.*             If unwelcome,
I might have found a grave there.
   *Crot.*             Sure, your business
Was soon dispatch'd, or your mind alter'd quickly.
   *Org.*   'T was care, sir, of my health cut short my journey;
For there a general infection
Threatens a desolation.
   *Crot.*         And I fear
Thou hast brought back a worse infection with thee, —

---

  **3** Instruct.               **4** Success.

Infection of thy mind; which, as thou say'st,
Threatens the desolation of our family.

 *Org.* Forbid it, our dear genius![5] I will rather
Be made a sacrifice on Thrasus' monument,
Or kneel to Ithocles, his son, in dust,
Than woo a father's curse. My sister's marriage
With Prophilus is from my heart confirm'd.
May I live hated, may I die despis'd,
If I omit to further it in all
That can concern me!

 *Crot.*     I have been too rough.
My duty to my king made me so earnest;
Excuse it, Orgilus.

 *Org.*   Dear sir! —

 *Crot.*      Here comes
Euphranea with Prophilus and Ithocles.

*Enter to them* Prophilus, Euphranea, Ithocles, **Groneas,**
*Lemophil*

 *Org.* Most honoured! — ever famous!

 *Ith.*     Your true friend,
On earth not any truer. — With smooth eyes
Look on this worthy couple; your consent
Can only make them one.

 *Org.*    They have it. — Sister,
Thou pawn'st to me an oath, of which engagement
I never will release thee, if thou aim'st
At any other choice than this.

 *Euph.*    Dear brother,
At him, or none.

 *Crot.*  To which my blessing 's added.

 *Org.* Which, till a greater ceremony perfect, —
Euphranea, lend thy hand. — Here, take her, Prophilus.
Live long a happy man and wife; and further,
That these in presence may conclude an omen,
Thus for a bridal song I close my wishes:

[*Sings.*]

  *Comforts lasting, loves increasing,*
  *Like soft hours never ceasing:*
  *Plenty's pleasure, peace complying,*
  *Without jars, or tongues envying;*
  *Hearts by holy union wedded,*

[5] Spirit that watches over the family.

> *More than theirs by custom bedded;*
> *Fruitful issues; life so graced,*
> *Not by age to be defaced;*
> *Budding, as the year ensu'th,*
> *Every spring another youth:*
> *All what thought can add beside*
> *Crown this bridegroom and this bride!*

*Pro.*    You have seal'd joy close to my soul. — Euphranea,
Now I may call thee mine.
   *Ith.*                    I but exchange
One good friend for another.
   *Org.*                    If these gallants
Will please to grace a poor invention
By joining with me in some slight device,
I 'll venture on a strain my younger days
Have studied for delight.
   *Lem.*                    With thankful willingness
I offer my attendance.
   *Gro.*             No endeavour
Of mine shall fail to show itself.
   *Ith.*                    We will
All join to wait on thy directions, Orgilus.
   *Org.*   O, my good lord, your favours flow towards
A too unworthy worm; — but as you please.
I am what you will shape me.
   *Ith.*                    A fast friend.
   *Crot.*   I thank thee, son, for this acknowledgment;
It is a sight of gladness.
   *Org.*             But my duty.             *Exeunt omnes.*


[SCENE V]

*Enter Calantha, Penthea, Christalla, Philema*

*Cal.*   Whoe'er would speak with us, deny his entrance.
Be careful of our charge.
   *Chris.*             We shall, madam.
   *Cal.*   Except the king himself, give none admittance;
Not any.
   *Phil.*   Madam, it shall be our care.
                    *Exeunt [Christalla and Philema].*
   *Cal.*   Being alone, Penthea, you have granted

The opportunity you sought, and might
At all times have commanded.
    *Pen.*                    'T is a benefit
Which I shall owe your goodness even in death for.
My glass of life, sweet princess, hath few minutes
Remaining to run down; the sands are spent;
For by an inward messenger I feel
The summons of departure short and certain.
    *Cal.*   You feel too much your melancholy.
    *Pen.*                        Glories
Of human greatness are but pleasing dreams
And shadows soon decaying: on the stage
Of my mortality my youth hath acted
Some scenes of vanity, drawn out at length
By varied pleasures, sweet'ned in the mixture,
But tragical in issue. Beauty, pomp,
With every sensuality our giddiness
Doth frame an idol, are unconstant friends,
When any troubled passion makes assault
On the unguarded castle of the mind.
    *Cal.*   Contemn not your condition for the proof
Of bare opinion[6]: to what end
Reach all these moral texts?
    *Pen.*               To place before ye
A perfect mirror, wherein you may see
How weary I am of a ling'ring life,
Who count the best a misery.
    *Cal.*               Indeed
You have no little cause; yet none so great
As to distrust a remedy.
    *Pen.*            That remedy
Must be a winding-sheet, a fold of lead,
And some untrod-on corner in the earth. —
Not to detain your expectation, princess,
I have an humble suit.
    *Cal.*        Speak, and enjoy it.
    *Pen.*   Vouchsafe, then, to be my executrix,
And take that trouble on ye to dispose
Such legacies as I bequeath, impartially.
I have not much to give, the pains are easy;
Heaven will reward your piety, and thank it
When I am dead; for sure I must not live;
I hope I cannot.

    [6] Mere commonplace.

*Cal.*          Now, beshrew thy sadness;
Thou turn'st me too much woman.          [*Weeps.*]
    *Pen.* [*Aside.*]                    Her fair eyes
Melt into passion. Then I have assurance
Encouraging my boldness. — In this paper
My will was character'd; which you, with pardon,
Shall now know from mine own mouth.
    *Cal.*                         Talk on, prithee;
It is a pretty earnest.
    *Pen.*               I have left me
But three poor jewels to bequeath. The first is
My youth; for though I am much old in griefs,
In years I am a child.
    *Cal.*          To whom that?
    *Pen.*   To virgin-wives, such as abuse not wedlock
By freedom of desires, but covet chiefly
The pledges of chaste beds for ties of love,
Rather than ranging of their blood; and next
To married maids, such as prefer the number
Of honourable issue in their virtues
Before the flattery of delights by marriage:
May those be ever young!
    *Cal.*               A second jewel
You mean to part with?
    *Pen.*               'T is my fame, I trust
By scandal yet untouch'd: this I bequeath
To Memory, and Time's old daughter, Truth.
If ever my unhappy name find mention
When I am fall'n to dust, may it deserve
Beseeming charity without dishonour!
    *Cal.*   How handsomely thou play'st with harmless sport
Of mere imagination! Speak the last.
I strangely like thy will.
    *Pen.*                  This jewel, madam,
Is dearly precious to me; you must use
The best of your discretion to employ
This gift as I intend it.
    *Cal.*               Do not doubt me.
    *Pen.*   'T is long agone since first I lost my heart.
Long I have liv'd without it, else for certain
I should have given that too; but instead
Of it, to great Calantha, Sparta's heir,
I do bequeath, in holiest rites of love,
Mine only brother, Ithocles.

*Cal.*                        What saidst thou?

*Pen.*   Impute not, heaven-bless'd lady, to ambition
A faith as humbly perfect as the prayers
Of a devoted suppliant can endow it.
Look on him, princess, with an eye of pity;
How like the ghost of what he late appear'd
'A moves before you.

*Cal.*                  Shall I answer here,
Or lend my ear too grossly?

*Pen.*                        First his heart
Shall fall in cinders, scorch'd by your disdain,
Ere he will dare, poor man, to ope an eye
On these divine looks, but with low-bent thoughts
Accusing such presumption.  As for words,
'A dares not utter any but of service:
Yet this lost creature loves ye. — Be a princess
In sweetness as in blood; give him his doom,
Or raise him up to comfort.

*Cal.*                        What new change
Appears in my behavior, that thou dar'st
Tempt my displeasure?

*Pen.*                        I must leave the world
To revel in Elysium, and 't is just
To wish my brother some advantage here:
Yet, by my best hopes, Ithocles is ignorant
Of this pursuit.  But if you please to kill him,
Lend him one angry look or one harsh word,
And you shall soon conclude how strong a power
Your absolute authority holds over
His life and end.

*Cal.*            You have forgot, Penthea,
How still I have a father.

*Pen.*                        But remember
I am a sister, though to me this brother
Hath been, you know, unkind, O, most unkind!

*Cal.*   Christalla, Philema, where are ye? — Lady,
Your check lies in my silence.

*Enter Christalla and Philema*

*Both.*                                Madam, here.

*Cal.*   I think ye sleep, ye drones: wait on Penthea
Unto her lodging. — [*Aside.*] Ithocles?  Wrong'd lady!

*Pen.*   My reckonings are made even; death or fate
Can now nor strike too soon, nor force too late.          *Exeunt.*

### *Actus Quartus:  Scæna prima*

#### *Enter Ithocles and Armostes*

*Ith.*    Forbear your inquisition: curiosity
Is of too subtle and too searching nature,
In fears of love too quick, too slow of credit. —
I am not what you doubt[7] me.

*Arm.*                        Nephew, be, then,
As I would wish; — all is not right. — Good heaven
Confirm your resolutions for dependence
On worthy ends, which may advance your quiet.

   *Ith.*    I did the noble Orgilus much injury,
But griev'd Penthea more: I now repent it, —
Now, uncle, now; this "now" is now too late.
So provident[8] is folly in sad issue,
That after-wit,[9] like bankrupts' debts, stands tallied,[1]
Without all possibilities of payment.
Sure, he 's an honest, very honest gentleman;
A man of single meaning.

   *Arm.*                        I believe it:
Yet, nephew, 't is the tongue informs our ears;
Our eyes can never pierce into the thoughts,
For they are lodg'd too inward: — but I question
No truth in Orgilus. — The princess, sir.

   *Ith.*    The princess! ha!

   *Arm.*                        With her the Prince of Argos.

#### *Enter Nearchus, leading Calantha; Amelus,*
#### *Christalla, Philema*

*Near.*    Great fair one, grace my hopes with any instance
Of livery,[2] from the allowance of your favour.
   This little spark —     [*Attempts to take a ring from her finger.*]

*Cal.*            A toy!

*Near.*                Love feasts on toys,
For Cupid is a child; — vouchsafe this bounty:
It cannot be deni'd.

   *Cal.*            You shall not value,
Sweet cousin, at a price what I count cheap;
So cheap, that let him take it who dares stoop for 't,
And give it at next meeting to a mistress.
She 'll thank him for 't, perhaps.     *Casts it to Ithocles.*

---

   7 Suspect.              8 Prolific.              9 Remorse.
   1 Marked up.        2 Delivery, i.e., success.

*Ame.*                                                  The ring, sir, is
The princess's; I could have took it up.

*Ith.*   Learn manners, prithee. — To the blessed owner,
Upon my knees —                        [*Kneels and offers it to Calantha.*]

*Near.*           Y' are saucy.

*Cal.*                           This is pretty!
I am, belike, "a mistress" — wondrous pretty!
Let the man keep his fortune, since he found it.
He 's worthy on 't. — On, cousin!

*Ith.* [*To Amelus.*]                 Follow, spaniel;
I 'll force ye to a fawning else.

*Ame.*                         You dare not.

*Exeunt. Manent Ith. and Arm.*

*Arm.*   My lord, you were too forward.

*Ith.*                           Look 'ee, uncle.
Some such there are whose liberal contents[3]
Swarm without care in every sort of plenty;
Who after full repasts can lay them down
To sleep; and they sleep, uncle: in which silence
Their very dreams present 'em choice of pleasures,
Pleasures — observe me, uncle — of rare object;
Here heaps of gold, there increments of honours,
Now change of garments, then the votes of people;
Anon varieties of beauties, courting,
In flatteries of the night, exchange of dalliance:
Yet these are still but dreams. Give me felicity
Of which my senses waking are partakers,
A real, visible, material happiness;
And then, too, when I stagger in expectance
Of the least comfort that can cherish life. ——
I saw it, sir, I saw it; for it came
From her own hand.

*Arm.*           The princess threw it t' ye.

*Ith.*   True; and she said — well I remember what.
Her cousin prince would beg it.

*Arm.*                     Yes, and parted
In anger at your taking on 't.

*Ith.*                     Penthea!
O, thou hast pleaded with a powerful language!
I want a fee to gratify thy merit;
But I will do —

*Arm.*       What is 't you say?

*Ith.*                       In anger!

[3] Bountiful satisfactions.

In anger let him part; for could his breath,
Like whirlwinds, toss such servile slaves as lick
The dust his footsteps print into a vapour,
It durst not stir a hair of mine. It should not;
I 'd rend it up by th' roots first. To be anything
Calantha smiles on, is to be a blessing
More sacred than a petty prince of Argos
Can wish to equal, or in worth or title.

  *Arm.*  Contain yourself, my lord. Ixion, aiming
To embrace Juno, bosom'd but a cloud,
And begat Centaurs: 't is an useful moral.
Ambition hatch'd in clouds of mere opinion
Proves but in birth a prodigy.[4]

  *Ith.*               I thank 'ee;
Yet, with your licence, I should seem uncharitable
To gentler fate, if, relishing the dainties
Of a soul's settled peace, I were so feeble
Not to digest it.

  *Arm.*        He deserves small trust
Who is not privy-counsellor to himself.

*Re-enter Nearchus, Orgilus, and Amelus*

  *Near.*  Brave me!

  *Org.*  Your excellence mistakes his temper;
For Ithocles in fashion of his mind
Is beautiful, soft, gentle, the clear mirror
Of absolute perfection.

  *Ame.*          Was 't your modesty
Term'd any of the prince his servants "spaniel"?
Your nurse, sure, taught you other language.

  *Ith.*                Language!

  *Near.*  A gallant man-at-arms is here, a doctor[5]
In feats of chivalry, blunt and rough-spoken,
Vouchsafing not the fustian[6] of civility,
Which rash spirits style good manners!

  *Ith.*              Manners!

  *Org.*  No more, illustrious sir; 't is matchless Ithocles.

  *Near.*  You might have understood who I am.

  *Ith.*                 Yes.
I did; else — but the presence calm'd th' affront —
Y' are cousin to the princess.

  *Near.*        To the king, too;
A certain instrument that lent supportance

---

  [4] Monster.         [5] One learned.        [6] Rant.

To your colossic greatness — to that king too,
You might have added.
  *Ith.*      There is more divinity
In beauty than in majesty.
  *Arm.*      O fie, fie!
  *Near.*  This odd youth's pride turns heretic in loyalty.
Sirrah! low mushrooms never rival cedars.
           *Exeunt Nearchus and Amelus.*
  *Ith.*  Come back! — What pitiful dull thing am I
So to be tamely scolded at! come back! —
Let him come back, and echo once again
That scornful sound of "mushroom"! painted colts —
Like heralds' coats gilt o'er with crowns and sceptres —
May bait a muzzled lion.
  *Arm.*      Cousin, cousin,
Thy tongue is not thy friend.
  *Org.*      In point of honour
Discretion knows no bounds. Amelus told me,
'T was all about a little ring.
  *Ith.*      A ring
The princess threw away, and I took up.
Admit she threw 't to me, what arm of brass
Can snatch it hence? No; could 'a grind the hoop
To powder, 'a might sooner reach my heart
Than steal and wear one dust on 't. — Orgilus,
I am extremely wrong'd.
  *Org.*      A lady's favour
Is not to be so slighted.
  *Ith.*      Slighted!
  *Arm.*      Quiet
These vain unruly passions, which will render ye
Into a madness.
  *Org.*  Griefs will have their vent.

    *Enter Tecnicus* [*with a scroll*]

  *Arm.* Welcome; thou com'st in season, reverend man,
To pour the balsam of a suppling[7] patience
Into the festering wound of ill-spent fury.
  *Org.* [*Aside.*] What makes he here?
  *Tec.*      The hurts are yet not mortal,
Which shortly will prove deadly. To the king,
Armostes, see in safety thou deliver
This seal'd-up counsel; bid him with a constancy

  [7] I.e., making supple.

Peruse the secrets of the gods. — O Sparta,
O Lacedæmon! double-nam'd, but one
In fate: when kingdoms reel, — mark well my saw, —
Their heads must needs be giddy.  Tell the king
That henceforth he no more must inquire after
My aged head; Apollo wills it so.
I am for Delphos.

   *Arm.*             Not without some conference
With our great master?

   *Tec.*             Never more to see him:
A greater prince commands me. — Ithocles,
*When youth is ripe, and age from time doth part,*
*The lifeless trunk shall wed the broken heart.*

   *Ith.*   What 's this, if understood?

   *Tec.*              List, Orgilus!
Remember what I told thee long before.
These tears shall be my witness.

   *Arm.*          'Las, good man!

   *Tec.*   *Let craft with courtesy a while confer,*
         *Revenge proves its own executioner.*

   *Org.*   Dark sentences are for Apollo's priests;
I am not Œdipus.

   *Tec.*       My hour is come.
Cheer up the king; farewell to all. — O Sparta,
O Lacedæmon!                  *Exit Tecnicus.*

   *Arm.*      If prophetic fire
Have warm'd this old man's bosom, we might cónstrue
His words to fatal sense.

   *Ith.*            Leave to the powers
Above us the effects of their decrees;
My burthen lies within me.  Servile fears
Prevent no great effects. — Divine Calantha!

   *Arm.*   The gods be still propitious!

                     *Exeunt [Ith. and Arm.].  Manet Org.*

   *Org.*                  Something oddly
The book-man prated, yet 'a talk'd it weeping;
      *Let craft with courtesy a while confer,*
      *Revenge proves its own executioner.*
Con it again; — for what?  It shall not puzzle me;
'T is dotage of a wither'd brain. — Penthea
Forbade me not her presence; I may see her,
And gaze my fill.  Why see her, then, I may,
When, if I faint to speak — I must be silent.    *Exit Orgilus.*

## [Scene II]

*Enter Bassanes, Grausis, and Phulas*

*Bass.* Pray, use your recreations. All the service
I will expect is quietness amongst ye:
Take liberty at home, abroad, at all times,
And in your charities appease the gods,
Whom I, with my distractions, have offended.

*Grau.*  Fair blessings on thy heart!

*Phu.* [*Aside.*]  Here 's a rare change!
My lord, to cure the itch, is surely gelded;
The cuckold in conceit[8] hath cast his horns.

*Bass.*  Betake ye to your several occasions;
And wherein I have heretofore been faulty,
Let your constructions[9] mildly pass it over.
Henceforth I 'll study reformation, — more
I have not for employment.

*Grau.*  O, sweet man!
Thou art the very "Honeycomb of Honesty."

*Phu.*  The "Garland of Good-will." — Old lady, hold up
Thy reverend snout, and trot behind me softly,
As it becomes a moil[1] of ancient carriage.[2]  *Exeunt. Manet Bass.*

*Bass.*  Beasts, only capable of sense, enjoy
The benefit of food and ease with thankfulness;
Such silly creatures, with a grudging, kick not
Against the portion nature hath bestow'd:
But men, endow'd with reason and the use
Of reason, to distinguish from the chaff
Of abject scarity the quintessence,
Soul, and elixir of the earth's abundance,
The treasures of the sea, the air, nay, heaven,
Repining at these glories of creation
Are verier beasts than beasts; and of those beasts
The worst am I. I, who was made a monarch
Of what a heart could wish for, — a chaste wife, —
Endeavour'd what in me lay to pull down
That temple built for adoration only,
And level 't in the dust of causeless scandal.
But, to redeem a sacrilege so impíous,
Humility shall pour, before the deities

8 Imagination.　　　9 Interpretations.
1 Mule.　　　2 Elderly demeanor.

I have incens'd, a largess of more patience
Than their displeased altars can require.
No tempests of commotion shall disquiet
The calms of my composure.

*Enter Orgilus*

*Org.*                    I have found thee,
Thou patron of more horrors than the bulk
Of manhood, hoop'd about with ribs of iron,
Can cram within thy breast. Penthea, Bassanes,
Curs'd by thy jealousies, — more, by thy dotage, —
Is left a prey to words.
　　*Bass.*            Exercise
Your trials for addition to my penance;
I am resolv'd.
　　*Org.*        Play not with misery
Past cure. Some angry minister of fate hath
Depos'd the empress of her soul, her reason,
From its most proper throne; but, — what 's the miracle
More new, — I, I have seen it, and yet live!
　　*Bass.*   You may delude my senses, not my judgment;
'T is anchor'd into a firm resolution;
Dalliance of mirth or wit can ne'er unfix it.
Practise yet further.
　　*Org.*            May thy death of love to her
Damn all thy comforts to a lasting fast
From every joy of life! Thou barren rock,
By thee we have been split in ken[3] of harbour.

*Enter Ithocles, Penthea, her hair about her ears;*
*[Armostes,] Philema, Christalla*

*Ith.*   Sister, look up; your Ithocles, your brother,
Speaks t' ye; why do you weep? Dear, turn not from me. —
Here is a killing sight; lo, Bassanes,
A lamentable object!
　　*Org.*            Man, dost see 't?
Sports are more gamesome; am I yet in merriment?
Why dost not laugh?
　　*Bass.*            Divine and best of ladies,
Please to forget my outrage; mercy ever
Cannot but lodge under a roof so excellent.
I have cast off that cruelty of frenzy

[3] Sight.

Which once appear'd, impostor, and then juggled
To cheat my sleeps of rest.

*Org.*                              Was I in earnest?

*Pen.*    Sure, if we were all Sirens, we should sing pitifully.
And 't were a comely music, when in parts
One sung another's knell.  The turtle sighs
When he hath lost his mate; and yet some say
'A must be dead first.  'T is a fine deceit
To pass away in a dream; indeed, I 've slept
With mine eyes open a great while.  No falsehood
Equals a broken faith; there 's not a hair
Sticks on my head but, like a leaden plummet,
It sinks me to the grave.  I must creep thither;
The journey is not long.

*Ith.*                         But, thou, Penthea,
Hast many years, I hope, to number yet,
Ere thou canst travel that way.

*Bass.*                              Let the sun first
Be wrapp'd up in an everlasting darkness,
Before the light of nature, chiefly form'd
For the whole world's delight, feel an eclipse
So universal!

*Org.*        Wisdom, look 'ee, begins
To rave! — Art thou mad too, antiquity?

*Pen.*    Since I was first a wife, I might have been
Mother to many pretty prattling babes.
They would have smil'd when I smil'd, and for certain
I should have cri'd when they cri'd: — truly, brother,
My father would have pick'd me out a husband,
And then my little ones had been no bastards.
But 't is too late for me to marry now,
I am past child-bearing; 't is not my fault.

*Bass.*    Fall on me, if there be a burning Ætna,
And bury me in flames!  Sweats hot as sulphur
Boil through my pores!  Affliction hath in store
No torture like to this.

*Org.*              Behold a patience!
Lay by thy whining gray dissimulation,
Do something worth a chronicle; show justice
Upon the author of this mischief; dig out
The jealousies that hatch'd this thraldom first
With thine own poniard. Every antic rapture[4]
Can roar as thine does.

----

[4] Fit.

*Ith.*                          Orgilus, forbear.

*Bass.*    Disturb him not; it is a talking motion[5]
Provided for my torment. What a fool am I
To bandy passion! Ere I 'll speak a word,
I will look on and burst.

 *Pen.*                          I lov'd you once. [*To Orgilus.*]

 *Org.*    Thou didst, wrong'd creature: in despite of malice,
For it I love thee ever.

 *Pen.*                          Spare your hand;
Believe me, I 'll not hurt it.

 *Org.*                          Pain my heart too!

 *Pen.*    Complain not though I wring it hard. I 'll kiss it;
O, 't is a fine soft palm! — hark, in thine ear:
Like whom do I look, prithee? — Nay, no whispering.
Goodness! we had been happy; too much happiness
Will make folk proud, they say — but that is he —

           *Points at Ithocles.*

And yet he paid for 't home; alas, his heart
Is crept into the cabinet of the princess;
We shall have points and bride-laces. Remember,
When we last gather'd roses in the garden,
I found my wits; but truly you lost yours.
That 's he, and still 't is he.          [*Again pointing at Ithocles.*]

 *Ith.*                          Poor soul, how idly
Her fancies guide her tongue!

 *Bass.* [*Aside.*]                    Keep in, vexation,
And break not into clamour.

 *Org.* [*Aside.*]               She has tutor'd me:
Some powerful inspiration checks[6] my laziness. —
Now let me kiss your hand, griev'd beauty.

 *Pen.*                          Kiss it. —
Alack, alack, his lips be wondrous cold.
Dear soul, h'as lost his colour: have ye seen
A straying heart? All crannies! every drop
Of blood is turned to an amethyst,
Which married bachelors hang in their ears.

 *Org.*    Peace usher her into Elysium! —
If this be madness, madness is an oracle.          *Exit Org.*

 *Ith.*    Christalla, Philema, when slept my sister?
Her ravings are so wild.

 *Chris.*                    Sir, not these ten days.

 *Phil.*    We watch by her continually; besides,
We can not any way pray her to eat.

  [5] Puppet.                    [6] Reproves.

*Bass.*   O, misery of miseries!

*Pen.*                     Take comfort;
You may live well, and die a good old man.
By yea and nay, an oath not to be broken,
If you had join'd our hands once in the temple, —
'T was since my father died, for had he liv'd,
He would have done 't, — I must have call'd you father. —
O, my wrack'd honour! ruin'd by those tyrants,
A cruel brother and a desperate dotage!
There is no peace left for a ravish'd wife,
Widow'd by lawless marriage; to all memory
Penthea's, poor Penthea's name is strumpeted:
But since her blood was season'd by the forfeit
Of noble shame with mixtures of pollution,
Her blood — 't is just — be henceforth never heighten'd
With taste of sustenance! Starve; let that fulness
Whose pleurisy[7] hath fever'd faith and modesty —
Forgive me; O, I faint!     [*Falls into the arms of her Attendants.*]

*Arm.*                     Be not so wilful,
Sweet niece, to work thine own destruction.

*Ith.*                                   Nature
Will call her daughter monster! — What! not eat?
Refuse the only ordinary means
Which are ordain'd for life? Be not, my sister,
A murth'ress to thyself. — Hear'st thou this, Bassanes?

*Bass.*   Foh! I am busy; for I have not thoughts
Enow to think: all shall be well anon.
'T is tumbling in my head; there is a mastery
In art to fatten and keep smooth the outside;
Yes, and to comfort up the vital spirits
Without the help of food, fumes or perfumes,
Perfumes or fumes. Let her alone; I 'll search out
The trick on 't.

*Pen.*   Lead me gently; heavens reward ye.
Griefs are sure friends; they leave without control
Nor cure nor comforts for a leprous soul.

                    *Exeunt the maids supporting Penthea.*

*Bass.*   I grant ye; and will put in practice instantly
What you shall still admire: 't is wonderful,
'T is super-singular, not to be match'd;
Yet, when I 've done 't, I 've done 't: — ye shall all thank me.

                              *Exit Bassanes.*

*Arm.*   The sight is full of terror.

[7] Excess.

*Ith.*                              On my soul
Lies such an infinite clog of massy dulness,
As that I have not sense enough to feel it. —
See, uncle, th' angry thing returns again;
Shall 's welcome him with thunder? We are haunted,
And must use exorcism to conjure down
This spirit of malevolence.
     *Arm.*                      Mildly, nephew.


*Enter Nearchus and Amelus*

     *Near.* I come not, sir, to chide your late disorder,
Admitting that th' inurement[8] to a roughness
In soldiers of your years and fortunes, chiefly,
So lately prosperous, hath not yet shook off
The custom of the war in hours of leisure;
Nor shall you need excuse, since y' are to render
Account to that fair excellence, the princess,
Who in her private gallery expects it
From your own mouth alone: I am a messenger
But to her pleasure.
     *Ith.*                      Excellent Nearchus,
Be prince still of my services, and conquer
Without the combat of dispute; I honour ye.
     *Near.* The king is on a sudden indispos'd,
Physicians are call'd for; 't were fit, Armostes,
You should be near him.
     *Arm.*                      Sir, I kiss your hands.
                    *Exeunt. Manent Nearchus & Amelus.*
     *Near.* Amelus, I perceive Calantha's bosom
Is warm'd with other fires than such as can
Take strength from any fuel of the love
I might address to her. Young Ithocles,
Or ever I mistake, is lord ascendant
Of her devotions; one, to speak him truly,
In every disposition nobly fashioned.
     *Ame.* But can your highness brook to be so rival'd,
Considering th' inequality of the persons?
     *Near.* I can, Amelus; for affections injur'd
By tyranny or rigour of compulsion,
Like tempest-threaten'd trees unfirmly rooted,
Ne'er spring to timely growth: observe, for instance,
Life-spent Penthea and unhappy Orgilus.

     [8] Habituation.

*Ame.*   How does your grace determine?

*Near.*                                    To be jealous

In public of what privately I 'll further;

And though they shall not know, yet they shall find it.

*Exeunt omnes.*

[SCENE III]

*Enter Lemophil and Groneas leading Amyclas, and placing him
in a chair; followed by Armostes [with a box], Crotolon, and
Prophilus*

*Amy.*   Our daughter is not near?

*Arm.*                              She is retir'd, sir,

Into her gallery.

*Amy.*         Where 's the prince our cousin?

*Pro.*   New walk'd into the grove, my lord.

*Amy.*                                 All leave us

Except Armostes, and you, Crotolon;

We would be private.

*Pro.*               Health unto your majesty!

*Exeunt Prophilus, Lemophil, and Groneas.*

*Amy.*   What!  Technicus is gone?

*Arm.*                            He is to Delphos;

And to your royal hands presents this box.

*Amy.*   Unseal it, good Armostes; therein lies

The secrets of the oracle; out with it:

[*Armostes takes out the scroll.*]

Apollo live our patron!  Read, Armostes.

*Arm.* [*Reads.*]   *The plot in which the vine takes root*

*Begins to dry from head to foot;*

*The stock soon withering, want of sap*

*Doth cause to quail the budding grape;*

*But from the neighbouring elm a dew*

*Shall drop, and feed the plot anew.*

*Amy.*   That is the oracle: what exposition

Makes the philosopher?

*Arm.*                   This brief one only.

[*Reads.*] *The plot is Sparta, the dri'd vine the king;*

*The quailing grape his daughter; but the thing*

*Of most importance, not to be reveal'd,*

*Is a near prince, the elm: the rest conceal'd.*

*Tecnicus.*

*Amy.*   Enough; although the opening of this riddle
Be but itself a riddle; yet we construe
How near our labouring age draws to a rest.
But must Calantha quail too? that young grape
Untimely budded! I could mourn for her;
Her tenderness hath yet deserv'd no rigour
So to be cross'd by fate.

   *Arm.*                        You misapply, sir, —
With favour let me speak it, — what Apollo
Hath clouded in hid sense. I here conjecture
Her marriage with some neighb'ring prince, the dew
Of which befriending elm shall ever strengthen
Your subjects with a sovereignty of power.

   *Crot.*   Besides, most gracious lord, the pith of oracles
Is to be then digested when th' events
Expound their truth, not brought as soon to light
As utter'd. Truth is child of Time; and herein
I find no scruple, rather cause of comfort,
With unity of kingdoms.

   *Amy.*                        May it prove so,
For weal of this dear nation! — Where is Ithocles? —
Armostes, Crotolon, when this wither'd vine
Of my frail carcass, on the funeral pile
Is fir'd into its ashes, let that young man
Be hedg'd about still with your cares and loves.
Much owe I to his worth, much to his service. —
Let such as wait come in now.

   *Arm.*                        All attend here!

*Enter Ithocles, Calantha, Prophilus, Orgilus, Euphranea,*
*Lemophil, and Groneas*

   *Cal.*   Dear sir! king! father!
   *Ith.*                        O my royal master!
   *Amy.*   Cleave not my heart, sweet twins of my life's solace,
With your forejudging fears; there is no physic
So cunningly restorative to cherish
The fall of age, or call back youth and vigour,
As your consents in duty. I will shake off
This languishing disease of time, to quicken
Fresh pleasures in these drooping hours of sadness.
Is fair Euphranea married yet to Prophilus?

   *Crot.*   This morning, gracious lord.
   *Org.*                        This very morning;
Which, with your highness' leave, you may observe too.

Our sister looks, methinks, mirthful and sprightly,
As if her chaster fancy could already
Expound the riddle of her gain in losing
A trifle maids know only that they know not.
Pish! prithee, blush not; 't is but honest change
Of fashion in the garment, loose for strait,
And so the modest maid is made a wife.
Shrewd business — is 't not, sister?

  *Euph.*        You are pleasant.
  *Amy.*   We thank thee, Orgilus; this mirth becomes thee.
But wherefore sits the court in such a silence?
A wedding without revels is not seemly.
  *Cal.*   Your late indisposition, sir, forbade it.
  *Amy.*   Be it thy charge, Calantha, to set forward
The bridal sports, to which I will be present;
If not, at least consenting. — Mine own Ithocles,
I have done little for thee yet.
  *Ith.*        Y' have built me
To the full height I stand in.
  *Cal.* [*Aside.*]     Now or never! —
May I propose a suit?
  *Amy.*      Demand, and have it.
  *Cal.*   Pray, sir, give me this young man, and no further
Account him yours than he deserves in all things
To be thought worthy mine: I will esteem him
According to his merit.
  *Amy.*      Still th' art my daughter,
Still grow'st upon my heart. — [*To Ithocles.*] Give me thine
  hand. —
Calantha, take thine own: in noble actions
Thou 'lt find him firm and absolute. — I would not
Have parted with thee, Ithocles, to any
But to a mistress who is all what I am.
  *Ith.*   A change, great king, most wish'd for, 'cause the same.
  *Cal.* [*To Ithocles.*]   Th' art mine. Have I now kept my word?
  *Ith.*           Divinely.
  *Org.*   Rich fortunes guard, the favour of a princess
Rock thee, brave man, in ever-crowned plenty!
Y' are minion of the time; be thankful for it. —
[*Aside.*]   Ho! here 's a swing in destiny! Apparent,
The youth is up on tiptoe, yet may stumble.
  *Amy.*   On to your recreations. — Now convey me
Unto my bed-chamber: none on his forehead
Wear a distemper'd look.

*Omnes.*                    The gods preserve ye!

*Cal.* [*Aside to Ithocles.*]    Sweet, be not from my sight.

*Ith.*    My whole felicity!

   *Exeunt, carrying out of the king. Orgilus stays Ithocles.*

*Org.*    Shall I be bold, my lord?

*Ith.*                         Thou canst not, Orgilus.
Call me thine own; for Prophilus must henceforth
Be all thy sister's: friendship, though it cease not
In marriage, yet is oft at less command
Than when a single freedom can dispose it.

 *Org.*    Most right, my most good lord, my most great lord,
My gracious princely lord, — I might add, royal.

 *Ith.*    Royal! A subject royal?

 *Org.*                         Why not, pray, sir?
The sovereignty of kingdoms in their nonage
Stoop'd to desert, not birth; there 's as much merit
In clearness of affection[9] as in puddle
Of generation. You have conquer'd love
Even in the loveliest; if I greatly err not,
The son of Venus hath bequeath'd his quiver
To Ithocles his manage, by whose arrows
Calantha's breast is opened.

 *Ith.*                         Can 't be possible?

 *Org.*    I was myself a piece of suitor once.
And forward in preferment too; so forward
That, speaking truth, I may without offence, sir,
Presume to whisper that my hopes, and — hark 'ee —
My certainty of marriage stood assured
With as firm footing — by your leave — as any's
Now at this very instant — but —

 *Ith.*                         'T is granted:
And for a league of privacy between us,
Read o'er my bosom and partake a secret:
The princess is contracted mine.

 *Org.*                         Still, why not?
I now applaud her wisdom: when your kingdom
Stands seated in your will, secure and settled,
I dare pronounce you will be a just monarch:
Greece must admire and tremble.

 *Ith.*                         Then the sweetness
Of so imparadis'd a comfort, Orgilus!
It is to banquet with the gods.

 *Org.*                         The glory

 [9] Nobility of disposition.

Of numerous children, potency of nobles,
Bent knees, hearts pav'd to tread on!
  _Ith._        With a friendship
So dear, so fast, as thine.
  _Org._       I am unfitting
For office; but for service —
  _Ith._       We 'll distinguish
Our fortunes merely in the title; partners
In all respects else but the bed.
  _Org._       The bed!
Forfend it Jove's own jealousy! — till lastly
We slip down in the common earth together.
And there our beds are equal; save some monument
To show this was the king, and this the subject. —   _Soft sad music._
List, what sad sounds are these? — extremely sad ones.
  _Ith._   Sure, from Penthea's lodgings.
  _Org._       Hark! a voice too.

       _A Song_ [_within_]

     _O, no more, no more! too late_
      _Sighs are spent; the burning tapers_
     _Of a life as chaste as fate,_
      _Pure as are unwritten papers,_
     _Are burnt out: no heat, no light_
     _Now remains; 't is ever night._

     _Love is dead; let lovers' eyes,_
      _Lock'd in endless dreams,_
      _Th' extremes of all extremes,_
     _Ope no more, for now Love dies,_
      _Now Love dies, — implying_
     _Love's martyrs must be ever, ever dying._

  _Ith._   O, my misgiving heart!
  _Org._       A horrid stillness
Succeeds this deathful air; let 's know the reason.
Tread softly; there is mystery in mourning.      _Exeunt._


       [SCENE IV]

_Enter Christalla and Philema, bringing in Penthea in a chair, veiled:
  two other Servants placing two chairs, one on the one side, and
  the other with an engine on the other. The Maids sit down at_

*her feet, mourning. The Servants go out: meet them Ithocles*
*and Orgilus.*

*1 Ser.* [*Aside to Orgilus.*]   'T is done; that on her right hand.
  *Org.*                              Good: begone. [*Exeunt Servants.*]
  *Ith.*   Soft peace enrich this room!
  *Org.*                              How fares the lady?
  *Phil.*   Dead!
  *Chris.*        Dead!
  *Phil.*                Starv'd!
  *Chris.*                Starv'd!
  *Ith.*                        Me miserable!
  *Org.*                                Tell us,
How parted she from life?
  *Phil.*                        She call'd for music,
And begg'd some gentle voice to tune a farewell
To life and griefs. Christalla touch'd the lute;
I wept the funeral song.
  *Chris.*                    Which scarce was ended
But her last breath seal'd up these hollow sounds,
"O, cruel Ithocles and injur'd Orgilus!"
So down she drew her veil, so died.
  *Ith.*                        So died!
  *Org.*   Up! you are messengers of death; go from us.
Here 's woe enough to court without a prompter.
Away! and — hark ye — till you see us next,
No syllable that she is dead. — Away!
Keep a smooth brow.                *Exeunt Philema and Christalla.*
                    My lord, —
  *Ith.*                        Mine only sister!
Another is not left me.
  *Org.*                    Take that chair;
I 'll seat me here in this. Between us sits
The object of our sorrows; some few tears
We 'll part among us. I perhaps can mix
One lamentable story to prepare 'em. —
There, there; sit there, my lord.
  *Ith.*                        Yes, as you please.
            *Ithocles sits down and is catch'd in the engine.*
What means this treachery?
  *Org.*                    Caught! you are caught,
Young master. 'T is thy throne of coronation,
Thou fool of greatness! See, I take this veil off.
Survey a beauty wither'd by the flames

Of an insulting Phaëthon, her brother.

*Ith.*    Thou mean'st to kill me basely?

*Org.*                              I foreknew

The last act of her life, and train'd[1] thee hither

To sacrifice a tyrant to a turtle.

You dreamt of kingdoms, did ye? How to bosom

The delicacies of a youngling princess;

How with this nod to grace that subtle courtier,

How with that frown to make this noble tremble,

And so forth; whiles Penthea's groans and tortures,

Her agonies, her miseries, afflictions,

Ne'er touch'd upon your thought. As for my injuries,

Alas, they were beneath your royal pity;

But yet they liv'd, thou proud man, to confound thee.

Behold thy fate, this steel!                    [*Draws a dagger.*]

*Ith.*                    Strike home! A courage

As keen as thy revenge shall give it welcome.

But prithee, faint not; if the wound close up,

Tent[2] it with double force, and search it deeply.

Thou look'st that I should whine and beg compassion,

As loath to leave the vainness of my glories.

A statlier resolution arms my confidence,

To cozen thee of honour. Neither could I

Wish equal trial of unequal fortune

By hazard of a duel: 't were a bravery

Too mighty for a slave intending murther.

On to the execution, and inherit

A conflict with thy horrors.

*Org.*                    By Apollo,

Thou talk'st a goodly language! For requital

I will report thee to thy mistress richly.

And take this peace along: some few short minutes

Determin'd,[3] my resolves shall quickly follow

Thy wrathful ghost; then, if we tug for mastery,

Penthea's sacred eyes shall lend new courage.

Give me thy hand: be healthful in thy parting

From lost mortality! thus, thus I free it.          **Kills him.**

*Ith.*    Yet, yet, I scorn to shrink.

*Org.*                    Keep up thy spirit:

I will be gentle even in blood; to linger

Pain, which I strive to cure, were to be cruel.    [*Stabs him again.*]

---

[1] Lured.              [2] Reopen.

[3] Concluded.

*Ith.*    Nimble in vengeance, I forgive thee.  Follow
Safety, with best success: O, may it prosper! —
Penthea, by thy side thy brother bleeds,
The earnest[4] of his wrongs to thy forc'd faith.
Thoughts of ambition, or delicious banquet
With beauty, youth, and love, together perish
In my last breath, which on the sacred altar
Of a long-look'd-for peace — now — moves — to heaven. *Moritur.*[5]

*Org.*    Farewell, fair spring of manhood!  Henceforth welcome
Best expectation of a noble suff'rance.
I 'll lock the bodies safe, till what must follow
Shall be approv'd. — Sweet twins, shine stars for ever! —
In vain they build their hopes whose life is shame:
No monument lasts but a happy name.                    *Exit Orgilus.*


### Actus Quintus:  Scæna prima

#### Enter Bassanes, alone

*Bass.*    Athens — to Athens I have sent, the nursery
Of Greece for learning and the fount of knowledge;
For here in Sparta there 's not left amongst us
One wise man to direct; we 're all turn'd madcaps.
'T is said Apollo is the god of herbs,
Then certainly he knows the virtue of 'em:
To Delphos I have sent too.  If there can be
A help for nature, we are sure yet.

#### Enter Orgilus

*Org.*                                             Honour
Attend thy counsels ever!

*Bass.*                         I beseech thee
With all my heart, let me go from thee quietly;
I will not aught to do with thee, of all men.
The doubles[6] of a hare, — or, in a morning,
Salutes from a splay-footed witch, to drop
Three drops of blood at th' nose just and no more, —
Croaking of ravens, or the screech of owls,
Are not so boding mischief as thy crossing
My private meditations.  Shun me, prithee;
And if I cannot love thee heartily,
I 'll love thee as well as I can.

*Org.*                         Noble Bassanes,
Mistake me not.

---

⁴ Part payment.                    ⁵ He dies.                    ⁶ Twistings.

*Bass.*    Phew! then we shall be troubled.
Thou wert ordain'd my plague — heaven make me thankful, —
And give me patience too, heaven, I beseech thee.
    *Org.*    Accept a league of amity; for henceforth,
I vow, by my best genius, in a syllable,
Never to speak vexation.  I will study
Service and friendship, with a zealous sorrow
For my past incivility towards ye.
    *Bass.*    Hey-day, good words, good words!  I must believe 'em,
And be a coxcomb for my labour.
    *Org.*                        Use not
So hard a language; your misdoubt[7] is causeless.
For instance, if you promise to put on
A constancy of patience, — such a patience
As chronicle or history ne'er mentioned,
As follows not example, but shall stand
A wonder and a theme for imitation,
The first, the index pointing to a second, —
I will acquaint ye with an unmatch'd secret,
Whose knowledge to your griefs shall set a period.
    *Bass.*    Thou canst not, Orgilus; 't is in the power
Of the gods only: yet, for satisfaction,
Because I note an earnest in thine utterance,
Unforc'd and naturally free, be resolute.
The virgin-bays shall not withstand the lightning
With a more careless danger than my constancy
The full of thy relation.  Could it move
Distraction in a senseless marble statue,
It should find me a rock: I do expect now
Some truth of unheard moment.
    *Org.*                        To your patience
You must add privacy, as strong in silence
As mysteries lock'd up in Jove's own bosom.
    *Bass.*    A skull hid in the earth a treble age
Shall sooner prate.
    *Org.*            Lastly, to such direction
As the severity of a glorious action
Deserves to lead your wisdom and your judgment,
You ought to yield obedience.
    *Bass.*                    With assurance
Of will and thankfulness.
    *Org.*                With manly courage
Please, then, to follow me.
    *Bass.*                Where'er, I fear not.        *Exeunt omnes.*

7 Suspicion.

## Scene 2

*Loud music. Enter Groneas and Lemophil, leading Euphranea;*
*Christalla and Philema, leading Prophilus; Nearchus supporting*
*Calantha; Crotolon and Amelus. Cease loud music; all make a*
*stand.*

*Cal.* We miss our servant Ithocles and Orgilus;
On whom attend they?

    *Crot.*               My son, gracious princess,
Whisper'd some new device, to which these revels
Should be but usher: wherein I conceive
Lord Ithocles and he himself are actors.

    *Cal.* A fair excuse for absence: as for Bassanes,
Delights to him are troublesome. Armostes
Is with the king?

    *Crot.*        He is.

    *Cal.*              On to the dance! —
Dear cousin, hand you the bride; the bridegroom must be
Intrusted to my courtship. Be not jealous,
Euphranea; I shall scarcely prove a temptress. —
Fall to our dance.

*Music. Nearchus dance with Euphranea, Prophilus with Calantha,*
*Christalla with Lemophil, Philema with Groneas.*

        *They dance the first change;[8] during which Enter*
                         *Armostes*

*Arm.* (*In Calantha's ear.*)   The king your father 's dead.

*Cal.* To the other change.

*Arm.*            Is 't possible?        *Dance again.*

                  *Enter Bassanes*

*Bass.* [*Whispers Calantha.*]   O, madam!
Penthea, poor Penthea 's starv'd.[9]

    *Cal.*               Beshrew thee! —
Lead to the next.

    *Bass.*     Amazement dulls my senses.    *Dance again.*

                  *Enter Orgilus*

*Org.* [*Whispers Calantha.*]   Brave Ithocles is murther'd, mur-
    ther'd cruelly.

    *Cal.* How dull this music sounds! Strike up more sprightly;

[8] Figure of the dance.
[9] Dead of starvation.

Our footings are not active like our heart,
Which treads the nimbler measure.

*Org.*                                    I am thunderstruck.

                            *Last change. Cease music.*

*Cal.*   So! let us breathe awhile. — Hath not this motion
Rais'd fresher colour on your cheeks?

*Near.*                                Sweet princess,
A perfect purity of blood enamels
The beauty of your white.

*Cal.*                              We all look cheerfully;
And, cousin, 't is, methinks, a rare presumption
In any who prefer[1] our lawful pleasures
Before their own sour censure, to interrupt
The custom of this ceremony bluntly.

*Near.*   None dares, lady.

*Cal.*   Yes, yes; some hollow voice deliver'd to me
How that the king was dead.

*Arm.*                      The king is dead:
That fatal news was mine; for in mine arms
He breath'd his last, and with his crown bequeath'd ye
Your mother's wedding ring; which here I tender.

*Crot.*   Most strange!

*Cal.*   Peace crown his ashes! We are queen, then.

*Near.*   Long live Calantha! Sparta's sovereign queen!

*Omnes.*   Long live the queen!

*Cal.*                          What whisper'd Bassanes?

*Bass.*   That my Penthea, miserable soul,
Was starv'd to death.

*Cal.*                      She 's happy; she hath finish'd
A long and painful progress. — A third murmur
Pierc'd mine unwilling ears.

*Org.*                      That Ithocles
Was murther'd; — rather butcher'd, had not bravery
Of an undaunted spirit, conquering terror,
Proclaim'd his last act triumph over ruin.

*Arm.*   How! murther'd!

*Cal.*                  By whose hand?

*Org.*                              By mine; this weapon
Was instrument to my revenge: the reasons
Are just, and known; quit him of these, and then
Never liv'd gentleman of greater merit,
Hope or abiliment[2] to steer a kingdom.

[1] Put, place.
[2] Ability.

*Crot.*  Fie, Orgilus!

*Euph.*          Fie, brother!

*Cal.*                    You have done it?

*Bass.*   How it was done let him report, the forfeit
Of whose allegiance to our laws doth covet
Rigour of justice; but that done it is,
Mine eyes have been an evidence of credit
Too sure to be convinc'd.  Armostes, rent not
Thine arteries with hearing the bare circumstances
Of these calamities.  Thou 'st lost a nephew,
A niece, and I a wife: continue man still.
Make me the pattern of digesting evils,
Who can outlive my mighty ones, not shrinking
At such a pressure as would sink a soul
Into what 's most of death, the worst of horrors.
But I have seal'd a covenant with sadness,
And enter'd into bonds without condition,
To stand these tempests calmly.  Mark me, nobles:
I do not shed a tear, not for Penthea;
Excellent misery!

*Cal.*          We begin our reign
With a first act of justice: thy confession,
Unhappy Orgilus, dooms thee a sentence;
But yet thy father's or thy sister's presence
Shall be excus'd. — Give, Crotolon, a blessing
To thy lost son; — Euphranea, take a farewell; —
And both be gone.

*Crot.* [*To Orgilus.*] Confirm thee, noble sorrow,
In worthy resolution!

*Euph.*              Could my tears speak,
My griefs were slight.

*Org.*   All goodness dwell amongst ye!
Enjoy my sister, Prophilus: my vengeance
Aim'd never at thy prejudice.

*Cal.*                    Now withdraw.
          *Exeunt Crotolon, Prophilus, and Euphranea.*
Bloody relater of thy stains in blood,
For that thou hast reported him, whose fortunes
And life by thee are both at once snatch'd from him,
With honourable mention, make thy choice
Of what death likes thee best; there 's all our bounty. —
But to excuse[3] delays, let me, dear cousin,
Intreat you and these lords see execution
Instant before ye part.

    [3] Avoid.

*Near.*                Your will commands us.

*Org.*   One suit, just queen, my last: vouchsafe your clemency,
That by no common hand I be divided
From this my humble frailty.

 *Cal.*                     To their wisdoms
Who are to be spectators of thine end
I make the reference.[4] Those that are dead
Are dead; had they not now died, of necessity
They must have paid the debt they ow'd to nature
One time or other. — Use dispatch, my lords;
We'll suddenly prepare our coronation.

                          *Exeunt Calantha, Philema, Christalla.*

*Arm.*   'T is strange these tragedies should never touch on
Her female pity.

*Bass.*          She has a masculine spirit;
And wherefore should I pule, and, like a girl,
Put finger in the eye? Let's be all toughness,
Without distinction betwixt sex and sex.

*Near.*   Now, Orgilus, thy choice?

*Org.*                    To bleed to death.

*Arm.*   The executioner?

*Org.*               Myself, no surgeon;
I am well skill'd in letting blood. Bind fast
This arm, that so the pipes may from their conduits
Convey a full stream; here's a skilful instrument.

                          [*Shows his dagger.*]

Only I am a beggar to some charity
To speed me in this execution
By lending th' other prick to th' tother arm,
When this is bubbling life out.

 *Bass.*                   I am for 'ee;
It most concerns my art, my care, my credit. —
Quick, fillet both his arms.

*Org.*               Gramercy, friendship!
Such courtesies are real which flow cheerfully
Without an expectation of requital.
Reach me a staff in this hand.     [*They give him a staff.*]
                    —If a proneness
Or custom in my nature from my cradle
Had been inclin'd to fierce and eager bloodshed,
A coward guilt, hid in a coward quaking,
Would have betray'd fame to ignoble flight
And vagabond pursuit of dreadful safety:
But look upon my steadiness, and scorn not

 [4] Refer the matter.

The sickness of my fortune, which, since Bassanes
Was husband to Penthea, had lain bed-rid.
We trifle time in words: — thus I show cunning
In opening of a vein too full, too lively

         *[Pierces the vein with his dagger.]*

 *Arm.* Desperate courage!
 *Org.*        Honourable infamy!
 *Lem.* I tremble at the sight.
 *Gro.*       Would I were loose!
 *Bass.* It sparkles like a lusty wine new broach'd;
The vessel must be sound from which it issues. —
Grasp hard this other stick — I 'll be as nimble —
But prithee, look not pale — have at ye; stretch out
Thine arm with vigour and unshook virtue.  **[Opens the vein.]**
Good! O, I envy not a rival, fitted
To conquer in extremities. This pastime
Appears majestical; some high-tun'd poem
Hereafter shall deliver to posterity
The writer's glory and his subject's triumph.
How is 't, man? Droop not yet.
  *Org.*        I feel no palsies.
On a pair-royal[5] do I wait in death;
My sovereign, as his liegeman; on my mistress,
As a devoted servant; and on Ithocles,
As, if no brave, yet no unworthy enemy.
Nor did I use an engine to entrap
His life, out of a slavish fear to combat
Youth, strength, or cunning; but for that I durst not
Engage the goodness of a cause on fortune,
By which his name might have outfac'd my vengeance.
O, Tecnicus, inspir'd with Phœbus' fire!
I call to mind thy augury: 't was perfect;
*Revenge proves its own executioner.*
When feeble man is bending to his mother,
The dust 'a was first fram'd on, thus he totters.
  *Bass.* Life's fountain is dri'd up.
  *Org.*       So falls the standard
Of my prerogative in being a creature!
A mist hangs o'er mine eyes, the sun's bright splendour
Is clouded in an everlasting shadow:
Welcome, thou ice, that sitt'st about my heart!
No heat can ever thaw thee.       **Dies.**
  *Near.*     Speech hath left him.
   5 In some card games, three of a kind.

*Bass.* 'A has shook hands with time; his funeral urn
Shall be my charge: remove the bloodless body.
The coronation must require attendance;
That past, my few days can be but one mourning.          *Exeunt.*


[SCENE III]

*An altar covered with white; two lights of virgin wax, during which
music of recorders; enter four bearing Ithocles on a hearse, or in
a chair, in a rich robe, and a crown on his head; place him on one
side of the altar. After him enter Calantha in a white robe and
crown'd; Euphranea, Philema, Christalla, in white; Nearchus,
Armostes, Crotolon, Prophilus, Amelus, Bassanes, Lemophil, and
Groneas.*

*Calantha goes and kneels before the altar, the rest stand off, the
women kneeling behind. Cease recorders, during her devotions.
Soft music. Calantha and the rest rise, doing obeisance to the
altar.*

*Cal.* Our orisons are heard; the gods are merciful. —
Now tell me, you whose loyalties pays tribute
To us your lawful sovereign, how unskilful
Your duties or obedience is to render
Subjection to the sceptre of a virgin,
Who have been ever fortunate in princes
Of masculine and stirring composition.
A woman has enough to govern wisely
Her own demeanours, passions, and divisions.
A nation warlike and inur'd to practice
Of policy and labour cannot brook
A feminate authority: we therefore
Command your counsel, how you may advise us
In choosing of a husband whose abilities
Can better guide this kingdom.
*Near.*                    Royal lady,
Your law is in your will.
*Arm.*                    We have seen tokens
Of constancy too lately to mistrust it.
*Crot.* Yet, if your highness settle on a choice
By your own judgment both allow'd and lik'd of,
Sparta may grow in power, and proceed
To an increasing height.

*Cal.*                         Hold you the same mind?

*Bass.*   Alas, great mistress, reason is so clouded
With the thick darkness of my infinite woes,
That I forecast nor dangers, hopes, or safety.
Give me some corner of the world to wear out
The remnant of the minutes I must number,
Where I may hear no sounds but sad complaints
Of virgins who have lost contracted partners;
Of husbands howling that their wives were ravish'd
By some untimely fate; of friends divided
By churlish opposition; or of fathers
Weeping upon their children's slaughter'd carcases;
Or daughters groaning o'er their fathers' hearses:
And I can dwell there, and with these keep consort[6]
As musical as theirs.  What can you look for
From an old, foolish, peevish, doting man
But craziness of age?

*Cal.*   Cousin of Argos, —

*Near.*                         Madam?

*Cal.*                                     Were I presently
To choose you for my lord, I 'll open freely
What articles I would propose to treat on
Before our marriage.

*Near.*                     Name them, virtuous lady.

*Cal.*   I would presume you would retain the royalty
Of Sparta in her own bounds; then in Argos
Armostes might be viceroy; in Messene
Might Crotolon bear sway; and Bassanes —

*Bass.*   I, queen! alas, what I?

*Cal.*                               Be Sparta's marshal.
The multitudes of high employments could not
But set a peace to private griefs.  These gentlemen,
Groneas and Lemophil, with worthy pensions,
Should wait upon your person in your chamber. —
I would bestow Christalla on Amelus, —
She 'll prove a constant wife; and Philema
Should into Vesta's Temple.

*Bass.*                     This is a testament!
It sounds not like conditions on a marriage.

*Near.*   All this should be perform'd.

*Cal.*                                   Lastly, for Prophilus,
He should be, cousin, solemnly invested
In all those honours, titles, and preferments

---

6 Harmony.

Which his dear friend and my neglected husband
Too short a time enjoy'd.

    *Pro.*                I am unworthy
To live in your remembrance.

    *Euph.*                 Excellent lady!

    *Near.*    Madam, what, means that word, "neglected husband"?

    *Cal.*    Forgive me: — now I turn to thee, thou shadow
Of my contracted lord! Bear witness all,
I put my mother's wedding-ring upon
His finger; 't was my father's last bequest.

                   [*Places a ring on the finger of Ithocles.*]

Thus I new-marry him whose wife I am;
Death shall not separate us. O, my lords,
I but deceiv'd your eyes with antic gesture,
When one news straight came huddling on another
Of death, and death, and death! still I danc'd forward;
But it struck home, and here, and in an instant.
Be such mere women, who with shrieks and outcries
Can vow a present end to all their sorrows,
Yet live to vow new pleasures, and outlive them?
They are the silent griefs which cut the heartstrings;
Let me die smiling.

    *Near.*          'T is a truth too ominous.

    *Cal.*    One kiss on these cold lips, my last! [*Kisses Ithocles.*] —
Crack, crack! —
Argos now 's Sparta's king. — Command the voices
Which wait at th' altar now to sing the song
I fitted for my end.

    *Near.*         Sirs, the song!


### A Song

    *All.*    *Glories pleasures, pomps, delights, and ease,*
              *Can but please*
            *Outward senses when the mind*
             *Is not untroubled or by peace refin'd.*
*1* [*Voice.*] *Crowns may flourish and decay,*
              *Beauties shine, but fade away.*
*2* [*Voice.*] *Youth may revel, yet it must*
              *Lie down in a bed of dust.*
*3* [*Voice.*] *Earthly honours flow and waste,*
              *Time alone doth change and last.*
    *All.*    *Sorrows mingled with contents prepare*
             *Rest for care;*

*Love only reigns in death; though art*
*Can find no comfort for a broken heart.*

[*Calantha dies.*]

*Arm.*    Look to the queen!
*Bass.*                    Her heart is broke, indeed.
O, royal maid, would thou hadst miss'd this part!
Yet 't was a brave one.  I must weep to see
Her smile in death.
*Arm.*                Wise Tecnicus! thus said he:
*When youth is ripe, and age from time doth part,*
*The Lifeless Trunk shall wed the Broken Heart.*
'T is here fulfill'd.
*Near.*            I am your king.
*Omnes.*                    Long live
Nearchus, King of Sparta!
*Near.*                Her last will
Shall never be digress'd from: wait in order
Upon these faithful lovers, as becomes us. —
The counsels of the gods are never known
Till men can call th' effects of them their own.    [*Exeunt.*]

FINIS

꧁꧂

## The Epilogue

Where noble judgments and clear eyes are fix'd
To grace endeavour, there sits truth, not mix'd
With ignorance: those censures may command
Belief which talk not till they understand.
Let some say, "This was flat;" some, "Here the scene
Fell from its height;" another, that the mean[7]
Was ill observ'd in such a growing passion
As it transcended either state or fashion.
Some few may cry, " 'T was pretty well," or so,
"But — " and there shrug in silence; yet we know
Our writer's aim was in the whole address'd
Well to deserve of *all*, but please the *best*:
Which granted, by th' allowance of this strain
The BROKEN HEART may be piec'd up again.

[7] The middle way, i.e., moderation.

# RIVERSIDE EDITIONS

* In preparation